DÉTENTE

By the Same Author

Aftermath: The Makers of the Postwar World (I B Tauris, 2015)

DÉTENTE

The Chance To End the Cold War

Richard Crowder

To Lord Hennessy
With many thanks for your
support and encouragement,
Richard.

I.B. TAURIS

LONDON • NEW YORK • OXFORD • NEW DELHI • SYDNEY

I.B. TAURIS
Bloomsbury Publishing Plc
50 Bedford Square, London, WC1B 3DP, UK
1385 Broadway, New York, NY 10018, USA

BLOOMSBURY, I.B. TAURIS and the I.B. Tauris logo are trademarks of Bloomsbury
Publishing Plc

First published in Great Britain 2021

Cover design by Adriana Brioso
Cover image: Richard Nixon and Premier Brezhnev wave from the doorway of Air Force
One at San Clemente, California, 23 June, 1973. (© Corbis via Getty Images)

A catalogue record for this book is available from the British Library.

A catalogue record for this book is available from the Library of Congress.

ISBN: HB: 978-1-3501-4794-2
         ePDF: 978-1-3501-4796-6
         eBook: 978-1-3501-4795-9

Typeset by RefineCatch Limited, Bungay, Suffolk
Printed and bound in Great Britain

To find out more about our authors and books visit www.bloomsbury.com
and sign up for our newsletters.

Dedication

To My Mother, Pauleen.

'The old order changeth, yielding place to new,
And God fulfils himself in many ways,
Lest one good custom should corrupt the world.'

Tennyson

CONTENTS

List of Illustrations ix
Preface x
Dramatis Personae xv
Maps xx

Introduction
DEEP HEARTS 1

Chapter 1
SEEING GLORY 19

Chapter 2
TIME ENDING 35

Chapter 3
COMING DARKNESS 45

Chapter 4
THE COCK CROWS 63

Chapter 5
COURAGE TO CHANGE 85

Chapter 6
THE TOPMOST BRANCH 103

Chapter 7
HURTING EACH OTHER 125

Chapter 8
SWEET RAIN 145

Chapter 9
MONSTER RISING 163

Chapter 10
THE HUMILIATED MAN 187

Contents

Chapter 11
AWFUL WISDOM   207

Chapter 12
HORIZON OF DREAMS   223

Bibliography   237
Index   243

ILLUSTRATIONS

1. President Richard Nixon and National Security Adviser Dr Henry Kissinger, 1972. White House Photo Collection.
2. National Guardsmen advance towards student protestors at Kent State University, May 1970. Kent State University Libraries. Special Collections and Archives.
3. Nixon mingles with anti-war protestors at the Lincoln Memorial, May 1970. Getty Images.
4. West German Chancellor Willy Brandt kneeling at the Warsaw Ghetto memorial, December 1970. Getty Images.
5. Richard and Pat Nixon at the Great Wall of China, February 1972. US National Archives and Records Administration.
6. Nixon and Chinese Premier Zhou Enlai share a toast, February 1972. Richard Nixon Presidential Library and Museum.
7. Kissinger briefs the White House press corps that 'Peace is At Hand' in Vietnam, October 1972. Shutterstock.
8. Kissinger and Soviet leader Leonid Brezhnev hunting outside Moscow, May 1973. Getty Images.
9. Nixon and Brezhnev en route to California aboard presidential aircraft *Spirit of '76*, along with Treasury Secretary John Connally and interpreter Viktor Sukhodrev, June 1975. US National Archives and Records Administration.
10. Brezhnev and interpreter Sukhodrev meet actor Chuck Connors at San Clemente, California, June 1975. US National Archives and Records Administration.
11. Nixon, Kissinger, Alexander Haig and new vice-president Jerry Ford in the White House, late 1973. Getty Images.
12. Premier Golda Meir and Defence Minister Moshe Dayan visit Israeli troops on the Golan Heights after the Yom Kippur War, November 1973. Getty Images.
13. Writers Alexander Solzhenitsyn and Heinrich Boll meet after the former's exile from the Soviet Union, February 1974. Associated Press.
14. Nixon hugs his daughter Julie after announcing his resignation watched by sister Tricia and husband David, August 1974. US national Archives and Records Administration.
15. President Jerry Ford swaps his fur coat with Brezhnev, Vladivostok Summit, December 1974. Associated Press.
16. Fleeing Americans board a US Marine Helicopter at Tan Son Nhut Airbase in Saigon, Vietnam, April 1975. Getty Images.

PREFACE

'It's subjunctive history,' Hector tells his pupils in Alan Bennett's *The History Boys*. 'You know, ... the mood used when something may or may not have happened.' Some periods in time seem decisive, clear-cut. My first book, *Aftermath*, was about such an era, with the Second World War and onset of the struggle between East and West which followed it. This second volume picks up that story two decades later, in the middle passage of the Cold War. Beginning with the summer of 1968, when Soviet tanks quelled the Prague Spring in Czechoslovakia, and the Democratic Party convention in Chicago collapsed amid scenes of popular protest at the Vietnam War, the book runs through to 1975, with America's final exodus from Saigon, and the twilight period of Jerry Ford's caretaker presidency.

During these seven years, the world changed, and yet didn't. The leaders of the United States and the Soviet Union, Richard Nixon and Leonid Brezhnev, hoped to forge a new relationship between East and West. 'An era of negotiation, rather than confrontation', as Nixon called it, for which Brezhnev coined the name 'détente' – a French word for an easing of tension, which had first entered the diplomatic lexicon to describe failed efforts to defuse competition between the great powers before the First World War. The quagmire of Vietnam and the strain of the Czechoslovakia invasion had forced both men to question old thinking, and wonder whether it might be possible to channel the Cold War away from the brink of conflict, towards a peaceful coexistence, in the phraseology of the time. In parallel, Nixon reached out to communist China, in a dramatic break with her isolation over the previous decades. And, within Europe, West German leader Willy Brandt imagined a new start for his country, burying the shame of the Nazi past in a reconciliation with her Eastern neighbours that was dubbed Ostpolitik.

Détente was not to be. The high point came in 1972, with a first visit for Nixon to Moscow, close behind his trip to Beijing. Nixon and Brezhnev signed agreements on limiting nuclear weapons and other matters, posing for the world's cameras with champagne glasses in hand. But by 1974, when Nixon returned for a second visit amid tumult in Washington over the Watergate affair, it was clear that the initiative had run its course. Détente limped on through the subsequent presidency of Jerry Ford, with agreement of the Helsinki Accords on peace and human rights in Europe, and enjoyed a brief revival under his Democrat successor Jimmy Carter. With the arrival of Ronald Reagan to the presidency, a new chapter opened in the Cold War, and a dramatic return of tension between the superpowers. Détente fell apart for many reasons – lack of support in both countries; geopolitical tensions, including in the Middle East; Nixon's own political demise. At its core, it failed because it assumed that the superpowers could park differences in their values to work on common interests. That tension – whether voiced by the neoconservative hawks in Washington or dissidents under persecution inside the Soviet Union – made long-term cohabitation impossible.

There is much tactical mastery during this period to admire. Nixon and Kissinger were players at the top of the game, drawing together different threads – nuclear talks; agreement over Berlin; Middle East; Vietnam; China – to pursue their goals. It was diplomatic tradecraft of the highest order, if cynical and secretive at the same time. The channel between Kissinger and Anatoly Dobrynin, the wily veteran who served as Soviet ambassador in Washington, was a thrilling blend of intellect, battle of wits, and moments of genuine friendship. In the closing months of Nixon's presidency, the shuttle diplomacy that Kissinger conducted in the Middle East after the Yom Kippur War is another case study in first-class diplomacy, as he coaxed historic adversaries towards a path of peace.

Détente left some important traces. The agreements on missile defence and limiting strategic arms that Nixon and Brezhnev signed have, until recently, been a bedrock to international arms control. The Helsinki Accords enabled creation of groups like Solidarity in Poland or Charter 77 in Czechoslovakia, whose opposition to communism eventually led to the revolutions of 1989 in eastern Europe. Nixon's opening to China paved the way for the reforms that unleashed the Chinese economy as a global powerhouse. 'As we look at this wall,' commented Nixon during his visit, 'what is most important is that we have an open world.'[1] Fifty years on, that has come true in ways unimaginable at the time, as people, information, finance and ideas swirl around our planet at a speed and with consequences that we sometimes find hard to comprehend.

Yet, the greatest changes of the era took place outside the sphere of international diplomacy. The 1960s brought social collision across the world, from the anti-war protests in America to the student demonstrations on the streets of Paris, or Mao Tse-tung's Red Guards in China. A new generation, whom advertising executives dubbed the baby boomers, brought new attitudes. Musicians of the era – Bob Dillon, Jimmy Hendrix, John Lennon – preached a new set of values, and attitudes towards sex, gender, race, the environment and religion were all transformed. The landmark ruling on abortion, *Roe vs Wade*, came from the US Supreme Court in the same month (January 1973) that Henry Kissinger completed a peace deal on Vietnam. We now take these freedoms for granted, perhaps to our peril. To contemporaries, they were the hard-won gains of a genuine social revolution.

Technology, too, was changing the world. The 1960s saw the advent of satellite communications, travel by jet airliner, and mainframe computing. Colour television spread across homes in America and Europe. It was an age of vivid images – Vietnam; the Apollo moon landings; Woodstock; Nixon in China. The world was coming together at a speed which people found thrilling and at times bewildering. The space race seemed to define a new era in a way which seems almost quaint now, with the expectation that technology would bring not just opportunity, but a better human spirit.

This globalization brought new vulnerabilities, too. For a thirty-year period after the Second World War, economies across the Western world had enjoyed steady growth, secure within the currency relationships established at Bretton

Woods. Under the strain of the Vietnam War, and then the oil shock imposed by the Organisation of Petroleum-Exporting Countries (OPEC) after the Yom Kippur War with Israel in 1973, that fell apart. The immediate impact was dislocation, as governments and consumers were exposed to spiralling prices. In time, these adjustments would usher in a new era, of free market economics, capital flows and floating exchange rates. Higher oil prices would also give an unexpected flip to the Soviet economy, and give the Kremlin leeway to pull back from engagement with the West. *Aftermath* described a post-war liberal order based on international institutions and rules. The era covered in *Détente* would bring a different kind of liberalism, with new social freedoms and unbridled capitalism. Today, we live in a world still being shaped by those changes.

With upheaval came uncertainty, or the subjunctive mood that playwright Alan Bennett describes. The 1960s and 1970s were a time of questioning, of old values colliding with the new. 'Our country is founded on as decent principles as exist in human society,' wrote the journalist Martha Gellhorn to Daniel Ellsberg, the academic who leaked the Pentagon Papers on America's involvement in Vietnam, 'but of course principles become contemptible hypocrisy when they are only used for rhetoric, not as a faithful guide to action.'[2] Inside the Soviet Union, a new wave of dissidents led by Alexander Solzhenitsyn and Andrei Sakharov found the courage to voice similar challenges to authority. Leadership lacked the moral compass of a previous era, with clarity between good and evil in human affairs. At times, posterity has treated Nixon, Brezhnev and Kissinger as black-and-white characters, tainted by Watergate or the bombing of Hanoi. I hope that readers of this book will find them more multilayered, struggling with a messy blend of high aims and low politics.

There are parallels with our own day. Some are easy to spot – an American president wrestling with the threat of impeachment by Congress, under criticism over engagement with Moscow, while seeking to disengage with honour from war in a distant country. Others are more subtle. The United Kingdom is largely invisible from the détente era, consumed with seeking entry to the European Community and domestic tensions over Northern Ireland. An ageing Russian leader zigzags between aggression and engagement with the outside world, while trying to mask a failing economy. As a serving diplomat, and writing with others from my profession in mind, I hope that we can draw out the best which this period has to tell us, and reflect on the worst.

The years between 1968 and 1975 do not seem a distant time. We still listen to the songs, and enjoy the fashion. The student rebels of that era are now our elder statesmen. The fiftieth anniversary of the moon landings in 2019 was greeted with a fresh wave of wonderment, tinged with nostalgia. But in other ways it was a different time, now almost lost. Even for those who lived through it, the constant sense of fear that the Cold War brought, of the ever-present threat of nuclear annihilation, has dwindled with time. The optimism has faded, too. Recent years have seen new waves of political protest by young people around the world, over climate change or political freedoms, but not quite that idealistic hope in progressive politics which their forebears nursed.

Recreating these years on paper, I am conscious that they coincide with my own lifespan. I was born in November 1973, the same week that the OPEC oil shock took hold. My parents met as colleagues at an English public school, where my father served as chaplain. Even there, the distant drumbeat of protest could be heard, among young men increasingly determined to question the world around them. While this is not exactly my era, it is one in which I can claim to have roots.

My aim is to bring the past alive. What follows is a narrative account, tracing the main events and protagonists. Each episode draws entirely on the sources that they left behind. This is a uniquely well-documented period, in which official records, memoirs and archive footage enable the historian to recreate much of what happened, down to the level of individual conversations and mood. The Nixon tape recordings are an additional bonus. On just a few occasions, such as the White House conversations around Watergate, I have been obliged to use a narrower and more partisan range of sources. Nonetheless, I have recreated as an authentic depiction of events as possible, as the story weaves around the globe, drawing together politicians, diplomats, soldiers and activists of the age.

I am grateful to those who have offered me advice and guidance along the way – Luke Nichter, John Farrell, Rodric Braithwaite, Vladislav Zubok, Robert Cooper, Nat Copsey, Robert Hands, F S Aijazuddin – as I have navigated the different strands. Particular thanks go to I.B. Tauris, and editors Jo Godfrey and Olivia Dellow, for their commitment to my work. And, once more, I am indebted to my wife Hilary, my mother Pauleen and my two sons Daniil and Seriosha for all their support and love through the challenges of both my writing and working life as a diplomat. I owe them a debt beyond measure.

Notes

1   Quoted in Perlstein (2008), 627.
2   Gellhorn (2006), 376.

DRAMATIS PERSONAE

Americans

Dean Acheson. 1893–1971. Lawyer and Politician. Democrat. Secretary of State, 1949–53.

Spiro Agnew. 1918–96. Politician. Republican. Governor of Maryland, 1967–69. Vice President, 1969–73.

Carl Bernstein. 1944–. Journalist. *The Washington Post*, 1966–77.

Ellsworth Bunker. 1894–1984. Business and diplomat. President, National Sugar Refining Company. Ambassador to South Vietnam, 1967–1973.

Alexander Butterfield. 1926–. US Air Force officer and administrator. Deputy assistant to President Nixon, 1969–73. Federal Aviation Administration, 1973–75.

Richard (Dick) Cheney. 1941–. Politician. Republican. Deputy, then Chief of Staff, White House, 1974–77. Secretary of Defence, 1989–93. Vice President, 2001–09.

Clark Clifford. 1906–98. Lawyer, presidential aide and politician. Democrat. Secretary of Defence, 1968–69.

Charles (Chuck) Colson. 1931–2012. Lawyer and presidential aide. White House staff, 1969–73. Later evangelical preacher.

John Connally. 1917–93. Politician. Democrat. Governor of Texas, 1963–69. Secretary of the Treasury, 1971–72.

John Dean. 1938–. Lawyer and presidential aide. White House Counsel, 1970–73.

John Ehrlichman. 1925–1999. Lawyer and presidential aide. White House staff, 1969–73.

Dwight D Eisenhower. 1890–1969. Soldier and politician. Republican. Supreme Commander, Allied Expeditionary Force, 1942–45. President 1953–61.

Daniel Ellsberg. 1931–. Academic and journalist.

Sam Ervin. 1896–1985. Politician. Democrat. Senator, 1954–74. Chair, Senate Watergate Committee, 1973–74.

Gerald Ford. 1913–2006. Politician. Republican. Congressman, 1949–73. Minority Leader, 1965–73. Vice President, 1973–74. President, 1974–77.

Barry Goldwater. 1909–98. Politician. Republican. Senator, 1953–65 and 1969–87. Presidential candidate, 1964.

William (Billy) Graham. 1918–2018. Evangelical preacher.

Alexander Haig. 1924–2010. Soldier and politician. National Security Council, 1969–73. White House Chief of Staff, 1973–74. Supreme Allied Commander Europe, 1974–79. Secretary of State, 1981–82.

Harry Robbins (Bob) Haldeman. 1926–93. Businessman and political aide. White House Chief of Staff, 1969–73.

Richard Helms. 1913–2002. Government official and diplomat. Director, Central Intelligence Agency, 1966–73.

John Edgar Hoover. 1895–1972. Government official. Director, Federal Bureau of Investigation, 1924–72.

Hubert Humphrey. 1911–78. Politician. Democrat. Senator, 1949–64 and 1971–78. Vice President, 1965–69. Presidential candidate, 1968.

Howard Hunt. 1918–2007. Government official and author. CIA 1949–70.

Henry 'Scoop' Jackson. 1912–83. Politician. Democrat. Senator, 1953–83.

Leon Jaworski. 1905–82. Lawyer. Watergate Special Prosecutor, 1973–74.

Lyndon Baines Johnson. 1908–73. Politician. Democrat. Senator, 1949–61. Vice President, 1961–63. President, 1963–69.

Robert Kaiser. 1943–. Journalist. *The Washington Post*, 1963–2014.

John Fitzgerald Kennedy. 1917–63. Politician. Democrat. Congressman, 1947–53. Senator, 1953–1960. President, 1961–63.

Robert Kennedy. 1925–68. Politician. Democrat. Attorney General, 1961–64. Senator, 1965–68.

Henry Kissinger. 1923–. Academic, diplomat and politician. National Security Adviser, 1969–73. Secretary of State, 1973–77

Egil 'Bud' Krogh. 1939–2020. Lawyer and presidential aide. White House staff, 1969–73.

Melvin Laird. 1922–2016. Politician. Republican. Congressman, 1953–69. Secretary of Defence, 1969–73.

Gordon Liddy. 1930–. Lawyer and FBI agent. White House staff, 1970–71. Committee to Re-elect the President, 1971–72.

Michael (Mike) Mansfield. 1903–2001. Politician. Democrat. Senator, 1953–77. Majority Leader, 1961–77.

George McGovern. 1912–2012. Politician. Democrat. Senator, 1963–81. Presidential candidate, 1972.

John Mitchell. 1913–88. Lawyer and politician. Republican. Attorney General, 1969–72. Chair, Nixon Presidential Campaign, 1968 and 1972.

Roger Mudd. 1928–. Journalist and broadcaster.

Thomas Moorer. 1912–2004. US Naval officer. Chairman, Joint Chiefs of Staff, 1970–74.

Paul Nitze. 1907–2004. Businessman and public servant. Deputy Secretary of Defence, 1967–69. Member of US delegation to SALT, 1969–73.

Richard Nixon. 1913–94. Politician. Republican. Congressman, 1947–50. Vice-President, 1953–61. President, 1969–74.

Dan Rather. 1931–. Journalist and broadcaster.

Ronald Reagan. 1911–2004. Politician. Republican. Governor of California, 1967–75. President, 1981–89.

James (Scotty) Reston. 1909–95. Journalist. *The New York Times*, 1945–89.

Peter Rodino. 1909–2005. Politician. Democrat. Congressman, 1949–89. Chair, House Judiciary Committee, 1973–89.

William (Bill) Rogers. 1913–2001. Politician. Republican. Attorney General, 1957–61. Secretary of State, 1969–73.

Donald Rumsfeld. 1932–. Politician. Republican. White house Chief of Staff, 1974–75. Secretary of Defence, 1975–77 and 2001–06.

William Safire. 1929–2009. Journalist and presidential aide. White House staff, 1969–73.

James Schlesinger. 1929–2014. Politician and public servant. Secretary of Defence, 1973–75. Secretary of Energy, 1977–79.

Joseph (Joe) Sisco. 1909–2004. Diplomat. Assistant Secretary of State, 1969–74.

Gerard Smith. 1914–94. Diplomat. Director, Arms Control and Disarmament Agency, 1969–74.

Hedrick Smith. 1933–. Journalist. *The New York Times*, 1962–88.

Helmut (Hal) Sonnenfeldt. 1926–2012. Diplomat. National Security Council, 1969–74.

John Stennis. 1901–1995. Politician. Democrat. Senator, 1947–89. Chair, Armed Services Committee, 1969–81.

Vernon Walters. 1917–2002. Soldier and diplomat. Deputy Director, Central Intelligence Agency, 1972–76.

Robert (Bob) Woodward. 1943–. Journalist. *The Washington Post*, 1971–.

Earle 'Bus' Wheeler. 1908–75. Soldier. Chairman, Joint Chiefs of Staff, 1964–70.

Ronald (Ron) Ziegler. 1939–2002. Presidential aide. White House Press Secretary, 1969–74.

Soviets

Aleksandrov-Agentov, Andrei. 1918–93. Diplomat.

Yuri Andropov. 1914–82. Government official and politician. Chairman, Committee for State Security (KGB), 1967–82. General Secretary, 1982–84.

Arbatov, Georgy. 1923–2010. Academic.

Bonner, Elena. 1923–2011. Dissident. Married to Andrei Sakharov.

Leonid Brezhnev. 1906–82. Politician. General Secretary, 1964–82.

Anatoly Chernyaev. 1921–2017. Government official. Central Committee, 1961–76.

Dobrynin, Anatoly. 1919–2010. Diplomat. Ambassador to Washington, 1962–86.

Andrei Grechko. 1903–76. Soldier. Minister of Defence, 1967–76.

Andrei Gromyko. 1909–1989. Diplomat and politician. Ambassador to the United States, 1943–46. Ambassador to the United Nations, 1946–48. Foreign Minister, 1957–85.

Alexei Kosygin. 1904–80. Politician. Premier, 1964–80.

Nikita Khrushchev. 1894–1971. Politician. General Secretary, 1953–64.

Nikolai Podgorny. 1903–83. Politician. Chairman, Praesidium of the Supreme Soviet, 1965–77.

Andrei Sakharov. 1921–89. Scientist and dissident. Nobel Peace Prize, 1975.

Alexander Solzhenitsyn. 1918–2008. Writer and dissident. Nobel Prize for Literature, 1970.

Vladimir Semenov. 1911–92. Diplomat. Chief of Delegation to SALT, 1968–78.

Viktor Sukhodrev. 1932–2014. Diplomat. Interpreter to Soviet leaders from 1950s to 80s.

Others

Hafez Al-Assad. 1930–2000. Syrian politician. President, 1971–2000.

Willy Brandt. 1913–1992. German politician. Chancellor of West Germany, 1969–74.

Rene Cassin. 1887–1976. French lawyer. Member, UN Commission on Human Rights, 1946–59. President, European Court of Human Rights, 1965–68.

Nikolai Ceausescu. 1918–1989. Romanian politician. General Secretary, 1965–89.

Moshe Dayan. 1915–81. Israeli soldier and politician. Chief of General Staff, 1953–58. Minister of Defence, 1967–74. Foreign Minister, 1977–79.

Alexander Dubcek. 1921–92. Czechoslovak politician. First Secretary, 1968–69.

Hussain bin Talal. King of Jordan, 1952–99.

Mao Tsetung. 1893–1976. Chinese revolutionary leader and politician. Chairman, People's Republic of China, 1949–76.

Golda Meir. 1898–1978. Israeli politician. Prime Minister, 1969–74.

Yitzhak Rabin. 1922–1995. Israeli soldier, diplomat and politician. Chief of Staff, 1964–68. Prime Minister, 1974–77 and 1992–95.

Nguyen Van Thieu. 1923–2001. Vietnamese politician. President, Republic of (South) Vietnam, 1967–75.

Le Duc Tho. 1911–90. Vietnamese revolutionary, diplomat and politician. Lead negotiator in peace talks with US, 1970–73.

Anwar Sadat. 1918–81. Egyptian soldier and politician. President, 1970–81.

Ludvik Svoboda. 1895–1979. Czechoslovak soldier and politician. President, 1968–75.

Zhu Enlai. 1898–75. Chinese revolutionary leader and politician. Premier, 1954–76.

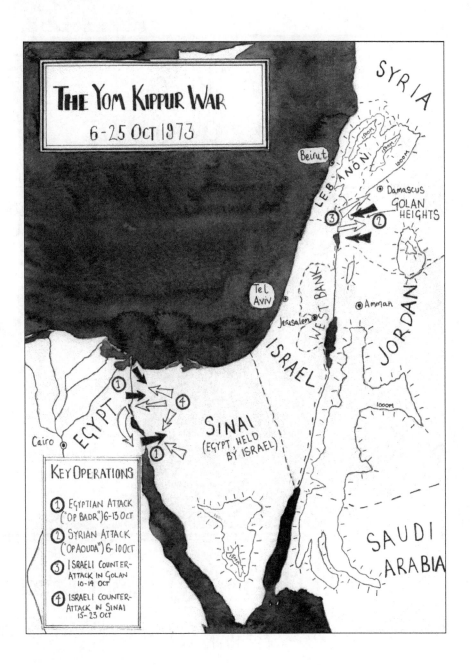

THE YOM KIPPUR WAR
6-25 OCT 1973

SYRIA

Beirut

LEBANON

Damascus
GOLAN
HEIGHTS

③ ②

Tel
Aviv

WEST BANK

Amman

Jerusalem

ISRAEL

JORDAN

① ④

Cairo

EGYPT

①

SINAI
(EGYPT, HELD
BY ISRAEL)

SAUDI
ARABIA

KEY OPERATIONS

① EGYPTIAN ATTACK
("OP BADR") 6-13 OCT

② SYRIAN ATTACK
("OP AOUDA") 6-10 OCT

③ ISRAELI COUNTER-
ATTACK IN GOLAN
10-14 OCT

④ ISRAELI COUNTER-
ATTACK IN SINAI
15-23 OCT

THE COLD WAR & DETENTE 1968-75

CANADA

UNITED STATES

UK
FRANCE
W. GER

① ③ ⑥ ①

⑦

KEY EVENTS

① BRANDT "OSTPOLITIK"

③ BERLIN QUADRIPARTITE AGREEMENT - SEPT 1971

④ NIXON VISIT TO CHINA

⑥ PARIS PEACE ACCORDS ON VIETNAM - JAN 1973

⑦ WASHINGTON SUMMIT NIXON - BREZHNEV –

⑨ MOSCOW SUMMIT NIXON - BREZHNEV - JUNE 1974

⑩ VLADIVOSTOK SUMMIT FORD - BREZHNEV –

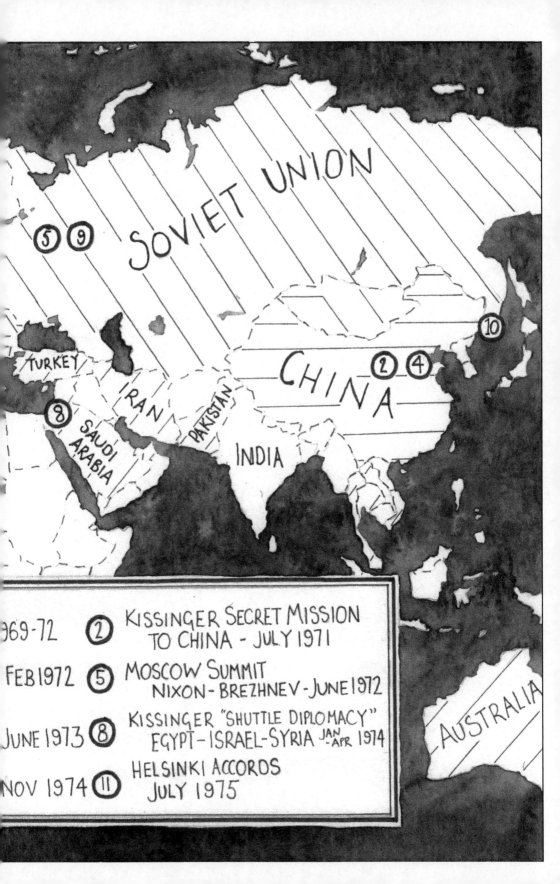

Introduction

DEEP HEARTS
(August 1968)

'Comrade Dubcek, you are to come with us straight away.'

It was nine o'clock on the morning of Wednesday, 21 August 1968. The men spoke in urgent tones. A colonel led the group, short in stature and dressed in Soviet uniform. Two others accompanied him, with tweed jackets and open shirts. One spoke Czech. They stood in Alexander Dubcek's office, in the Central Committee building. Around them, young soldiers formed a circle behind Dubcek and his colleagues, guns pointing at their heads. Outside, armoured vehicles had surrounded the building. All the phone lines were cut.

The colonel reached forward to shake Dubcek's hand, but the Slovak pulled away. He looked at the intruders. Dubcek was a tall man, with a youthful, shy smile and receding hair swept back from his brows.

'Who are you, what do you want?' he asked.

'The Revolutionary Committee.'

'What and who are you?' Dubcek repeated his question.

'The Revolutionary Security Committee.'

A colleague asked what authority the intruders held. But Dubcek cut him short. Silently, the captors led them out of the room.[1]

It had been a long night. Prime Minister Oldrich Cernik first informed General Secretary Alexander Dubcek late the previous evening that forces of the Soviet Union had entered Czechoslovakia. They were joined by allied contingents from Hungary, Poland, East Germany and Bulgaria under the Warsaw Pact, as the military grouping within the communist bloc was known. Planes carrying special forces and operatives from the KGB, or Soviet intelligence agency, flew into Prague's main airport, at Ruzyne, while mechanized troops poured across the borders. Paratroops seized Brno and Bratislava. More than 500,000 troops were involved, and 4,600 tanks.

When Cernik broke the news, Dubcek was sitting with his fellow members of the Presidium – the governing cabinet – in the Central Committee building. Bewildered, he rose and walked around the room.

It was clear that armed resistance was pointless. By midnight, Defence Minister Martin Dzur had issued orders for the Czech military to remain in their barracks.

Alexander Dubcek was 46. He had only served as general secretary of the Czech Communist Party since January. The Central Committee elected him in place of Antonin Novotny, a hardliner who had led communist Czechoslovakia for the previous fifteen years. The period since his appointment had been tumultuous. Dubcek and his colleagues sought to modernize the communist system. In March, the Central Committee published an Action Program, which envisaged economic reform, rehabilitation for victims of political oppression, and free elections within ten years. 'We shall experiment, give socialism new forms,' the document declared. 'If we did not use such an opportunity, nobody could ever forgive us.'[2] It became known as 'Socialism with a Human Face'.

Visiting in late spring, exiled journalist Zybnek Zeman was caught by the new mood. For men, politics had banished football and women as the usual topics of conversation. There was a casualness in the air. Zeman noted that the ceremonial guards outside Hradcany Castle, overlooking the centre of Prague, sported sunglasses.[3] The annual May Day parade that year turned into a joyful celebration. Ordinary citizens took part, carrying flowers. A group of former political prisoners joined in. As Dubcek and his wife Anna watched, the sun shone from a cloudless sky.[4]

It could not last. Events started to run out of control. While writers such as Ludvik Vaculik, Milan Kundera, Pavel Kohout and Vaclav Havel called for faster and more ambitious reform, Dubcek prevaricated. A convinced communist, he had lived in the Soviet Union as a child, when his father worked as a car engineer, and again during the war. By conviction and experience, he wanted to preserve ties with Moscow. But his fellow countrymen saw a different future for Czechoslovakia. They doubted that the communist system alone could reform itself. At the end of June, Vaculik issued a radical manifesto, called *Two Thousand Words*. 'We have no choice but to complete our plan to humanize the regime,' Vaculik wrote. 'The time now approaching will decide events for years to come.'[5]

Elsewhere in eastern Europe, leaders watched with unease. In mid-July, Soviet General Secretary Leonid Brezhnev met in Poland with his counterparts from the other Warsaw Pact countries. They sensed a threat. News from Czechoslovakia was leaking out. The Prague Spring, as it had become known, could undermine them, too. 'We must frankly say that what is going on in Czechoslovakia could have grave consequences,' declared Wladyslaw Gomulka, leader of the Polish Communist Party. 'The whole system of socialism is in danger of being weakened.'[6]

Over the next five weeks, Brezhnev sought to reach an accommodation. Meeting at Cierna nad Tisou, on the border between Czechoslovakia and the Soviet Union, Dubcek agreed to give commitments on restoring controls over the press. But, back in Prague, there was little evidence that the general secretary could deliver on his word. The Czechoslovak party was due to hold its Fourteenth Congress in September. The Soviets feared it would be a tipping point. The military had already drawn up plans for 'fraternal assistance', to intervene. On 17 August, the Politburo in Moscow decided to act.

Following Dubcek's arrest, he was marched down to the courtyard of the Central Committee building. The soldiers shoved him into an armoured carrier.

Shortly after noon, they arrived at Ruzyne airport. He was held there for the rest of the day.

Late that night, Dubcek was placed in an Antonov transport plane. They waited. Then he was moved to a larger Tupolev, which eventually took off. After a couple of hours, the aircraft touched down, at a rough dirt-track airfield. Dubcek was led to a wooden barracks, where the same colonel who had arrested him that morning was waiting. After a short delay, they took off again.

This time, the flight was shorter. Cernik was on the same aircraft. When they arrived at their destination, a squad of tall, athletic KGB operatives marched the captives to military vehicles. As they pushed Cernik into a car, Dubcek protested.

'What are you doing?' he cried in Russian. 'Don't you know this man is the prime minister of a sovereign state?'

The men were startled, and stood back. Cernik climbed into the car himself.

Dubcek took note. That morning, his captors had treated their charges rudely. They seemed more courteous now. The frequent changes suggested that something was not going to plan.

The convoy drove for about an hour, uphill. Late at night, they arrived at a group of houses. Dubcek was led to a room.

The following day was Thursday 22 August. Dubcek was left alone with his thoughts. The next morning he was summoned. His guards placed heavy dark glasses over his eyes, and led him outside to a car. It drove off, down the same road as two days before.

The car pulled up. Dubcek was still wearing the dark glasses. The Soviets marched him to the entrance of a building and into a lift. It rose. The group climbed out, and the glasses were removed from Dubcek's face. He was standing in an office, with a phone on the desk in front of him.

The phone rang. Dubcek picked it up. A Russian voice, soft-spoken and polite, spoke at the other end of the line. Dubcek recognized it as that of Nikolai Podgorny, Chairman of the Supreme Soviet.

'We will have to talk,' said Podgorny.

'About what, and where?' asked Dubcek.

'How about Moscow?' came the reply.[7]

Anatoly Dobrynin knew how to follow instructions.

Aged 49, the veteran Soviet diplomat had already served as ambassador in Washington for six years. The son of a plumber, he had first trained as an aircraft engineer, and built fighter planes. Then, in 1944, Dobrynin was drafted into the diplomatic service. Soviet leader Josef Stalin had instructed that the foreign ministry be enlarged with new talent, to prepare for the challenges that the Soviet Union would face after the end of the Second World War. He wanted to broaden recruitment, and change the mindset of the service. Men like Dobrynin were in demand.[8]

Dobrynin rose quickly. He was, recalled his colleague Arkady Shevchenko, 'imaginative and suave, [with] an intuitive grasp of what makes people tick'.[9] He served as a personal assistant to foreign minister Vyacheslav Molotov, and then his successor, Andrei Gromyko. In 1957, Dobrynin was sent to New York, on a secondment as Assistant Secretary General at the United Nations. Five years later, in March 1962, he arrived in Washington.

Within months, Dobrynin found himself at the sharp end of confrontation between the Soviet Union and the United States. The Kremlin had ordered a secret deployment of Soviet nuclear missiles to Cuba, within striking distance of the American mainland. In early October, US reconnaissance planes spotted preparations. President John F. Kennedy ordered a blockade of the island. During the tense fortnight that followed, Dobrynin acted as a confidential channel between Kennedy, his brother Robert, and Soviet leader Nikita Khrushchev. In a series of private messages, the two sides struck a deal. Moscow agreed to halt the deployment. In return, six months later, Washington withdrew American missiles based in Turkey.

It was a powerful experience. Dobrynin, along with other Soviet ambassadors around the world, had not known about the missile plan in advance. Suddenly, he had been plunged into handling contacts of the highest sensitivity. With Robert Kennedy, who acted as emissary for his brother, Dobrynin developed a certain trust. Robert took the Soviet ambassador into his confidence. He described the pressures that John was experiencing from the American military, who wanted to force armed confrontation.[10]

Six years on, in August 1968, Dobrynin still held his post in Washington. He had watched the escalation of events around Czechoslovakia. But he remained unsure that the Kremlin would decide to invade. Though on most issues the embassy in Washington was better informed than other Soviet missions around the world, on this occasion details of debate inside the Politburo had not been shared. On 18 August, even as Brezhnev was briefing his fellow socialist leaders on the decision, Dobrynin attended a party hosted by the Secretary of the United States Navy, aboard the yacht *Honey Fitz*. He was unaware of what was about to happen.[11]

Two days later, Dobrynin received an urgent instruction from Moscow. He was to seek an audience with President Lyndon Baines Johnson that evening, between 6 p.m. and 8 p.m. It would be midnight in Prague, by which time the invasion would have begun. Separately, a highly classified telegram arrived about the situation in Czechoslovakia, sent on a personal basis to Soviet ambassadors around the world. All diplomats, the text concluded, should 'behave stolidly and must strictly observe party and professional discipline'.[12]

Dobrynin decided to call Johnson direct. The president had given him a private number for his White House quarters, to use in emergencies. They agreed to meet that evening.

Just after 8 p.m., Dobrynin arrived for his audience. The White House barber had just given Johnson a trim, and he was in a cheerful mood. The National Security Adviser, Walt Rostow, joined them. They met in the cabinet room.

Outside, the setting sun cast shadows over the Rose Garden. It had been one of the hottest days of the year. That afternoon, the temperature had reached 90 °F. Now it was cooling with the dusk. Johnson ordered a lime and grapefruit fresca drink. It was, he proudly told Dobrynin, free of alcohol and calories. The president had embarked on a diet, and already lost seven or eight pounds.

For several minutes, the two men exchanged small talk. Then Dobrynin seized his moment.

'Mr President, I have an urgent instruction from my government.'

Dobrynin proceeded to read out the statement which he had been sent by telegram. The text was in Russian, and the ambassador translated as he read. Czechoslovakia, it declared, had requested assistance from fellow socialist states to prevent a conspiracy by internal and external forces. The Soviet Union had decided to act, in the interests of peace. 'Current events,' the statement concluded, 'should not harm the Soviet–American relations.'

As Dobrynin read, Johnson strained to catch his words. He confided to the ambassador that he was going a little deaf, but refused to wear a hearing aid.

The previous year, Johnson had held a summit with Soviet Prime Minister Alexei Kosygin, who held power along with Brezhnev and Nikolai Podgorny. Kosygin was reputed to be more liberal, and Johnson believed that the two men could create an opening to defuse tensions between East and West, with talks on limiting nuclear weapons.

Time was running out for Johnson, who had held office since the assassination of John F. Kennedy almost five years before. New presidential elections were due in November, when Johnson would step down from office. Before that, Johnson had set his heart on a further summit with the Soviets. In recent days, the White House and Kremlin had seemed close to agreement. Earlier that Tuesday, over weekly lunch with members of his cabinet, Johnson had served a glass of sherry to celebrate. 'This,' he had told them, 'could be the greatest accomplishment of my administration.'[13]

Even now, Johnson had not absorbed Dobrynin's full message. Instead, he launched into talking about timing for the summit announcement, and fixing a date. Dobrynin did not miss a beat. He would, he said, get back to the president in the morning, with further details. He had hardly expected the president to react so placidly to the news about Czechoslovakia.

Business over, the men resumed small talk. Johnson offered the ambassador a whisky, which Dobrynin readily accepted. It had been a long day. The president started talking about his home state of Texas. Dobrynin asked about the song, 'Yellow Rose of Texas'. Johnson explained that it had first been sung by the Hood Brigade, a Confederate unit in the American Civil War. Johnson's grandfather had served in the ranks. 'It's a good marching hymn,' he commented. 'It gets you excited, and so on and so forth.'

After half an hour, Dobrynin rose. He thanked the president for his time.[14]

Rostow had largely been silent. But the full importance of what Dobrynin had said was clear to him. This was a major international crisis. After the ambassador had left, the national security adviser pulled his president aside, and explained his concern. Johnson instructed Rostow to convene the National Security Council.[15]

Over the next hour, the president's most senior foreign policy advisers converged on the White House. Secretary of State Dean Rusk had served almost eight years in the role, under Kennedy and then Johnson. Secretary of Defence Clark Clifford first started in the White House as an assistant to Harry Truman. Clifford had joined the cabinet earlier that year, following the resignation of long-serving defence secretary Robert McNamara over the war in Vietnam. Vice President Hubert Humphrey had served fifteen years in the Senate, then as Johnson's running mate in the 1964 presidential election. They were joined by Richard Helms, director of the Central Intelligence Agency, and Earle 'Bus' Wheeler, chairman of the Joint Chiefs of Staff.

The group met at 10.15 p.m., around the same cabinet table where Johnson, Rostow and Dobrynin had met earlier. It was now dark outside.

Over recent months, this team had been preoccupied with finding a resolution to the war in Vietnam. During his years in office, Johnson had poured American forces into the south of the country, in an effort to resist infiltration by the communist north. But the conflict escalated, and the administration was forced to call up young American men through a draft system. By 1968, there were over half a million troops in Vietnam, with around two hundred dying each week. The war became deeply unpopular. In colleges across America, protests grew against Johnson. 'LBJ, LBJ,' ran one chant, 'how many boys did you kill today?'

To win, Johnson believed that America must be prepared to escalate the conflict still further, and launch aerial bombing against the north. He hoped it would force the North Vietnamese to accept a negotiated solution. Desultory contacts had begun, led by the veteran wartime envoy Averell Harriman. But without pressure from Moscow on North Vietnam, compromise would be impossible. Johnson had hoped that a further summit with Kosygin would produce such a breakthrough.

Now that the news about Czechoslovakia had sunk in, Johnson could see that such hopes had been dealt a heavy blow. Wheeler, Helms and Rostow updated the group on events. Discussion then turned to future relations with Moscow.

'It is aggression,' stated Johnson bluntly. 'There is danger in aggression everywhere.' Could the United States still talk to the Soviets, or would it look like condoning the invasion?

General Wheeler stated the obvious. Washington and her allies could not halt the Soviet action with military force. The Soviets had engaged in a calculated insult.

Johnson felt betrayed. 'Maybe I was sucked in by honeyed messages about the summit from Kosygin,' he fumed. Clifford, who had watched Soviet politics for almost a quarter of a century, thought that power had shifted inside the Politburo. Hitherto, Brezhnev had ceded space to Kosygin on foreign policy, but now he seemed more in control.

Reluctantly, the group agreed that the summit announcement must be postponed. A message should reach Dobrynin that night. The task was delegated to Rusk. It was, Clifford later recalled, a shattering moment. 'History was taking a wrong turn that day,' he wrote, 'and there was nothing that anyone could do about it.'

The last word fell to Humphrey. He had sat silent through the hour-long meeting, hunched in depression. Now, as the men prepared to leave, he spoke.

What the Czechs had done, he commented, had touched the heart of the communist revolution. All that the Americans could do in response was to 'snort and talk'. As the principals walked out of the room, Clifford tried to offer the vice president some words of consolation.[16]

'Come all you rebels, youth spirits, rock minstrels, truth seekers, peacock freaks, poets, barricade jumpers, dancers, lovers and artists,' ran the invitation. 'New tribes will gather in Chicago.'[17]

The Yippies had long been planning this moment. Eight months before, on New Year's Eve, student activist Jerry Rubin had met with friends Abbie and Anita Hoffman at their home on New York's Lower East Side. Paul Krassner, editor of the satirical magazine *Realist*, was also there. Wreathed in marijuana smoke, the group sat on the floor of the sparsely furnished apartment and hatched a new idea.

1967 had been a good year for the protest movement. Mounting anger at Johnson's war in Vietnam, and the drafting of young men to fight in the army, had stoked demonstrations on university campuses across the United States. Berkeley in California, where Rubin was based, had become a hotbed of discontent. In late October 1967, more than 100,000 people had descended on Washington, and besieged the Pentagon. It had contributed to the resignation of Defence Secretary McNamara.

Rubin, Krassner and the Hoffmans were older than most of the student protesters. Rubin was in his late twenties, Krassner his thirties. But they believed that they could harness the mood of a new generation. During the 1950s, television had swept across America. By 1960, around 90 per cent of households had a set. Three major networks – ABC, CBS and NBC – dominated the airwaves. Evening bulletins, such as that led by Walter Cronkite on CBS, set the news agenda. In 1964, colour broadcasting was launched. Pictures each night from Vietnam had shaped American views of the war.

Hoffman argued that television had created a new reality. People over 50 still needed words. But younger audiences absorbed news through images. Political protest should create visual drama.

In August, the Democratic Party was due to hold its convention in Chicago. Working with host-city mayor Richard Daley, Johnson hoped to dominate the event. Hoffman and his friends decided, as Rubin put it, that 'Chicago is LBJ's stage and we are going to steal it'.[18] They would host a Festival of Life, to rival the 'Convention of Death' run by Daley and Johnson, and launch a new Youth International Party – or 'Yippie' for short.

As 1968 progressed, it was clear that the convention would bring drama of its own. In the first primaries, held in New Hampshire, Johnson was challenged by Senator Eugene McCarthy, running on an anti-war ticket. He won a narrow victory, but was bloodied. Days later, Senator Robert Kennedy announced that he was entering the race. At 42, Kennedy offered the same youthful exhilaration as his brother running for the presidency eight years before. 'Whatever Robert Kennedy said,' recalled veteran commentator Theodore White, 'rang with a passion, a cry, a call on emotions.'[19] He quickly picked up support from liberals and Catholics. Reluctantly, Johnson withdrew. He hoped to swing backing for the nomination behind Vice President Humphrey.

In June, Kennedy beat McCarthy in the crucial California primary. 'And now it's on to Chicago,' he declared in his victory speech at Ambassador Hotel in Los Angeles. Moments later he was shot as he left through the hotel kitchen. Alistair Cooke, a BBC commentator who had covered American politics since the 1940s, was a bystander. Kennedy sustained devastating injuries to his head. As he slumped into unconsciousness, Cooke thought he looked like 'the stone face of a child, lying on a cathedral tomb'.[20] Twenty-six hours later, Kennedy was dead, four and a half years after the assassination of his brother John in Dallas, Texas.

Shockwaves flooded the nation. 'The Kennedys,' reflected journalist Norman Mailer, 'had seemed magical because they were a little better than they should have been, and so gave promise of making America a little better than it ought to be.'[21] Following on from the murder of civil rights leader Martin Luther King, in April that same year, the assassination seemed to plunge America into new crisis. It was, recalled the veteran *New York Times* journalist James 'Scotty' Reston, 'a time of profound political and even spiritual bewilderment'.[22]

Competing visions were descending on the Chicago convention. A further candidate, Senator George McGovern of South Dakota, entered the race. Many delegates had been elected behind Johnson or Kennedy. Now they would have to choose a new candidate. Vietnam dominated the debate. Johnson wanted to continue the war, using escalation to force the North Vietnamese to negotiate. Humphrey supported him. McCarthy and McGovern argued for withdrawal.

The convention would take place in the Chicago Amphitheatre, close to the city's stockyard district. The formal opening was scheduled for Monday 26 August. Daley ordered massive preparations, with police and national guardsmen placed on alert. Police practised anti-riot drills, against officers dressed up as hippies, in long-haired wigs and ponchos. The venue was surrounded by a ring of barbed wire, over two thousand feet in length. Beyond, the Yippies gathered on the open expanse of Lincoln Park, with tents, flags and the sound of chanting, along with drugs and free love. Pictures from Czechoslovakia were on television screens; the mood of revolt was in the air. In solidarity, the Yippies dubbed Chicago 'Prague West'.

'Off we go into battle,' Humphrey told journalists as he departed Washington for Chicago. 'And I can hardly wait.'[23]

It was 11 p.m. on Friday 23 August 1968. Alexander Dubcek's watch had stopped during his detention. But he knew that it was late: even at this time of year, when the lingering sun gave long summer evenings in Moscow, it was past twilight.

Dubcek was standing in the Kremlin. He still wore the clothes in which he had been taken prisoner, three days before. He had not washed. In front of him was Soviet leader Leonid Brezhnev, along with his colleagues Alexei Kosygin and Nikolai Podgorny.[24]

'How is Comrade Cernik feeling?' asked Brezhnev.

The attempt at small talk fell flat. Czech Prime Minister Oldrich Cernik had been beaten during detention. Dubcek had been allowed to see him briefly the previous day. He was in no mood to reciprocate.

'Bad, like everyone else,' answered the Slovak.

Brezhnev persisted. 'Is it his health that's bad or his mood?' he offered.

'It's the situation that's difficult,' Dubcek snapped back.[25]

Brezhnev and his colleagues might have said the same. Things were not going to plan.

The initial military advance into Czechoslovakia had been smooth. The Red Army seized the country within hours. The worst violence occurred at the headquarters of Radio Prague, which continued to transmit in the hours after the invasion. Seventeen people were killed when Soviet tanks attacked the building. 'Sad brothers,' declared the announcer in a final broadcast, 'when you hear the national anthem you will know that it is over.'[26]

Even under Soviet control, however, the Czechs were determined to resist. People surrounded tanks, haranguing the young Soviet soldiers. Some threw Molotov cocktails or petrol bombs, setting vehicles on fire. Graffiti appeared on the streets, telling the invaders to go home. Underground radio stations sprung up. Activists had staged the Fourteenth Party Congress, which the Soviets had hoped to stall, at a factory in a Prague suburb. The Politburo planned to hand over power to Dubcek's opponents, led by Moscow sympathizer Vasil Bilak. But it was clear that this faction could not command popular authority. 'Our friends have gone to pieces,' reported Kirill Mazurov, a point man for Brezhnev on the ground. Bilak and his acolytes were 'not showing the initiative and firmness of purpose that they should have displayed immediately'.[27]

This was dangerous. Brezhnev and his colleagues were acutely conscious of public reactions inside the Soviet Union. Pyotr Shelest, First Secretary for Ukraine, was particularly concerned. His territory bordered Czechoslovakia. In factory canteens, universities and on the streets, the KGB was picking up murmurs of discontent.[28]

Pleasantries over, Brezhnev did not attempt to shake hands with Dubcek. Podgorny motioned to take a seat, on the opposite side of a rectangular table.

The atmosphere was strained. Dubcek was exhausted, and angry. Brezhnev was nervous. The previous December, he had travelled to Prague, to oversee the transition from Antonin Novotny, the previous leader of Czechoslovakia. It was a first step into foreign policy – the space which, during his initial years in power, Brezhnev had left to Kosygin. He had gambled on Dubcek as a fresh new choice, telling his Czech comrades that 'it's your business'. Eight months on, that judgement looked questionable. In the ruthless world of Kremlin politics, a misstep in foreign policy could be fatal. Indeed, Brezhnev had himself exploited Khrushchev's mishandling of the Cuban crisis to seize power with Podgorny and Kosygin four years before.

Now Brezhnev was trying a new tack. Unknown to Dubcek, the Politburo had invited the rest of the Czech leadership to Moscow. Earlier that day, President

Ludvik Svoboda arrived at Vnukovo Airport, along with Defence Minister Martin Dzur, Bilak and others. Svoboda was a former general who had led Czechoslovak forces fighting alongside the Red Army during the Second World War. He and Brezhnev had both taken part in the liberation of Czech territory from the Nazis, during the spring of 1945. That experience had left a deep imprint on the Soviet leader.[29] As a visiting head of state, Svoboda had been given a formal welcome, with Brezhnev, Podgorny and Kosygin all waiting for him on the tarmac. The leaders drove into the centre of Moscow together, in an open limousine. The roadside was filled with crowds of onlookers, drafted in to create a display of friendship towards the Czech delegation.

That afternoon, the two sides held talks without Dubcek. Brezhnev and Podgorny made an impassioned appeal to work together. Svoboda outlined a compromise. The Soviets should allow Dubcek and Cernik to return to Prague, and let them defuse the situation. It was, Kosygin replied, a 'basis for agreement'.[30]

Nevertheless, the plan needed Dubcek on board. His support would be crucial, in winning over the Czech population. Hence this late night meeting.

Brezhnev's tone became serious. Dubcek noted that he used the familiar Russian form of address, '*ty*', rather than the more formal '*vy*'. In their correspondence over recent months, Brezhnev had switched between the two. Now he was signalling warmth. Brezhnev had built his career through charm, or what his niece later called a 'mysterious ability to motivate and manipulate without causing resentment'.[31] But on this occasion it wasn't working. Dubcek stuck firmly to '*vy*' in reply.

The Soviet leader tried to sound reasonable. 'We have to conduct negotiations in a prudent and sober way,' he told his Czech visitor. Events in Prague had run out of control. Dubcek was not personally responsible for all that had happened. The Soviets wanted to reach a businesslike solution.

'We are ready to listen,' he added. 'We are not dictating anything.'

Dubcek was in little mood to engage. He launched into a diatribe against his captors. The invasion, he told them flatly, was 'a terrible political mistake that will have tragic consequences'. The communist movement might even face breakdown.

The discussion wore on, past midnight. The Politburo members tried to calm Dubcek. It was no use.

'I'm in such a state,' he exclaimed at one point. 'Soldiers, guns pointed at me all the time, I couldn't get out of the car for seven hours, men with machine guns both sides, armoured cars. You think it was easy?'

'It was a matter of your security,' offered Brezhnev. Dubcek thought that the Soviet leader was avoiding his eye as they spoke.

Cernik joined the meeting later, equally tired and largely silent. Then, in the early hours, the gathering broke up. Dubcek was led out, through a different door to that by which he had entered. He was taken into a waiting room.

There, he found a surprise. His colleagues from Prague were waiting for him. In their midst, he saw the white hair of Svoboda, with his stiff, military bearing. For a moment, their eyes met. To Dubcek, exhausted and traumatized, it felt as though a chill ran between the two men. Through the heady months of the Prague Spring, the Slovak had counted Svoboda among his supporters. But now, in that brief exchange of glances, something had changed.

Alexander Solzhenitsyn did not often come into Moscow. The summer heat was oppressive in the city. The writer preferred to spend his days at Rozhdestvo, a hamlet south of Moscow where he owned a dacha, or wooden cottage. There was no electricity, gas or running water. Only his closest friends knew about the spot. It was a perfect hideaway.

Solzhenitsyn was approaching his fiftieth birthday. He had become used to a life in the shadows. As a young man, he had fought in the Red Army during the Second World War, serving in an artillery regiment at the great battle of Kursk, and the advance into Germany. Arrest had followed, on trumped-up charges, and eight years' imprisonment in the gulag camps of Siberia and Kazakhstan. In exile, Solzhenitsyn turned to writing for consolation. In 1962, it brought him fame. Soviet leader Nikolai Khrushchev agreed to the publication of a short novel entitled *A Day in the Life of Ivan Denisovich*. It was a searing depiction of life in the camps. Solzhenitsyn was welcomed into the Union of Writers, among the Soviet Union's literary elite. He had discovered a vocation.

With the succession from Khrushchev to Brezhnev, writing became more difficult. Censorship was reimposed. In 1965, the author Yuli Daniel and critic Andrei Sinyavsky were arrested. They were charged with anti-Soviet propaganda and agitation. The KGB launched a crackdown on underground literature, known as *samizdat*, which opponents of the regime passed secretly from one to another, in well-thumbed carbon copies.

Solzhenitsyn was determined to resist. He was engaged on a vast new work, recounting the stories of the camps and their inmates. It was called *The Gulag Archipelago*. The text could be smuggled out to the West on microfilm, where friends would arrange publication. Through the spring and summer of 1968, Solzhenitsyn plugged away at Rozhdestvo to complete his work. A circle of female helpers typed up manuscripts and hid them in the homes of trusted accomplices.

On Monday 26 August, the writer travelled into Moscow. The city had changed from his youth. Soviet planners had opened up a vast ring road around the centre, eight lanes wide in either direction. It was called the Garden Ring. Along the western side, Khrushchev had built a line of huge apartment blocks, which towered over the old Arbat roadway. On festival days they were hung with banners, displaying communist slogans.

Solzhenitsyn's first appointment took him to the north-west of the city centre, close to the House of Cinema. A few blocks away was Pushkin Square, where two years before a group of supporters had braved the KGB to stage a demonstration against the trial of Sinyavsky and Daniel.

He called at a small flat. It was occupied by 28-year-old Alya Svetlova, who lived with her young son, mother and her stepfather. Svetlova was working on a doctorate in mathematics, but had a deep love of literature. In her teens she had worked for the poet Nadezhda Mandelstam. She was connected to dissident circles, as the underground intellectuals who opposed the regime were known. Friends had suggested that she might help Solzhenitsyn. After a short meeting, they agreed that she would start some typing, doing a couple of hours each evening after her son was asleep.

Two hours later, Solzhenitsyn arrived for his second meeting. It was in the flat of Yevgeny Feinberg, a theoretical physicist and member of the Academy of Sciences. Feinberg had arranged for the writer to meet a friend. Solzhenitsyn arrived first. He insisted on drawing the curtains, against possible surveillance by the KGB, and unplugged the telephone.

A few minutes later, Andrei Sakharov walked through the door.

Born in 1921, he was slightly younger than Solzhenitsyn. Whereas the writer had been punished during the Stalin years, Sakharov had enjoyed a dizzying career, at the heart of the scientific establishment. As a nuclear physicist, Sakharov was of immense value to the Soviet state. In 1945, Stalin had been shocked by American use of the atom bomb to end the war with Japan. He ordered KGB chief Lavrenti Beria to build a rival device as fast as possible. Sakharov was recruited to this top-secret project. In the early 1950s, when the Americans developed a hydrogen bomb, it was Sakharov who played a key role in creating a Soviet equivalent. He was elected to the Academy of Sciences, at the pinnacle of Soviet academia.

Like nuclear scientists in America, Sakharov hoped that his discoveries might bring a path to peace. 'May all our devices explode as successfully as today's,' he declared when the first hydrogen bomb detonated at a testing ground in Kazakhstan, 'but over test sites and not cities.' Army generals and KGB officers looked on in stern silence. Such decisions were for politicians, not academics.[32]

Sakharov became troubled. During the early years of the Cold War, the United States enjoyed a substantial lead over the Soviet Union in quantity of nuclear bombs and capability. But by the mid-1960s, the Soviets were catching up. New technologies, with long-range bombers and intercontinental missiles, were changing the balance. The Cuba crisis had shown how quickly the world might descend into a nuclear war.

He decided to speak out. In the spring of 1968, as Solzhenitsyn was working on his *Gulag Archipelago*, Sakharov composed an essay for his fellow citizens. It was entitled *Reflections on Progress, Peaceful Coexistence and Intellectual Freedom*. 'He alone is worthy of life and freedom,' ran the epigraph, in a line from Goethe's *Faust*, 'Who each day does battle for them anew!' Copies rapidly circulated in *samizdat*. Then, in late July, *The New York Times* published a text. The top-secret scientist had burst onto the world stage.[33]

Sakharov had arrived for his meeting in a jacket and tie, carefully knotted. Solzhenitsyn was more informally dressed, used to the relaxed pattern of dacha life.

Initially, the writer was awkward and tongue-tied. 'I could not get used to the feeling,' he recalled, 'that I could reach out and touch, through that dark-blue sleeve, the arm that had given the world the hydrogen bomb.' The two men started talking about events in Czechoslovakia. The previous day, a group of seven young Soviet citizens had staged a protest on Red Square, opposite the Kremlin. They included the wife of Daniel and Pavel Litvinov, grandson of commissar Maxim Litvinov who led Soviet foreign policy during the 1930s. For a few, brief moments, the group had waved banners. 'Long Live Free and Independent Czechoslovakia' read one. 'For Your Freedom and Ours' ran another, quoting the words of nineteenth-century Poles who fought to liberate their country from Russian control. KGB officers moved in and bundled the protesters into cars.

Solzhenitsyn had read *Reflections*. Sakharov called for a new, liberal order, in which scientific progress brought countries closer together, and nuclear weapons were dismantled. Solzhenitsyn disagreed. Convergence with the West was, he argued, impossible. Western countries were lost in materialism and permissiveness, while the Soviet system was beyond rescue. The only hope lay in spiritual renewal.

Carried away, the writer had talked for two hours. In the stuffy evening air, Sakharov loosened his tie. When Solzhenitsyn had finished, he offered a response. It was delivered, the older man recalled, 'mildly . . . with an embarrassed little smile'. American journalist Hedrick Smith, who later got to know both men, noticed the same dynamic between them. Solzehntisyn thrust himself into the centre of a conversation, relishing the limelight, while Sakharov 'would hover in the wings . . . content to listen and reflect'.[34]

The physicist acknowledged that his argument contained some simplifications. But he hoped it might influence people over the longer term. His aim had been to expose the dangers that the world faced.

As they prepared to go, the two men talked again about the demonstrators. What punishment would they face? Since Stalin's time, the Soviet system had become more legalistic. The KGB and police authorities would seek to present their actions in terms framed by the law. Yet it could still be harsh. Sinyavsky had been sentenced to seven years in a labour camp, and Daniel to five.

A few days later, Sakharov decided to take action. Following publication of *Reflections*, he had been barred from the top-secret laboratory where he worked. But the scientist still had access to the Atomic Energy Institute in Moscow.

He entered and went to the director's study. There he made a phone call. It was on the special, secure network that senior officials used for communication.

His call was to Yuri Andropov, head of the KGB. Sakharov had only spoken with Andropov once before.

'I am concerned about the people arrested,' Sakharov said. Czechoslovakia had become the centre of world attention. 'It will make matters worse,' he explained, 'if the demonstrators are tried and sentenced.'

Andropov was brisk, but not cold. He had held the post for a year, following the dismissal of his predecessor, Vladimir Semichastny, over the defection of the daughter of former Soviet leader Josef Stalin to the West. A quiet, abstemious man, Andropov had served as ambassador to Hungary in 1956, during the bloody suppression of an anti-Soviet uprising. He was no stranger to the ruthless side of the Soviet state. But he was a newcomer to the ranks of the KGB and its notorious building at Lubyanka, just north of the Kremlin. 'All my life I have been walking past this building with a feeling of unease and awkwardness,' he confided to a friend after his appointment. 'Imagine, now I'm going to become its boss.'[35]

His response to Sakharov was brief. He had, he said, hardly slept for a week, due to events in Prague. He understood that the public prosecutor, and not the KGB, was investigating the demonstration.

Then Andropov added a thought. The court sentences, he told the scientist, would probably not be severe.[36]

Alexander Dubcek had been dreading this moment.

Throughout the weekend, intense discussions had continued in the Kremlin, among the Czech delegation, and with the Soviet Politburo. Dubcek left the negotiations with Soviet leader Leonid Brezhnev and his colleagues to Prime Minister Oldrich Cernik. He spent much of Saturday in bed, exhausted.

The Soviets offered Cernik a draft protocol. This would commit the Czechoslovak government to roll back many of the reforms, and reimpose censorship. They also identified individual reformers who should be removed from public office. It was a bitter pill to swallow, with painful overtones of the agreement in 1939, by which Czechoslovakia had accepted a Nazi protectorate over Bohemia and Moravia. The text also stated that the invasion had been legitimate. To soften the blow, the Politburo agreed to remove this reference. By the early hours of Monday morning, Cernik, President Ludvik Svoboda and their colleagues were leaning towards compromise.

Dubcek realized that he was isolated. He loathed the proposed agreement. But he could also see that it was the only realistic way forward. The Red Army held Czechoslovakia. The Czech foreign minister, Professor Jiri Hajek, had appeared before the United Nations Security Council, to protest against the invasion. But it was clear that the international community could do nothing. Though galling, Dubcek thought that the draft protocol would allow the Czechs to preserve at least some of the reforms they had introduced.

On Monday afternoon, Dubcek and his colleagues met with the Politburo.

As he walked into the conference room, Dubcek felt shaky, and had to steady himself against the table. 'Hang on! Hang on!' he muttered under his breath. When Brezhnev launched into a lengthy opening statement, Dubcek let the words pass over him. He left Cernik to speak in reply.

It couldn't last. As the meeting wore on, his temper snapped. The draft protocol was concealing brute force with falsehood and pretence. Dubcek wanted Brezhnev and his colleagues to hear the truth. He started speaking, in Russian and without notes.

'You, too,' he declared, 'must see the situation in our country and in our party realistically.' The invasion had been a tragedy. It had damaged the communist movement.

Brezhnev erupted. He rose to his feet, face red and thick black eyebrows bristling. Since the Second World War, he shot back, Czechoslovakia had been part of the Soviet security zone. The Prague Spring was a bid for independence. For that reason, the Soviet Union had been forced to intervene.

'If what you're saying here is also what you intend to say back home,' he added darkly, 'things will get even worse ...'

Brezhnev turned, slowly. He walked out of the room. The rest of the Politburo followed.

Left alone, the Czech delegation burst into debate. Cernik urged realism. If they did not sign now, they could not hope for better in the future. His colleague Jan Smrkovsky drew a bleak parallel with the 1939 agreement. It had 'managed to slow things down and to save a lot of people'.

Isolated, Dubcek gave way, and the meeting reconvened. It was now after dark. This time, there were no opening statements. The two sides worked through details in the text, until, around midnight, it was done. The Czechs left for the airport. Their flight for Prague took off at 3 a.m.[37]

The following afternoon, Dubcek faced a grim duty. The leaders had agreed that he should deliver a radio address to the Czechoslovak people. He would not refer explicitly to the protocol, which remained secret, but describe the provisions in general terms. He spoke seated at a desk, wearing suit and tie. Horn-rimmed glasses framed his long face. Behind him stood Margita Kollarova, a radio journalist. She wore a sleeveless top with a floral print. Her black hair was tied back.

Dubcek thanked the people for their support. He described the talks in Moscow, setting out the facts as well as he could. In the future, activities 'would be conducted in a situation that would not depend on our will alone'. Only unity could save the Czech people.

His voice was strained. After a few sentences, Dubcek choked up. He apologized to his listeners.

There was a long, awkward pause. Kollarova waved at her colleagues to bring a glass of water. Eventually, Dubcek started to speak again. Tears were streaming down his face.[38]

Mayor Daley felt in control. 'We are talking to the hippies, the Yippies, the flippies and everything else,' he told the press before the Democratic Convention opened.[39] Calm, orderly demonstrations would be allowed. In April, riots that followed the death of Martin Luther King passed off more peacefully in Chicago than other big American cities. The police knew what to do.

The Yippees had other ideas. Arriving in Chicago the previous week, they had quickly seized the initiative. Jerry Rubin arrived at the Chicago Civic Center with a 200-pound pig, dubbed 'Pigasus'. As television cameras rolled, he announced that it was the Yippy nominee for president. When Rubin delivered an endorsement speech, police stepped in. They arrested activist and pig.

The next day, undeterred, the Yippies produced a female pig. They called her 'Mrs Pigasus', and declared that she wanted her husband to be released. By now, tensions were rising. The police tried to clear protesters from their encampments, on Lincoln Park. The Yippies resisted.

'Pigs eat shit! Pigs eat shit!' they taunted the officers. 'Oink, oink!'

Over the weekend, demonstrators and police fought running battles across Chicago. Tear gas was deployed, in choking, rolling clouds. The police had been trained to wield their batons as a deterrent, with light jabs to move protesters along. But, under provocation, they lashed out. 'It was hard to control your emotions – people were so against us, you just wanted to hit them,' recalled one policeman. Blood flowed. The National Guard were called in. 'This is fantastic,' declared Rubin. 'And it's only Sunday night. They might declare martial law in this town.'

In the early hours of Monday, an ecstatic Hoffman called Deputy Mayor David Stahl.

'Hi, Dave. How's it going?' he taunted. 'Your police have got to be the dumbest and most brutal in the country.'[40]

The convention opened on Monday, inside the heavily fortified Chicago Amphitheatre. BBC journalist Alistair Cooke thought it felt like a 'circus in the middle of a plague'.[41] Debate focused on the so-called 'peace plank', which Senators George McGovern, Eugene McCarthy and their supporters had drafted as a challenge to President Johnson's policy on Vietnam. By Wednesday afternoon, the motion was defeated. Outside, the crowd reacted in fury. At the bandstand in Grant Park, overlooking Lake Michigan, a teenager pulled down the Stars and Stripes from a flagpole. Others hoisted a red T-shirt in its place. Onlookers cheered, while, enraged, the police moved in. Watching, journalist Norman Mailer was reminded of the bulls at Pamplona.[42]

That evening, thousands of protesters surged onto Michigan Avenue, in the heart of the city. Lines of police and National Guard drew up around the Hilton Hotel. They wore helmets, and held plexiglass shields. The protesters had been sleeping rough for the last week. A stink of unwashed bodies wafted across into the hotel lobby. It was, recalled one witness, 'an amazing Satanic smell . . . this exotic moral stink had drifted halfway around the world, after all, from Vietnam'.[43]

Squads of police waded into the crowd. Enraged, George McGovern watched from his fourth-floor hotel room. 'Do you see what those sons of bitches are doing to those kids down there?' he shouted at visitors.

'The whole world is watching! The whole world is watching!' chanted the protesters.

Within a couple of hours, news bulletins were screening images of the violence across America. Over 80 million people watched.[44] The convention and the Democratic Party, concluded Cooke, had been 'wounded beyond recognition'.[45]

Later that night, delegates held a vote on the nomination.

Senator Abraham Ribicoff from Connecticut spoke in support of McGovern. Under his presidency, Ribicoff told delegates, 'we wouldn't have Gestapo tactics on the streets of Chicago'.

The cameras zoomed in on Daley, sitting among the Illinois delegation. He was puce with anger.

'Fuck you, you Jew son of a bitch!' cursed the Irish American.

'How hard it is,' Ribicoff shot back, 'to accept the truth.'[46]

Voting took place at 11.30 p.m. As expected, Vice President Hubert Humphrey swept the board. Johnson and Daley had ensured that delegates swung behind their man.

On the following day, Humphrey delivered his acceptance speech. Beforehand, delegates watched a film commemorating the life of Robert Kennedy. Emotion flooded the amphitheatre. 'Bobby, We Will Miss You' ran one sign, in letters eight feet high. Delegations from New York and California launched into 'The Battle Hymn of the Republic' – the marching song first composed in the American Civil War.

Others joined in. 'He has sounded forth the trumpet that shall never call retreat,' they sung. 'Oh, be swift my soul to answer him, be jubilant my feet.'

Eventually, Humphrey stepped up to the podium. His voice was soft, high-pitched.

'Put aside recrimination and dissension,' the candidate declared. 'Turn away from violence and hatred. Believe – believe in what America can do, and believe in what America can be.'[47]

Notes

1 See Dubcek (1993), 182–3; Navratil (2006), 418–19 and 467.
2 Action Program, p. 29, as published in *Rude Pravo*, 8 April 1968.
3 Zeman (1969), 49.
4 Dubcek (1993), 150.
5 Quoted in Navratil (2006), 179.
6 Quoted in Navratil (2006), 214.
7 See Dubcek (1993), 183–6 and Navratil (2006), 420–3.
8 Dobrynin (1995), 15–16.
9 Shevchenko (1985), 194.
10 Dobrynin (1995), 75–6.
11 See Bohlen (1973), 531 and FRUS 1964–8 Vol. XVII, item 89.
12 Quoted in Navatil (2006), 409.
13 Clifford (1991), 559.
14 FRUS 1964–8 Vol. XVII, item 80; Dobrynin (1995), 180–1.
15 See Johnson daily diary for Tuesday 20 August 1968, LBJ Presidential Library.
16 FRUS 1964–8, Vol. XVII, item 81; Clifford (1991), 561–2.
17 Quoted in Farber (1988), 17.
18 Farber (1988), 22.
19 White (1969), 201.
20 Cooke *Letter from America*, 9 June 1968.
21 Mailer (1968), 91.
22 Reston (1991), 263.
23 Kurlansky (2004), 278.
24 Dubcek (1993), 187–200.
25 Navatil (2006), 465.
26 Kurlansky (2004), 292.
27 Navatil (2006), 452.
28 See Shelest report to Central Committee, 29 August 1968, at Wilson Centre archive.
29 Brezhnev (1978), 87 ; Brezhneva (1995), 252.
30 Navatil (2006), 469–71.
31 Brezhneva (1995), 17.

32 Lourie (2002), 154.
33 Sakharov (1990), 283.
34 Smith (1977), 534.
35 Doder (1986), 151. See also Aleksandrov-Agentov (1994), 265, for Andropov's reaction to his appointment.
36 Sakharov (1990), 292–4; Solzhenitsyn (1975), 369–71; Lourie (2002), 205–9.
37 Dubcek (1993), 206–14; Navatil (2006), 471–3 and 481–3.
38 Dubcek (1993), 216–17; Kollarova account at www.radio.cz/en/section/archives.
39 Farber (1988), 160.
40 Rivers (2016) Chp 4.
41 Cooke *Letter from America*, 30 August 1996.
42 Mailer (1968), 174.
43 Rivers (2016) Chp 4.
44 Farber (1988), 205.
45 Cooke *Letter from America*, 30 August 1996.
46 Rivers (2016) Chp 4; Mailer (1968), 191.
47 Mailer (1968), 223–4; White (1969), 356–9.

Chapter 1

SEEING GLORY
(January–December 1969)

It was a bright, autumnal New York morning. Henry Kissinger arrived at the Hotel Pierre, on the Upper East Side. The time was just before ten o'clock, on Monday 25 November 1968. He crossed the ornate lobby and took an elevator to the thirty-ninth floor. First opened in 1930, the 41-storey hotel enjoyed views across Central Park and downtown Manhattan. The building was crowned by a distinctive penthouse, with arched windows and pillars modelled on the Royal Chapel at the Palace of Versailles. Kissinger had come to the transition headquarters for the president-elect of the United States.

Almost three weeks before, Richard Nixon had won the presidency. Nixon fought a disciplined campaign, targeting the largest states and projecting an image of calm control at staged rallies. His Democrat opponent, Hubert Humphrey, was behind in the polls following the convention in Chicago. Nixon held his lead through the first half of the autumn. But Vietnam nearly cost him the race. In late October, Johnson declared a halt to bombing of the north. When Hanoi seemed ready to engage in peace talks, a wave of relief swept the nation and Humphrey edged ahead in the polls.

The election took place on Tuesday 5 November. Nixon spent that night at the Waldorf Towers, a few blocks south of the Pierre, joined by his wife Pat and two daughters, Julie and Tricia. Earlier, the mood aboard the aircraft which brought him back from his last campaign event in Los Angeles had been sombre, pensive. Speech-writer Pat Buchanan thought the race lost.[1] As results from individual states came in, Nixon started with a lead on Humphrey. Then, by midnight, his opponent had moved ahead in the popular vote. But, through the early hours, the lead tipped back. In the end, Nixon beat Humphrey by a margin of just 500,000. In the Electoral College, with ballots from each state, his margin was more decisive. Nixon had won by 301, against 191 for Humphrey.

For the president-elect, it had been a long journey. Richard Milhous Nixon was born on 9 January 1913, in California, the son of Quaker smallholders. He was a determined, intense child, who drove himself through the local high school, and on to study law at Duke University. 'He seemed so lonely, and so solemn,' recalled a former girlfriend. 'Sometimes I think I never really knew him, and I was as close to him as anyone.'[2]

After war service in the Pacific, Nixon threw himself into politics. He was elected to Congress in 1946, among the same intake as John F. Kennedy. As freshmen on Capitol Hill, the two men shared an office. Nixon scored early fame in the investigation of Alger Hiss, a State Department diplomat suspected of spying for the Soviet Union. Four years after arriving in Washington, Nixon was elected to the Senate. Then, in 1953, he joined the administration of Dwight Eisenhower as vice president. For eight years, he travelled the world as deputy-in-command. In 1959, Nixon visited Moscow, and found himself in an impromptu debate with Soviet leader Nikita Khrushchev, at a mock-up kitchen in the American exhibition centre. The exchange dramatized a clash between capitalism and communism.

The following year, in 1960, Nixon ran for the presidency. His opponent was Kennedy. The Democrat scored a very narrow victory in the popular vote, of just over 100,000, but a decisive margin in the Electoral College. Kennedy managed to project a youthful, vibrant image, which left Nixon looking outclassed. In a first televised debate between candidates, Nixon appeared haggard and perspiring on screen, while Kennedy was fresh.

At the age of 47, Nixon's career seemed over. He tried running for the governorship of California, but his heart was not in holding state office, and he lost. 'This,' he told journalists afterwards, 'is my last press conference.' Nixon travelled, wrote and practised law.

As the decade went on, the former vice president found himself drawn back into politics. In 1964, the Republicans selected a right-wing candidate, Barry Goldwater, who lost badly against incumbent Lyndon Johnson. Nixon offered a more centrist alternative for 1968 – with a record of being tough on communism, but open to the social policies of Eisenhower and Johnson. He assembled a new team, built around his chief of staff, Bob Haldeman, and John Ehrlichman, a former lawyer from Seattle. They developed a new campaign strategy. In 1960, Nixon had tried to visit every state, and exhausted himself. In 1968, the candidate would concentrate on projecting himself through television, mastering what Haldeman called the 'news cycle'. As America became further mired in Vietnam and racial tensions, Nixon cast himself as a leader of experience who could reunite the nation. Commentator Theodore White was struck that this relaunched candidate seemed more able to listen, to understand himself and others.[3] 'I always felt that a man cannot seek the presidency and get it simply because he wants it,' he told journalists at the Republican Convention in Miami. 'I think that he can seek the presidency and obtain it only when the presidency requires what he may have to offer.'[4]

Kissinger waited in a large room, at the end of the suite where Nixon had established his transition team. He did not know what the president-elect wanted to discuss. Aged 45, Kissinger was the son of Jewish émigrés from Nazi Germany. The family had arrived in New York in 1938, on the eve of the Second World War. Kissinger served in the US Army, including as part of the occupation force which remained in Germany after the war. Following demobilization, he had studied at Harvard University. Kissinger thrived in academia. His mind generated original ideas and expressed them in clear, compelling language. He gained tenure, and built a career as a public intellectual on foreign policy, specializing in nuclear weapons and the statecraft of nineteenth-century Europe.

During the 1960s, Kissinger edged his way onto the political scene. He was briefly attached to the Kennedy White House, in an advisory capacity. Subsequently, he was linked to Nelson Rockefeller, scion of the wealthy New York family, who sought the Republican nomination against Goldwater and then Nixon.

Nixon and Kissinger had only met once before, at a party in New York. Nixon had read Kissinger's influential book, *Nuclear Weapons and Foreign Policy*, and made reference to it. Written in 1957, the study argued that statesmen should be prepared to contemplate the limited use of nuclear weapons, in a calculated exchange of force. Experts were sceptical, but the provocative argument launched the academic as a public figure.

The president-elect walked in. He sat on a sofa, while Kissinger took an armchair. Behind them, the view looked down onto Fifth Avenue.

Neither man was much interested in small talk. Nixon launched into a description of what he hoped to achieve in foreign policy. In the early stages of his career, Nixon had built a reputation as a hardline opponent of communism. But during the years out of office his views had evolved. 'We live in a new world,' he told an audience of business and political elite at the annual gathering of the Bohemian Grove summer camp in 1967. 'The new generation has neither the old fears nor the old guilts of the old generation.' It was, he later recalled, the speech which gave him the greatest satisfaction in his political career.[5] Now, with Kissinger, he elaborated his ideas. America has an opportunity to influence the global balance of power. She needed to end the war in Vietnam, but from a position of strength that would allow her to recalibrate relationships with European allies, the Soviets, and with communist China.

As he watched, Kissinger was struck by Nixon's physical movements. His gestures seemed oddly out of sync with the ideas running through his head, and expressed in his low, gravelly voice. Following the candidate at the Republican Convention in Miami, journalist Norman Mailer had been struck by the same phenomenon.[6] It was, Kissinger recalled, as if 'two different impulses were behind speech and gesture'.

The conversation moved on to structures in government. Nixon said that he was suspicious of the State Department. He wanted a strong foreign policy, driven from the White House. Kissinger agreed. His brief exposure to the Kennedy and Johnson administrations had left him convinced that a more disciplined, centralized effort was required, built around the National Security Adviser's staff.

Nixon discreetly reached for a buzzer. Bob Haldeman entered the room. The chief of staff was tall, with a neat crew cut. He clutched a yellow notepad. Nixon instructed him to establish a secure phone line to Kissinger's office at Harvard. Haldeman wrote down the order.

The men rose to their feet. The meeting was over. Haldeman escorted Kissinger from the suite, stopping for a few moments in his own office. His role, he explained to the academic, was to prevent 'end-runs', where uncoordinated advice reached the president without squaring with relevant staff members first.

Kissinger shook hands, and left. He was due back at Harvard that afternoon, to teach a seminar. It wasn't clear what, if anything, Nixon and his team wanted.

The next day, Kissinger received a phone call. It was from John Mitchell, a New York lawyer and campaign manager to Nixon. He asked Kissinger to return to the Pierre Hotel.

'What have you decided about the national security job?' asked Mitchell, when Kissinger presented himself again at the thirty-ninth floor.

'I did not know that I had been offered it,' replied the academic.

'Oh, Jesus Christ!' exclaimed Mitchell. 'He has screwed it up again.'[7]

The following Monday, Nixon announced the appointment to a press conference at the Pierre. He focused on the chance for Kissinger to overhaul the machinery on foreign policy, creating what he called a 'very exciting new procedure' to make sure the president got the advice that he needed.

In Johnson's presidency, key decisions were reached at the weekly cabinet lunch on Tuesdays. Under this, issues were thrashed out in a so-called Senior Interdepartmental Group, chaired by the deputy secretary of state. Nixon and Kissinger thought this model inefficient, and that it ceded too much ground to the State Department. They wanted a more centralized structure, in which National Security Council (NSC) staff worked through options from line departments, and ensured that policy was driven from the presidency.

To play this centralized role, Kissinger needed a strong team. His predecessor Walt Rostow had been supported by a staff of specialists, drawn from across the Washington bureaucracy and based in the White House. Kissinger followed the same approach, but wanted new people, who owed their loyalty to him.

His first requirement was a deputy. Much of NSC business would deal with military matters. Kissinger realized that this was not his field of expertise. Rostow had employed a liaison officer, linked to the Joint Chiefs of Staff. Kissinger wanted someone who could be his own man, willing to stand up for the White House in any difference of view with the Pentagon, as the building which housed the Department of Defence was known. He also wanted a 'rough-cut' type, with experience of front-line operations.[8]

Fritz Kraemer was an old mentor who had known Kissinger since the war. He made a suggestion. Alexander Haig was 44, a West Point graduate who had fought in Korea and then Vietnam. Serving with the First Infantry Division, he had won a Purple Heart and promotion to the rank of colonel. During one encounter at night, on the Cambodian border, Haig was in a helicopter that was hit. The pilot crash-landed. He and Haig ran back to the battalion positions, under fire from Viet Cong troops. Bullets whipped between them, and mortar rounds exploded in the darkness. The Vietnamese advanced in waves, throwing satchel charges into the American positions. At dawn, F4 Phantom jets struck back, tearing through the attackers with chain guns, napalm and cluster bombs. When the fighting was over, Haig's men counted almost five hundred Vietnamese dead, including one group of twenty-nine men still lying in assault positions, where a cluster bomb had cut them down.[9]

In December 1968, Haig called on Kissinger at the Pierre. The adviser-designate had been assigned to a small room, with oversized furniture. Haig thought that it looked rather shabby.

'Are you a military intellectual?' asked Kissinger. Chairman of the Joint Chiefs 'Bus' Wheeler had offered him various names for the post, with strong academic credentials. It was not what the Harvard professor wanted.

Haig demurred, pointing to his service record. He was, he said, a 'combat commander by intention, training and instinct'. The two men talked about Vietnam. Haig described his experiences, and shared his scepticism about the direction of the war.

Kissinger nodded, smiled and offered Haig the job. He was to start immediately.[10]

Richard Nixon was Anatoly Dobrynin's third president. After six years in Washington, the Soviet ambassador had become used to visiting the Oval Office. Presidents had worked there since William Howard Taft, who remodelled the West Wing of the White House in 1909, creating a new office from the half-rounded corner room used by his chief of staff. With each new incumbent, the style changed. Kennedy had decorated the room with a deep red rug and pale curtains. Johnson opted for a blue-grey decor instead. During his first weeks in the job, Nixon had not yet had an opportunity to make his own mark. His Irish setter, King Timahoe, proved reluctant to lie down next to the president's desk and Chief of Staff Bob Haldeman was reduced to bribing the dog with biscuits.[11]

For Dobrynin, the arrival of a new president was a moment of opportunity, and of risk. As Moscow's representative in Washington, he must judge how to balance the two. Nixon had built his reputation as a tough opponent of communism. But on the campaign trail he suggested that he was open to negotiation under the right conditions. Since taking office, the administration had given further hints. In giving evidence before the Senate Committee on Foreign Relations, Nixon's nominee as secretary of state, Bill Rogers, sought to be conciliatory. 'As the impact of Czechoslovakia wears off a little bit,' he told the senators, 'it is a good thing to try to probe for initiatives toward peace.'[12] Moscow had taken note. This might be the moment to change gear.

Nevertheless, the international scene remained delicate. Through the autumn of 1968, the Soviet Union had tightened its control over Czechoslovakia. Alexander Dubcek remained in office, but found himself marginalized. Moscow was grooming new leadership in Jan Husak, a fellow Slovak who was prepared to toe the Soviet line. The joyful atmosphere of the Prague Spring was a fading memory. Days before Nixon's inauguration, a young philosophy student called Jan Palach set fire to himself on Wenceslas Square, in the heart of Prague. Horribly burned, he later died in hospital.

Western governments largely kept their counsel. Realism prevailed, as Johnson and his colleagues had anticipated it would on the first night of the invasion. But it was not a moment to make overt gestures. 'While showing willingness to do official business with them,' the British Foreign Office instructed its embassies in Warsaw Pact countries, 'you should avoid public expression of goodwill.'[13]

Even before Nixon's inauguration, the Soviets had opened up lines of communication. Just after New Year, Boris Sedov, an official from the Soviet Embassy in Washington, travelled up to New York. Sedov was a KGB officer. He met Kissinger at the Pierre Hotel. The emissary read out a lengthy message, which Kissinger noted down. Moscow had watched the US elections carefully. The Soviets did not take a 'pessimistic view ... of the accession of the Republicans to power'. They were willing to build mutual trust, and work towards a goal of peaceful coexistence. But it would need both sides to take steps towards this end.[14]

Three weeks later, in his address at the traditional inauguration ceremony held on the steps of the Capitol building, Nixon picked up on the theme. It was a cold and windy day. The new president took the oath of office with his hand resting on a family Bible, open to the verse in Isaiah 2:4 calling on nations to 'beat their swords into plowshares'. Then, in his address afterwards, he set out the case for peace. 'Those who would be our adversaries,' he declared, 'we invite to a peaceful competition – not in conquering territory or extending dominion, but in enriching the life of men.' The new president went on to invoke a photograph taken by astronauts on the Apollo 8 space mission, which at the end of 1968 had made the first manned orbit of the moon. As the men emerged from behind the far side, they saw the earth reappear over the lunar horizon. It was, he said, quoting the poet Archibald MacLeish, a chance 'to see ourselves as riders on the earth together, brothers on that bright loveliness in the eternal cold'.[15]

With the new administration in office, Dobrynin no longer needed to act through Sedov. He met Kissinger for the first time on Valentine's Day. It was a Friday evening. Kissinger rarely appeared on the diplomatic cocktail circuit. But he accepted an invitation to the Soviet Embassy, for a reception in honour of Georgy Arbatov, a well-connected Soviet expert on America who was visiting Washington. Dobrynin was unwell, and remained in his private apartment upstairs. A junior official pulled Kissinger aside and suggested that he come up to meet the ambassador.

Kissinger found Dobrynin in his dressing gown. The ambassador explained his reason for asking to see the presidential adviser. He had spent much of January back in the Soviet Union, and met Leonid Brezhnev, Andrei Kosygin and Nikolai Podgorny. He had a message from these leaders to convey to the new president. There was an opportunity to strengthen relations between the two superpowers, which should not be lost. Kissinger agreed. The new administration, he said, was ready to move, but it must be on a reciprocal basis.[16]

On the Monday morning, Dobrynin came to the White House. He waited in a windowless room at the centre of the West Wing. Wartime president Franklin Roosevelt had used it to display his aquarium, and dubbed it the Fish Room. Nixon greeted his visitor, and escorted him across the corridor to the Oval Office.

They were joined by Kissinger, together with Malcolm Toon, Assistant Secretary from the State Department. Toon was there as a compromise. Nixon's new Secretary of State, Bill Rogers, had demanded to attend the meeting, but Nixon wanted to establish his primary role over relations with the Soviets. Kissinger and Haldeman spent much of the weekend standing Rogers down.

Nixon invited the ambassador to speak.

Dobrynin took the same line as Sedov. The president, he noted, had talked about an era of negotiations, rather than confrontation. Moscow was keen to begin as soon as possible. Talks could take place on various levels and cover different subjects at the same time.

Nixon was intrigued by this last point. What did the ambassador mean?

Dobrynin explained. In his first press conference as president, a couple of weeks before, Nixon had talked about the race in nuclear weapons and conflict in the Middle East. It should, the ambassador said, be possible to pursue such issues in tandem. Was the president open to such an approach?

Nixon sounded interested. Progress in one area might influence that in others. He talked about Vietnam, and about the confrontation over the city of Berlin, which was located within East Germany, but under arrangements made at the end of the Second World War was divided into sectors run by the Soviets, Americans, British and French. The Soviet Union and the United States had the power to maintain peace in the world. They must ensure that their differences did not lead to confrontation, nor be drawn into it by the action of others.

Dobrynin thanked the president. He handed over a memorandum, prepared by Moscow. As Kissinger and Toon rose to leave, Nixon asked Dobrynin to stay behind for a moment.

Once alone, Nixon explained that he had a sensitive request to make. To navigate relations between Moscow and Washington, he wanted a direct channel for confidential communication. Dobrynin, he said, should establish such a link with Kissinger, and not the State Department.

Dobrynin thanked the president again. In principle, such a proposal was no surprise. During the war Roosevelt had handled contacts with British premier Winston Churchill and Soviet leader Josef Stalin through his emissaries Harry Hopkins and Averell Harriman. Kennedy had also worked with trusted assistants. The nature of presidential power was to centralize authority in the White House. But it was a delicate business. If Nixon was serious, it could mean Dobrynin became privy to secrets that the president was not prepared to share even with his own cabinet colleagues. Already a veteran of almost a decade in Washington, Dobrynin's posting was about to enter a new phase. He shook Nixon's hand, and took his leave of the president.[17]

Nixon found such encounters stressful. He had prepared carefully, underlining sections of the briefing paper which Kissinger provided in advance and memorizing lines to use in the meeting. Afterwards, he sought reassurance. Four times that afternoon, he called Kissinger into his office.

The academic was upbeat. At the Pierre Hotel, Nixon and Kissinger had discussed at length how to handle relations with the Soviet Union. They hit on a set of guiding principles. Progress should be built on concrete initiatives, rather than general declarations; both sides should restrain themselves from pursuing advantage at the expense of the other; and, most importantly, there should be linkage between different issues, so that progress on one might be tied to others.[18]

Nixon had alluded to these in his meeting with Dobrynin. Now, as Kissinger read through the note which the ambassador had left behind, he could see the raw elements which might make them work in practice. Quoting Nixon's words from his inaugural address, the note listed those areas on which the United States and the Soviet Union could make progress: nuclear weapons; Vietnam; Germany; the Middle East. It was, he told the president, 'extraordinarily forthcoming'. This was a moment which Washington should not let pass.[19]

Dean Acheson was not an easy man.

A lawyer by training, he had served as deputy and then secretary of state in the post-war administration of Harry Truman. Acheson had a sharp mind, bristling moustache and a cutting manner. When, as a young congressman, Nixon had made his name by investigating the diplomat Alger Hiss on suspicion of communist espionage, Acheson was unimpressed. He was a personal friend of Hiss, and did not view the accusation kindly.

Now approaching his seventy-sixth birthday, the former secretary of state remained as sharp as when he had served in public office, almost twenty years before. It was mid-March, and the new president had asked Acheson for his advice.

Acheson arrived in the Oval Office alone. As secretary of state, he had frequently made the short walk across from Foggy Bottom, home to the State Department. He and Truman had formed a close partnership, despite very different backgrounds. While Acheson had enjoyed a privileged upbringing in Connecticut and Truman came from a small town in Missouri, they established a deep mutual respect. Acheson dedicated his memoirs to the former president, calling him 'the captain with a mighty heart'.

Truman and Acheson's partnership had lasted through the ordeal of the Korean War. In May 1950, communist forces invaded South Korea, without warning. The Americans intervened, only to be thrown back when China entered the war a few months later. Bogged down in stalemate, Truman saw his popularity sink as his administration ground through the remainder of his presidential term.

For Nixon, it was the current conflict in Vietnam, rather than Korea, that preyed on his mind. Every month, America was spending $2.5 billion on the war, and losing more than 800 men.[20] The previous day, at a ceremony held in the Oval Office, the president had presented the Medal of Honour to the family of Private First Class Melvin Newlin. The Marine had been mortally wounded in fighting around Nong Son, on the coast of South Vietnam. Hit by mortar and grenade explosions, he continued to man a machine gun post, and broke up Viet Cong attacks against the rest of his company's position. 'His indomitable courage, fortitude and unwavering devotion to duty in the face of almost certain death,' ran the presidential citation, 'reflected great credit upon himself and the Marine Corps.'[21]

Before his inauguration, Nixon and Kissinger had sent word to Hanoi, through a trusted French intermediary, that the new administration was open to negotiation.

But the approach had met with silence, and then a resumed offensive by communist forces, based along the Cambodian border within reach of Saigon. Rocket attacks fell on the South Vietnamese capital. In retaliation, Nixon ordered covert bombing against the main base areas, located in enclaves of Cambodian territory dubbed the Fish-Hook and Parrot's Beak. The first strikes by strategic bomber B-52 aircraft, code-named Breakfast, had taken place two days before.

Against this backdrop, administration policy wavered. Averell Harriman had served as Johnson's representative at peace talks in Paris. He now argued strongly for a deal.[22] Emboldened, Secretary of State Bill Rogers had met with Dobrynin in early March, and suggested that Washington was ready to open private talks with Hanoi. Kissinger was incandescent. Nixon instructed him to pass a corrective message to the Soviets.

Speaking with Acheson, Nixon confessed that he found the situation 'frustrating and puzzling'. He could see the business establishment was reaching a view that America should simply cut its losses and withdraw. This was, he believed, unacceptable.

Acheson agreed. He drew a parallel with the war in Korea. Fighting had ended only when the Chinese realized that they could not win militarily. The United States should take the same approach in Vietnam, and not engage in negotiations.

Was it, Nixon asked, a good time to talk with the Soviets?

Acheson had been impressed with the new president. Nixon seemed to project a sense of orderliness and concentration. He could be given frank advice.

No, Acheson replied. There was never a good time.[23]

A few days later, Nixon met with his National Security Council. They gathered in the Cabinet Room. In addition to the usual cast of Washington officials, the group was joined by Ellsworth Bunker, the American ambassador in Saigon. Kissinger's deputy Alexander Haig completed the group as the most junior officer in the room.

Two weeks before, Defence Secretary Melvin Laird and 'Bus' Wheeler, chairman of the Joint Chiefs, had visited Vietnam. They reported that the war was, in effect, at a stalemate. American forces could prevent the communists from overrunning the south. But they could not achieve victory. The fighting had already cost $100 billion and 33,000 American lives. These were now in effect, Laird reported, 'sunk costs'.[24] Meanwhile, public support in the United States continued to decline.

Laird believed that he had a solution. Washington should accelerate investment in strengthening the South Vietnamese army, so that it could take over the burden. This would create space for American forces to withdraw in an orderly fashion.

For two hours, the NSC wrestled with the issue. Nixon liked the proposal. Rogers agreed, describing it as 'de-Americanization'. But, Nixon reminded his colleagues, his administration was up against the clock. Mid-term elections were due in eighteen months' time. They could not afford to suffer the fate of Truman and Acheson over Korea. Indeed, at best they had a window of six to eight months in which to make progress. Bunker said that he was hopeful that conditions might exist to reach a political solution.

Laird suggested that they use the phrase 'Vietnamization', rather than 'de-Americanizing' the war. Nixon agreed. It was, Haig reflected, a skilful touch of public presentation.[25]

The meeting finished just after noon. Nixon walked back to the Oval Office, with Laird, Kissinger and Haldeman. After a few minutes, Haldeman stepped outside, and found Walter Tkach, the White House doctor. He had brought news. Haldeman ushered the medic back into the Oval Office.

'Mr President,' Haldeman said. 'President Eisenhower just died.'

It was expected. Eisenhower was 78, and had been in declining health. He spent the last year in the Walter Reed Military Hospital, nursed through a series of heart attacks. But the announcement still came as a shock.

Nixon was silent for a moment. Then he stood and looked out of the window. Tears ran down his face. 'He was such a strong man,' the president said.

The bond between past and present president ran deep. Nixon first saw Eisenhower leading a celebratory ticker-tape parade in New York at the end of the Second World War. Seven years later, in 1952, the veteran picked Nixon to be his running mate, even though the latter was still a junior senator. They had served together as president and vice president for eight years. Early in his first term, Eisenhower had reached a ceasefire agreement in Korea. He went on to preside over a period of rising prosperity across America.

During Eisenhower's final decline, the president had been a frequent visitor to his bedside. Now, his eyes red with grief, Nixon recalled their last conversation together. It had taken place two days before. Awkwardly, Kissinger, Laird, Haldeman and Rogers, who had joined the group, listened to their president.

Nixon had found Eisenhower lying in his hospital bed, pale and drawn. It was clear that the end was close. They spent fifteen minutes together. As he rose to leave, Nixon felt a sudden impulse to say a last farewell. Eisenhower's eyes were already closed.

'General,' he told the dying soldier, 'no man in our history has done more to make America and the world a better and safer place in which to live.'

'Mr President,' replied Eisenhower, opening his eyes and lifting his head weakly from the pillow. 'You do me great honor in what you have just said.'

And, slowly, the general raised his hand, in a salute to the president.[26]

'We said to ourselves, even if we have to die on the ice, we have to beat them.'

Jozef Golonka had come to Stockholm with one objective. The Czech team was competing in the International Ice Hockey World Championship. The Soviet Union had won the last six such contests, in an unbroken run. The Czechs were determined to dent their record. When the team arrived in Stockholm, they found hundreds of telegrams, sent by fans back in Czechoslovakia.

Two matches were scheduled with the Soviet Union. The first had taken place on Friday 21 March, at the Johanneshov stadium. The Czechs won 2-0. After the first goal, striker Jaroslav Holik taunted the Soviet goalkeeper, calling him a 'bloody communist'. Back home, the fans were ecstatic.[27]

The second match came a week later. Holik scored two goals. The final result was 4-3 to Czechoslovakia.

That night, crowds massed on the streets of Prague. Hundreds of cars drove up and down Wenceslas Square in the centre of the city, honking their horns and headlights blazing. By 11 p.m., police estimated over 100,000 had gathered. 'Score, score,' they shouted. 'One, two, three, four!'

The offices of Soviet airline Aeroflot were in a building at the lower end of Wenceslas Square. Loose paving stones were piled outside, apparently left by workmen. The crowd surged forwards. Stones were thrown, smashing the office windows. People clambered inside. Furniture and office items were hurled outside onto a bonfire. Eventually police arrived, and pushed the looters back. 'Gestapo! Beat them!' shouted the crowd.[28]

Three days later, Soviet Defence Minister Marshal Andrei Grechko flew in to Milovice military airfield, outside Prague. He was joined by Deputy Foreign Minister Vladimir Semyonov. Grechko had first joined the Red Army at the age of 16, as a cavalryman in the Russian Civil War. During the Second World War, he commanded the First Guards Army, which liberated Czechoslovakia at the end of the war. He and Semyonov were determined not to lose the country now.

The next day, Dubcek and other members of the Executive Committee of the Czechoslovak Praesidium met. As general secretary, Dubcek still chaired the gathering. But his authority was much reduced since the events of the previous summer. Pro-Soviet hardliners led by Jan Husek had gained ground, with Moscow's support. These new disturbances further weakened Dubcek's position.

The meeting began with a report from Jan Pelnar, the interior minister. His officials had received police reports from across the country following the ice hockey match. There had been provocations against Soviet troops, and scuffles.

President Ludvik Svoboda had joined the gathering. Like Grechko, he was a veteran of the war. 'One must feel ashamed over what has happened,' he commented. 'Would something like that be possible in another country? We must be ashamed for that.'

Prime Minister Oldrich Cernik was downbeat. 'We have deeply underestimated the situation and its political ramifications,' he warned his colleagues.[29]

At ten o'clock that night, Grechko met Defence Minister Martin Dzur and senior members of the Czech military. He was blunt. The situation was worse than in August 1968. Action was needed. 'I personally liberated many of the places where there were disturbances,' he told the assembled officers. 'We will not tolerate a repetition ... we shall not let Czechoslovakia go.'[30]

The next day, Grechko and Semyonov met Dubcek at Prague Castle. What, Dubcek asked, did the Soviets want?

'The counter-revolution must be beheaded,' replied Semyonov.

Inside the Praesidium, support for Dubcek was melting away. During the months after August 1968, he had hoped that it might be possible to retain some of the reforms that he had introduced, while placating the Soviets. But now even his loyal supporters feared that he had become a liability.

Dubcek went to consult Svoboda. Might the president be prepared to weigh in behind him, and prevent Husek from taking over? The two men sat in Svoboda's office, in Prague Castle. Dubcek set out his case. The older man listened in silence. He seemed, Dubcek thought, to sink deeper into the sofa as the conversation went on.

At last Svoboda spoke, cutting Dubcek short. 'For God's sake, Sasha,' he interjected. 'Forgive me, but I must tell you this. I have already promised Grechko that you would soon resign.'

Dubcek looked away. The game was up.[31]

Midway Island was not used to visitors. The tiny atoll lay on the International Date Line in the Pacific Ocean, halfway between America and Asia. San Francisco was 2,800 nautical miles to the east; Japan just over 2,200 to the west.

In June 1942, the Japanese and American fleets fought for control of the seas around Midway. It was the first naval battle conducted entirely by aircraft, launched from carriers, rather than surface ships. The encounter was a crucial turning point. In the attack on Pearl Harbor, six months before, the Japanese had failed to catch the US carriers in their base. Planes from these ships provided enough firepower to sink four Japanese carriers and prevent Japan from establishing naval domination over the Pacific.

Twenty-seven years later, Midway remained a US naval station. It was led by Captain Albert Yesensky, a veteran of the Pacific War. Airstrips covered both the main islands on the atoll, and radio communication masts. It was a remote posting, but not without attractions. Personnel could live with their families, enjoy the empty white beaches and stunning sunsets. They shared their remote home with thousands of gooney birds, a rare species of albatross which had colonized the reef long before the US Navy.[32]

In late May 1969, Petty Officer Tom Helvig received a call from base headquarters. The president was coming. Helvig and his colleague Jim McMullin were detailed to act as drivers. The base was thrown into a frenzy of preparation. Twenty cars were flown in from the naval base on Hawaii, more than 1,000 nautical miles away. Thousands of droppings from the gooney birds were swept away. Along the short road linking the airstrip to the base commander's house buildings were given a fresh coat of paint and shrubs pruned. The backs, facing away from the road, were left untouched.

It was Vietnam which brought Nixon to this remote spot. In April, North Vietnam had changed tack, announcing a ten-point plan to achieve peace. The starting point for the communist leadership in Hanoi was that the US should withdraw its forces prior to any settlement. Nixon had responded with his own proposals, which envisaged sequencing withdrawal alongside negotiations. This would allow for 'Vietnamization' to proceed, as the South Vietnamese took over the lead in defending their country. But it would only work if the government in Saigon was willing to go along. And the South Vietnamese remained fearful of losing their American ally. While the South Vietnamese army was a million strong, it was staffed by conscripts, and beset with poor leadership and low morale. Nixon had invited President Nguyen Van Thieu to Midway to hear a tough message.[33]

Nixon arrived on 8 June 1969. The previous day, he and National Security Adviser Henry Kissinger had met in Hawaii with their key advisers on Vietnam, including Secretary of State Bill Rogers, Defence Secretary Melvyn Laird, Chairman of the Joint Chiefs 'Bus' Wheeler and Ambassador Ellsworth Bunker from Saigon. They were joined by General Creighton Abrams, who led ground forces in Vietnam, and Admiral John McCain, commander of the US Navy in the Pacific. Abrams was a former tank officer, who led the battalion that relieved the embattled 101st Airborne Division at Bastogne during the battle of the Bulge in 1944. McCain, himself the son of an admiral, had served as a submariner against the Japanese during the war. His son John had been shot down in 1967 on a bombing mission over Hanoi, and taken prisoner by the North Vietnamese. Reluctantly, the two commanders agreed to begin the withdrawal of US forces.[34]

Captain Yesensky had prepared throughly. As Nixon descended the steps from the presidential aircraft, Air Force One, a Marine band played *Ruffles and Flourishes*, followed by *Hail to the Chief*. Five howitzers, flown in from Hawaii, performed a 21-gun salute. White House Chief of Staff Bob Haldeman noted with satisfaction in his diary that it was a smooth operation.[35]

A few minutes later, Thieu arrived, on a Pan American aircraft. The two presidents boarded a Lincoln Continental limousine, chauffeured by McMullin. Petty Officer Helvig was assigned to drive Kissinger. Sailors from *USS Arlington* lined the route to the base commander's house, dressed in white uniforms. Kissinger was more intrigued by the gooney birds. 'They squat[ted] arrogantly,' he recalled, 'in the middle of the road, producing traffic jams to amuse themselves.'[36]

Nixon and Kissinger met privately with Thieu and Nguyen Phu Doc, his military chief. Their talks lasted for four hours, running over lunch.[37] Haldeman and Rose Mary Edwards, Nixon's secretary, slipped away to the beach for a swim.[38]

The president said that he wanted to speak in confidence. The press was trying to drive a wedge between him and Thieu. While America was committed to resisting North Vietnam, and to achieving peace, neither side could win militarily. And the domestic situation inside the United States had become a 'weapon in the war'.

Thieu agreed that a negotiated peace was essential. He was open to talks, but did not want to be pushed around. People thought that the United States would force South Vietnam to make concessions. Spirits were sagging in Saigon.

In public, both men had to put on a brave face. Nixon had arrived in Midway with a travelling entourage of over 350 people, including the White House press corps. With a difference of five hours behind the East Coast, his media team were anxious to broadcast in time to meet evening news bulletins. So the talks broke up after an hour and a half, to hold a press conference outside the commander's house.

Speaking at a microphone alongside Thieu, Nixon announced the withdrawal of 25,000 US troops. It was the first time that America had reduced its forces in Vietnam. Thieu looked on, impassively.[39]

Three days later, back in Washington, Kissinger met Dobrynin. The adviser and ambassador had settled into a rhythm for such private meetings. They would see each other in the East Wing of the White House, to avoid attention from the press corps. Kissinger had taken to agreeing his talking points in advance with Nixon. The president would annotate and initial a paper copy. Kissinger would then show this to Dobrynin, to make clear that he was speaking with direct presidential authority.

Dobrynin explained that he was due to return to Moscow, for consultations. His link to Kissinger had further bolstered his standing back home, as what one colleague called 'the Soviet Union's knight in the international chess game'.[40] He had noted the announcement from Midway. The administration seemed to be moving in a deliberate and precise way, on Vietnam, and on the Middle East and nuclear arms.

Kissinger agreed. It was a very careful policy, with moves for the next few months worked out. The president was prepared to see changes in Saigon which produced a fair political contest, but not a 'disguised defeat' for the United States and her South Vietnamese allies. Dobrynin acknowledged that Hanoi was difficult. It was hard for the Soviet Union to dictate what position the North Vietnamese took. Kissinger pointed out that they supplied 85 per cent of military equipment used by the north.

What message, Dobrynin asked, should he convey back to Moscow?

Everything, Kissinger said, depended on Vietnam. If the war could be brought to a close, there was no limit on what could be achieved.[41]

Notes

1   White (1969), 454; Price interview, 4 April 2007, p. 78.
2   Ambrose (1987), 67.
3   White (1969), 165.
4   Mailer (1968), 43.
5   Address to Bohemian Club, San Francisco, 29 July 1967, at FRUS 1969–76 Vol. I, item 2; Nixon (1978), 284.
6   Mailer (1968), 34.
7   Nixon (1978), 340–1; Kissinger (1979), 10–14. See also Haig interview with Brinkley and Naftali, 30 November 2006, p. 7.
8   Kissinger (1982), 106–7.
9   Haig (1992), 174–9; Haig interview with Brinkley and Naftali, 30 November 2006, p. 8.
10 Haig (1992), 189–91.
11 Haldeman interview with Raymond Geselbricht, 11 April 1988, p. 98–9.
12 FRUS 1969–72 Vol. I, item 8.

13 Bischof et al. (2010), 249.

14 FRUS 1969–76 Vol. XII, item 1.

15 Nixon, First Inaugural, 20 January 1969; Nixon (1978), 346–7.

16 Kissinger (1979), 111–14.

17 FRUS 1969–76 Vol. XII, item 14; Dobrynin (1995), 198–9; Nixon (1978), 369–70, Kissinger (1979), 141–3.

18 Kissinger (1979), 128–30; Nixon (1978) 346–7.

19 FRUS 1969–76 Vol. XII, item 17.

20 Hastings (2018), 446.

21 Nixon official diary, 18 March 1969; www.ohioheroes.org/inductees/2008/newlin/htm.

22 FRUS 1969–76 Vol. XII, item 13, p. 47; Kissinger (1979), 256–8.

23 Ambrose (1989), 259–60; CHECK memo of conversation at Acheson papers Series 4 Sterling Library Yale University Box 4.

24 FRUS 1969–76 Vol. XII, item 38, p. 108.

25 FRUS 1969–76 Vol. XII, item 49, p. 164–76 and item 51, p. 179–80; Haig (1992), 224–9.

26 Nixon (1978), 375–6, 379–80; Haldeman (1994), 25–6; Price (1977), 60–1; Nixon daily diary; Haldeman interview with Raymond Geselbricht, 11 April 1988, p. 114.

27 www.iihf.com story #18.

28 Report by Czech Interior Minister Jan Pelnar, 31 March 1969, at www.digitalarchive. wilsoncentre.org.

29 Minutes of 18th meeting of the Executive Committee of the Czech Praesidium, 1 April 1969. At digitalarchive.wilsoncentre.org.

30 Navratil (2006), 564–70.

31 Dubcek (1992), 236–41.

32 midway-island.com. Notes by Tom Helvig, CTRCM, USN (Ret.).

33 FRUS 1969–75 Vol. VI, p. 243–6.

34 Kissinger (1979), 272–3.

35 Haldeman (1994), 64.

36 Kissinger (1979), 273.

37 Nixon daily diary, 8 June 1969, at www.nixonlibrary.gov.

38 Haldeman (1994), 64.

39 Kissinger (1979), 274; FRUS 1969–75 Vol. VI, p. 248–52.

40 Shevchenko (1985), 195.

41 FRUS 1969–75 Vol. XII, p. 178–80.

Chapter 2

TIME ENDING
(July–December 1969)

White House chief of staff Bob Haldeman stood on the flight deck of the aircraft carrier *USS Hornet*. It was just before 7 a.m., on the morning of Friday 25 July. *Hornet* was in the Pacific Ocean, some 1,000 nautical miles south of Midway Island, where Nixon and Haldeman had met Thieu the month before. Far above, an arc of flame carved through the early morning sky. Over the past week, the world had watched with mounting excitement as astronauts from the American Apollo 11 mission successfully travelled to and landed on the moon, for the first time in the history of space exploration. Mission almost complete, the main spacecraft, named *Columbia*, was returning to earth.

As *Columbia* plunged downwards, air collided with the craft's resin heat shield, creating bursts of flame. Layers peeled away, leaving a trail of flaming particles. Haldeman thought it looked like a meteor.[1]

At 24,000 feet above the ocean, three orange and white parachutes opened to slow the *Columbia's* descent. During re-entry to the earth's atmosphere, the intense heat had blocked out radio signals from the spacecraft. Once the parachutes had opened, communication was resumed. Rescue helicopters from *USS Hornet* flew towards the craft.

'Swim 1. Have a visual dead ahead about a mile,' announced the first helicopter pilot.

'*Hornet*. Roger,' replied the control tower from the aircraft carrier.

'300 feet,' confirmed the astronaut Neil Armstrong, reporting a final altitude reading for *Columbia*. It was Armstrong who, four days before, had stepped out of the lunar module *Eagle* as the first human to set foot on the surface of the moon. Nixon had called to congratulate him, in a phone call from the Oval Office patched through the *Eagle's* radio system.

'Roger. You're looking real good . . . Splashdown!'[2]

Nixon was waiting aboard the *Hornet*. Once the three astronauts had transferred to the ship they assembled to meet the president. As a precaution against the remote risk of infection from space, they were confined to a glass-fronted isolation unit. Outside, the president attempted to engage them in conversation. Nixon was elated. It was, he announced to accompanying journalists, 'the greatest week in the history of the world since the creation.'[3]

As Armstrong and his fellow astronauts 'Buzz' Aldrin and Michael Collins settled into the isolation routine, the presidential party flew on to Asia. It was the most extensive tour of the continent that an American president had yet completed: Guam in the Pacific, then the Philippines, Indonesia, Thailand, South Vietnam, India and Pakistan. In honour of Apollo 11, the journey was code-named Moonglow.

For security, the Vietnam leg was kept secret until arrival. Nixon flew in to Saigon, for a meeting with Thieu, and then to the military base at Di Am, twelve miles north of the capital, where he met soldiers from the First Infantry Division. The men thronged round him, dressed in fatigues and helmets with camouflage covers, while Nixon engaged in banter about baseball. Nicknamed the Big Red One, after the divisional shoulder badge, it was a veteran formation, with a combat record stretching back to the Western Front in the First World War. During 1968, the division saw action in the Tet Offensive. Major-General Keith Ware, divisional commander, was killed when his helicopter was shot down by anti-aircraft fire.

For Nixon's visit, the secret service took no chances. At each stop, the presidential helicopter landed and took off with a rapid, stomach-churning vertical motion. Kissinger, in the travelling party, found himself wondering whether he was at greater risk from anti-aircraft fire or from the pilot.[4]

From Asia, the party flew on westwards. At just after midday on Saturday 2 August, the presidential Boeing arrived at Bucharest airport, capital of communist Romania. The tarmac was lined with the red, yellow and blue Romanian flag, fluttering alongside the Stars and Stripes. 'If human beings can reach the moon,' Nixon declared, 'human beings can reach an understanding with each other on earth.'

It was the first time that an American president had visited a country in the Eastern bloc, and indeed the first visit to any communist state since Roosevelt attended the Yalta Conference in February 1945. But Romania was a special case. Alone among the Warsaw Pact countries, her forces had not taken part in the invasion of Czechoslovakia. Indeed, General Secretary Nikolai Ceausescu had delivered a dramatic speech in response, to an audience gathered in the main Palace Square in Bucharest. He denounced the invasion as a 'grave error' and 'a serious danger to peace in Europe'.

Ceausescu and Nixon rode in together from the airport in an open-topped limousine, along the main boulevard. The president stretched out both arms with a wave. It was a familiar gesture from the US campaign trail. A million people had thronged onto the streets of the capital to see them. Police outriders flanked the motorcade, with white helmets, leather gloves and sunglasses. The crowds looked on, dozens of rows deep. Young men ran alongside to catch a view of the visitor. At several points the two leaders stopped the motorcade and walked over to greet onlookers. Even after the cars had passed, people milled around on the streets for hours, soaking up the atmosphere.[5]

Nixon was ecstatic. He and his team stayed in an opulent state guest house, complete with bathrooms and a swimming pool lined with green marble. Late that night, the president sat out in the garden with Haldeman and Kissinger. He was wearing pyjamas, and smoking a cigar. 'Exceeded all expectations,' Haldeman noted in his diary. 'Really unbelievable.'[6]

The next day, Air Force One took off. It made one final stop in Britain, before the flight back over to the Atlantic. But Henry Kissinger was bound on a different path, for Paris.

The pretext was to brief Georges Pompidou, the new French president, on Nixon's world tour. But Kissinger's real objective was much more sensitive. On the afternoon of Monday 4 August, he slipped out of the American Embassy and went to the Rue de Rivoli. There, he entered the apartment of Jean Sainteny, a former academic acquaintance who had served in the French colonial administration in Vietnam. Three weeks before, Sainteny had called on Nixon in the Oval Office and offered to act as a private go-between with North Vietnam.

Kissinger was joined by Major-General Vernon Walters, the American military attaché in Paris, and his assistant, Anthony Lake. Walters had served as interpreter to Eisenhower, spoke nine languages and had a photographic memory, such that he could recall conversations almost verbatim.[7] The Vietnamese delegation was led by Xuan Thuy, former foreign minister in Hanoi. Sainteny sat the guests down in his living room, with a view over the Jardin des Tuileries. It was decorated with Vietnamese antiques. 'I hope if you disagree you will not throw the crockery at each other,' the Frenchman commented dryly.

The warning was unnecessary. The Vietnamese were soft-spoken, undramatic. Three months before, Hanoi had unveiled a ten-point plan to end the war in the south. This, Xuan Thuy explained, remained their basis for negotiations. The United States should make a total withdrawal of its forces. In Saigon, the Thieu government was a 'warlike, dictatorial administration'. It would be difficult to settle the Vietnam problem if it remained.

The meeting lasted three and a half hours. Kissinger asked various questions to clarify his understanding. The most difficult problems, he said, were not where good people meet evil people, but where two strong people with strong convictions confront each other. Xuan Thuy smiled.

Walters was encouraged. He had dealt with the North Vietnamese before. This encounter seemed more positive. He offered his phone number to act as a contact point. The Vietnamese agreed to address him by the cover name 'André' over the phone.

Back in Washington the next evening, Kissinger gave Nixon a read-out. Before the meeting at Rue de Rivoli, he said, he would have put the chances of success in Vietnam at one in ten. Perhaps now they were one in three or four.[8]

Troop withdrawals would, Kissinger warned, be like salted peanuts. Each handful would only fuel the public appetite for more.[9]

With students back for the fall semester, pressure was again mounting on university campuses against the Vietnam War. Activists had devised a new campaign, called the Moratorium. They planned a nationwide day of protest each month, until the administration pulled out of Vietnam. The first was scheduled for 15 October 1969.

The White House was rattled. In an attempt to forestall the protest, Nixon announced withdrawal of a further 60,000 troops by the end of the year, and cancelled call-up of new recruits to the military draft. It made little impact. Demonstrations erupted on campuses across the US. Seventy-nine college presidents signed a letter, calling for an accelerated withdrawal. In a bid to buy time, Nixon pledged to deliver a major speech on Vietnam the following month.

On Wednesday 15 October, the demonstrators arrived in the national capital. Tens of thousands converged on the White House and the Washington Monument. Many wore black armbands and carried candles. A few even waved North Vietnamese flags.

'Ho, Ho, Ho Chi Minh is going to win,' they chanted, naming the veteran Hanoi leader who had died earlier that autumn.[10]

Inside the White House, Nixon met with his National Security Council. Afterwards, Defence Secretary Melvin Laird and Secretary of State Bill Rogers lingered for a private chat in the Oval Office. They complained about Kissinger. The adviser, they argued, had become an obstacle between the president and his cabinet colleagues. Wearily, Nixon asked Haldeman to look into the problem.[11]

The difficulties facing the administration were more than just personal. Nixon and his colleagues were being boxed into a corner over Vietnam. If the protests and troop withdrawals continued, Hanoi would have no incentive to engage in substantive negotiations. The opening which Kissinger had found in Paris would fade. Nor was there any sign that the Soviets would lean on the North Vietnamese. Without negotiations, retreat would end in ignominy.

It was a path that Nixon was determined to avoid. 'By 1972 the war is going to be over,' he told Kissinger. 'I am going to be the man who ended it . . . there's a lot of rough stuff coming up, but the thing to do is to sail along.'[12]

The military chiefs had prepared more drastic options. On the eve of the election in November 1968, Johnson had called a halt to bombing missions against North Vietnam, in an apparent gesture towards peace. Kissinger instructed the Pentagon to assemble plans to resume, with a decisive four-day assault on port, rail and command facilities. These included the possible use of tactical nuclear weapons. It was given the code name Pruning Knife. The White House changed the name to Duck Hook.

Laird disassociated himself. Such escalation would, he warned Nixon, bring little benefit. Kissinger came to the same conclusion, warning of 'explosive confrontations' inside the administration. The departure of Robert McNamara as defence secretary had been a heavy blow to the Johnson administration. Nixon could not afford a repeat.

Two days after the Moratorium protest, Nixon and Kissinger met Robert Thompson, a former British civil servant who had served in Malaya, overseeing counter-insurgency operations against the communist insurgency there during the 1950s. What, they asked, did he think of escalation? Thompson was sceptical.

In Malaya, the British adopted a 'hearts and minds' approach, seeking to win round the local population and deny support to the insurgents. The United States should beat the communists in the same way, by winning over political support in South Vietnam. Kissinger advised the president to defer the Duck Hook bombing operation.[13]

This left Vietnamization, or handing over the military effort to Saigon, as the only realistic option. But, for the policy to work, Nixon needed time. Ahead of the speech which he had pledged to make on Vietnam, expectations were mounting. CBS news anchor Dan Rather suggested that the president would announce a faster timetable for withdrawal, or even a unilateral ceasefire. If the speech fell short, anti-war pressure would only increase. 'They are intentionally building him up,' Haldeman confided in his diary, 'for the biggest possible fall.'[14]

Through the last week of October, Nixon and Haldeman wrestled with drafts. As he geared himself up for a big speech, the president was, the chief of staff realized, like a dog circling to make its bed. Nixon worked off yellow legal pads, jotting notes and phrases. 'Don't get rattled – don't waver – don't react,' he scribbled, at the top of a first draft.[15] Former Secretary of State Dean Acheson came into the Oval Office to offer advice. The president should, he said, appeal to the 'great majority who really agree with him'.[16]

At lunchtime on Friday 31 October, Nixon left Washington for a long weekend at Camp David, the presidential retreat in the Catoctin Mountains, about sixty miles north-west of Washington. It was Franklin Roosevelt who first built a getaway at the remote military base. He called in Shangri-La, after the mythical Himalayan paradise in the novel *Lost Horizon* by British writer James Hilton. Eisenhower remodelled the site and called it David, the name of both his father and his grandson, later Nixon's son-in-law through marriage with his elder daughter Julie.

The text of the speech had already been through twelve drafts. Acheson's advice had given him an idea. The president worked further on it that evening, and into the night. By 8 a.m. the following morning, it was finished.

That afternoon, the president called Haldeman. His voice sounded relaxed. 'The baby's just been born,' he told the chief of staff.[17]

Nixon delivered his speech on Monday night, at nine o'clock. Haldeman had calculated that this was the optimum spot to reach prime-time audiences on both coasts of the USA.[18] Nixon spoke from the Oval Office, reading from a typed script. Hot television lights could cause the president to perspire. His make-up assistant had prepared a special foundation, which blocked the pores. He wore a dark blue tie, and sat against a yellow curtain, flanked by the presidential and Union flags. A picture of his family stood on the table behind him.

He begun by recalling the situation he had inherited. It would have been easy to pursue a unilateral withdrawal, and blame the war on Johnson. But as president Nixon had a greater obligation, to win 'America's peace'.

Nixon went on. He alluded to the secret contacts with Hanoi through Sainteny, and Kissinger's conversations with Dobrynin. His goal was a just peace, reached through a negotiated settlement. There were honest and patriotic American citizens who took a different view. But, while vocal and fervent, they were a minority. If their view prevailed, America's future as a free society would be at risk.

'And so tonight,' Nixon concluded, glancing down at his script, 'to you, the great silent majority of my fellow Americans – I ask for your support.' His voice sounded deep, the delivery steady. This was how Nixon wanted to project himself.

Acheson had talked about a 'great majority'. The previous year, on the campaign trail, speech-writers William Safire and Pat Buchanan had both encouraged Nixon to pitch at a 'silent majority' of ordinary voters across the country who rejected the politics of protest. Now the president was making that appeal. It was this very swathe of American society which he believed had brought him to the White House.[19]

Once the speech was complete, Haldeman and his team hit the phones. They hoped to influence the late-evening television bulletins and newspapers for the next morning. But, inside Washington, reactions were sceptical. The speech did not contain any new announcements. The next day, journalist Scotty Reston wrote in *The New York Times* that it would 'merely divide and polarize the debaters in the United States'.[20]

As the evening went on, Haldeman noticed that the White House was taking incoming calls, too. They were from ordinary people, expressing support for what Nixon had said. By the following morning, the calls had swelled to a flood. The switchboard was jammed. More than 50,000 telegrams flowed in. During the subsequent week, they were followed by letters. Some 30,000 arrived in the White House.

It was the silent majority, speaking out. Nixon was thrilled. He kept the letters and telegrams in piles on his desk, and proudly showed them to visitors. The president had won his mandate.[21]

The doorbell rang. Alexander Solzhenitsyn was deep in work. The Soviet writer was living in Ryazan, about 125 miles south-east of Moscow, and engaged on a new novel. The work was entitled *August 1914*. It was an assault on the events leading up to the Bolshevik Revolution. Outside, it was a crisp November morning, with winter in the air.

The last year had been an intense time for Solzhenitsyn, since his encounter with Sakharov in the summer of 1968. He had engaged as a researcher Alya Svetlova, the young woman he had met on the same day as his meeting with the scientist. At 30, she was twenty-two years his junior. They formed an intense partnership, and their attraction became more than just intellectual. Solzhenitsyn found himself juggling a new relationship with Alya alongside marriage to his wife Natasha. At the same time, his novels *Cancer Ward* and *The First Circle* were published in the West, to huge publicity. Solzhenitsyn had become a literary celebrity.

The writer opened the door, to find a young woman outside with a message. Flustered, she pushed it into his hand and left.

It was a summons to the Ryazan Writers' Union. Solzhenitsyn was requested to join a meeting at 3 p.m. that day on the ideological education of writers.

Sensing that something was wrong, he decided to attend. He arrived at the venue early, but no one was there apart from Vasily Matushkin, the acting secretary. He was perched on a window ledge.

'Hello,' said Solzhenitsyn. 'Is the meeting off then?'

'No. It's on, alright,' answered the other man. He seemed depressed, and avoided looking at his colleague.

Then, at the appointed time, the others arrived. There were five writers, and a group of officials. The writers were known to him. One, Nikolai Rodin, was clearly running a fever. He had been summoned from his sick bed, 120 miles outside town, and obliged to drive in for the occasion.

Sitting at a round table, the group explained. Charges had been laid against several authors in Moscow on ideological grounds. They included Solzhenitsyn. 'Bitter though it is,' concluded Matushkin, 'I am bound to say, Alexander [...], that our paths differ from yours and we will have to part company.'

Solzhenitsyn bristled.

'No!' he declared. 'It will not be possible indefinitely to keep silent about Stalin's crimes or go against the truth.'

The others were unmoved. They read out a draft resolution. 'In view of his anti-Soviet behaviour ... the writer Solzhenitsyn is hereby expelled from the USSR Union of Writers.'

Solzhenitsyn stormed home. This was a blatant attempt to reverse the tide started under Khrushchev. Publication of his first novel, *A Day in the Life of Ivan Denisovich*, had brought Solzhenitsyn fame and recognition, as a member of the literary elite. Now that same club was turning its back on him. Enraged, he compiled a letter of protest to the Writers' Union.

'Blow the dust off the clock,' Solzhenitsyn wrote. 'Your watches are behind the times ... the time is near when each of you will seek to erase his signature from today's resolution!'

But it was not just his literary colleagues that the writer needed to worry about. Opposite the house where Solzhenitsyn was living stood a huge portrait of Lenin, displayed on the street. It had inspired him to pour his frustration and anger with the Soviet regime into *August 1914*. Next to it, in the early winter snow, stood a truck. Two men sat in the cab, assigned as watchers from the KGB. Yuri Andropov's secret agents were on his trail.[22]

The days were drawing in. For Helsinki, northernmost capital city in mainland Europe, November brought dusk in the middle of the afternoon.

During the chaos of the Bolshevik Revolution, Finland had won independence from the Russian Empire. But it remained in Moscow's shadow. In the winter of 1939–40, the Red Army attempted to seize back the country, only to be thwarted by the snow and heroic defence from Finnish troops. After the end of the Second World War, Finland settled into precarious neutrality, caught between East and West.

The Smolna Palace stood in the heart of Helsinki. It was a former home of the governor-general from Tsarist times. The palace was built in the Russian classical style, with white columns and a stucco facade painted lemon yellow. Inside, elaborate reception rooms were decorated in gilt and ornate mirrors. Here, on 17 November 1969, Finland hosted delegations from the Soviet Union and the United States. They had come to Helsinki to discuss nuclear weapons. The negotiations were known as Strategic Arms Limitation Talks, or SALT, and formed another strand in the complex web of de-escalation between East and West which Kissinger and Dobrynin hoped to weave.

The previous decade had seen a shift in the nuclear landscape. During the 1960s, the United States enjoyed a substantial superiority, both in the technology and size of her arsenal. It was a major reason for Khrushchev's retreat over Cuba in 1962. In that year, the United States possessed 229 land-based launchers for intercontinental ballistic missiles (known as ICBMs), and 144 sea-based launchers for submarine missiles (SLBMs). The Soviet Union had approximately 50 and 97 of each.[23] If the crisis had led to a full nuclear exchange, the greater American numbers stood a better chance of surviving an initial Soviet strike, and inflicting crippling destruction on Soviet cities in retaliation.

Soviet leader Leonid Brezhnev, along with his colleagues Alexei Kosygin and Nikolai Podgorny, was determined to redress the balance. By the end of the 1960s, the Soviet arsenal had risen to over 1,400 ICBM and 280 SLBM launchers. In America, too, there was a major increase. But Vietnam, and Johnson's expansion of medical care and civil rights under the 'Great Society' programme, put other pressures on the budget. Congress became reluctant to authorize new spending. The administration was forced to accept a self-imposed limit, of just over 1,000 ICBM and 650 SLBM launchers. These constraints drove the military to seek other, cheaper options. In the late 1960s, plans were developed for a defensive screen to protect key targets, called Anti-Ballistic Missile defence, or ABM, and warheads which could separate in flight to hit several targets at once (Multiple Independently Targeted Re-entry Vehicles, or MIRVs).

In Moscow and Washington, calculations were made more complicated by the long lead times required. On average, new American systems took six years to develop before they could be deployed. It produced an unstable dynamic, in which each raced to acquire new weaponry, driven by fear that they might be outclassed by the other.

The 1960s also saw steps towards containing the nuclear threat. In 1963, the main nuclear states – the Soviet Union, United States, United Kingdom and France, followed by China – signed the Partial Test-Ban Treaty. This prohibited testing of nuclear devices above ground, and thus the spread of radioactive particles in the atmosphere. It was followed by the Non-Proliferation Treaty, concluded in 1968 by a wider cast of countries from both East and West. Those without nuclear weapons committed themselves not to acquire them, while the nuclear states pledged to share nuclear technology for civilian use, under safeguards. They also vowed to pursue disarmament.

The superpowers were ambivalent about arms control. They feared ceding advantage to each other. But, by mid-1969 the stars were sufficiently aligned for both sides to give it a try, and they agreed to launch the SALT negotiations. The American delegation was led by Gerard Smith, a veteran nuclear expert who had served in the US Navy during the war. His Soviet counterpart was Vladimir Semenov, a deputy to Gromyko in the Soviet Foreign Ministry. Helsinki was chosen at the venue for the first round of talks.

After an initial ceremony at the Smolna Palace, the two delegations elected to switch venue, holding alternate days in each others' embassies. The atmosphere was tense. Across the street from the US mission, the Americans spotted a KGB watch post, with eavesdropping and photographic equipment.[24] At the first working session, held in the Soviet embassy, one participant opened a bottle of sparkling water, laid out on the table alongside packets of Russian cigarettes. It gave a loud pop.

'Rocket!' exclaimed a Soviet general.

There was a nervous round of laughter.

A week in, Smith played his first card. In preparation, he and National Security Adviser Henry Kissinger had wrestled with a basic dilemma. Should the Americans put a proposal on the table first, or wait for the Soviets to do so? To get round this, the Americans offered a paper entitled 'Illustrative Elements'. This offered general parameters. An agreement to limit arms might, it suggested, cover ICBMs, SLBMs and ABM. There was no mention of MIRVs, nor of bomber aircraft, which could also deliver nuclear weapons. Semenov quickly picked up on the latter, but remained silent over MIRVs. Smith and his colleagues concluded that it was a significant omission. This was the field where the Soviets lagged most behind the Americans. They did not want to raise a subject where they felt exposed.[25]

Over the next month, the talks settled into a rhythm. Twice a week, at ten o'clock in the morning, the delegations would arrive. They would shake hands and mumble greetings in each others' language. Smith had learnt Russian earlier in his career, and made an effort to brush up again. He started to deliver his opening statements in the language, though with an interpreter present to handle the follow-up discussion. After the plenary, Smith and Semenov would adjourn for a more private meeting. In the Soviet embassy, they met in a room decorated with a picture of Lenin, surrounded by children. The delegations would then report back, by secure communications, and await instructions for the next session.[26]

This format was stiff and slow-moving. Both sides were reduced to scouring for the smallest clues. At one point, Smith spoke of an 'initial' agreement in the course of 1970. The American delegation thought that they caught a flash of disappointment across Semenov's face.[27] The Soviet diplomat had served as a military adviser during the war, and entered Berlin in 1945. On several occasions, he described the terrible destruction he had seen. 'If weapons ever talked instead of men,' he liked to say, 'it would be an undesirable evil for both our countries.'

Back at the US embassy, in a secure, soundproofed room, Smith and his colleagues pored over satellite images of nuclear facilities inside the Soviet Union. These showed the construction of new submarines and missile silos. Washington assessed that the Soviets were building 250 new launchers each year. The drive for strategic nuclear parity seemed to be continuing unchecked. Smith found the grainy pictures sinister. At a personal level, Semenov was a pleasant colleague. But the photos told a different story. What, he wondered, did Moscow really want?[28]

Notes

1 Haldeman (1994), 75.
2 Parry (2009), 259.
3 Ambrose (1989), 285.
4 Kissinger (1979), 276–7.
5 Price (1977), 303; Buchanan (2017), 55; FRUS Vol. XL, item 23, p. 71.
6 Haldeman (1994), 77; Hildebrand (1998), 276.
7 Haldeman interview with Raymond Geselbricht, 13 July 1987, p. 13.
8 FRUS 1969–76 Vol. VI, items 105–7, p. 328–43; Kissinger (1979), 278–82; Walters (1978), 508–11.
9 Kissinger (1979), 284.
10 Ambrose (1989), 304.
11 Nixon daily diary, 15 October 1969; Haldeman (1994), 100.
12 FRUS 1969–76 Vol. VI, item 135, p. 450–3.
13 FRUS 1969–76 Vol. VI, item 134, p. 446–50, item 137, p. 460–6; Kissinger (1979), 284–5.
14 Haldeman (1994), 102.
15 Haldeman interview with Raymond Geselbricht, 13 July 1987, p. 73; Nixon (1978), 405.
16 Ambrose (1989), 308.
17 Nixon (1978), 409; Haldeman (1994), 103.
18 Haldeman interview with Raymond Geselbricht, 13 August 1987, p. 79 and 12 April 1988, p. 56–7.
19 Safire (1975), 50; Buchanan (2017), 68; Safire interview, 27 March 2008, p. 8.
20 Ambrose (1989), 310.
21 Haldeman (1994), 104–5; interview with Raymond Geselbricht, 12 April 1988, p. 118.
22 Solzhenitsyn (1975), 257–64; Pearce (1999), 202–4; Thomas (1998), 343–6.
23 Figures from Nitze (1989), 287.
24 Nitze (1989), 305.
25 Smith (1985), 88–90.
26 Smith (1985), 55–6.
27 FRUS 1969–75 Vol. XXXII, item 44, p. 168–70.
28 Smith (1985), 66–7, 105.

Chapter 3

COMING DARKNESS
(January–December 1970)

'You have sowed the wind, and you must reap the whirlwind.'[1]

Le Duc Tho was direct. It was a Sunday afternoon in early April 1970, and the Vietnamese envoy's third meeting with Henry Kissinger. Their talks had reached an impasse.

The two men had first met in late February, at Kissinger's instigation. Major-General Vernon Walters passed word to his contact in the North Vietnamese delegation. Kissinger and Walters deployed elaborate subterfuge to conceal the former's absence from Washington. The National Security Adviser travelled on a Boeing 707 from the presidential fleet, disguised as a routine training flight. The plane touched down at an airforce base in central France, dropped Kissinger and proceeded on to Frankfurt airport. The former academic took an executive jet belonging to French president Georges Pompidou to Villacoublay Airport outside Paris. He was met by Walters, who drove them in a rented Citroën to Choisy-le-Roi, an anonymous suburb on the outskirts of the city. The cloak-and-dagger operation gave both men a thrill.[2]

The talks followed a similar format to Kissinger's initial encounter with Xuan Thuy the previous summer. The two sides sat in opposite rows of red upholstered chairs, in the downstairs front room of a small suburban house. Between them, as Kissinger recalled, lay 'four or five feet of floor space and eons of perception.'[3]

The new element was Le Duc Tho, who flew from Hanoi to join the talks. As a politburo member, he outranked Xuan Thuy, though the latter remained formal head of the North Vietnamese delegation. Born in 1911, Le Duc wore a dark Mao suit, with a high collar, and grey hair swept back in a parting. He had been a communist activist against the French colonial administration in Vietnam until the 1950s, and helped to found the Viet Minh independence movement. At points, Kissinger found that he could draw out a smile with self-deprecating references to his academic background. Professors, he noted, were trained to speak in class-length chunks of fifty-five minutes. As each side exchanged lengthy statements, it became a running joke between them. At one point, Kissinger said that it was like reading the philosopher Kant. A student had to plough through nine volumes in order to find a verb, in the tenth.[4]

At first, Kissinger was hopeful. Nixon's 'silent majority' speech the previous November had shored up a measure of domestic support in the US. The path might be open to pressure Hanoi into substantive negotiations. Returning from his first meeting, in February, Kissinger told the president that it had been 'the most important since the beginning of your administration'.[5] At the second encounter, in mid-March, he trailed a potential timetable for drawdown of US forces from Vietnam over a sixteen-month period.[6]

Beyond Paris, however, the dynamic was changing. War was spilling outside Vietnam. In February, Hanoi had launched an offensive to support communist insurgents in Laos. The United States responded with bombing by B-52s and covert support from US troops. Then, as Kissinger and Le Duc Tho held their second meeting in mid-March, the ruler of Cambodia, Norodan Sihanouk, was overthrown in a military coup. A former king, who had abdicated the throne and assumed the role of prime minister, Sihanouk had trod a careful path between Washington, Hanoi and Saigon. The new military administration took a tougher line against communism, including the left-wing Khymer Rouge insurgency inside Cambodia.

By the third meeting, the tone had become more direct. In manner, Le Duc Tho remained polite, but his message was blunt. As the meeting drew to a close, he launched into a long speech. The US had miscalculated in Vietnam. While it might have military superiority, the Vietnamese were stronger, because they were united in fighting against foreign aggression. America would face the same fate as France, which had been forced to abandon its colony in Vietnam after a bitter war of liberation during the 1950s. Nixon would, he warned, 'sink deeper into the quagmire'.[7]

As Le Duc Tho closed, Kissinger looked at his watch. The North Vietnamese had spoken for exactly fifty-five minutes, he noted. Perhaps he could recommend him for the faculty at Harvard.[8]

Back in Washington, Nixon was in little mood for academic jokes. The president's polling figures had lifted at the end of 1969, following the 'silent majority' speech. But now they were slipping again, down below the 60-per-cent mark. With Chief of Staff Bob Haldeman, he fretted that he had lost his feel for the job, after the adrenalin of the early months. Nixon performed best, by his own admission, when there was a crisis at hand.[9]

Mid-April brought more drama. Apollo 13 was intended as a routine space mission, to land a third craft on the moon after the successes of Apollo 11 and then Apollo 12, which had completed a moon landing in November 1969. But the flight suffered an explosion on board during the outward journey. For four, tense days, the crew and team at mission control in Houston struggled to bring the crippled ship back to earth. The world watched on. At the SALT talks, meeting in Vienna for a second round, Soviet negotiator Vladimir Semenov interrupted normal business to offer his hope for a successful return to earth.[10] In Rome, Pope Paul VI led prayers for the astronauts. When the craft landed safely in the Pacific, south-east of American Samoa, Nixon ordered cigars for his staff in celebration.[11]

The next day, Nixon flew to Hawaii, to greet the returned crew of Apollo 13. During the visit, he met with Admiral John McCain, commander of US naval forces in the Pacific. The situation in Cambodia was deteriorating. Communist forces were closing in on the capital, Phnom Penh. A senior CIA officer was sent into the country, along with covert supplies of military equipment. But it did not look enough. If the country fell to communists, South Vietnam would be isolated, to the north and the west. Kennedy had first sent troops to South Asia from fear of a 'domino effect', that communism would spread across the region. Now another domino seemed about to fall.

One option remained. Kissinger developed plans with Chairman of the Joint Chiefs 'Bus' Wheeler and CIA director Richard Helms for a military incursion into the Viet Cong base areas inside Cambodia. The Americans believed that the Central Office for South Vietnam, or 'COSVN' as they designated it, was located in a Cambodian enclave along the Vietnamese border which they called the Fishhook. An attack by American and South Vietnamese ground forces on this and a neighbouring enclave, dubbed Parrot's Beak, might halt the offensive on Phnom Penh. But it would amount to significant escalation. The bombing offensive against the same areas a year earlier had produced a popular outcry in the United States. A land assault would be even more controversial. Three of Kissinger's staffers resigned when they learned of the plans. Both Secretary of State Bill Rogers and Defence Secretary Melvyn Laird were sceptical.

On Saturday 25 April, Kissinger travelled up to Camp David to brief Nixon. As the president paddled in the facility swimming pool, his national security adviser walked along the edge, talking him through the military plans. Nixon was clear. Two days earlier, he had sent Kissinger a minute, recalling the Soviet invasions of Hungary and Czechoslovakia. 'Over and over again,' he concluded, 'we fail to learn that the Communists never need an excuse to come in.'[12] That evening, the two men travelled back to Washington, and cruised along the Potomac River aboard the presidential yacht *Sequoia*. They were joined by Nixon's friend and golf partner Bebe Rebozo, and by John Mitchell, the attorney general and a close political ally. The alcohol flowed. As the *Sequoia* passed former president George Washington's home at Mount Vernon, the men rose to attention, somewhat unsteady on their feet. Afterwards, back at the White House, Nixon insisted on a late-night screening of the film *Patton*, about the Second World War tank commander. Starring George C. Scott in the title role, the movie had been released at the start of April. It became Nixon's favourite.[13]

The attack was launched six days later, under the code name Operation Rockcrusher. At first light, B-52s pounded the border of the Fishhook zone. They were followed by troops of the US Air Cavalry Division, mounted in helicopters.

With the time difference, it was still evening in Washington from the previous day. As the assault began, Nixon delivered a live television address from the White House. Gesturing to a map, he described COSVN and the challenge in Cambodia. Then the president returned to his desk, clutching his printed script. The camera zoomed in on his head and shoulders, framed against a blue curtain backdrop. 'It is not our power,' he declared, 'but our will and character which is being tested tonight.'

Afterwards, Nixon talked with allies and supporters on the phone. They included Gerald Ford, Republican leader in the House of Representatives, and Bob

Hope, the television entertainer. Eventually, at three o'clock in the morning, the president returned to his bedroom. There, he found a note from his daughter Julie. 'I know you are right,' she had written. 'I am so proud.'[14]

'I thought it was fireworks.' Chryssie Hynde was an 18-year-old art student at Kent State University in Ohio. Along with other protesters, she had gathered on the Commons, a raised, grassy area in the centre of the campus. After a few seconds, the bangs ceased. She remembered hearing a young man's voice.

'They fucking killed somebody!'

America's universities were in uproar. Following news of the incursion into Cambodia, campuses erupted with protest. At Kent State, demonstrators gathered on the morning after Nixon's televised address. One group of history students staged a symbolic burial ceremony for a manuscript copy of the US Constitution.

Demonstrations continued through the weekend. The campus building for the Reserve Officers' Training Corps was set on fire. That night, the Ohio National Guard was called out. State Governor James Rhodes called the protesters 'the worst type of people we have in America'.

A further rally was scheduled for noon on Monday 4 May. More than five hundred students gathered, including Hynde. Just under a hundred guardsmen faced them. Many had barely slept. They fired tear gas, but it dispersed in the breeze. Protestors threw back the canisters, and hurled rocks.

'One, two, three, four,' they chanted. 'We don't want your fucking war!'

The guardsmen loaded their M1 carbine rifles, and fixed bayonets. The crowd had now swollen to over two thousand, with protesters and bystanders. Some edged up to the soldiers, taunting them.

'Kill the pigs! Stick the pigs!'

A shot rang out. Then another, and another. As the troops unleashed volleys, officers ran frantically along the skirmish line, ordering them to cease fire.

Thirteen students had been hit. Four were dead. One survivor, struck by a bullet fragment in the spine, would be paralysed for the rest of his life.[15]

Shock waves rippled across America. On Wall Street, demonstrators clashed with workmen who were building the new twin skyscrapers of the World Trade Center. Washington was in turmoil. The anti-war movement called for a national day of protest, set for Saturday 9 May. Thousands of demonstrators converged on the capital. Haldeman and fellow presidential aide John Ehrlichman watched through binoculars from the roof of the White House.[16] Meeting with university presidents, Nixon was struck at how frightened they seemed. Events were running out of control.[17]

At first, the mood inside the White House was frozen with horror. Nixon and Haldeman were reluctant to be pressurized into a public response. The president had been due to visit Stone Mountain in Georgia, for the unveiling of a relief sculpture of the Civil War figures Robert Lee, Jefferson Davis and Stonewall Jackson. Speech-writer William Safire had composed a speech for Nixon which, the two men hoped, would restore the historical reputation of the Southern leaders, and unite the country. But it was clear that the president could not afford to leave Washington. Vice President Spiro Agnew went in his place.[18]

Instead, Nixon decided to hold a live televised press conference. It was scheduled for ten o'clock on Friday night, ahead of the protests expected on Saturday. Inside the White House, tension built up through the afternoon and evening. Advisers were divided over whether he should confront the protesters, or strike a more conciliatory note. As he entered the East Room, Nixon later wrote he could 'feel the emotions seething below the hot T V lights'.[19]

Afterwards, the president and his team worked the phones. While Haldeman spoke with newspaper editors, spinning coverage for the morning headlines, Nixon talked with old friends and supporters. It was a familiar means of relaxation, after the stress of the public performance. His first call was to his daughter Tricia. Other conversations followed, with Kissinger, Safire, Haldeman, Rogers, Laird, and Billy Graham, the television evangelist. Wandering down to the national security staff in the basement, Nixon paused in front of the desk of Al Haig, Kissinger's deputy on the NSC staff.

'We've had a tough day, Al,' he commented. 'Things are bad out there. But we've got to stick to our guns. We've done the right thing and we have to go on.'

Usually, Nixon was immaculately dressed. But that evening Haig noticed the tie was slightly askew, and hair tousled.[20]

Haldeman left just after midnight, weaving through a circle of public buses drawn up around the White House as a barrier against the protests. Nixon continued his phone calls, until after two o'clock in the morning. William Safire thought that he was in an odd mood, both keyed up and relaxed, too exhausted to sleep. 'The country's been through a terrible experience this week,' Nixon commented to his speech-writer.[21]

The president slumbered for about an hour. But then he woke again, and went to the Lincoln Sitting Room, on the first floor of the White House. He sat listening to a record of Rachmaninov's Second Piano Concerto. It was a performance by the Hungarian conductor Eugene Ormandy, with the Philadelphia Orchestra. Manolo Sanchez, his valet, heard the sound, and entered. He offered to bring some coffee.

Nixon was looking out of the window, towards the Washington Monument. Groups of students were beginning to gather for the demonstration.

'Have you ever been to the Lincoln Memorial at night?' he asked Sanchez.

The Mexican American replied that he had not.

'Get your clothes on,' responded Nixon. 'We'll go.'

The two men set off. They walked down the stairs, and out onto the White House lawn. To the consternation of the secret service, Nixon requested a car. Six minutes later, they arrived at the memorial. It was just before five o'clock in the morning.

Nixon and Sanchez climbed up the long steps. Above them sat the sculpted form of the sixteenth president of the United States. Nixon pointed out the inscription. 'In this temple,' it ran, 'as in the hearts of the people for whom he saved the Union, the memory of Abraham Lincoln is enshrined forever.'

Nixon introduced himself to a group of students. Half were from upstate New York. He asked their names, and what they were studying. Others came up, until the circle was about twenty-five in number. The protest marches had been noisy, angry affairs. Al Haig thought them a mix between demonic ceremony, class picnic, collective tantrum and a mating ritual.[22] But in the early morning this group was quiet, reflective.

'I know that probably most of you think that I'm a son-of-a-bitch,' explained Nixon, 'but I want you to know that I understand just how you feel.'

He went on. Nixon remembered hearing British prime minister Neville Chamberlain on the radio, with news of the Munich Agreement in 1938. It was just after Nixon had left law school. As a Quaker, he had believed that the United States should stay out of war. But events had proven him wrong.

The group grew larger. Older students joined in. They seemed to be leaders for the demonstration. Behind them the dawn was breaking, and the Washington Monument in the distance was bathed with a soft shade of pink.[23]

'I hope you realize that we are willing to die for what we believe in,' commented one.

Nixon responded, his manner intense. He had felt the same way when he was young. So had others of his generation. The world was going to become much smaller in the next twenty-five years. Young people must understand those living in other countries. They were searching for answers, just as Nixon himself had done forty years before.

It was time to go. Back in the limousine, Nixon asked Sanchez if he had visited the Capitol. His valet replied that he had not. The car sped up Constitution Avenue. A white Volvo with a couple of demonstrators followed behind. The secret service were already on edge. This pursuit added to their jitters.

The convoy arrived at the Capitol. Inside, they took an elevator up to the Senate. The door was locked. Undeterred, the group walked under the Great Rotunda, across to the House of Representatives. That, too, was locked. There was a delay while they waited for a custodian to bring a key.

Once inside, Nixon showed Sanchez around. He pointed out the chair where he had sat as a new Congressman, in 1947. The president was pleased to find that he could still fit into the wooden seat.

They walked up to the Speaker's Chair, at the centre of the chamber. At Nixon's invitation, Sanchez delivered a few remarks. Three African-American cleaning women had joined the party, and listened. Sanchez spoke of his pride at being an American citizen. The audience applauded.

As Nixon made to leave, one of the cleaning women made a request. She carried a Bible with her, and asked that the president sign it. Nixon did so.

'The trouble,' he commented, 'is that most of us these days don't read it enough.'

'Mr President,' replied the woman. 'I read it all the time.'

Nixon paused for a moment, holding her hand. A thought seemed to enter his mind.

'You know, my mother was a saint,' he said at last. 'She died two years ago. She was a saint.'

There was a pause.

'You be a saint, too,' Nixon said to the cleaning woman.

'I'll try, Mr President.'[24]

Gerard Smith had been in Vienna for almost three months. The second round of SALT negotiations opened in mid-April. The venue was the Belvedere Palace, on the south-eastern side of the city centre. Austrian foreign minister Kurt Waldheim presided over the opening ceremony. Fifteen years before, the Soviet Union, United States and the other former allied powers had signed a treaty in the same building that restored Austria to independence after the Second World War. Like Finland, Austria was a neutral country.

The Americans had come to the former imperial capital in an expectant mood. The opening round in Helsinki had exposed a complex landscape. It was clear that negotiations would need to range across both offensive and defensive weapons systems. At a meeting of the National Security Council ahead of the Vienna round, Nixon and his senior advisers agreed to offer the Soviets a package approach. The United States would be prepared to accept mutual limits on land-based (ICBM) and submarine (SLBM) missile launchers, along with restrictions on anti-ballistic missile defences, and on multiple warheads (the so-called 'MIRVs'). The Americans dubbed it the 'Vienna Option'.

Smith had unveiled this package soon after the talks began. It produced little impact. By early May, American action in Cambodia had cast a chill over the talks. 'Negotiations are built on trust,' warned Soviet premier Alexei Kosygin in a statement from Moscow. 'This action by the United States does not in the least strengthen trust between our states.' Privately, Soviet expert Georgy Arbatov warned Kissinger that if the bombing continued the Soviets might have to break off talks.[25]

Vladimir Semenov was Smith's Soviet counterpart. A few weeks into the talks, the two men met privately to take stock. Smith hosted, at his office on the Strudelhof Gassel. His objective was to persuade Semenov on the package approach. To reinforce his point, Smith pointed out a plaque on the wall. It recorded that the room was used by Count Leopold Berchtold, foreign minister to the Hapsburg Empire. From this very spot, Berchtold drew up the ultimatum against Serbia which ignited the First World War.

Semenov took note. But he showed little enthusiasm for the package approach. It was, Semenov told Smith, reminiscent of the Greek philosopher Empedocles. Prior to the creation of mankind, Empedocles believed, arms, legs and torsos had been clumped together in random clusters. The American proposal showed a similar lack of coherence.[26]

More than just philosophy lay behind Semenov's reaction. Within the Soviet Foreign Ministry, he had the reputation of a skilled diplomat, shrewd enough to avoid placing himself in an exposed position. Semenov well understood the tensions back in Moscow over the Soviet negotiating position on SALT, between diplomats and the military establishment. The Politburo had been conflicted over whether to open talks at all. Arms negotiation was a shifting kaleidoscope of strategic and political calculation. After a decade of rapid expansion, the Soviets had more missile launchers. But they lagged behind America in the field of anti-ballistic missile defence (known as ABM). It scarcely suited their interests to trade their lead on the former for limitations on the latter. As a precaution to ensure cohesion within the Soviet delegation, Foreign Minister Gromyko had imposed the unusual requirement that reporting telegrams be signed off by all seven members, including those from the military, rather than just Semenov as the lead.[27]

In any case, American domestic politics might be about to do the job for them. That summer, Congress was due to vote on whether to authorize funding for the American ABM programme, called Safeguard. The year before, the Senate had given approval by a margin of one vote. Although the Democrats held a majority, by fifty-eight to forty-two seats, the debate cut across party lines. A group of Democrats opposed Safeguard on the grounds that it was an unnecessary expense, and risked stoking a further arms race with the Soviets. They were led by Albert Gore, chair of the disarmament subcommittee of the Committee on Foreign Relations, along with William Fulbright and Ted Kennedy, younger brother of John and Robert. Some Republicans took a similar view, including Margaret Chase Smith, a moderate from Maine. The opposite camp was led by another Democrat, Henry 'Scoop' Jackson. He was hawkish on defence issues, and backed more spending for the military. Jackson had recruited a team of ambitious young staffers around him, including graduate students Richard Perle and Paul Wolfowitz.[28]

Over the summer, the two camps battled to win support. On 17 July, the Senate held a closed session for five and a half hours. Jackson presented charts, prepared by Perle and Wolfowitz. 'When it came down to it,' recalled Wolfowitz, 'it was not the intellectual argument, but who you believed ... [Jackson] spoke with such authority that when he really believed something on a defence issue, few members of the Senate were comfortable challenging him.'[29]

The opponents of Safeguard had tabled amendments to the budget, which would prohibit or limit expenditure on the system. A vote was scheduled for 12 August.

Three weeks before, on 24 July, Jackson called on Nixon in the White House. He was joined by John Tower, Republican senator for Texas. Tower had taken over the seat when Lyndon Johnson moved to the vice presidency in 1961. They ran through the likely vote count. It looked very close. Fifty senators were expected to support the administration. Forty-eight or forty-nine were likely to oppose, depending on how Margaret Chase Smith voted. Jackson noted that diplomats from the Soviet embassy were 'all over the Hill', discussing the vote with senators and their staffs.[30]

The pressure continued. Gerard Smith was still in Vienna. In the days running up to the vote, he received phone calls from several senators, calling at the suggestion of the White House. They asked what effect limiting ABM would have on the SALT negotiations.

The reality was that it would be devastating. Removal of funding would knock one of the key negotiating cards out of Smith's hand. But his instinct was to tread carefully. He did not want to look panicked, or suggest that as a diplomat he was trying to influence elected politicians back home. The envoy agreed a short script with Kissinger, which he used to speak with senators over the phone. A 'significant split between executive and legislative branches', it explained, could prejudice a SALT agreement. Smith concluded each phone call by confirming that the conversation remain confidential.[31]

The vote took place on Wednesday 12 August. Margaret Chase Smith offered an amendment, which would ban Safeguard but authorize research spending on other potential ABM systems. The vote was tied, fifty-fifty. Presiding over the Senate, Vice President Spiro Agnew cast a deciding vote, in favour of the administration. Safeguard had survived, but only just.

The next day, Smith read that *The New York Times* had published details of his conversations with senators. The SALT delegation was thrown into the political fray. Furious, he called Kissinger.

'I find it hard to believe that I am getting a fair deal here,' fumed Smith.

'Gerry,' replied Kissinger weakly. 'The trouble is that some of these things are not being done from my office.'

Smith was scarcely reassured.

'I feel,' he concluded, 'that my prospects of doing anything for you in the future are sadly diminished.'

'I don't think so,' Kissinger replied. 'But at any rate you deserve much better.'[32]

'Situation deteriorating dangerously ... I request immediate physical intervention both air and land.'[33] King Hussein of Jordan was in trouble. His plea arrived in the White House by telegram, from the American embassy in Amman. The message was passed to Kissinger and Joe Sisco, Assistant Secretary of State for the Middle East.

The Nixon administration had inherited a region in turmoil. In June 1967, Israeli forces staged a dramatic surprise attack, on Egypt, Jordan and Syria. Caught unprepared, Arab forces were heavily defeated. In the space of six days, the Israelis seized control of Egyptian territory in the Sinai peninsula, the West Bank, and the Golan Heights in Syria. Almost twenty years after the creation of Israel, the new state had seemingly achieved strategic dominance over its neighbours.

Israel and Egypt continued armed confrontation, with regular Israeli air strikes across the Suez Canal, deep into Egyptian-held territory. Palestinians displaced from the Israeli occupation of the West Bank established camps inside Jordan and Lebanon. Jordanians became a minority within their own country. From within the camps, the Palestinian Liberation Organization (PLO) led by Yasser Arafat staged guerilla attacks against Israel. In May 1970, rocket-propelled grenades were fired at a school bus from Avivim, in the north of the country. Nine children died.

Tension mounted inside Jordan. At the start of September, King Hussein had survived an assassination attempt by Palestinian guerillas. Fighting broke out between the Jordanian Army and the Palestinians. Days later, PLO terrorists seized four international airliners, and forced them to land in Amman. Several hundred passengers were taken hostage, including Israelis, Americans and Europeans.

To restore order, the Jordanian Army entered Amman. Fighting broke out on the streets. Hostages from the airliners were held in houses around the city, and found themselves caught up in the fighting. American ambassador Dean Brown was forced to take shelter in a protected bunker within his embassy.[34]

In Washington, Nixon and Kissinger watched with alarm. King Hussein was an ally of the United States. If he fell from power, it could plunge the region further into chaos. Two aircraft carriers from the US Sixth Fleet were dispatched to the eastern Mediterranean, along with an amphibious task force of Marines.

This move was intended to win space for Hussein. But there was a wider game afoot, between the superpowers. Iraq and Syria backed the Palestinian cause. They were in turn supported by the Soviet Union. By signalling that the United States might intervene behind the Jordanian king, Washington was increasing the stakes for all sides.

The Syrians decided to take a gamble. Early on the morning of 20 September, Syrian tanks crossed the border into Jordan. At first, the Jordanians had the upper hand. Their equipment, provided by the British and Americans, was superior to the Soviet-made armour used by the Syrians. Some thirty Syrian tanks were destroyed.[35] But then two more armoured brigades joined the invasion. Jordanian forces were split between fighting Palestinians and Syrians. Defeat beckoned.

For the White House, it was a different kind of crisis. Handling the invasion of Cambodia was primarily about domestic US opinion. Conflict in the Middle East required fast-paced diplomacy, as Washington juggled her Israeli and Arab allies. Coordination across the administration was essential. Kissinger adapted his regular official-level body, called the Washington Special Actions Group, to ensure a consistent approach. They met each day in the White House Situation Room, in the basement of the West Wing. The facility was built a decade before, following the Kennedy administration's abortive invasion of Cuba at the Bay of Pigs. Dark panelling lined the walls, with neon lighting overhead. Staffer Steve Bull thought it looked like the games room in the basement of a suburban house.[36]

The Syrian invasion broke in the early hours of a Sunday morning for Washington. By the afternoon, it was clear the situation was deteriorating in Amman. Nixon had spent the day at Camp David. He returned to Washington in the evening, for a quiet game in his private bowling alley, under the Executive Office Building. Kissinger and Sisco interrupted him with the news from Jordan.[37] As the three men talked, the president cradled a ball in his hand. They agreed that urgent action was required. The 82nd Airborne Division was based in Germany and could reach Jordan within hours. Nixon ordered it to immediate readiness. Meanwhile, Washington would approach Tel Aviv over possible Israeli air strikes to halt the Syrian invasion.

A few minutes later, King Hussein's plea reached the White House. Nixon, Kissinger and Sisco conferred again. It was clear that events were moving fast. The following day might bring a decision point about military action. Israeli air strikes seemed the most effective option available to blunt the Syrian attack. Carrier planes based with the Sixth Fleet could fly 200 sorties a day, while the Israelis could carry out 700.

Straight afterwards, Kissinger called Israeli ambassador Yitzhak Rabin. The latter was in New York, accompanying Prime Minister Golda Meir on a visit to the United States. They were at a formal dinner. Over the phone, Kissinger could hear chatter in the background. Nixon wandered into his office and stood listening to the call. In the bowling alley he had been dressed in shirtsleeves, but now Kissinger noticed that he had put his jacket and tie back on.

Rabin was clear, and to the point. If Israel took action, would the president support them? And would Washington manage tensions with Moscow?

'That is correct,' replied Kissinger. 'We are taking some immediate precautionary measures,' he added, referring to messages which Secretary of State Bill Rogers had passed to the Soviets earlier that evening.[38]

Rabin called back just under an hour later. It was 11.30 p.m. Meir and the ambassador had been in contact with Tel Aviv. Israeli planes would conduct reconnaissance flights overnight. But air strikes alone might not be enough to halt the Syrian advance. Ground forces could also be required. And that would raise the stakes to another level.[39]

It was a long night for the White House team. The Special Actions Group met again at midnight, to run through preparations. Kissinger left at two o'clock in the morning.

His deputy Al Haig followed a couple of hours later. As he crept into his bedroom, the phone rang. The officer groaned. It was the American ambassador in Amman. The situation was deteriorating. A few minutes later, the phone rang again. It was Rabin. He wanted American agreement to use of Israeli ground forces. For what remained of the night, Haig sat on the bedroom floor, phone in hand. His wife Pat brought him cups of coffee. A car ride back to the White House would last twenty minutes, and Haig calculated that he could not afford to be out of contact for that long.[40]

From his flat, Kissinger called Nixon. He explained Rabin's request. The president's immediate reaction was to agree. But Kissinger then spoke with Rogers and Laird, who were both less certain. He recommended a meeting of the National Security Council. At moments like these, it was essential that all the key players were on the same page.[41]

Afterwards, Haig and Kissinger spoke privately on the phone for a moment. It was about 7.30 a.m.

'I don't know what I'd do without you,' said the national security adviser. 'We will be snapping at each other all afternoon we'll be so tired.'

Haig laughed.

'Except that we don't snap on big things,' Kissinger added. 'It takes little ones'.

'Right,' replied Haig.[42]

The National Security Council met that morning, at 8.45. Rogers and Laird were present, along with Kissinger, Haig, Sisco and Admiral Thomas Moorer, who had taken over from 'Bus' Wheeler as chairman of the Joint Chiefs of Staff. Nixon hosted, in the Cabinet Room. During his presidency, Johnson had used the Situation Room for NSC meetings. But Nixon preferred the lighter surroundings of the Cabinet Room, on the ground floor of the White House.

Kissinger opened with a summary of the Israeli request and diplomatic contacts overnight. Laird and Moorer gave an update on the military situation. A spearhead of forty Syrian tanks was moving south, towards Amman.

Both Laird and Rogers were cautious. Laird argued that the administration needed to engage with Congress before taking action, so as to ensure support. Rogers urged further consultation with Hussein. It was possible that the Syrians might slow their advance, and the king could handle matters without outside intervention.

Nixon was dubious. Intervention carried risks. But not to do so could lead to more serious consequences. The worst thing that the United States could do would be to delay too long.

The meeting concluded just after ten o'clock. Nixon instructed Kissinger and Sisco to pass a message back to Rabin. Washington could support an Israeli ground operation in principle, subject to the views of the king.[43] Soviet ambassador Anatoly Dobrynin was out of Washington. His deputy, Yuli Vorontsov, was holding the fort. That afternoon, he called on Sisco. Vorontsov brought a message from Moscow.

The Soviet Union considered outside intervention in Jordan unacceptable. It hoped that the Americans were taking this approach with Israel. 'The Soviet government,' the message concluded, 'adheres to the same line in its contacts with the government of Syria.'[44]

Behind the stern words, Sisco sensed an opening. If Moscow was indeed distancing itself from Syrian action, it would give Damascus pause for thought.

The next morning brought a change of fortune. The Royal Jordanian Air Force was flying round-the-clock sorties, using its small fleet of British- and American-made aircraft. The Syrian air force remained in its bases. Unprotected, Syrian tanks suffered heavy losses. They began to fall back.[45]

Late that night, Dobrynin returned to Washington. The crisis was on the turn, with Syrian forces in retreat. The Arab League called an emergency summit, in Cairo, to broker a ceasefire agreement. King Hussein had survived.

The next day, the Soviet ambassador called Kissinger. It had been a tense few days.

'You didn't keep your word not to organize anything during my absence,' commented Dobrynin in mock reproach.

'Don't speak about who isn't keeping his word,' the presidential adviser shot back. 'You stayed away longer than we thought.'[46]

The news from Stockholm broke on 8 October. Alexander Solzhenitsyn had been awarded the Nobel Prize for literature, the sixty-sixth recipient since the award was established. In its official citation, the Swedish Academy said that the accolade was made 'for the ethical force with which he has pursued the indispensable traditions of Russian literature'.

It was an earthquake. Twelve years earlier, the Russian author Boris Pasternak was awarded a Nobel Prize for his novel *Doctor Zhivago*. Publication had been banned within the Soviet Union. Under pressure, Pasternak was obliged to turn down the honour. But the controversy left the Soviet authorities damaged. It was one factor which led Khrushchev to loosen control over the literary establishment and thus create the environment in which Solzhenitsyn launched his career. Now that the former prison inmate had himself been named for the Nobel Prize, how would he respond?

The ceremony was due to take place on 10 December. Solzhenitsyn immediately wrote back, accepting the award. He said that he would come to Stockholm if he could.

Messages of congratulations poured in. One came from a group of political prisoners, smuggled out from their camp in secret. 'Barbed wire and automatic weapons,' it ran, 'prevent us from expressing to you personally the depth of our admiration for your courageous, creative work.'

Solzhenitsyn's award was a humiliation for the Soviet authorities. But they still had one card to play. To visit Stockholm, the author would need an exit visa. Even if he were to receive it, there would be no guarantee of entry back into the Soviet Union. In Moscow, Leonid Brezhnev and his colleagues weighed up the choice. KGB chief Yuri Andropov circulated copies of private reactions from leading intellectuals. 'This is going to be a story with a tragic ending,' concluded the poet Yevgeny Yevtushenko, 'whether he is allowed to go and then return, or go and not return.'

That autumn, relations between Solzhenitsyn and his wife deteriorated further. His lover Alya was pregnant with a child. Natasha was devastated. A few days after news of the Nobel Prize, she decided to take matters into her own hands. The couple were staying at a cottage in Zhukovka, outside Moscow. They were guests of the famous cellist Mstislav Rostropovich and his wife. One night, Natasha told Solzhenitsyn that she was going out for a walk. She went into a separate bedroom, and took out two boxes of sleeping pills.

The next morning, Solzhenitsyn found his wife unconscious. He and Rostropovich rushed her to the local hospital. From there, she was moved to a facility in Moscow.

KGB agents kept a close eye on Natasha's recovery. In her drugged and angry state, she opened up about her marriage to the hospital doctors. Andropov circulated updates to his Politburo colleagues.

'Success always spoiled him,' Natasha railed. 'He who calls on people to tell the truth, who stands up for the truth in all his works, and at home all lies!'[47]

Nixon was determined to attend Charles de Gaulle's memorial service. The former French president and wartime leader fascinated him. A volume of De Gaulle's memoirs was one of the most heavily annotated books in Nixon's library.[48]

In 1963, on a visit to Paris during Nixon's years in the political wilderness, De Gaulle had hosted the American for lunch at the Elysée Palace, and offered a toast to the hope that he would return to serve his country once more. Six years later, during his first visit to Europe as president, Nixon called once more on De Gaulle, as the veteran leader prepared to step down amid student protests. The Frenchman spent his final months at his home in the village of Colombey-les-Deux-Eglises, in north-eastern France. There, he wrote his memoirs, and tended the grounds of his modest country house, La Boisserie. The Frenchman died in early November from aneurism, at the age of 80.

At De Gaulle's wish, he was to be buried in a simple ceremony at Colombey. But the occasion required a more public commemoration, too. The French authorities scheduled an official memorial service for the same day, 12 November, at the cathedral of Notre Dame in Paris. It drew attendance from around the world. Nixon was the first major world leader to announce that he would go. Dozens followed, including the Shah of Iran, Haile Selassie of Ethiopia, Emperor Hirohito of Japan, David Ben Gurion, the first prime minister of Israel, and Indira Gandhi, prime minister of India. The United Kingdom was represented by Prime Minister Edward Heath, along with his predecessors Anthony Eden, Harold Macmillan and Harold Wilson. They were joined by Prince Charles, the 22-year-old heir to the British throne.

Chief of Staff Bob Haldeman wanted to keep the visit short. A week before, America had gone to the polls in midterm elections. Nixon campaigned strongly in support of Republican candidates, but the Democrats held their majority in the Senate, and made gains in the House of Representatives. It was not a time for the president to be away from Washington longer than necessary.

Georges Pompidou had succeeded De Gaulle to the presidency. He invited guests to a reception, at the presidential quarters in the Elysée Palace. Haldeman wanted Nixon to skip it, and head straight for the airport. On the flight across, Kissinger challenged him, on the grounds that not to attend would be an affront to their French hosts. Nixon acquiesced. Aside from protocol, there were good policy reasons. The Americans were worried at the potential for fracture among their European allies, as West Germany under Chancellor Willy Brandt sought improved relations with the Soviet bloc, while the United Kingdom under Heath made a renewed attempt to join the European Economic Community which Germany and France had established in the 1950s.[49]

At Notre Dame, mourners arrived in a series of motorcades. Gendarmes flanked the entrance, along with Garde Civile in uniform. Civilians wore black ties and morning dress, while the military were in full regalia. Harold Macmillan carried a silk top hat. At the end of the service, the organ played the Marseillaise. The mourners processed out of the cathedral. Nixon turned back for a final look at the altar, and placed his hand over his heart.[50]

The party moved to the Elysée Palace, for the official reception. Amid the crowd, Nixon shared a moment with Pompidou.

The American waited for the Frenchman to speak. There was silence. He looked up, and realized that Pompidou was choked for words. It reminded Nixon of his own feelings over Eisenhower's death, the previous year. A generation of great wartime leaders were leaving the stage.

Eventually, Pompidou broke the silence.

He sighed, and looked at Nixon. 'Well,' he said. 'We're on our own.'[51]

Eighteen months before, Soviet physicist Andrei Sakharov had lost his wife Klara. They met as young researchers during the war, and been married for twenty-six years. She died from stomach cancer. The end was agonizing. Confined to bed in her final weeks, she found some solace in watching coverage of the International Ice Skating Championships in Ljubljana on television, through the blurred images available on the Soviet domestic channel. But then the pain became too much, and she motioned for the screen to be turned off. Sakharov took it as a final gesture of farewell to life.

Heartbroken, the scientist spent the months after her death in a daze. In an impulsive moment, he withdrew his life's savings from the bank, and signed them away to a cancer hospital and children's charities.[52]

Time began to heal. It begun with a fellow scientist, Valentin Turchin. A specialist in the new field of computer science, Turchin wanted to assemble a joint letter from a group of scientists, calling on the authorities to allow more intellectual freedom for the advancement of research. Sakharov was supportive.

Through Turchin, Sakharov found himself drawn into a new circle. They were intellectual dissidents, who questioned the direction of the Soviet regime. The group included the leading physicist Pyotr Kapitsa, and Roy Medvedev, a historian who had published a critical assessment of Stalin entitled *Let History Judge*. In March 1970, Turchin, Sakharov and Medvedev published a letter in *The New York Times*. It was a blunt critique of the Soviet state. 'Anti-democratic traditions,' they wrote, had led to 'cruel distortions in the system.'[53]

A few weeks later, Sakharov received a phone call. It was from Valery Chalidze, a junior researcher at the Institute of Physics, and author in *samizdat* underground literature circles. Chalidze had a favour to ask. Pyotr Grigorenko was a former major-general in the Red Army and dissident activist. He had been confined to a psychiatric hospital. Might Sakharov be able to intervene with the authorities for his release? Medvedev called a few days later, over a similar case involving his brother. Sakharov realized that the Soviet authorities had adopted a new tactic. He was appalled at the use of psychiatric facilities to incarcerate dissidents.[54]

Kapitsa and Sakharov lobbied over the cases. Their pleas were successful. The former atomic scientist had found a new vocation. He saw more of Chalidze, joining meetings in the young man's apartment and involving himself in other cases. At one meeting, he was introduced to a woman called Elena Bonner. Approaching 50, Bonner had dark hair, heavy glasses and a serious manner. Her father had been killed during the purges under Stalin. Since the mid-1960s, she had been involved in the dissident movement. Sakharov was entranced.

As news of the Nobel Prize awarded to Solzhenitsyn spread, Bonner, Sakharov and Chalidze expanded their activities. In October, they travelled together to Kaluga, south-west of Moscow, to intervene in the trial of two dissidents. Revolt Pimenov was a mathematician, while Boris Vail worked in a puppet theatre. Both men were charged with distributing *samizdat*.

Back in Moscow, Chalidze and Sakharov decided to up the stakes. They held a press conference with Western journalists, launching a Human Rights Committee. It was, Chalidze explained, a 'voluntary, non-governmental association' that would study and publicize cases about human rights.[55]

KGB chief Yuri Andropov sensed a problem. Sakharov was different to Solzhenitsyn. Like his fellow writer, he could carry huge moral authority, both inside the Soviet Union's borders and beyond. Solzhenitsyn, however, had not sought to mobilize a political movement. Sakharov now seemed to be heading in that direction. In the two years since the invasion of Czechoslovakia, the KGB hoped that they had successfully curtailed the dissident movement. But these latest developments left Andropov concerned. Sakharov's involvement might, he warned the Central Committee, lead into 'something akin to an opposition'. The Soviet state needed to fight back. But how to be sure it would succeed?[56]

Notes

1 FRUS 1969–76 Vol. VI, p. 783.
2 Kissinger (1979), 439; Walters (1978), 512–13.
3 Kissinger (1979), 440.
4 FRUS 1969–76 Vol. VI, item 222, p. 774.
5 FRUS 1969–76 Vol. VI, item 191, p. 627–9.
6 FRUS 1969–76 Vol. VI, item 201, p. 663–82; Kissinger (1979), 445.
7 FRUS 1969–74 Vol. VI, item 222, p. 784.
8 FRUS 1969–74 Vol. VI, item 222, p. 787.
9 Haldeman (1994), 150.
10 Smith (1980), 57.
11 Haldeman (1994), 151.
12 Nixon (1978), 448–9.
13 Kissinger (1979), 498.
14 Ambrose (1989), 345; Nixon (1978), 453.
15 www.kentstate1970.org.
16 Dean interview with Naftali, 30 July 2007, p. 52.
17 Haldeman (1994), 162
18 Safire (1975), 191–3, 202–3; Buchanan (2017), 165.
19 Haldeman (1994), 162; Nixon (1978), 459.
20 Haig (1992), 238–9.
21 Nixon daily diary, 8 May 1970; Haldeman (1994), 163; Nixon (1978), 459; Safire (1975), 203.
22 Haig (1992), 238.
23 Buchanan (2017), 166.
24 Nixon (1978), 459–66; Safire (1975), 205–10; Krogh interview, 5 September 2007, p. 10–11, 13–20.
25 Smith (1985), 136–7; FRUS 1969–76 Vol. XXXIII, item 76, p. 263–4.
26 Smith (1985), 138.

27 Shevchenko (1985), 202–5.

28 Yanarella (2002), 156-57; Kaufman (2000), 210-11.

29 Quoted in Kaufman (2000), 211.

30 FRUS 1969–76 Vol. XXXIII, item 98, p. 322-5.

31 FRUS 1969–76 Vol. XXXIII, item 101, p. 337–8; Smith (1985), 148–9.

32 FRUS 1969–76 Vol. XXXIII, item 102, p. 338–40.

33 FRUS 1969–76 Vol. XXIV, item 284, p. 787.

34 Kissinger (1979), 618.

35 FRUS 1969–76, item 281, p. 775.

36 Bull interview with Naftali, 25 June 2007, p. 30.

37 Haig (1992), 249.

38 FRUS 1969–76 Vol. XXIV, item 287, p. 795-6, Haig (1992), 249; Kissinger (1979), 623.

39 FRUS 1969–76 Vol. XXIV, item 289, p. 798–9, Kissinger (1979) p624.

40 Haig (1992), 249–50.

41 FRUS 1969–76 Vol. XXIV, item 297, p. 826–8; Kissinger (1979), 625.

42 FRUS 1969–76 Vol. XXIV, item 298, p. 829–30.

43 FRUS 1969–76 Vol. XXIV, item 299, p. 831–9; Kissinger (1979), 626.

44 Kissinger (1979), 627.

45 Richard Mobley, *US Joint Military Contributions to Countering Syria's 1970 Invasion of Jordan*, ndupress.ndu.edu.

46 FRUS 1969–76 Vol. XII, item 216, p. 656.

47 Thomas (1998), 357–62; Pearce (2000), 207–9; Scammel (1995) doc. 31, p. 107–10.

48 Thomas (2016), 145.

49 Kissinger (1979), 936–7; (1999), 58.

50 Fenby (2010), 634.

51 Nixon (1978), 386.

52 Sakharov (1990), 297–9; Rubenstein and Gribanov (2005), 97.

53 Rubenstein and Gribanov (2005), 98–9.

54 Sakharov (1990), 309–11.

55 Lourie (2002), 226.

56 Rubenstein and Gribanov (2005), 104–11.

Chapter 4

THE COCK CROWS
(January–June 1971)

It was not an optimistic start to the year. At the beginning of 1971, KGB chief Yuri Andropov and Foreign Minister Andrei Gromyko offered a joint assessment to Politburo colleagues on relations between the superpowers. 'Confrontation,' they advised, would 'cover a historically long period.' Since taking office two years before, the Nixon administration had done little to change the dynamic. But a breakthrough was not impossible. In a whirlwind of diplomacy the previous autumn, West German Chancellor Willy Brandt had visited Moscow and then Warsaw, where he made the dramatic gesture of kneeling in repentance before a memorial to victims of the Jewish ghetto uprising against the Nazis in 1943. Ostpolitik was attracting support among many Germans. Perhaps Nixon might seek an equivalent step eastwards to position himself for re-election in 1972, through a meeting at summit level with the Soviet leadership.[1]

The president spent the New Year break at Camp David. The compound was swathed in snow, and Nixon remained indoors, mulling over what to do in the year ahead. The death of De Gaulle, he told Chief of Staff Bob Haldeman, had elevated his position. He was now the pre-eminent leader left. It was a real opportunity.[2]

Returning to Washington, Nixon gave an hour-long interview with a panel of journalists from the main TV networks. It was filmed in the library, on the ground floor of the White House. John Chancellor from NBC led off the questions, asking if Nixon had changed after two years in the job. The president replied that he had learned to be more realistic. 'We must not become impatient,' he declared, 'and we must plow forward.'

The interview continued, with questions on domestic policy and Vietnam. Nancy Dickerson from PBS stepped in. She asked if the two superpowers were back in 'something of a cold war situation.'

Nixon outlined the progress in talks on arms control. 'I am not without the confidence that I had at the beginning,' he concluded, choosing his words with care. 'The United States and the Soviet Union owe it to their own people and the people of the world, as superpowers, to negotiate rather than confront.'[3]

The interview over, Nixon flew to San Clemente, to celebrate his fifty-eighth birthday. Press Secretary Ron Ziegler persuaded the president to pose for photos on the beach. It was not a success. Nixon struggled to look at ease. He strode along the sand wearing a windbreaker with an embroidered presidential seal over his office shirt and trousers. His Yorkshire terrier, Pasha, scampered around him. At one point, caught in the Pacific surf, the president stiffened, with arms straight at his sides.[4]

Back in Washington, Soviet ambassador Anatoly Dobrynin and National Security Adviser Henry Kissinger met at the Soviet embassy. The Soviets had seen Nixon's interview. They wanted to test if the president meant what he said. A few days before, Moscow had sent the White House a note on Berlin. It was an exploratory probe.

Kissinger gave Dobrynin a response, both on Berlin and on arms control. Nixon, he said, was prepared to move forward on both issues, using the channel through Dobrynin. But it had to be on precise issues. For Berlin, the United States wanted to negotiate improved access between West Germany and West Berlin, guaranteed by the Soviets, and not just the East Germans. And, on SALT, there should be two negotiations, on ABM and about limits on offensive weapons, which were concluded together. These two issues would be a package, managed swiftly and in secrecy by those at the highest levels of government. Kissinger warned against including the Middle East as a third element.

Dobrynin took note. He was due to fly to Moscow for consultations, and indeed had delayed his flight in order to meet with Kissinger. He would report back. Though he said nothing, he already knew what his advice would be. This was an opening, and the Soviets should take it.

As Kissinger rose to leave, the ambassador offered a token of friendship. It was a book about art, for Kissinger's 9-year-old son David. Dobrynin had written a short inscription inside.[5]

Two weeks later, the ambassador returned. This time, he and Kissinger met at the White House, in the Map Room. Dobrynin was, his counterpart recalled, 'bubbling with enthusiasm'. He did most of the talking.

In Moscow, Dobrynin had met with the top Soviet leadership. They were open to a summit meeting. The ambassador was even instructed to offer dates, in the second half of the summer. It should deliver a concrete achievement. The Soviet Union was willing to work towards agreement on Berlin, and on nuclear weapons. While Moscow had not reached a final view on the linkage between ABM and offensive weapons proposed by Kissinger, they were sympathetic to the approach.

Kissinger welcomed the news. He took the opportunity to sharpen his warning about working in secrecy. Dobrynin, he said, must understand the 'extreme delicacy' of working directly with the White House on these issues, and thus bypassing Secretary of State Bill Rogers and his department. He could see that the Soviets might be tempted to play off different parts of the American system against each other. But it could not work. Dobrynin replied that he had never done so, and that it was not in his own self-interest.

Dobrynin rose to take his leave. 'So,' he said as he put on his coat, 'the future of Soviet–US relations is in our hands. I want you to know that we are going to make a big effort to improve them.'

Afterwards, Kissinger gave Nixon a read-out. The meeting was, he said, perhaps the most significant that he had held with Dobrynin since their first, two years before. After all their shadow-boxing over the time since, things might now really come together. The game had begun.[6]

Decision time had arrived. It was early February. Two weeks earlier, Nixon and his national security team had approved plans for an incursion into neutral Laos. Under the code name Lam Son 719, preparations were set.

The Americans believed that the invasion of Cambodia had been crucial to reducing the North Vietnamese war effort in 1970. But the north continued to infiltrate troops and material into Vietnam from Laos, a landlocked country which adjoined both North and South Vietnam. An elaborate network of jungle trails and supply depots ran along the border, known as the Ho Chi Minh Trail. These allowed Hanoi to bypass the narrow direct frontier between North and South. An attack into Laos might disrupt supply. And disruption would buy time for the South Vietnamese army, known as the ARVN, to develop into a force capable of holding its own while America continued to withdraw its troops.

General Creighton Abrams and his team in Saigon developed a plan in great secrecy. They operated under a new constraint. In the aftermath of the Cambodian invasion, Senators John Cooper and Frank Church had introduced an amendment, preventing deployment of American ground forces in either Cambodia or Laos without congressional approval. The amendment did not cover air forces. So the attack into Laos would need to be spearheaded by ARVN ground troops, with logistics, helicopters and firepower provided by the Americans in support.

The target was a town called Tchepone, about twenty-five miles inside Laos. This sat on a hub in the Ho Chi Minh Trail. As a prelude, American troops would reoccupy a support base at Khe Sanh, close to the Laotian border. This strategic point had been the scene of heavy fighting during the so-called Tet Offensive in 1968. To disguise the move, it would be given the same code name – Dewey Canyon – used for an operation by US Marines in the area two years before.

Abrams' plan called for an airborne assault by South Vietnamese paratroops, while armoured forces advanced along a road called Highway 9, which linked Khe Sanh and Tchepone. 'Fire bases' for supporting artillery would be established along either flank.

News leaked out. Communist spies and American journalists in Saigon each got hold of the story. In Congress, opponents of the war swung into action.

Should the operation go ahead? In early February, Nixon met in the Oval Office with Rogers and Kissinger, along with Defence Secretary Melvyn Laird, Chairman of the Joint Chiefs Thomas Moorer and Richard Helms, from the CIA. Al Haig and Ambassador Elsworth Bunker from Saigon were also present. In advance, Kissinger had circulated a five-page note, summarizing the arguments for and against going ahead with the operation. No one present spoke against.[7]

The next morning, CBS anchor Dan Rather reported that the meeting had taken place. He claimed that the national security team was seeking to dissuade

Nixon from going ahead. Somewhere, the story had leaked. And someone seemed to be having second thoughts. Kissinger, for one, was torn. He was concerned that the element of surprise had been lost. Shortly after Nixon had arrived at his desk, Kissinger came into the Oval Office. Haldeman joined them, along with Attorney General John Mitchell and Treasury Secretary John Connally. It was the same that had happened over Cambodia. Faced with an agonizing choice, Nixon would retreat into a huddle with his most trusted advisers.[8]

The group went back and forth over the options. The problem, Kissinger declared, was that the bureaucracy seemed determined to thwart them. If so, why go ahead with an operation that was already doomed?

By late morning, Nixon and Kissinger had swung round. To cancel would look weak. Their authority over State and Defence Departments would be lost. Haldeman agreed, for the reason that Lam Son 719 was essential if Vietnamization was to succeed.

In the late afternoon, Nixon had an appointment with the White House doctor, Walter Tkach, and Kenneth Riland, his physiotherapist. He stripped to his underpants in the outer room from the Oval Office and lay down, while Riland massaged his back. Somewhat awkwardly, Haldeman and Kissinger continued the conversation about Laos. Afterwards, Nixon sat back in a chair. He was still undressed, and still talking.[9]

Just after 6 p.m., the group broke up. The operation was on.

That evening, the Nixon family was hosting special visitors to the White House. Jackie Kennedy, presidential widow and now remarried to the shipping magnate Aristotle Onassis, had not set foot in the building since the assassination of her former husband. At the time, Nixon had written to offer his condolences. 'I would not have had Jack live his life any other way,' she wrote in her reply, 'though I know his death could have been prevented, and I will never cease to torture myself with that. We never value life enough when we have it.'[10]

Now, eight years on, she had decided to return. The occasion was to see new official portraits of John F. Kennedy and herself, which would shortly be unveiled. Her children John and Caroline joined her. John had lost his father just days before his third birthday. He was now aged 10, while Caroline was 13.

Jackie was on lively form. Allen, the butler, remembered the Kennedy's, and greeted the family group warmly. He served the former First Lady white wine with an ice cube, just as she had preferred during her time in the White House. John and Caroline opted for a glass of milk, which John managed to spill over Nixon's lap.

The portrait of Kennedy hung in the Great Hall. It was by the artist Aaron Shikler, and painted at the request of Jackie. Shikler had chosen to depict the thirty-fifth president of the United States seated, with head sunk on his chest in thought and arms folded. Jackie looked at the work in silence. Caroline and John took a quick glance, and said that they wanted to carry on looking round their old home.[11]

The group dined in a room on the second floor. Dinner was shrimp and steak, followed by a soufflé. It did not take long. The party sat down just before seven o'clock, and finished little over an hour later. Afterwards, they wandered down to the Oval Office, where John and Caroline had played with their father as young children. Throughout, Nixon and his wife Pat tried to keep conversation light. They did not want to bring distress to the former First Family. But it was hard to hold back the memories.

At one point, Jackie stopped for a moment. She looked directly at Nixon. 'I always live in a dream world,' said the former First Lady.[12]

Five days later, Operation Lam Son 719 was launched. American helicopters airlifted 1,000 South Vietnamese paratroops to Tchepone. Meanwhile, as planned, a much larger ground force set off from Khe Sanh.

Forewarned, the North Vietnamese had moved thousands of their own troops into the area, equipped with Soviet tanks and heavy artillery. Heavy rain reduced Highway 9 to mud, and the ground force became bogged down about halfway to Tchepone. Isolated, some South Vietnamese soldiers broke and fled.

A worried Kissinger and Nixon spoke on the phone.

'We're not going to lose it. That's all there is to it,' declared the president.

'In Laos . . .' interjected Kissinger.

'We can't. We can't lose,' repeated Nixon.

'No, Mr President.'

'. . . We can't lose. We can lose an election, but we're not going to lose this war, Henry. That's my view.'[13]

Fighting raged through February, and into early March. Hanoi committed more than 40,000 soldiers to the battle, while American aircraft flew over 150 sorties a day.[14] Determined to secure their objective, the ARVN threw additional airborne forces into Tchepone. Looking back, Kissinger was reminded of the struggle for Verdun in the First World War, or Stalingrad in the Second. Tchepone had assumed a similar psychological importance.[15]

Both Nixon and Kissinger began to lose confidence in Abrams. A series of tense cables followed, to Ambassador Bunker in Saigon. 'I am,' Kissinger warned in a private message, 'profoundly concerned at the way that the situation is evolving.'[16] At one point, Nixon angrily summoned Haig into the Oval Office, and told him to assume direct command. For a moment, the ambitious subordinate was tempted. But he thought better of it, and suggested that the president reflect on his decision overnight.[17]

Instead, Haig flew out to Saigon, to assess the situation for himself. The officer now held the rank of brigadier, while Abrams was a full general. But it was clear who had the president's confidence. Haig toured the fighting zone, interviewing combat commanders and headquarters staff. He reported his conclusions back to Washington. The picture was stark. Individual ARVN units had fought courageously. But they could not hold their own against the North Vietnamese without massive US firepower in support. Almost half the South Vietnamese committed to the offensive had been killed, wounded or taken prisoner.[18] Though Abrams and his subordinates did not admit as much, Haig left convinced that they had held US troops back to minimize American casualties. For now, at least, Vietnamization hung in the balance. And without success on the battlefield, there was little prospect of progress at the negotiating table.[19]

'You and I are going steady. We should exchange numbers.'

It was evening in late March, and Kissinger had just arrived at San Clemente. He had already spoken with Dobrynin three times that day. Matters were urgent.[20]

Through February and March, their secret dialogue on Berlin and Strategic Arms Limitation Talks (SALT) had continued apace. A week before, Dobrynin had shared a draft agreement on the former with Kissinger. It was, the adviser told Nixon, an 'acceptable' starting point.[21] This was followed by a Soviet proposal which set out the relationship between a deal on Anti-Ballistic Missile defence (ABM) and that on offensive weapons. Though more problematic for the Americans, because it implied that agreement on ABM should come first, it was also a step forward.

That progress had been possible despite the fighting in Laos suggested that the Soviets were interested in a deal. But the pressures were mounting, on each side.

In principle, Dobrynin and Kissinger could use this secret channel to draw together the different negotiations, from behind the scenes. They could make linkages and trade-offs, just as Nixon and Kissinger had envisaged when they first took office. But it added to tensions inside the Nixon administration. Though Secretary of State Bill Rogers was not aware of the details, he could sense that he was being frozen out. The relationship between Kissinger and himself fell to new depths. With Haldeman, Nixon lamented that his national security adviser nursed a 'psychotic hatred' for the secretary of state.[22] Over a three-hour lunch, Haldeman heard out Rogers' side of the story. Both men were, he confided to his diary, just set on a 'collision course'.[23]

The position was complicated for Rogers' subordinates. Kenneth Rush was American ambassador in West Germany and representative in the Quadripartite talks on Berlin. Kissinger shared details with him of the Soviet proposals on Berlin that he received through Dobrynin, and of his contacts with Egon Bahr, adviser to Chancellor Willy Brandt, who had visited the United States earlier that year for secret talks with Kissinger, under the pretext of watching an Apollo moon rocket launch at Cape Canaveral. Rush and Kissinger communicated by telegrams in a special cipher, routed through a US Navy officer based in Frankfurt. But Gerard Smith, who led the US delegation to the SALT talks, had no such line into Kissinger's secret parallel negotiations. 'He's a small player and I don't trust him,' commented Nixon in private.[24]

In Moscow, different pressures applied. Brezhnev remained part of a collective leadership. Decisions were reached in the Politburo by consensus. Dobrynin took Kissinger into his confidence, to explain the process. Under Stalin, one man had set policy on all the big questions. But Brezhnev lacked the same freedom. KGB chief Andropov, Marshal Grechko and Premier Alexei Kosygin were key on foreign policy, along with Foreign Minister Gromyko. All of them were entitled to see the same papers, and to debate issues at Politburo meetings, held each Thursday. When agreement could not be reached, Gromyko would be invited to redraft position papers, and circulate a new version, for fresh discussion a week later.[25]

Nonetheless, as Brezhnev grew in authority within the Kremlin, he had greater scope to shape and drive debate. To support him, he had assembled a kitchen cabinet of younger advisers, to write speeches and prepare policy documents. They included speech-writer Andrei Bobin, diplomatic adviser Andrei Aleksandrov-Agentov, academic Georgy Arbatov, and Anatoly Chernyaev, deputy head of the international department in the central party secretariat. Brezhnev would convene the group at his dacha at Zavidovo, 75 miles north-west of Moscow, for intense working sessions. The advisers lodged in spartan rooms, with metal bedsteads and a shared bathroom. They would work with the general secretary in a glass-roofed conservatory called the 'winter garden', seated round a large table. Among this circle of intimates, who were imbued with the more liberal mindset of the 1960s, Brezhnev felt able to talk openly.[26]

At the end of March, the Communist Party of the Soviet Union was due to hold its 24th Party Congress. The first took place in Minsk, in 1898. By the 1960s, they had settled into a rhythm, convening every five years. Almost 5,000 delegates were due to assemble from across the USSR. The venue was the Palace of Congresses, a conference hall inside the Kremlin walls which Khrushchev had built a decade before. The Congress would elect a new Central Committee and Politburo, in order of seniority. While the public sessions were carefully scripted, the build-up to these gatherings involved intense competition behind the scenes. Brezhnev had to watch his back.

Dobrynin knew where he needed to be. When Kissinger asked for his phone number, he gave the line for his residence in Moscow, where he would be based during the Congress. It was 290-2520. Kissinger wrote it down in the margin of his copy of the Soviet proposal on SALT.[27]

Andropov, too, was taking no chances. The KGB head was, recalled diplomatic adviser Aleksandrov-Agentov, 'intelligent, erudite and shrewd', but he could be uncompromising in defence of the communist system.[28] He had been watching closely since Andrei Sakharov and Valery Chalidze had launched their Human Rights Committee at the end of 1970. A spate of hijacking incidents had broken out over the winter months, as Jews and other persecuted minorities within the Soviet Union sought to draw attention to their plight, and flee to the West. Sakharov had become involved in the trials of detained hijackers. He worked closely with Elena Bonner, the activist whom he had first met at Chalidze's birthday party the previous autumn. As the KGB watched, their partnership flourished into romance.

Andropov believed that Sakharov might be open to persuasion. During his years as a nuclear physicist, he had enjoyed privileged access to the top of the Soviet state. Andropov urged Brezhnev to meet himself with Sakharov. The former scientist was, he believed, 'honest, compassionate and conscientious'. Attention from the top might help to draw his sting. Kosygin and Podgorny supported the proposal. But Brezhnev stalled, fearing that a meeting carried risks.[29] As a leader in the Komsomol youth movement in the 1920s, he had been awarded with a handcrafted knife, inscribed with the words 'Save Us, Dear Lord, From Our Friends – I'll Save Myself From Our Foes'. In the ruthless world of Soviet politics, it was sound advice. Now at the pinnacle of his career, the general secretary still needed to tread carefully ahead of a Party Congress that he hoped would consolidate his hold on power.[30]

Instead, the KGB tightened the net. Protests by Jewish dissidents were broken up, and more opponents of the regime incarcerated in psychiatric hospitals. Then, on the night before the Congress, security agents moved against Chalidze, with a surprise raid on his flat.

It was already late evening. Sakharov was called by another member of the committee, and rushed to Chalidze's address. He waited outside until the KGB had finished their business. Elena was with him. A car carrying more agents pulled up. 'We'll soon make your whole lot knuckle under,' snapped one woman officer. Sakharov thought that she looked like the guard of a Nazi concentration camp.

Eventually, around midnight, the door opened. The KGB squad filed past, carrying two large sacks filled with papers and books. It was a heavy blow for the dissident group. Months of secret work had been lost. Nor could it be easily replaced. In the Soviet Union, access to typewriters and paper was tightly controlled. Sakharov and Elena entered. They sat and listened while Chalidze made tea.

Beneath a calm, retiring manner, Sakharov could be relentless in pursuit of a cause. *New York Times* correspondent Robert Kaiser thought him like a 'gentle old cat', but one that was capable of moving 'with a deliberate sense of purpose and control'.[31] Now, faced with this fresh setback, his mood was defiant. A few weeks ago, Sakharov had told Elena that he was not interested in fame. But it was too late. The game had changed.[32]

The next morning, Brezhnev addressed the opening session of the Party Congress. He was dressed simply, in a dark suit and tie. On his left breast he wore the most important of the medals which he had been awarded over his career: Hero of the Soviet Union, and Hero of Socialist Labour. Behind the podium sat members of the Politburo and Central Committee, beneath a vast mosaic image of Lenin, founder of the Soviet state. In front of him sat thousands of delegates, in the stalls and upper levels of the Palace of Congresses.

These were the men and women who had built the Soviet Union. Brezhnev's generation was in charge. Now entering their fifties and sixties, they had been young enough to fight against Nazi Germany on the front line. That wartime service remained their defining experience. Beneath them were those now in their thirties and forties. Theirs had been a different experience. Too young to have suffered directly under Stalin, they had enjoyed the new opportunities of the postwar era, with places at university, better housing and jobs in the new fields of engineering and science through which the Soviet Union hoped to become the most advanced society in the world.

Brezhnev's formal position was General Secretary of the Party. In that role, he was required to report to the congress. His address lasted for six hours. Theirs, he told the delegates, had been a 'generation of peace'. The Soviet Union had lived without conflict for the last quarter century. But the threat of war had not been eliminated. It was essential that people should not become accustomed to the idea that the arms race was an unavoidable evil.

Turning to the future, Brezhnev set out his prescription for a 'peace programme'. The Soviet Union and the United States should work towards resolving conflict in Vietnam, and in the Middle East. They should reach a final settlement of borders in Europe, thus ending the territorial divisions in Germany and elsewhere which remained from the war. And they should work towards nuclear disarmament. Using a French word, for the first time, Brezhnev declared that he was seeking a 'détente', or relaxation, in relations between East and West. The expression had first crept into diplomatic jargon some sixty years before, during the period of rivalry between the great powers before the First World War.

The general secretary had experienced war at first hand. During the conflict with Nazi Germany, he served as a political commissar, engaged in intense fighting around the Black Sea port of Novorossisk. Later, his unit liberated the Ukrainian city of Dnipropetrovs'k, where as a young man he had worked in the regional party committee before the war. It was a bitter homecoming. 'There is no smell more acrid than that of homes burned to ashes,' he later recalled. 'Disfigured by fire and metal, lying in ruins, was my native land.' Years later, he would recount stories of wartime service to his niece, Ludmilla. It had, she recalled, left her uncle and his contemporaries with deep feelings, masked by hard shells on the outside.[33]

Over on the west coast of America, Nixon was spending the day at San Clemente. He was in a reflective mood. Earlier in his stay, he had taken a long drive along the coast, from Beverly Hills to Santa Monica and back northwards. Glimpses of everyday life were a rare thrill for the president. Fascinated, he gazed through the bulletproof windows of his limousine. Hippies wandered along the sidewalk, in jeans and long hair.

That evening, he and Haldeman were served a steak dinner by his valet Manolo, with onion rings and a cheese soufflé. Afterwards, Nixon walked out with the chief of staff to his car, chatting in a relaxed way.

Back in his quarters, Haldeman reflected on the encounter. Nixon's presidency seemed at something of a low point. Polling suggested a new drop in support, to the low 40s. But somehow he felt optimistic. Others in the White House had the same sense. There were, Haldeman noted in his diary, a number of 'monumentally optimistic possibilities' on the horizon, with Berlin, SALT and even Vietnam. Perhaps the turning point was just around the corner.[34]

Glenn Cowan was not a diplomat. The 19-year-old student from Santa Monica was a table tennis player. At the end of March 1971, Cowan and his teammates arrived in Nagoya, Japan, for the 31st World Table Tennis Championships.

After a first week of matches, Sunday was a rest day. Cowan spent the afternoon at practice, exchanging rallies with a player called Liang Geliang from the communist People's Republic of China. The Chinese were the team to beat. Geliang and his team mates had already established themselves as the dominant force in the competition.

When a Japanese official told them that it was time to close the training facility, Cowan looked round to board his team bus for the journey back to the hotel. But it had already gone. The Chinese suggested that he join them instead.

At first, the passengers sat in silence. With his long hair and tracksuit emblazoned 'USA', the Californian seemed from another planet. The Chinese had grown up during the Cultural Revolution of the 1960s, when America was reviled as the imperialist enemy. 'We were all tense,' recalled Zhuang Zedong, another Chinese player. 'We had all been advised not to speak to Americans, not to shake their hands, and not to exchange gifts with them.'

Zedong decided to break the ice. At 31, he was a full decade older than Cowan. A year before, Chinese leader Mao Tse-tung had met with the American writer Edgar Snow, at the national day parade in Tiananmen Square. Zedong felt that he should show the same hospitality towards the lone American. After all, they were just athletes together, not politicians. It was, he later remembered, 'really out of instinct'.

The two young men started a haltering conversation, through an interpreter. When the bus reached the hotel, Zedong dug around in his bag for a gift. He offered the American a silk screen print, of the Huangshan Mountains in Hangzhou. Cowan looked for something to give in return, but found himself empty-handed.

The next day, Cowan came up to Zedong, with a gift. He had bought a T-shirt, decorated with the symbol for peace and the words 'Let It Be'.

The encounter had been noticed. As Cowan and Zedong stepped off the bus at the end of their ride together, Japanese journalists snapped pictures of the pair. The image appeared in Japanese newspapers, and then around the world.[35]

Back in China, it was carried in *Dacankao*, a private paper for senior party officials. Chairman Mao Tse-Tung had led the revolution and run the country for the previous quarter of a century. When he heard the news, he saw an opportunity. Contacts between China and the United States had been frozen since the days of the Korean War. Washington continued to recognize the nationalist regime of Chiang Kai-shek, who had held power prior to the communist takeover, and then retreated to the island of Taiwan, off the coast of mainland China. But the plates were shifting. Through the 1960s, a rift had opened up between Beijing and Moscow. Extending a hand to Washington was no longer unthinkable. And sport provided a channel through which to test the ground.

The Chinese foreign ministry had previously counselled that a visit by American sports teams would be premature. Mao overruled the advice, and ordered that the team in Nagoya be instructed to invite their counterparts back to Beijing, for a friendly tour. 'This Zhuang Zedong not only plays table tennis well,' he declared, 'but he is good at foreign affairs, and he has a mind for politics.'[36]

The Laos operation was over. It was time for Nixon to address the nation once more. The president did so from the White House. Speaking from notes, and with a chart on a stand behind him, he traced the level of American forces in Vietnam since the early 1960s. 'Cambodia' and 'Laos' were both marked on the chart, to show how these operations had contributed to the overall reduction in troops. 'Every decision made has accomplished what I said it would accomplish,' he declared. 'They have reduced American involvement. They have drastically reduced our casualties.' Vietnamization, he assured his audience, was succeeding.

As he neared the end of his address, Nixon set his notes to one side. In preparation, the president had scripted this moment, too, and rehearsed it with Haldeman earlier in the day. He wanted to create the impression that he was speaking impromptu.

A few weeks earlier, at the height of the Laos operation, Nixon had presided over a medal ceremony in the Oval Office. He presented the Medal of Honour to the widow of Staff Sergeant Karl Taylor, a marine gunnery specialist. Taylor had charged a Viet Cong machine gun. His action saved his unit, but cost him his own life. Taylor's three children attended the ceremony, including the youngest, Kevin, who was 4 years old. As the family filed out afterwards, he stood to attention, and saluted the president.

Nixon recounted the scene to his audience. Presenting such a posthumous award was, he said, the hardest task that a president had to face. When the boy saluted, he had found it difficult to maintain his composure.

Later that night, Nixon made his usual round of phone calls to friends and supporters. He spoke with the Christian evangelist Billy Graham. The two men had become close. Four years before, Graham had conducted the funeral service for Nixon's mother. Afterwards, Nixon sobbed on the preacher's shoulder.[37] Now, in the White House, Graham would offer the president a listening ear, and counsel. They chatted for a few minutes. The preacher said that the reference to the young boy had reduced him to tears.

'It's awful tough, isn't it?' commented Nixon.

'Well, God Bless,' replied Graham. 'You've got a lot of people praying for you and pulling for you.'

'Believe me, Billy, it means an awful lot. And you keep the faith, huh?'

'Ah, you betcha.'

'Keep the faith.'

'Yes, sir,' said the preacher.

'We're going to win.' Nixon finished the call.[38]

'You say Dobrynin will be back tomorrow night?'

Nixon was getting impatient. Almost a fortnight had passed since his television address on Vietnam, and nearly a month since Dobrynin had flown back to Moscow for the Party Congress. In a notable honour for a serving diplomat, the ambassador had been elected to the Central Committee. But Nixon and Kissinger were anxious to know what had happened behind the scenes, on SALT and on Berlin. Was a deal in sight?

'Tomorrow, late afternoon,' replied the national security adviser. 'I've got it – we've – I've got the FBI checking passenger lists.' Haig was on the case with the Bureau. They would know as soon as Dobrynin was on a flight.

'Oh, he'll bring something back,' Kissinger added.

Nixon was more cautious. It might not be the answer for which they were hoping. 'No fooling round,' he snapped back. 'If he ain't going to play, then we'll explore the Chinese one to the hilt if there's any way of exploring it.'[39]

'Ping-Pong diplomacy', as the press had dubbed the contact between Chinese and American teams, had given the two men a new card. That week, Cowan and his teammates had visited Beijing, travelling via Hong Kong. They had received a lavish welcome. Zhou Enlai, premier of the People's Republic and second in the hierarchy to Mao, had welcomed the young Americans in the Great Hall of the People, on Tiananmen Square. Back in the United States, *The Washington Post* and *Newsweek* had been quick to suggest that the Chinese initiative would put pressure on Moscow to be more forthcoming. Privately, Kissinger had suggested to Nixon that there might be a 30-per-cent chance of landing closer relations with both Beijing and Moscow.[40]

The next morning, Nixon received a visitor. Graham Steenhoven was president of the US Table Tennis Association. He had accompanied the national team on their trip to Beijing. For Americans, China was a remote and unknown land. Nixon and his advisers wanted to hear all about it. Steenhoven described his encounter with Zhou Enlai. They spoke through an interpreter, but it was clear that Zhou understood what was being said.

'Please criticize us,' Zhou had told his visitor. 'We want to do better.'

Steenhoven recounted the conversation to Nixon. The president was fascinated. Had Zhou, he asked, really been telling the American visitors to critique Communist China?

Steenhoven elaborated. At first he had been confused by Zhou's invitation. It seemed rude to criticize his host, especially when the Chinese made such a visible effort to honour their American guests. But when he was sitting alone with the Zhou later, he had thought of something to say. 'Well,' he told Zhou, 'you feed us too much.' When the Americans had sat down to dine, the menu cards were in Chinese. The visitors were offered a serving of cold meat. Unable to read the menu, they assumed it was all that was on offer and cleared their plates. The Chinese went on to produce another ten courses. Undeterred, the young American players kept eating.

'Was the food good?' Nixon asked.

'Excellent,' Steenhoven replied. 'We just got everything. Everything.'[41]

Dobrynin was back. He met Kissinger over lunch at the White House.

With him, the ambassador brought a draft letter, from the Soviet leadership to the president. The text was intended to be made public in its final form. By sharing it with the Americans in advance, and negotiating over the wording, the Soviets could narrow down agreement on the key issues for a summit. Kissinger judged it a draw. On SALT, the draft letter implied that agreement on ABM and a freeze in offensive weapons should be linked and simultaneous. This was a move towards the American position. But on Berlin, Dobrynin said that Moscow was disappointed with progress in the Quadripartite negotiations. US Ambassador to West Germany Kenneth Rush seemed to have hardened his line. What was going on?[42]

Kissinger reacted sharply. The American side would not be pressured into a deal as the price for a summit meeting. Afterwards, when Kissinger debriefed him, Nixon agreed.

On the following Monday, Kissinger and Dobrynin met again. A further meeting followed on Tuesday. Dobrynin seemed to be aware of a fix on Berlin which the national security adviser had discussed with West German envoy Egon Bahr at the weekend, in which both sides might agree to focus on practical undertakings, rather than opposing claims over the legal status of the city. He was prepared to accept it.

The ambassador sensed that the atmosphere had cooled. Kissinger implied that the Soviets had been slow to make progress on SALT, and suggested that the American side was not in a position to discuss dates for a summit. Dobrynin realized that he must respond. He said that he hoped developments in recent weeks between Beijing and Washington were not an attempt to blackmail Moscow. The reaction on the Soviet side would be very negative.

The two men took leave of each other. It was just after four o'clock.[43]

China was indeed a factor. In fact, events were moving even while Kissinger and Dobrynin had been talking. Since the early months of the Nixon administration, the president and his adviser had sought to open a private channel of communication with Beijing. They had sent messages through Nikolai Ceausescu, the Romanian president, and through President Yahya Khan of Pakistan, who enjoyed good relations with both the United States and the People's Republic. Kissinger would meet with the Romanian or Pakistani ambassadors in Washington, and dictate a form of words which they would pass in confidence to the authorities in Beijing. But progress had been slow. Communications were cloaked in secrecy, misunderstanding and caution. The most recent message from the American side had been delivered, through the Romanians, at the end of January. Until now, there had been no reply.

Kissinger returned to his office after the meeting with Dobrynin. His assistant, Harold Saunders, told him that the Pakistani ambassador, Agha Hilaly, had called. He wanted to meet for five minutes, as soon as possible.

Hilaly arrived at the White House just after six o'clock. His message was too sensitive to transmit over the phone.

The Pakistani president had visited Beijing. Zhou dictated a communication, to pass back to the Americans. It had taken almost a week to reach Hilaly, carried by courier from Beijing to Islamabad, and then to Washington.

The note was two sides in length. It was written by hand, in an elegant script. Hilaly handed it across to Kissinger.

The preamble was familiar diplomatic wording. The People's Republic reaffirmed its commitment to the 'crucial question' of Taiwan, and its demand that US military forces be withdrawn from the region. This had been a familiar position since

America broke off diplomatic relations in the wake of the communist takeover in China, more than twenty years before.

The crucial sentence came in the middle of the letter. 'The Chinese Government,' it read, 'reaffirms its willingness to receive publically in Beijing a special envoy of the President of the United States.' In Kissinger's experience, diplomacy seldom produced obvious turning points. Most diplomatic business was the steady grind of daily pressures and tensions, in which a trend might only be discerned in retrospect. But this was indeed a breakthrough moment. An invitation to Beijing was a chance to reset the relationship with China, and at the same time turn the tables on Moscow.

Kissinger rushed to call Nixon. He was trembling with excitement as he broke the news.[44]

'We have played a game,' reflected the president, 'and we've gotten a little break here. We were hoping that we'd get one, and I think we have one now.'

Kissinger agreed. 'When we talked about "linkage",' he commented, 'everyone was sneering.'

'Yeah, I know,' replied Nixon.

'But we've done it now.'

'That's right.'

'We've got it all hooked together.'

Nixon rang off, and Kissinger put the phone down. For the first time in his role as national security adviser, the former academic felt a moment of elation and inner peace.[45]

Dean Acheson was back in the White House. Over the previous two years, the former secretary of state had been drawn into the president's circle. 'Nixon and Kissinger had been most considerate of me and some of my ageing colleagues,' he wrote to the former British prime minister, Anthony Eden. White House technicians even installed a secure phone line to his holiday home, on Antigua in the Caribbean.[46]

Acheson had been dismayed by the invasion of Cambodia. His relationship with Nixon had cooled. But now, once again, the president needed help.

Mike Mansfield was Democrat senator for Montana and majority leader in the Senate since Kennedy's presidency. He had sprung a trap. Mansfield was a long-standing opponent of the US military presence in Europe, stationed as part of conventional forces from the countries of the North Atlantic Treaty Organization (NATO) against the Soviet Union and its allies in the Warsaw Pact. The deployment dated back to the end of the Second World War.

Mansfield believed that the Nixon administration had failed to capitalize on the opportunities presented by détente with the Soviet Union. He had proposed an amendment to the Selective Service Bill, to halve US troops in Europe.

The administration was caught unawares. Mansfield's amendment was tabled on 11 May. He sought a vote on the following day. The White House managed to obtain an extension, for a further five days. Nixon ordered his team to spring into a counteroffensive. Haldeman found himself arbitrating between Rogers and Kissinger, over who would lead.[47]

On the next day, in the afternoon, the president hosted Acheson in the Cabinet Room. As secretary of state, the veteran had negotiated the North Atlantic Treaty. He was joined by other figures from the postwar era: Lucius Clay, the general who oversaw administration of occupied Germany, John McCloy, who served as president of the newly established World Bank and then US High Commissioner in Bonn following the creation of West Germany, and Thomas Dewey, the Republican governor of New York who had run unsuccessfully against Roosevelt and then Truman, in 1948. The group had met Nixon and Kissinger the previous December, to offer advice about Germany and Brandt's Ostpolitik.[48]

Nixon and Acheson sat in the main armchairs, in front of the fireplace. Clay, McCloy, Dewey and Kissinger flanked them, on sofas. Kissinger sat opposite Clay, under whom he had served as a junior non-commissioned officer during the early months of the occupation in Germany. He realized that he was witness to what he later called a 'final meeting of the Old Guard', men who had built a bipartisan US foreign policy in the years after the war.

Acheson spoke to the press afterwards, on behalf of the group. He slammed the Mansfield initiative, calling it 'asinine'. The veterans were unanimously opposed. Their meeting with the president had lasted for an hour and a half. One reporter asked why it had taken so long. 'We are all old and we are all eloquent', Acheson snapped back.[49]

The next day, Friday 14 May, Brezhnev gave a speech. He was visiting Tbilisi, capital of the Soviet republic of Georgia. At the 24th Party Congress, the leader hailed the Soviet Union as a unified state, in which different nationalities were merged into a single identity. But the republics which made up the Union remained distinct entities. As a centerpiece to his visit, Brezhnev addressed the Georgian Communist Party's own congress, on the fiftieth anniversary of communist takeover in Georgia. It was a different audience to that in Moscow, six weeks before. As Georgians, they were a proud race, with a long history and distinct culture. Though ruled by Moscow since Tsarist times, they did not look kindly on outside interference. Before Brezhnev, the congress was addressed by Edvard Shevardnadze, head of the Tblisi city administration and a rising local star. Moscow was eyeing him as a clean pair of hands that might replace the local first secretary, Vasil Mzhavanadze, who was tainted by corruption.

Brezhnev used his speech to reinforce the message he gave to the 24th Party Congress. He appealed to European countries to engage with the Soviet Union on proposals for reducing armed forces in Europe. So far, he declared, the reaction had been like 'a person who tries to judge the taste of a wine by its appearance alone, without touching it'. It was time to engage in negotiations, which the Soviets saw as a necessary corollary to the Quadripartite talks over Berlin and Brandt's Ostpolitik diplomacy.

At the end of his speech, Brezhnev was presented with the flag of Soviet Georgia. The design featured a blue sun in the top left hand corner of a red rectangle, inlaid with the hammer and sickle. It was based on the Soviet Union flag but, like those of the other fourteen republics, given a local twist. Brezhnev and Mzhavanadze embraced, kissing on both cheeks.

Tblisi was more than a thousand miles south of Moscow. The US Embassy followed Brezhnev's speech through the Soviet media, and reported back to Washington. In the National Security Council, Soviet matters were handled by Hal Sonnenfeldt, a State Department diplomat who specialized in the region. Like Kissinger, Sonnenfeldt was a German Jew, whose family had escaped in the 1930s. He became close to the national security adviser.

When they read about the speech, Sonnenfeldt and Kissinger spotted an opportunity to wrong-foot Mansfield. It could, they told Nixon, 'be turned to our advantage'.[50] If Brezhnev was urging negotiations, it was no time for the United States to engage in unilateral troop withdrawals. To do so could undermine the American position on Berlin and other European matters. Nixon agreed. He instructed Haldeman to relay the point to Rogers, for use with key senators. To reinforce the point, the secretary of state announced that Jacob Beam, American ambassador in Moscow, had been instructed to follow up with the Kremlin.

Five days after Brezhnev's speech, the Mansfield amendment went to a vote. In the run-up, many senators favoured a compromise. They hoped that the administration might accept some drawdown of its forces in Europe. But Nixon, Kissinger and Rogers held firm. Not to do so, Kissinger thought, would lead to being 'driven from one position of disadvantage to another'.[51]

The final vote came before midnight. Mansfield was conclusively defeated. Only thirty-six senators voted in favour of his amendment, while sixty-one voted against. America would keep its military forces in Europe.

Nixon wrote to thank Acheson. A few years before, the former secretary of state had published his memoirs, *Present at the Creation*. It was a play on a line by King Alfonso X of Spain. The monarch was alleged to have said that, given the chance, he would have offered some useful hints to the Almighty on ordering the universe.

'You were among [those] at the Cabinet Room who could truly claim to have been "Present at the Creation",' wrote Nixon. 'All can now proudly look back to the events of the last few days and with some degree of truth say that they were "Present at the Resurrection".'[52]

'It isn't frustrating?' asked the president.[53]

Nixon was meeting US diplomat Gerard Smith and his fellow delegates to the SALT negotiations on nuclear weapons. It was mid-afternoon, on the same day as the Senate vote over the Mansfield Amendment. SALT was in a further round, this time in Vienna. During a break in the talks, Smith flew back to Washington. He suspected that something was afoot.

A few days before, the Soviet and American delegations had taken a boat cruise on the Worthersee, provided by their Austrian hosts. It was a welcome chance to relax. The talks were making little progress. During the cruise, Soviet delegation head Vladimir Semenov pulled Smith aside. The two men stepped below deck, for a quiet word in the bar. Semenov explained that he had a question to ask. Would there be scope in reaching an agreement on ABM defence first, rather than a comprehensive agreement which covered offensive weapons as well? At the same time, there would be a halt to deployment of intercontinental missiles, or ICBMs, and later intensive negotiations on such offensive systems. Semenov gave the impression that he was speaking informally, off the cuff. But both men knew that such a suggestion would not have been made without prior consultation with Moscow. Unknown to Smith, it was in effect the same deal which Dobrynin had outlined to Kissinger when they met in late April, just before the invitation to visit China arrived in the White House.[54]

Smith reported the conversation to Washington. It was met with silence. When he arrived back in the capital on 10 May, there was no further news. A week later he called in at the White House, for breakfast with Kissinger.

It was the moment that Smith had half expected. The national security adviser confessed to his contacts with Dobrynin and admitted that agreement had been struck over the heads of the two delegations. The next day, Nixon would announce the news at a major press conference. Perhaps, Kissinger suggested, Smith might wish to return back to Vienna before the story broke?

Privately, Smith was incensed. For the previous eighteen months his delegation had reported each nuance of the Soviet position, and followed instructions to the letter. Now he found himself bypassed.

The diplomat restrained himself. When Kissinger showed him a copy of the draft letters, Smith's only comment was to suggest that some of the wording looked a little loose.[55]

His meeting with the president followed that afternoon. Smith continued to hold his poise. He accepted the logic behind Kissinger's position. A comprehensive agreement which covered both ABM and offensive weapons was just not possible. And a deal on ABM was valuable in itself, as a way of ensuring that neither superpower could undermine the nuclear balance by making itself immune from attack.

But it was Nixon's question about frustration which cut closest to the bone. Had Smith ever been frustrated, asked the president?

Kissinger was also present. They were joined by 'Tommy' Thompson, from the State Department. Approaching 70, Thompson had served in Moscow during the war. He returned to be ambassador on two occasions, including in the Cuba missile crisis. Following his meeting with Kissinger, Smith was considering whether he should resign. Privately, Thompson thought that it was the right course to take.

Smith dodged the question. Five years ago, the Soviets wouldn't have been prepared even to discuss these issues. So it wasn't frustrating to find himself in actual negotiations.

Nixon pressed him. 'Do you all feel that way?' he asked.

Without waiting for an answer, he extended his question to Thompson. 'You've been around the track with these guys more than anyone else,' the president said.

Thompson also ducked the question. He hadn't been present in the recent round of negotiations.

Kissinger interjected. The recent exchanges had been on a 'higher level', in an oblique reference to his channel with Dobrynin.

'It's very interesting, Mr President,' replied Smith.[56]

Life in the White House had not been easy for presidential daughter Tricia Nixon. Her bedroom was located over the Grand Entrance Hall. Each weekday, the building was open to the public. Tricia was awoken by the sound of guards setting up barriers to direct the queues of visitors. Would-be boyfriends tried to reach her through the White House switchboard, while staff muttered about her absences from official receptions. A visit by British royal and heir to the throne Prince Charles in the summer of 1970 stirred further gossip. Tricia's elder sister Julie was already married, to the grandson of President Eisenhower. To forestall speculation about romance, Tricia arranged for Julie to dance in her stead with the British visitor.[57]

In any case, Tricia had other plans. She and Ed Cox had met at high school. By autumn 1970, they had decided to marry. The president was determined to give his daughter a magical day. That summer, he had been obliged to cancel attendance at her graduation, in the wake of student protests over Cambodia. She had been bitterly disappointed. The wedding would make amends.[58]

The ceremony took place in the Rose Garden, on 12 June. It was scheduled for four o'clock in the afternoon. But all morning rain fell over Washington. The ushers set up chairs in the East Room, as a fallback. By 4.15 p.m., the guests were waiting. Tricia wondered if they should stay indoors. Among the president's family, tension was running high. When Nixon asked for a last-minute update on the weather, an urgent request was passed to the Air Force. Word came back that a break in the clouds was expected, at 16:33 precisely. As the sun came through, the guests filed out onto the Rose Garden lawn. In the scramble, they failed to follow the elaborate seating plan. Shortly afterwards, the president emerged with his daughter. They walked along the South Portico, to the sound of Bach's cantata *Jesu Joy of Man's Desiring*. The family dogs watched on, their collars decorated with flowers.[59]

That evening, Tricia and Ed led the dancing. For their first waltz they chose 'Lara's Theme', from the popular film *Doctor Zhivago*. Nixon danced with his daughter, and then his wife Pat. Guests broke into applause. Later he danced with Julie. Her husband David was away, serving with the US Navy in the Mediterranean.[60]

The next day was a Sunday. Nixon read through the morning papers with pride. 'Tricia Nixon Takes Vows' was the lead story in *The New York Times*, complete with photos. He hardly glanced at the headline alongside. It was about the release of a Pentagon archive on Vietnam.

At midday, Haig reached the president on the phone. The soldier was shaken. The *Times* story about the Pentagon was, he told Nixon, 'the most devastating breach of the greatest magnitude of anything that I've ever seen'.

Haig explained. During his tenure as defence secretary, Robert McNamara had ordered a major internal study into the Vietnam War. More than thirty analysts worked in secret, assembling some 4,000 pages of documents. The report was completed in January 1969, just before Nixon's inauguration. Only fifteen copies were printed, under conditions of maximum security. But, the *Times* had got hold of the text. It intended to publish by instalments.[61]

At the Monday morning staff meeting, Kissinger was even more incensed. He paced up and down, thumping the antique Chippendale table. His colleagues had become used to the former academic's outbursts of temper, but this was truly memorable.

'No foreign government will ever trust us again,' he shouted. 'We might just as well turn it all over to the Soviets and get it over with. These leaks are destroying us.'

'Destroying us!' he repeated. Kissinger glared at Haldeman. 'I tell you, Bob, the president must act – today. There is wholesale subversion of this government under way.'[62]

As the week went on more details emerged. The leak had come from Daniel Ellsberg, a 40-year-old academic who had worked in the Pentagon, and the RAND Corporation. Ellsberg had known Kissinger at Harvard, and continued some contact with him in the White House.

The connection was uncomfortable. At a meeting with the president, Kissinger lashed out. The academic accused his former colleague of sexual perversion, drug abuse and misconduct while on duty in Vietnam. Ehrlichman, who was also present, thought that it 'fanned [Nixon's] flame white hot'. The president ordered John Mitchell, the Attorney General, to file an injunction against the *Times*, and to press criminal charges against Ellsberg.[63]

Politically, the issues were less clear-cut. The 'Pentagon Papers', as the *Times* had dubbed them, were about the Kennedy and Johnson administrations. Nixon's presidency was not implicated. The report exposed a tale of covert presidential actions to deepen America's involvement in Vietnam, without informing Congress or the public. By the end of the week, Johnson was, Haldeman noted in his diary, in a 'state of being totally unstrung'.[64] While Nixon and Kissinger were concerned at the implications from leaking of classified information, it was not clear that the substance was an issue for their administration. 'The rest of us might have concluded that the Papers were Lyndon Johnson's problem, not ours,' Ehrlichman later reflected.[65]

But Nixon was clear. The challenge to executive authority must be confronted. He and Haldeman spent the following weekend at Key Biscayne. The Papers were, he told his chief of staff, an issue of principle. It was like the Alger Hiss case more than twenty years before. The administration must establish that publication had been illegal.[66]

'You're going to be my Lord High Executioner from now on,' Nixon said.[67]

Notes

1   Dobrynin (1995), 209–10.
2   Haldeman (1994), 230.
3   FRUS 1969–76 Vol. XIII, item 81, p. 245–7.
4   Haldeman (1994), 232.

5   FRUS 1969–76 Vol. XIII, item 90, p. 276–9; Kissinger (1979), 802–3; Dobrynin (1995), 210–11.
6   FRUS 1969–76 Vol. XIII, item 103, p. 303–8; Kissinger (1979), 804–5; Dobrynin (1995), 211.
7   Kissinger (1979), 1001; FRUS 1969–76 Vol. VII, item 116, p. 339–43.
8   Kissinger (1979), 1001.
9   Haldeman (1994), 242–3.
10 Nixon (1978), 254–5; Farrell (2017), 312.
11 Eisenhower (1986), 467–70.
12 Nixon (1978), 502–3; Nixon daily diary, 3 February 1971; Matthews (1996), 293–7.
13 FRUS 1969–76 Vol. VII, item131, p. 403; Brinkley and Nichter (2014), 11.
14 Hastings (2018), 499.
15 Kissinger (1978), 1006.
16 FRUS 1969–76 Vol. VII, item 142, p. 438–40.
17 Haig (1992), 275.
18 Hastings (2018), 501.
19 Haig (1992), 276–7; FRUS 1969–76 item 153, p. 462–4.
20 FRUS 1969–76 Vol. XII, item 161, p. 465.
21 FRUS 1969–76 Vol. XIII, item 146, p. 419; Soviet text at FRUS Vol. XL, items 201, 202, p. 592–9.
22 Brinkley and Nichter (2014), 19.
23 Haldeman (1994), 249–50.
24 Brinkley and Nichter (2014), 27.
25 FRUS 1969–76 Vol. XIII, item 149, p. 427–8. See also Shevchenko (1985), 176–7 and 187.
26 Chernyaev (1995), 258–9.
27 FRUS 1969–76 Vol. XIII, item 161, p. 465.
28 Aleksandrov-Agentov (1995), 264.
29 Rubenstein and Gribanov (2005) docs 23–4, p. 114–17.
30 Brezhneva (1995), 21.
31 Kaiser (1977), 389.
32 Bonner (1988), 26.
33 Brezhnev (1978), 93; Brezhneva (1995), 251–2.
34 Haldeman (1994), 261–3.
35 See 'The Ping Heard Around the World' by Jamie FlorCruz, 28 February 2008 and 'Ping Pong Diplomacy Player Dies' by Katie Hunt, 11 February 2013, both on www.cnn.com.
36 Kissinger (2012), 232, quoting Lin Ke, Xu Tao and Wu Xujun, *The True Life of Mao Zedong – Eyewitness Accounts by Mao's Staff*, Hong Kong (1995).
37 Thomas (2016), 151.
38 Brinkley and Nichter (2014), 53–5.
39 Brinkley and Nichter (2014), 82.
40 FRUS 1969–76 Vol. XIII, item 186, p. 539–40.
41 Brinkley and Nichter (2014), 83–6.
42 FRUS 1969–76 Vol. XXII, items 189 and 190, p. 547–56; Kissinger (1979), 817; Dobrynin (1995), 220–1.
43 FRUS 1969–76 Vol. XIII, items 192 and 195, p. 559–61 and 566–7; Kissinger (1979), 817, 827–8; Dobrynin (1995), 221.
44 Haldeman diary, 10 July 1971.
45 Brinkley and Nichter (2014), 106–7; Kissinger (1979), 713–18.

46 Isaacson and Thomas (1986), 716.
47 Haldeman (1994), 286.
48 FRUS Vol. XL, item 140, p. 403.
49 Brinkley (1992), 299.
50 FRUS 1969–76 Vol. XIII, item 217, p. 646–8.
51 Kissinger (1979), 942.
52 Nixon letter to Acheson of 23 May 1971, Acheson papers, quoted in Ambrose (1989), 444.
53 FRUS 1969–76 Vol. XXXIII, item 159, p. 498–502.
54 Smith (1985), 219–21. See also Shevchenko (1985), 205.
55 Smith (1985), 222–4; Kissinger (1979), 819; FRUS 1969–76 Vol. XXXIII, item 157, p. 491–2; Nitze (1989), 313.
56 FRUS 1969–76 Vol. XXXIII, item 159, p. 498–502.
57 Eisenhower (1986), 383–7.
58 Nixon (1978), 447.
59 Eisenhower (1986), 473–7; www.presidentialpetmuseum.com/pets/vicky.
60 Nixon (1978), 504–8.
61 Brinkley and Nichter (2014), 170–2.
62 Colson (1976), 62–3.
63 Ehrlichman (1982), 300–2; Kissinger (1979), 729–30; Haldeman (1994), 300–2; Nixon (1978), 508–12; Ambrose (1989), 446–8; Haldeman interview with Raymond Geselbricht, 12 April 1988, p. 150–2.
64 Haldeman (1992), 302.
65 Ehrlichman (1982), 302; Buchanan (2017), 212–24.
66 Haldeman (1992), 303; see also Ellsberg interview with Naftali, 20 May 2008, p. 23.
67 Haldeman (1978), 111.

Chapter 5

COURAGE TO CHANGE
(July–December 1971)

For a moment, Henry Kissinger felt like a child again. He was flying across the Himalayas and it was early morning, on Friday 9 July 1971. The national security adviser later called it one of those magical moments in adult life, when humans rediscover the mystery of novelty that comes with childhood. Together with a small group of American officials, Kissinger was aboard a Pakistan International Airlines Boeing 707, on the way from Islamabad to Beijing.

Below them, the rising sun caught the peaks of the Hindu Kush, on the border between Pakistan and China. The plane flew close to Daughalgiri and then K-2, the second highest mountain in the world. John Holdridge was a State Department expert on China. He thought that K-2 looked like a shark's tooth, overshadowing the other peaks. The mountain had first been climbed by two Italian mountaineers, fifteen years before. Looking down, Holdridge wondered how anyone could manage such a feat.[1]

Kissinger and his associates were on a mission to Beijing. A month before, Pakistani ambassador Hilaly had brought a message from Chinese premier Zhou Enlai, confirming that the visit was on. Kissinger interrupted Nixon at a state banquet to break the news. It was, he said, the most important communication to reach a president since the end of the Second World War. The two men toasted their fortune with a private bottle of vintage brandy, in the Lincoln Sitting Room at the White House. It was Courvoisier, given to the Nixons for Christmas. 'Let us drink to generations to come,' announced the president.[2]

The trip was conducted in high secrecy. Kissinger concocted an elaborate cover plan. He made a ten-day journey through Asia, including Vietnam, Thailand, India and then Pakistan. Once in Islamabad, the Americans had agreed that the former academic would complain of a stomach bug, and cancel his schedule for a couple of days' rest. Undercover, he would then fly to Beijing, aboard a Pakistani aircraft. Winston Lord was a young NSC staffer accompanying him on the trip. He produced different versions of the schedule, for those in the travelling party who knew what was afoot, and those who, unawares, would remain behind in Pakistan. The only hitch was that, on his stop in India, Kissinger caught a genuine upset stomach. He had to suffer in silence, so that the cover story for the Pakistan leg remained intact.[3]

The aircraft had been specially equipped by the Pakistanis. Kissinger was given a separate cabin in the middle of the fuselage, with a double bed. His companions travelled in the front section. They were joined by a welcoming party of Chinese officials, who had flown in from Beijing. The Americans later learned that they had been selected two years before, when the Chinese first decided to explore a diplomatic opening with Washington. All spoke English. After breakfast had been served, the Pakistani cabin crew offered round cartons of cigarettes. When the Americans refused, Holdridge was amused to see the Chinese navigator quietly swipe the entire lot for himself.[4]

The flight arrived in Beijing at just after noon, local time. More officials greeted the Americans at the airport. They drove into the city centre aboard a convoy of limousines, with curtains closed across the passenger windows. Holdridge recognized that carrying his boss was a Hong Ki, or 'Red Flag' – a Chinese version of the Cadillac. The rest of the party was ushered into lesser Shanghai models. They swept past Tiananmen Square, and to a complex of guest houses, in the western quarter of the city.

Later that afternoon, Zhou Enlai arrived to greet the guests. He was accompanied by half a dozen other officials, and a swarm of photographers. During the drive in from the airport, Holdridge had been quizzed by an anxious Chinese official about whether Kissinger would offer a handshake. Meeting at Geneva, nearly twenty years before, John Foster Dulles had pointedly refused to extend his hand to representatives of Communist China. In an elaborate gesture, Kissinger thrust out his hand to the approaching Zhou. There was, the American thought, something like a coiled spring about his Chinese counterpart, intense, confident and controlled.[5]

The premier offered cigarettes round. Again, the Americans refused. Zhou laughed, and offered words of welcome. The two delegations sat down, in large wicker chairs around a table covered with a green cloth. Soda bottles and glasses stood in front of each participant.

After more pleasantries, Zhou invited his guest to begin. Kissinger launched into a lengthy opening statement. He spoke from notes, written out in a large briefing book on the table in front of him. Zhou produced a single of sheet of paper, with a few words jotted down to jog his memory. After a few minutes, Kissinger coyly tucked away his briefing book.

The former academic spoke of the historic occasion. America and China were meeting as equals. Reality had brought them together, and reality would shape the future.

Kissinger turned to his conclusion. 'Many visitors have come to his beautiful, and to us mysterious, land,' he read. His words were translated by Nancy Tang, translator with the Chinese foreign ministry who had grown up in the United States, and spoke with a Brooklyn accent.

'You will find it not mysterious,' interrupted Zhou. 'When you have become familiar with it, it will not be as mysterious as before.'

'We have come to the People's Republic of China with an open mind and an open heart,' declared Kissinger. 'We hope that when we leave we may have contributed to sowing seeds from which will grow peace.'

Discussion continued, with a break for dinner and then on into the evening. Holdridge and Lord scribbled down notes as the two men spoke, taking advantage of the delay during consecutive translation to catch as much as they could. This was a new kind of conversation for the Americans. With the Soviets, diplomatic encounters were brusque and confrontational, or buried behind long formal statements. But Zhou spoke freely, ranging across issues past and present. Kissinger found it exhilarating. His conversations with Zhou, he later reported to Nixon, represented 'the most searching, sweeping and significant' of his time in government.[6]

Next morning, the Americans were taken to visit the Forbidden City, in the heart of Beijing. The entire complex was closed to the public, to avoid news of their visit leaking. The visitors were enthralled. Holdridge had visited Beijing as a boy, before the communist takeover. He was thrilled to see the places that he remembered, over thirty years later. There were new things, too. The guides showed their guests items excavated from Han dynasty tombs, including priceless funeral suits of jade not previously seen by foreigners.[7]

The party dined in the Great Hall of the People, overlooking Tiananmen Square. They were served Peking Duck. One American fainted, overcome by the heat and cuisine. Uniformed assistants promptly carried him outside to recuperate. After lunch Zhou showed his guests the kitchens, with ovens in which the ducks were roasted with fruitwood, apple or cherry to impart flavour.[8]

Talks resumed in the afternoon, and on into the evening. The tone became more focused. Both men knew that the real purpose was to agree the announcement of a visit by President Nixon to Beijing. And the issue that lay between them was Taiwan. When the communist government won power, in 1949, the defeated nationalist forces under Chiang Kai-shek retreated to this island, a hundred miles off the coast of mainland China. Both sides claimed to represent China as a whole. Washington had maintained formal diplomatic recognition of the Taiwan government, not that in Beijing. The prospect of a visit by Nixon raised the question of whether this position would continue.

Kissinger and Zhou faced a real deadline. To maintain his cover story, Kissinger could not remain in Beijing for longer than forty-eight hours. He had to be back in Islamabad by Sunday evening, for a flight back to Paris, and thence Washington. He could, Kissinger told Zhou, delay by an hour, but no more.[9]

The crux would be a joint statement, announcing the visit. Zhou deferred to his colleague Huang Hua to negotiate a text. Huang spoke excellent English, which he had first learned at Yenching University in Beijing during the 1930s, under the American missionary John Leighton Stewart. For Kissinger, used to haggling over each sentence with the Soviets, it was a very different experience. At first, the Chinese produced a draft that was clearly unacceptable. It implied that the visit came at Nixon's request, thus presenting him as a supplicant, and that the sole purpose was to discuss Taiwan. When Kissinger objected, Huang set the text to one side. Instead, he suggested, both sides should explain their needs frankly to each other. The two men discussed until the early hours of Sunday morning.

At 9.40 a.m., with just three and a half hours to go before departure time for Americans, talks reconvened. The Chinese produced a revised text, based on discussion the night before. With the change of one word, Kissinger accepted it.

The purpose of the visit would be 'to see the normalization of relations between the two countries'. Taiwan was not mentioned.[10]

Four days later, on the evening of 15 July, Nixon gave a televised statement. It was just 386 words. 'I said what needed to be said,' he told his associates, 'and not one word more.'[11] The White House gave no indication in advance of what the statement would cover.

Speaking from the NBC studios in Burbank, California, Nixon described Kissinger's visit, and read out the joint statement. When he had done so, he added a few words of his own. This action was not directed against any other nation, the president explained, in a nod to Moscow, nor at the expense of America's old friends. 'We seek friendly relations with all nations,' he added. 'Any nation can be our friend without being any other nation's enemy.'

The news swept through Washington, and around the world. *New York Times* journalist Scotty Reston heard it in Beijing, where he was seeking an interview with Mao Tse-tung. A veteran who had covered American foreign policy since the Roosevelt administration, Reston had missed the scoop of a lifetime.

That evening, Nixon and his entourage went for a celebratory meal at Perino's restaurant in Los Angeles. Diners had already heard the news, and offered congratulations as the president walked to his table.

The wine waiter came over. The party had chosen beef, and he offered a suggestion to match.

'Well, yes, that wine sounds interesting,' replied the president. 'What do you think, Henry?' he asked, turning to his national security adviser.

'I believe that '64 was a fine year, Mr President,' Kissinger replied. 'I believe it was a wet season.' Presidential aide John Ehrlichman had joined the party. He could see that the national security adviser was bluffing.

'What about Château Lafite?' Nixon asked.

'We have a fine, rare selection,' the waiter replied. He went off, and returned with a huge bottle. A sample was poured for the president.

Nixon sniffed, and swirled the wine in his glass. He turned to Kissinger for a second view. Both men declared that it was outstanding.

Chief of Staff Bob Haldeman, Ehrlichman and Press Secretary Ron Ziegler struggled to keep a straight face. Later, when he tasted the vintage himself, Ehrlichman thought the wine a bit rough.

At the end of the meal, the party rose to leave. Nixon and Kissinger hovered in the foyer, shaking hands with other diners. The adviser thought that his boss seemed oddly vulnerable, wanting recognition but somehow unable to bridge the gap between himself and those who approached him.

Behind them, the presidential naval aide pulled Ehrlichman aside. He had been presented with a bill for the wine. It came to $600. The bottle was clearly overpriced.

The two men decided to offer $300, and quickly made their exit.[12]

'If we can't get anyone in this damn government to do something,' declared the president, 'then, by God, we'll do it ourselves.'[13]

Nixon, Ehrlichman and Haldeman were frustrated. The action that they had ordered against *The New York Times* and Daniel Ellsberg over the Pentagon Papers had produced little effect. In late June, the Supreme Court had ruled, by a 6–3 margin, against the administration's case for an injunction against the *Times*. The FBI had been slow to take action against Ellsberg. Attorney General John Mitchell learned that the long-serving Bureau director, John Edgar Hoover, was close friends with Ellsberg's father-in-law, a toy manufacturer called Louis Marx. Each Christmas, Marx would bring toys for children of FBI employees. Mitchell suspected that Hoover was playing for time.[14]

Meanwhile, Ellsberg had become a figurehead for opponents of the Vietnam War. As the Supreme Court considered its verdict, the academic gave a major interview to Walter Cronkite on CBS News. The veteran broadcaster asked him if anyone emerged from the Pentagon Papers in a positive light.

Ellsberg cited a private soldier, who had laid down his rifle in protest during the massacre of Vietnamese civilians by US troops at My Lai, in 1968. Otherwise, those in authority had not 'lived up to the responsibilities of their office'.[15]

By early July, Nixon and his associates were forming a plan. If the wider system could not prevent leaks, they would do so themselves, from the White House. They were assisted by Charles Colson, Special Counsel to the President, and Egil 'Bud' Krogh, a former lawyer who acted as liaison to the FBI and other agencies.

'I don't care how it is done,' exploded Nixon, at one late-night meeting with Haldeman and Colson. 'I want those leaks stopped. Don't give any excuses.'

'Bob,' he added. 'Do we have one man here to do it?'[16]

Colson and Haldeman had a suggestion. E. Howard Hunt was a former CIA officer, who had worked on the abortive Bay of Pigs operation against the communist regime in Cuba, and then led the Agency's Domestic Operations Division. Disillusioned with what he saw as the CIA's insufficiently tough line against Cuba, Hunt had resigned in the summer of 1970.

On the weekend after Nixon's statement about China, Hunt was appointed to a new role. He and Krogh would lead a secret team, called the Special Investigations Unit. They would work out of an office on the ground floor of the Old Executive Building. Only those with a strict need to know would be aware of their activities.

The following Monday morning, 19 July, Nixon briefed the congressional leadership on the opening with China. Seventeen of the key figures in the Senate and House gathered in the Cabinet Room of the White House. Senate Majority Leader Mike Mansfield, Senate Foreign Relations Chair William Fulbright, Speaker Carl Albert and House Minority Leader Gerald Ford were all present. Secretary of State Bill Rogers and Kissinger joined the group.[17]

These were the men who would determine the domestic fate of Nixon's foreign policy. The president had a blunt message to give.

'I will try to tell you as much as possible,' Nixon said. 'But without secrecy, there will be no success.'

'Self-discipline on our part is essential,' added Kissinger.

By necessity, the mission to China had to be conducted in absolute secrecy. It was the same for negotiations with the Soviet Union.

Of those present, Mansfield spoke last. It was he who had authored the amendment that attempted to limit US troop deployments in Europe, two months before.

'On our side, we're walking on eggshells,' he commented. So were the Chinese. But he was prepared to work with the administration. 'The attitude of this group, Mr President,' he concluded, 'is one of understanding.'

Later, Nixon joined a meeting of senior staffers to emphasize the same point. With the congressional leaders, his tone had been measured. Now, in private, he could vent his feelings more openly.

'The first element in trust is in dealing in confidence,' he declared. 'But then some little jackass on the White House staff, or at State or Defense, torpedoes the whole thing.'

Everyone present felt uncomfortable. Nixon's remarks seemed to be directed at each of them individually.

'Don't leak! Say nothing! Don't guess!' The president continued his tirade. Then checking himself, his voice became calmer.

'The stakes are too high,' he concluded, 'to indulge in the luxury of seeming to be smart when you meet people.'[18]

As Nixon spoke, Haldeman watched Kissinger. The former academic seemed to get more and more nervous. He fidgeted with his pencil as he listened. Eventually it broke.[19]

Dobrynin knew that he had been outsmarted. At lunchtime, on the same day that Nixon briefed the congressional leadership, the Soviet ambassador called on Kissinger at the White House. They met, as usual, in the Map Room. Both men knew that the terms of the equation between them had changed.

In a phone call from California, four days before, Kissinger had briefed Dobrynin on his visit to China. Both he and Nixon were keen to stress that the move towards Beijing was not, as the president had put it in his televised statement, 'directed at any other nation'. Kissinger had asked Dobrynin to convey a personal message from Nixon to the Soviet leadership, emphasizing this point.[29]

But Kissinger also used the occasion to chide the ambassador gently over the Kremlin's hesitation on agreeing to a summit meeting between the two leaders. Despite the joint statement on SALT, a few weeks earlier, the Soviets had continued to stall. Indeed, while Kissinger was travelling in the Far East, a further message had arrived to Haig and Nixon at the White House, with a vague offer to look at dates in the autumn of 1971 or into 1972. 'Well, bullshit,' reacted the president when Haig briefed him. 'We don't want to come [to Moscow] that badly.'[21]

With the tables turned, Dobrynin was in trouble back in Moscow for failing to spot the China move in advance. Since the news broke, Foreign Minister Gromyko had been in a black mood. Dobrynin needed to make up for lost ground, and fast. He was, Kissinger noted in his private record of their meeting, 'at his oily best and, for the first time in my experience with him, totally insecure'.[22] The ambassador had delayed his departure for holidays to meet. His host made a play of claiming that he would have been willing to reschedule. 'No, no, no,' replied Dobrynin. 'This is important.'

Moscow, the ambassador said, was very keen to confirm a summit. Indeed, would it be possible to find a date in advance of the president's visit to China? In his statement, Nixon had said that this would take place before May 1972.

Kissinger played it straight. Summits, he said, should take place in the order that they were announced. The visit to China had been announced first, so would take place first. But it should be possible to announce a visit to Moscow as well, and to do so before Nixon actually visited China.

The two men then reviewed the state of play on the different negotiations, over SALT and Berlin. The previous summer West German Chancellor Willy Brandt had used his visits to Moscow and Warsaw to strike provisional agreement over German recognition of post-war borders, pending conclusion of the Quadripartite talks on Berlin. Brandt hoped that the Western allies would secure equivalent Soviet concessions to enable greater ties between West Berlin and western Germany. Momentum had picked up during the spring, but then in anticipation of the China initiative Kissinger had instructed US negotiator Kenneth Rush to go slow. Now, with Dobrynin on the back foot, issues which had seemed blocked began 'magically to unfreeze', as Kissinger later described it.

As he took his leave, Dobrynin said that he would stay back in the States over the summer. He wanted to work on his relationship with Kissinger. The former academic suggested that he come over to California. They could visit a movie studio together.[23]

Nixon and Kissinger decided to move quickly. Jacob Beam was the US ambassador in Moscow. In a conversation with Foreign Minister Gromyko, Beam thought he had picked up a hint that Brezhnev would welcome a direct approach from the president. This would be a significant step. Previously, Nixon had communicated with the Soviet leadership as a collective. Formal correspondence was addressed to Alexei Kosygin, as premier. But with the 24th Party Congress, and his subsequent speech in Tbilisi, Brezhnev seemed to be emerging as first among equals within the Kremlin. To have impact, a summit meeting would need to be between Nixon and Brezhnev. The time had come for the president to appeal personally to the general secretary.

Kissinger checked with Dobrynin, reading out the relevant line of Beam's reporting telegram over the phone. Was this a deliberate hint from Gromyko? Dobrynin was in frequent, private contact with the Soviet foreign minister. The two men had worked together in their respective posts for almost a decade. They both well understood how to extract decisions from the Politburo machinery, and when Dobrynin could speak more freely to his American hosts. He was, the ambassador told Kissinger, 'a 100-per-cent sure' that the remark was intentional. 'My interpretation,' he added, 'is that [Gromyko] feels it is a good idea to have some human-being touch.'[24]

Kissinger and his staffer on Soviet issues, Hal Sonnenfeldt, worked on a draft. That same weekend, the first in August, Nixon and Haldeman retired to Camp

David. On the Sunday morning, the chief of staff snatched a game of tennis. Later, rain set in. Despite the summer warmth, Nixon instructed presidential valet Manolo to light a fire in his study. The flames took time to draw. When Haldeman entered, he found the room full of smoke, and the valet struggling with papers to generate a flow of air into the fireplace.

Nixon was tired. His schedule was weighing him down. He told his chief of staff to protect him. Being president was different to being a candidate. On the campaign trail, the only worry was the next speech. As president, he carried the emotional strain of all the problems on his mind. Talking with Kissinger a couple of weeks before, the adviser had praised Nixon for his 'ice-cold nerves'.[25] But the president was feeling the wear and tear.

Haldeman listened. He had tried to make the same point to Nixon before. But only now did it seem to be sinking in.[26]

Alexander Solzhenitsyn had become fascinated by the First World War. His latest novel, *August 1914*, was a blend of history and fiction. It described the great battle of Tannenberg, between Germany and Tsarist Russia in the opening weeks of that conflict. The action took place across the lakes and forests of East Prussia, where the writer had himself fought as a young artillery officer in the winter of 1944–5. The book had been published in June 1971, by the YMCA Press in Paris.

Later that summer, Solzhenitsyn decided to travel south. He wanted to track down veterans who were still alive from the conflict, and the civil war in Russia that followed it. While his wife Natasha remained at Rozhdestvo, Solzhenitsyn set out on the drive south, behind the wheel of his old Moskevich car. He planned to take two weeks on the road.

His destination was Rostov. Solzhenitsyn had spent much of his childhood in the Russian city on the edge of the Black Sea. One of the characters in *August 1914* came from Rostov. Solzhenitsyn wove a description of the city into his novel, with a scene of the early morning catch on sale at the stalls along the Taganrovsky quayside.[27]

Unknown to him, a reception was being prepared. In early August, the local KGB branch received a visitor. Boris Ivanov, an officer based in Rostov, was called into the office of his boss. A man in a grey suit was sitting there, who had come from Moscow. The visitor explained that Solzhenitsyn was heading towards the region. Ivanov was detailed to assist the grey-suited stranger.

On Sunday 8 August, the two men received word of Solzhenitsyn's whereabouts. The writer had been sighted in the cathedral at Novocherkassk, a smaller town to the west of Rostov. The local KGB were trailing him.

Ivanov and his companion arrived in the town. It was soon after 10 o'clock in the morning. They went to the cathedral, on the main Yermak Square. Inside, the two men hovered at the back of the congregation, holding their hats in their hands. The operative from Moscow pointed out Solzhenitsyn. He was with another man. The writer was kneeling in prayer, and crossing himself.

Outside, the pair followed Solzhenitsyn and his companion around the town. A third man joined the two KGB officers, sturdy and short, with close-cropped hair. He was wearing gloves.

The pace quickened. The trio caught up with Solzhenitsyn and his companion in a store. They closed in on their target. Ivanov was a couple of paces behind, and could not see clearly what was happening. The man with gloved hands seemed to make a movement, and to be holding something. Then, a moment later, the KGB men slipped out. The man with gloves left separately.

'That's it,' the visitor from Moscow said to Ivanov. 'It's all over. He won't last very long now.'

By midday, Solzhenitsyn became aware of an aching sensation on the skin down his left side. By the next morning, he had come up in huge blisters.

A couple of days later, his companion put Solzhenitsyn on a sleeper train back to Moscow. The writer was in agony. The blisters had spread across his trunk and legs. Friends met him at the Kursk station, in Moscow. He collapsed into bed.

There, Solzhenitsyn heard more bad news. While he had been away, his dacha in Rozhdestvo was raided and searched by the authorities. A friend, Aleksandr Gorlov, was badly beaten. At a local police station, he was warned to remain silent about what had happened.

Solzhenitsyn was incensed. Still in his sickbed, he wrote a letter to Andropov. 'For many years,' he declared to the KGB chief, 'I had borne in silence the lawlessness of your employees ... the spying around my house, the shadowing of visitors, the tapping of telephone conversations, the drilling of holes in ceilings ...'

'But after the raid yesterday, I will no longer be silent ...'[28]

The message came from Haldeman's office. William Safire, presidential speech-writer, was needed for the weekend. He was to report to the naval helipad at Anacostia, on the banks of the Potomac River. It was a Friday afternoon.

Safire took a car from the White House with Herb Stein, from the Council of Economic Advisers. What, he asked his colleague, was afoot?

'This could be the most important weekend in the history of economics since 4 March 1933,' declared Stein.

Safire mulled this over for a moment. He struggled to remember the action by Roosevelt to which Stein was referring.

'We closing the banks?' he asked at last.

'Hardly,' replied Stein. 'I would not be surprised if the president were to close the gold window.'

Safire was lost. He had read Stein's textbook on economics. But he was not sure to what the adviser was referring. He decided to keep quiet.

When he boarded the helicopter, Safire found himself sitting between Stein and an official from the US Treasury. It was hard to talk over the sound of the rotary blades.

The Treasury official asked Safire what was going on. The speech-writer repeated what Stein had said about the gold window.

'My God!' came the reply. Safire's fellow traveller leant forward, his face in his hands.

Safire sensed that something was up. He turned back to Stein.

'How would you explain to a layman the significance of the gold window?' he asked, hoping to mask his own ignorance.

'It's the suspension of the convertibility of the dollar,' Stein shouted back, into the other man's ear.

'Anyone knows that!' responded Safire, confidently. 'But how would you put it in one-syllable words?'

'I wouldn't try,' replied Stein. 'That's why you're along.'[29]

Their destination was Camp David. When Safire and Stein arrived, they found other officials already present. Earlier that afternoon, Nixon had met with his core economic advisers: Treasury Secretary John Connally; Arthur Burns, Chair of the Federal Reserve; George Schulz, Director of the Office of Management and Budget; and Paul McCracken, Chair of the Council of Economic Advisers. Together, this group of four seniormost officials was known as the Quadriad.

Some dozen other officials had been summoned to join the senior group. They met in conditions of the strictest secrecy. Along with Safire and Stein, Kissinger, Paul Volcker, deputy to Connally at the Treasury, and Cap Weinberger, deputy to Schulz, were all present. Nixon asked them all to sign the visitors' book as they arrived. The president did so first. Last was Haldeman, who completed the group.

Two days earlier, Connally had briefed Nixon. The president liked the tall, confident Texan. Connally had previously served as state governor, and been grazed by a bullet when he accompanied John F. Kennedy on the former president's fatal visit to Dallas in 1963. He was appointed as Treasury Secretary the previous September. Connally was a Democrat, whom Nixon had persuaded to break ranks with his party. He was, the president told Arthur Burns, one of a handful of men in America who 'understand the use of power'.[30]

America had a problem. Under the Bretton Woods system, established at the end of the Second World War, the United States was committed to ensure that the dollar was freely convertible with gold. Other countries then sought to keep their own currencies at a stable exchange rate with the dollar. This system had provided a bedrock to the world economy over the previous quarter of a century.

That arrangement was under pressure. In theory, the United States should have sufficient reserves to exchange every dollar in circulation for an equivalent sum in gold, at the rate of $35 an ounce. But, as the American economy and national debt had grown through the 1960s, the number of dollars outstripped US gold reserves. While investors retained confidence in the United States, this presented little problem. But during the first two and a half years of Nixon's term, inflation had accelerated. Speculative pressure was building that America would be obliged to break the link to gold, and let the dollar float on the open market.

Connally had received word that the United Kingdom wanted to exchange its holding of $3 billion into gold. This was worrying. If a close ally like the British were having doubts, the market would read it as a signal that the link was about to break. Decisive action was required.[31]

At Camp David, Nixon and his team talked over the options. Connally argued for suspending the link with gold. Burns, who had served in the White House under Eisenhower, was more cautious. But Nixon was swayed by the case for action. He drew a parallel with the invasion of Laos. It was better to take a tough decision quickly, accept the criticism, and then reap approval as the longer-term benefits became apparent.

A break with gold would likely produce a drop in the value of the dollar. The group had to work out accompanying policy measures which the president could announce, that would soften the impact and ensure that the US economy became more competitive. That night, at dinner, Connally took charge. He tapped on his glass, and ordered the group to divide into three working parties, each assigned a different set of problems.

Nixon had given his officials a stern warning against leaks. All but essential phone calls from Camp David were discouraged. Over dinner, Paul Volcker pointed out the market-sensitive nature of the issues. 'Fortunes could be made with this information,' he noted.

Haldeman leaned forward. 'Exactly how?' asked the chief of staff.

For a moment, his dinner companions looked startled. Then Haldeman grinned. It was a joke.[32]

Through Saturday, the group worked under Connally's instructions. Nixon was due to give a televised address the following evening, before markets opened on Monday. Safire produced a first draft, only to find that the president himself had worked through Friday night, on his own text. The speech-writer melded the two into a final text.

The president wanted to emphasize the challenge of competition. He found a quotation from 1775, just before the American Revolution. 'Many thinking people,' it ran, 'believe America has seen its best days.' Such sentiment, Nixon argued, was no more true in the 1970s than it was on the eve of America's birth as an independent country.

Late on Saturday night, Safire walked back to his cabin with Burns. It was cool, and the moon shone through the trees. Burns was wearing a windcheater, with the Camp David crest. At 66, he was more than twenty years Safire's senior. He reminisced about his time in the Eisenhower administration, and his impressions of Nixon.

In his diary, Burns wrote that the weekend left him with the sense that Nixon 'lacks true self-assurance'. The president, he felt, was drawn to dramatic actions to convince himself that he was a strong leader.[33] Speaking with the presidential staffer, the chairman offered a more coded version of the same view.

'He has a noble motive,' Burns commented, 'to reshape the world, or at least his motive is to earn the fame that comes from nobly reshaping the world. Who can say what his motive is? But it's moving him in the right direction.'[34]

The new team was up and running. Egil 'Bud' Krogh, Gordon Liddy, David Young and Howard Hunt occupied Room 16, on the ground floor of the Old Executive

Office Building. It was a suitably anonymous hideout for covert activities. The group called themselves the Plumbers. Their job was to stop leaks.

First target was Daniel Ellsberg, source of the Pentagon Papers. In late July, Nixon had summoned Krogh to the Oval Office, to vent his frustration at the former official. 'This crap is never ending,' he fumed. 'Now, goddamit, we're not going to allow that.'[35]

Hunt was keen to establish more background about Ellsberg, and his motivation. It could be used to discredit the former academic. Ellsberg had been seeing a psychiatrist, Dr Lewis Fielding, who was based in Beverley Hills. Young and Krogh devised a plan to break into Fielding's offices, and look through his patient's medical files. They submitted it to Ehrlichman on 11 August. He wrote his response on the paper in longhand. The presidential aide gave his approval, provided that the operation was not traceable. The Plumbers had their first job.[36]

To carry it out, the team needed men who could do the actual break-in. Hunt turned to a pair of Cuban exiles, Eugenio Martinez and Felipe de Diego, whom he had known in the CIA. They were joined by Bernard Barker, another CIA operative. To ensure security, Diego and Martinez were not told the background to their assignment. After years of working for the CIA, they were used to such covert methods. The men obtained disguises, with wigs and glasses, from Sears Roebuck, and photographic equipment. The cover story, if they were caught, was that they were addicts hunting for drugs.

The break-in was scheduled for Labor Day weekend, at the start of September. The team travelled to California. When they reached the office building, a cleaner was still at work, and they had to wait. Once the coast was clear, Liddy ordered the Cuban Americans to break through a window. He and Hunt stood on watch outside.

Martinez, Diego and Barker climbed inside. In Fielding's office, they found a cabinet with patient files, which the trio wrenched open with a crow bar. Inside, they rifled through the drawers. But there was nothing on Ellsberg.

It was time to leave. Martinez scattered some pills from Fielding's briefcase. They were vitamin supplements, which would be evidence to support the cover story of a break-in by drug addicts.

As the team drove away, the Cuban American noticed a police car in the distance. It did not approach. Martinez assumed that the vehicle had been assigned to protect them. He took it as a sign that their operation was authorized from the very top. 'That is the feeling you have,' he later recalled, 'when you are doing operations for the government.'[37]

A few days later, back at the White House, Ehrlichman briefed Nixon. 'We had one little operation,' he explained, 'which, I think, it is better that you don't know about.'

'But we've got some [other] dirty tricks underway,' the aide added.[38]

Andrei Gromyko had first entered the Oval Office almost thirty years before. As a young diplomat, in his early thirties, he was posted to Washington during the

Second World War. There, he served as ambassador for the Soviet Union, and called on Roosevelt in the White House. America had made a big impression on the young man. 'It was the breath of technology one felt,' he recalled, 'and innovation, and everywhere the buildings seemed to shout after you.'[39]

Gromyko became Soviet foreign minister in 1957, under Khrushchev. He held onto the position when Brezhnev, Podgorny and Kosygin took power. A survivor, the diplomat knew how to read the political currents in the Kremlin, and float with them. 'He can joke and he can rage,' recalled his aide Arkady Shevchenko, 'but underlying any such expression is a cold logic and discipline that can make him formidable.'[40]

Now, in late September 1971, Gromyko was calling on Nixon. The Californian was the sixth president with whom he had conducted business. Gromyko had been present in the Oval Office in April 1945 when Harry Truman berated wartime foreign minister Vyacheslav Molotov for the breakdown in relations between East and West amid defeat of Germany. In September 1963, he called on Kennedy just two months before the president was assassinated. The two men slipped out onto the terrace, for a private chat. Kennedy warned that it was difficult for him to improve relations with Moscow, because of domestic opposition inside the United States. But, the president told Gromyko, he was determined to try.[41]

Gromyko had come to Washington to pursue a new opening between the superpowers. Days before, the Quadripartite negotiations over Berlin had reached agreement, with a set of practical measures to improve access to the western half of the city and reduce tensions. It felt as though détente might be getting somewhere. Gromyko brought with him instructions from Brezhnev to follow up on the letter which Nixon had sent the previous month.

The encounter started with a plenary meeting, in which Nixon and Gromyko were joined by Dobrynin, Rogers and Kissinger. It was afternoon. The national security adviser had just lunched with former secretary of state Dean Acheson, with whom Gromyko had sparred during the early years of the Cold War.

Discussion ranged across the diplomatic agenda, including the SALT negotiations, security in Europe and the Middle East. Then, as with Kennedy before him, Gromyko and Nixon held a private meeting. Outside, the late summer warmth was still in the air. But, unlike his predecessor, Nixon preferred to remain indoors. No interpreter was required. Gromyko spoke English fluently.

In front of Rogers, the two men had avoided talking about a possible summit meeting, between Nixon and Brezhnev. The president had not briefed his secretary of state on his letter to Brezhnev. In making preparations with Dobrynin, Kissinger had been at pains to stress that Gromyko should not mention it during the plenary meeting.[42]

Now in private, Nixon spoke openly. A summit must deliver matters of substance. 'You see, the mountain cannot labour and produce a mouse,' he added, and then wondered if Gromyko had understood the expression.

The Soviet official laughed. His English was impeccable. Back at his office in Moscow, he would read copies of *The New York Times*, *Time* magazine and even American comic strips.[43] Gromyko reassured him. He had spoken with

Brezhnev, prior to the latter's departure to the Crimea, for a meeting with West German chancellor Willy Brandt. The general secretary hoped that both sides might reach the point where they could say that relations were 'good, and maybe even friendly'.

Nixon agreed. It would be a great signal to the world if Washington and Moscow could show that they were resuming the relationship which had existed during the Second World War. 'If we let the time slip by,' he added, 'events may drag us into something, so now is the time to get together if we can.'

Gromyko went on. The private channel between White House and Kremlin had served well in concluding the agreement over Berlin. The Soviet Union would be prepared to reach an understanding over the Middle East, too. Moscow was ready to reduce its supply of weapons to the region, and its military presence in Egypt. But, he emphasized, it would have to be a very private deal.

'I understand,' responded the president. The United States would be prepared to discuss the idea. But, he added, Gromyko should think about Vietnam as well.

'If we could get that out of the way,' he added, 'it opens other doors. You see?'[44]

As Gromyko and Dobrynin prepared to leave the White House, they noticed a motorcade outside. Nixon explained that it was bringing officials from the International Monetary Fund, to discuss currency matters, following America's decision to drop the gold standard. He ventured a joke. Would the Soviet Union be interested in joining the IMF?

Gromyko smiled. It was a club for millionaires. 'So we don't belong in there, after all.'[45]

Andrei Sakharov was in love. Through the summer and early autumn of 1971, his relationship with Elena Bonner deepened. He was a widower, recently turned 50. She was two years his junior. For both of them, it was a heady experience. American journalist Robert Kaiser, who got to know the couple when he was posted to Moscow with *The New York Times*, called theirs 'an almost adolescent passion'.[46]

At the end of August, Bonner took Sakharov up to Leningrad. She introduced him to a trio of retired female friends, living together in an apartment on Pushkinskaya Street. Their home was a whirl of cooking, conversation and literature. During the autumn, he met others from Bonner's circle. There was Bulat Okudzhava, an Armenia singer-songwriter, and the poet David Samilov, a war veteran. Sakharov was enchanted. 'Six months earlier,' he recalled later, 'and who would have imagined me in such company?'[47]

At the same time that his romance with Bonner gathered pace, Sakharov was drawn further into his work on human rights. He attended a series of trials during 1971, of different individuals who sought to emigrate from the Soviet Union. 'You're wasting your time with these drunken dissidents,' a KGB officer told him at one trial. 'Riff-raff! You can't be sure who is married to whom.'[48]

Sakharov was becoming a central figure in the dissident movement. The Committee of Human Rights, which the physicist had co-founded along with his friend Valery Chalidze, had contacted various international figures. They included Rene Cassin, a key figure in drafting the Universal Declaration of Human Rights, in 1948, and Amnesty International, a British-based pressure group.

The authorities were unsure how to respond. KGB chief Yuri Andropov urged an uncomprising line, both on Sakharov and the writer Solzhenitsyn. 'The Committee's members,' he warned the Politburo, 'are establishing contact with foreign organizations in an effort to raise its authority in world public opinion.' But others questioned whether a hard-line response would work. Where Solzhenitsyn was concerned, Interior Minister Nikolai Shchelokov advocated a more nuanced approach. 'Objectively,' he counselled his colleagues, 'Solzhenitsyn has talent.' The authorities risked looking 'incomprehensible and inconsistent'. When Brezhnev read the minute, he underlined these words and asked his staff to hold it on file.[49]

Sakharov would agree with the charge of inconsistency. He was deeply affected by the human rights cases championed by the Committee. Soviet Jews, and ethnic Germans, felt a deep patriotic urge to emigrate to their respective countries, in Israel and West Germany. They had been subject to injustice and persecution under Stalin. It was wrong for the authorities to prevent their departure from the Soviet Union.

In October 1971, the physicist decided to act. He dictated a letter to the Supreme Soviet. Bonner typed a first draft, and then the two of them refined the wording. It was the first time that they had produced a document together.

The centerpiece of Sakharov's case was an appeal to the Universal Declaration of Human Rights. Emigration was a personal decision, not a matter for the state. As such, it was one of the fundamental rights set out in the Declaration. 'The freedom to emigrate,' Sakharov concluded, 'is an essential condition of spiritual freedom.'[50]

'The admiral was cleaned out last night, lock stock and barrel.'[51]

It was Christmas Eve. John Ehrlichman was briefing Nixon on the latest episode of leaks to hit the White House.

Three weeks earlier, fighting had broken out between India and Pakistan. The main focus of fighting was in the territory known as East Pakistan. Following partition in 1947, Pakistan comprised of two halves. Separatist pressure grew in the eastern territory, later renamed Bangladesh. Indian forces massed on the border, then, on the evening of 3 December, the Pakistan Air Force launched a pre-emptive strike. Within two weeks, the Indian Army had overrun the territory. President Yahya Khan, who had facilitated Kissinger's visit to Beijing five months earlier, resigned.

The Nixon Administration was torn over how far it could support Pakistan, with whom America had enjoyed close ties since independence. Jack Anderson was an investigative journalist who fought in China during the Second World War.

On 14 December, he published an account of decision-making inside the White House. Anderson was later awarded a Pulitzer Prize for his work. It gave a detailed account of NSC official meetings in the opening days of the crisis. He reported that Kissinger had called for a 'tilt' towards Pakistan. Both Nixon and his national security adviser were furious at the leak. Ehrlichman and the Plumbers were ordered to investigate.

The team unearthed an unexpected source. Anderson was a Mormon. He had obtained copies of the key NSC records from a fellow Mormon working in the White House. Charles Radford was a young naval yeoman, assigned to the liaison office for the Joint Chiefs of Staff within the NSC staff. Radford had previously served in India, and felt strongly about the Indo-Pakistan conflict. He and Anderson were friends, and dined together, along with their wives.[52]

Ehrlichman ordered that Radford be interviewed using a polygraph lie detector. The naval yeoman revealed that Anderson was not his main client. Radford reported to Admiral Robert Welander, senior liaison officer for the Joint Chiefs. Together with his boss, the yeoman had developed an elaborate system to keep track of White House business and pass sensitive papers back to the Pentagon. 'He had systematically stolen documents out of Henry [Kissinger's] briefcase,' Ehrlichman reported to Nixon, 'Haig's briefcase, people's desks, anyplace and everyplace in the NSC apparatus that he can lay his hands on.'

'Jesus Christ!' responded the president.[53]

When Ehrlichman played a recording of the polygraph interview with Welander to Kissinger, the national security adviser reacted with fury. The admiral was dismissed.

'I tell you, Mr President, this is very serious,' Kissinger told Nixon the next day. 'We cannot survive the kinds of internal weakness we are seeing.'[54]

Nixon was less convinced. The exposure confronted him with a dilemma. If the president was to conclude a SALT deal on nuclear weapons with the Soviet Union, he needed the support of the Pentagon. Admiral Moorer, head of the Joint Chiefs, was due to be renewed in his post during 1972. A decision not to press charges over the Radford case would keep him on his toes.

'We can't do it,' Nixon told Ehrlichman and Kissinger. 'The military must survive.'[55]

That evening, the president hosted Christmas dinner for his family in the White House. Tricia's new husband Ed joined them for the first time, making six around the table.

Over their meal, the group talked about the role of women in society. David and Julie had recently read *The Feminine Mystique* by Betty Friedan, a writer and activist. Published in 1963, the book was inspired by Friedan's conversations with her Smith College classmates, at a fifteen-year reunion. Many had become frustrated with life as housewives and mothers, in 1950s America. The book sparked a new wave of feminist thinking.

Nixon was intrigued. He asked for a copy as a belated Christmas present. Pat argued that it was better for children under 5 to remain with their mothers, rather than be cared for in day centres. When her husband was running as a candidate in the House and Senate, she felt that she had not been able to give the attention to Tricia that she wished.

After dinner, the family opened presents around the tree. They were joined by their three dogs. King Timahoe, the Irish setter, belonged to Nixon, while Pasha, a Yorkie, and the poodle Vicky belonged to his daughters. Manolo had bought stockings for the pets. The dogs ripped them open with enthusiasm. As a present for his father-in-law, David had found a recording of *Jingle Bells* with barking dogs as the chorus. The girls realized that it was a gentle dig at Nixon's tendency to indulge his pets. A fortnight before, they had starred in a CBS television special entitled *Christmas at the White House*. Nixon was filmed romping on the floor with them.

Afterwards, the president settled down in the Lincoln Sitting Room with his diary. 'I think,' he wrote, 'that it is one of the best Christmases we have ever had.'[56]

Notes

1 Kissinger (1979), 742–3; Holdridge (1997), 54–5.
2 Nixon (1978), 552; Kissinger (1979), 728.
3 Kissinger (1979), 736–9.
4 Holdridge (1997), 55; Kissinger (2012), 237–8.
5 Holdridge (1997), 57; Kissinger (1979), 743–4.
6 Kissinger (1979), 742–9; Holdridge (1997), 57–8; FRUS 1969–76 Vol. XVII, item 139, p. 359–97 and item 144, p. 453.
7 Holdridge (1997), 58–9; Kissinger (1979), 749.
8 Holdridge (1997), 59–60.
9 FRUS 1969–76 Vol. XVII, item141, p. 432.
10 FRUS 1969–76 Vol. XVII, item 142, p. 437–9.
11 Safire (1975), 373.
12 Ehrlichman (1982), 292; Kissinger (1979), 760.
13 Haldeman (1978), 112.
14 Ehrlichman (1982), 165–6;
15 Transcript of Cronkite interview with Ellsberg, *The New York Times*, 24 June 1971.
16 Colson (1976), 65; Colson interview with Naftali, 17 August 2007, p. 23.
17 Nixon daily diary, 19 July 1971.
18 Safire (1975), 375–80.
19 Haldeman (1994), 323.
20 FRUS 1969–76 Vol. XIII, items 284 and 285, p. 834–7.
21 FRUS 1969–76 Vol. XIII, item 273, p. 807–8 and item 278, p. 813–19.
22 Shevchenko (1995), 200; Kissinger (1978), 836.
23 FRUS 1969–76, item 288, p. 842–6; Vol. XL, item 262, p. 764–5; Kissinger (1979), 766–7,, 835–6; Dobrynin (1995), 227–8.
24 FRUS 1969–76 Vol. XIII, item 305, p. 899–902; Kissinger (1979), 837; Dobrynin (1995), 228–32.
25 Brinkley and Nichter (2014), 205.
26 Haldeman (1994), 334–5.
27 Quoted in Thomas (1997), 46.
28 Thomas (1997), 370–8; Scammel (1995), 158–60.

29 Safire (1975), 509–10.
30 Safire (1975), 498.
31 Brinkley and Nichter (2014), 236.
32 Safire (1975), 518.
33 Burns (2010), 53.
34 Safire (1975), 524.
35 Krogh (2007), 45–6.
36 Krogh article in *The New York Times*, 30 June 2007.
37 Martinez and Barker, 'Mission Impossible', *Harpers* October 1974.
38 White House tapes, Nixon and Ehrlichman, 8 September 1971.
39 Gromyko (1989), 68.
40 Shevchenko (1985), 146. See also Vavilov (2016), 120–9 on Gromyko's character.
41 Gromyko (1989), 181–2.
42 FRUS 1969–76 Vol. XIII, item 336, p. 1021–31.
43 Shevchenko (1985), 156.
44 Brinkley and Nichter (2014), 286–96.
45 Dobrynin (1995), 234.
46 Kaiser (1977), 390.
47 Lourie (2002), 240–1.
48 Sakharov (1990), 342.
49 Rubenstein and Gribanov (2005) docs 34 and 35, p. 126–31; Scammel (1995) doc. 53, p. 161–3.
50 Sakharov (1990), 343–5.
51 Brinkley and Nichter (2014), 342.
52 Brinkley and Nichter (2014), 331.
53 Brinkley and Nichter (2014), 331–3.
54 Ehrlichman (1982), 307.
55 Brinkley and Nichter (2014), 344; see also Nixon (1978), 531–2; Haldeman interview with Raymond Geselbricht, 12 April 1988, p. 171.
56 Eisenhower (1986), 496.

Chapter 6

THE TOPMOST BRANCH
(January–June 1972)

It was the moment that Chief of Staff Bob Haldeman and Press Secretary Ron Ziegler had been planning for weeks.

Nixon's presidential Boeing 707 aircraft taxied across the tarmac at Beijing airport. In honour of the approaching 200th anniversary of the American Republic, it had been renamed *Spirit of '76*. Three hundred and fifty soldiers from the People's Liberation Army formed a guard of honour, dressed in overcoats and fur hats adorned with a single red star. Alongside them, a line of dignitaries prepared to welcome the president, with Premier Zhou Enlai at the head. Nixon had come to China.

It was 21 February 1972. The presidential party had set off three days earlier. As he boarded the flight at Andrews Air Force base, outside Washington, Nixon compared his journey to the Apollo space missions. He quoted a line from the plaque left by astronauts Armstrong and Aldwin on the moon: 'They came in peace for all mankind.' En route, *Spirit of '76* made a stop in Hawaii, so as to allow Nixon and Pat to adjust to the time change. They were, the president was later to remind his Chinese hosts, crossing 16,000 miles, and twenty-two years of isolation between the United States and the People's Republic.[1]

Nixon and his team were determined to create visual impact. Alexander Haig led an advance party in January, to negotiate logistical and press arrangements. Almost ninety journalists were due to travel with the president, chosen from more than two thousand who had applied to the White House.[2] Every detail mattered. The Chinese agreed to install a satellite television station, so that American broadcasters travelling with the president could relay their pictures back to the networks at home in real time. Unused to market pricing, Haig's counterparts insisted on paying a higher rate than that named by their guests.[3]

Nixon and his wife emerged from *Spirit of '76*. On the flight across, he had repeatedly instructed Kissinger and Rogers not to follow until he had descended the aircraft steps. The president was determined that television cameras should get a clear shot of his arrival. As a precaution, a secret service agent was assigned to block the exit until the descent was complete.

A military band played a revolutionary song, entitled 'The Three Rules of Discipline and the Eight Points of Attention'. As Nixon walked down the steps, the

Chinese officials waiting to greet him burst into applause. The president clapped his own hands, a smile broadening across his face. Pat walked with him, wearing a bright red coat. It stood out against the dark green and grey uniforms of their hosts.

Zhou Enlai was waiting at the bottom. Nixon stretched out his hand. The two men exchanged a vigorous handshake. It was bitterly cold, and breath hung in the air as they talked. The cameras rolled. Once the coast was clear, Kissinger and Rogers hurried down the steps to join their president.

The band struck up the *Star-Spangled Banner*. Zhou and Nixon inspected the honour guard, formed of soldiers over six feet tall. As the two officials walked along the ranks, each man silently turned his head towards them, in salute. Nixon thought the synchronized movement almost hypnotic. Then Zhou escorted his visitor to a line of Russian-made limousines. Turning to Nixon, the premier offered a thought. 'Your handshake,' he said, 'came over the vastest ocean in the world.'[4]

The motorcade sped into the city, along roads closed to traffic. Peering round the curtains which adorned each car, the Americans could just make out groups of curious onlookers in the distance, standing with bicycles. Ziegler and Haldeman had hoped for further pictures on Tienanmen Square, of Nixon greeting crowds of ordinary Chinese people. But the authorities were leaving nothing to chance. Pat thought it was as if most of the city was even unaware of their visit.[5]

The American delegation was housed in the same state guest houses where Kissinger had stayed the previous summer. Zhou's wife was waiting to greet them, and the visitors were shown to their rooms. Nixon was hoping to take a shower, after the flight.

Suddenly Kissinger burst into his room, breathless from running up the stairs. Chairman Mao Tse-Tung had invited them to an audience. Nixon grabbed his coat and sped off, along with the national security adviser and agent Bob Taylor, from the secret service. Left behind, the rest of the party was taken by surprise. This was not how presidential trips were supposed to work. Ziegler was eating a tangerine when he heard the news. Startled, he swallowed half of the fruit in surprise, peel and all.[6]

Nixon, Kissinger and Taylor were driven through a red gate, flanked by guards. They passed along the old city wall of Beijing, painted a shade of vermillion. Buildings lined the road, then after a mile, they gave way to a lake and woods. The cars drew up at a modest residence, with the front door was framed by a simple portico.

Inside, they crossed a hallway, and stepped into a room. It was average in size. Books lined the walls, and littered the floor. Easy chairs formed a semi-circle, covered in plain brown material. V-shaped tables were slotted into the gaps between them, with white cloths. A spittoon stood next to one of the chairs. It belonged to Mao.

The Chinese leader acknowledged his guests. A secretary helped him to his feet. Kissinger was struck at Mao's build, larger than most of his compatriots. His smile, the former academic recalled, was both penetrating and slightly mocking.

The group exchanged handshakes, and took their seats. Chinese cameramen jostled among them, to capture the moment. No American journalists were present.

Zhou later confided to the visitors that the pictures were of poor quality. The Chinese were nervous, and found it difficult to hold the heavy equipment steady.[7]

As the cameras rolled, the Americans ventured some small talk.

'I used to assign the Chairman's collective writings to my classes at Harvard,' offered Kissinger. He waited for the translation. Mao nodded, and replied.

'Those writings of mine aren't anything. There is nothing instructive in what I wrote.'

Mao shot a disapproving glance at the cameramen. 'They are trying to interrupt our meeting, our order here.'

Nixon was not to be deterred. 'The Chairman's writings moved a nation, and have changed the world,' he stated.

'I haven't been able to change it,' replied Mao. 'I've only be able to change a few places in the vicinity of Beijing.'[8]

The president was expecting this. He had spent the weeks before his trip assembling a picture of Mao. French writer Andre Malraux, who had known the Chinese leader, called at the White House. He warned Nixon that Mao saw himself as the last of a generation of leaders, alongside Churchill, De Gaulle and Gandhi. He would think that Nixon was a youngster in comparison. There was, the Frenchman added, 'something of the sorcerer in him.'[9]

The cameramen left the room. Conversation turned to more serious topics, on the relationship with India, and with the Soviet Union. But it remained elusive, general in tone. 'I discuss the philosophical questions,' Mao told his guests. Premier Zhou would handle more practical matters. Kissinger thought that it was like a walk through the Forbidden City, with each courtyard screening further mysteries within.[10]

Nevertheless, Nixon sensed he was making progress. At one point, Mao reached over to take his hand. He held it for a full minute, in silence.[11] Nixon could see that the old man was starting to tire. Zhou was discreetly checking his watch.

The president took his cue. But he wanted to register a final point before taking his leave.

'Mr Chairman,' he ventured, 'we know that you and the prime minister have taken great risks in inviting us here.'

'But,' he added, 'you must seize the hour and seize the day.' It was a quote from Mao's writings, which Nixon had learnt in preparation.

As the interpreter conveyed the meaning, the Chinese leader's face lit up. He repeated the line, pointing at Kissinger.

The meeting was over. Mao rose, to see his guests to the door. His feet shuffled as he walked, and his breathing seemed to come with effort. He confessed that he had not been feeling well.

'But you look very good,' responded Nixon.

'Appearances are deceiving,' retorted Mao. He gave a slight shrug.[12]

It was four o'clock in the afternoon. Back at the guest house, Haldeman and Ziegler were fretting. The visiting delegation was due to hold talks with Zhou and his government ministers. The press pack was waiting. As the minutes ticked by, the Americans started to worry. They had no way of contacting the president and, surrounded by guards, they could not leave their accommodation.[13]

That evening, Zhou hosted a banquet for his guests, at the Great Hall of the People. This vast structure was built in the space of ten months, between 1958 and 1959. Tired after a long day, the Americans had to climb a grand staircase. The walls were adorned with huge canvasses, of landscapes illustrating Chairman Mao's poetry. A red star, made from glass, hung at the centre of the ceiling. Zhou and his entourage greeted the visitors at the top. The two delegations assembled for a commemorative photo, perched on lines of wooden benches. Afterwards, as they entered the dining area, a military band played American folk songs, including 'The Arkansas Traveller' and 'Oh, Susanna'. Round tables were laid out across the huge room. Nine hundred guests attended in all. Nixon, Kissinger and Zhou sat at the centre, with their colleagues around them. Each table contained two or three Americans, with about eight Chinese.

Over dinner, the Americans were introduced to toasts in Mao Tai. This formidable Chinese spirit had first been drunk by Revolutionary Guards, when they passed through Guizhou province during the Long March in the 1930s. Haig had sampled the brew during his advance visit, drinking thirteen toasts at a dinner with Zhou Enlai. It was, he reckoned, about 90-per-cent proof. Concerned at Nixon's low tolerance for alcohol, he gave strict instructions that the president should not drain his glass. Diplomat John Holdridge found himself playing a drinking game with the minister of electric power. Each player was obliged to reveal a number of fingers, simultaneously guessing how many were on show from their opponent. The penalty was to down a full glass of Mao Tai. For good measure, the loser was required to invert the glass *gan bei*, or bottoms up, on top of their head.[14]

After dinner, Zhou and Nixon circled around the tables, exchanging toasts with their fellow guests. Haldeman was relieved to see that neither man drained their glass. As he toured the hall, Nixon squared up to each guest in turn, looked him in the eye and took a sip of his drink.[15]

The band played 'America the Beautiful' in the background. Zhou reminded Nixon that the president had played the tune at his inauguration.

'Here's to your next inauguration!' the premier added, offering a toast.[16]

On their second night in China, the Nixons were treated to a performance of the ballet *Red Detachment of Women*. The day after, they attended a gymnastic display, in front of an audience of 20,000 people. Athletes marched in, carrying a huge red flag. Floodlights illuminated each section of the audience in turn. First they fell on soldiers from the People's Liberation Army, in green and blue uniforms, then sportsmen in red and blue tracksuits. The groups applauded as they were picked out by the lights. Nixon thought the event was deeply impressive, but left a sense of foreboding, too. This was a nation entering the world stage, unified by total control.[17]

While the president held working meetings, Pat Nixon saw a different side of China. The First Lady visited a pig farm, watched doctors administering acupuncture and, in the kitchens of the Peking Hotel, saw 150 chefs in action. One gave a demonstration of how to chop a turnip into the shape of a chrysanthemum flower. At each stop, the television cameras rolled, taking pictures for the daily satellite feed to the United States. Back in the guest house, her hairdresser, Rita de Santis, struggled to ensure that the First Lady was presentable for the cameras. There were no showers, and the bathtub was built on gigantic proportions. Pat was obliged to kneel on top of a stool, with her head bent under the tap, while Rita shampooed her hair.[18]

Nixon and Kissinger spent more than fifteen hours with Zhou. Their talks ranged across foreign policy and the state of the world. His initiative in visiting Beijing, Nixon emphasized, was not intended to create a 'condominium' between China and America against the Soviet Union. The Russians were, Kissinger added, a 'bit hysterical' about the subject.

'If they had confidence in themselves,' replied Zhou, 'they would not be upset.'[19]

In their last session, discussion turned to the future. Nixon explained that his visit had bipartisan support back in Washington. He hoped that the opening to China would continue, regardless of who held the presidency.

In reply, Zhou cited a poem by Mao, entitled *Ode to a Plum Blossom*. He explained that he had hoped to take the president to Hangchow, so that he could see the blossom for himself. But they had already passed their bloom. The spring had come unusually early that year. Zhou reached into his pocket, and produced a small book with the text of the poem. He read it out, gesturing as he did so.

'That's very beautiful,' commented Nixon.

The premier went on. It was, he said, a comment about those who take the initiative. Just as the blossoms fade almost as soon as they bloom, so the originator might not still be around to see their actions bear fruit. But, Chou added, the 'Spirit of '76' would prevail, in a reference to the new name given to Air Force One.[20]

The American party spent their final night in Shanghai. The visit had lasted a week. Kissinger completed negotiation of the communiqué just in time for a press conference that afternoon, held at the Industrial Exhibition Centre. It had been a laborious process, with the wording on Taiwan thrashed out in late-night drafting sessions. Completing parallel versions in English and Chinese added to the strain. In the final scramble, there was no chance for the Americans to check the Chinese version before publication. With Moscow, Kissinger had learned to watch out for subtle divergences, introduced into a Russian text. After the press conference, Chinese-speaking diplomat John Holdridge nervously went through the document word for word. He was relieved to find that it matched the English one. Indeed, on some points, he judged that the Chinese wording even leaned towards the American position.[21]

The delegation stayed in the Jinjiang Hotel. It was a high-rise building, with the president lodged on one of the upper floors. Late that night, Nixon summoned Haldeman and Kissinger to his room. His chief of staff had enjoyed a week of relative relaxation, with time off to shop for souvenirs that the president could present to his colleagues back in Washington. But Kissinger was exhausted, and longing to turn in.

The president ordered a round of Mao Tai. He had already drunk several at lunchtime, and was acquiring a taste for the spirit. Haldeman suggested that they let Kissinger go to bed, but Nixon would have none of it. Zhou, he noted, would stay up all night over his work and he wanted to chew over the events of the week. By now, it was three o'clock in the morning.

Eventually, Haldeman coaxed his boss out onto the balcony. The three men looked out over the city. It was largely shrouded in darkness. 'The mass of China lay before us,' recalled Kissinger, 'all-pervasive but invisible.'

As Nixon gazed into the darkness, Kissinger and Haldeman seized the moment. They wished the president a good night, and slipped away to bed.[22]

'In a political year, never underestimate from which side it will come.'[23]

It was late March and the president was worried. The summit with Brezhnev was due to take place in two months' time. Diplomat Gerard Smith was in the Oval Office, talking through his instructions for the final round of SALT negotiations before Nixon met the Soviet leader. Alexander Haig joined them.

Through the previous winter, Smith had pursued further talks in Vienna with his Soviet counterpart, Vladimir Semenov. The contours of an agreement were within sight, based on the joint statement issued by the White House and the Kremlin in May 1971. But the details remained difficult. On defensive systems, covering anti-ballistic missile (ABM), both sides had agreed to include a carve-out, so that each superpower could maintain a protective shield around key strategic sites. But the number and dimension of these was still to be settled. The Americans were already constructing Safeguard defences around missile launch sites in North Dakota and Montana, whereas Soviet systems were concentrated around Moscow.

Alongside this, while both sides accepted that there should be an interim freeze on new offensive weapons, the duration and scope were still to be decided. In particular, they could not agree whether submarines should be included within the freeze. The Americans enjoyed a substantial strategic advantage in submarine-launched ballistic missiles (SLBMs), through their Poseidon and Polaris class vessels. The Pentagon envisaged replacing these with a new generation of missile system, called Trident. Construction was not due to begin until the late 1970s. The Soviets, too, hoped to close the gap, by building new submarines of their own. For Washington, there was some tactical advantage in securing a temporary ban on new submarines, which would hold the Soviets back until American shipyards were due to begin work on Trident.

Nixon was less interested in the detail. But he could see the implications for domestic politics in the United States.

The Democrats were holding primary contests to pick a candidate who could beat Nixon in the presidential election, in November 1972. Senator Edmund Muskie from Maine had started as frontrunner in the Democrat race, but at a press conference during the race in New Hampshire he appeared to break down in tears, over accusations against his wife from a conservative journalist. The senator went on to win, but by a reduced margin which left him vulnerable. George McGovern, senator for South Dakota, gave a strong performance from the left. Henry 'Scoop'

Jackson, senator for Washington State and a hawk on national security issues, was another potential challenger. He had sat out New Hampshire, but was in a good position to mount a run from the right of the party.

'The attack,' Nixon explained to Smith, 'warned to be from the Right ... the responsible Right will start raising hell.'

Half the battle about SALT, the president added, was about public opinion in the United States. 'It's got to be solid, strong, and tough, so that we can debate it, stand up for it, kick hell out of the critics.'

'Would you agree, Al?' he added, looking at Haig.

'Absolutely ...' replied the soldier.[24]

Smith steered the conversation into the detail. Objectively, he explained, the United States retained overwhelming power in the nuclear field. The development of Multiple Independent Re-Entry Vehicles (MIRVs), which allowed several warheads to be projected on one missile, was increasing the American arsenal at an exponential rate. One Poseidon submarine, equipped with sixteen missiles, could deploy four times more explosive force than that used by the United States against Germany and Japan during the whole Second World War.[25]

Nixon remained uncertain. Did the Soviets calculate that the Americans wanted a deal more than they did?

Yes, Smith conceded, they probably did. The upcoming summit, and the election, might make them believe that they had the advantage.

Llewellyn 'Tommy' Thompson, the State department veteran on Soviet affairs, had died a month before, from cancer. He was a few months short of his sixty-seventh birthday. Thompson had joined Nixon and Smith at their meeting the previous year, when the statement on reaching a deal with Moscow was first announced.

'What did Thompson think? Did he think they want a deal?' asked Nixon. 'Too bad he couldn't live to see it if we get one.'

Smith had been close to Thompson. The older man was a colleague and a friend.

'I believe Tommy would strongly endorse what we're saying here,' he replied.[26]

Back in Moscow, the Soviets had indeed been weighing up whether a deal on SALT was in their interest. At one point, Brezhnev had chaired a meeting for five hours, at which the diplomats argued for going ahead, while the military leadership resisted. Eventually, Brezhnev closed the debate by asking the latter whether, in the absence of a deal, they could guarantee that the USSR might achieve and maintain strategic parity with the USA. Defence Minister Andrei Grechko and his colleagues fell silent. They knew it would be unattainable.[27]

Just over a week later, Smith was in Helsinki. It was the same venue where the SALT negotiations had begun, two and a half years before.

Lieutenant General Konstantin Trusov was speaking. He was a missile specialist, who had previously served on the Soviet General Staff. Reading from a prepared paper, Trusov outlined the Soviet position on an interim freeze for offensive weapons. Limiting this to land-based missile systems would, he said, be 'sufficient'.

Smith pricked up his ears. Previously, the Soviets had described such a prospect as 'inappropriate'. This sounded like a move towards the American position.

After the plenary session was over, Smith sought out his Soviet opposite number, Vladimir Semenov. They spoke through an interpreter. Smith asked about the choice of word. Semenov was guarded. He merely promised to pass on a copy of the Soviet paper. But, after the interpreter had moved away, he turned back to Smith.

'You have very good antennae,' he said, speaking in Russian.

Smith had been brushing up the language. He nodded.[28]

It was the first time that Anatoly Chernyaev had attended a meeting of the Politburo.

Chernyaev was a few weeks short of his fifty-first birthday. As a young man, he had fought in the Second World War, commanding a mortar platoon in a battalion mounted on skis. After the war he gained a doctorate and taught at Moscow State University. In 1961, he joined the Central Committee of the Communist Party, in the International Department. Alongside the Foreign Ministry, the Soviet Union maintained direct links through the Central Committee with fraternal political movements in other socialist countries, and in the West. At Brezhnev's instigation, the department had grown in influence under an ambitious new director, Boris Ponomarev, who was seeking to build a rival centre of power to the ministry. Chernyaev had recently been promoted to be his deputy.

The Politburo met each week in the Kremlin on a Thursday. The group dated back to the creation of the Soviet Union. Since the days of Lenin and the Civil War, this inner circle of the top officials had formed and guided policy. The group still met close to Lenin's original office in the Kremlin, in a panelled room overlooking the medieval Palace of Facets. A portrait of the revolutionary leader hung over the long table, set with a chair for the current general secretary at the head.[29]

Chernyaev showed his security pass to the guards. They examined his photo. The former academic was a tall, athletic man, with black hair swept back and a thick moustache. They nodded him through.

Beyond, Chernyaev waited in a lobby. A dozen senior officials were gathered. Gromyko was there, and Defence Minister Grechko. He was flanked by men in uniform. Chernyaev fell into conversation with Konstatin Katushev, secretary to the Central Committee, about the situation in Germany. German Chancellor Willy Brandt was worried about winning sufficient support during an upcoming vote in the Bundestag on ratification of the treaties between West Germany and the Eastern bloc countries, which he had struck during his visits to Moscow and Warsaw eighteen months before. Without this, the Soviets would withhold their consent from ratification of the Quadripartite Agreement over Berlin, thus creating an impasse over German affairs. Brandt had contacted Moscow, asking for support from the Socialist International. Katushev suggested that Chernyaev might write an article for *Pravda*, the official Soviet newspaper.

The meeting was called. Members of the Politburo filed in, and filled their seats. Chernyaev glanced along the row. KGB chief Yuri Andropov was there, and Mikhail Suslov, second secretary and the main ideologue, who had served in the

Kremlin since Stalin. The seating order was carefully designed to reflect the hierarchy of power.

Leonid Brezhnev introduced the first item. Nixon was due to visit the Soviet Union, in just over a month. Papers had been distributed to the Politburo, setting out the key messages and potential wording for the communiqué. Brezhnev thanked the Foreign Ministry and the International Department for their contributions. When one of his aides prompted him, he remembered to thank Andropov's KGB, too.

'Of course,' Brezhnev told his colleagues, 'on many issues I will be speaking with Nixon without notes. But on paper every phrase has to be carefully weighed.'

The general secretary took issue with proposals for a reference to the struggle against colonialism. Days before, on 30 March, the North Vietnamese Army had entered South Vietnam in force, crossing the Demilitarized Zone which had divided the two countries since the French withdrawal, some fifteen years before. This was the most dramatic escalation in the war since Nixon had taken office. Rather than covert attacks, through the Ho Chi Minh Trail in Laos and Cambodia, North Vietnam had launched an open invasion of its neighbour. South Vietnamese forces were falling back, shaken and demoralized.

Communist orthodoxy demanded that the Soviet Union express solidarity with their brethren in Vietnam. Around the world, socialist parties would expect Brezhnev to take a firm stand with Nixon. But the Soviet leader was doubtful. 'We are teaming up with them on an issue in which we have nothing in common!' he declared.

Even if Nixon was prepared to accept such language in a communiqué, America was obliged to support South Vietnam in fighting back against the north. The logic of détente demanded that Nixon and Brezhnev find a way to manage their differences.

Discussion turned to what kind of protocol the Soviet hosts should extend to their guest. Brezhnev was worried about comparisons with the China trip.

'Nixon went to the Great Wall along with his wife,' he pointed out. 'With us she will be unaccompanied most of the time. They'll go to *Swan Lake* together – is that enough?'

'We'll have a crowd at the airport,' he added. 'Normally we'd line the route with flags and people shouting "Friendship!" That won't do on this occasion. But they can't be totally quiet. Perhaps we could get a few lads to shout something to the president like "Good luck in the negotiations", or whatever . . .'.

Podgorny suggested an outing to the Red Army Ensemble choir.

'No,' snapped Brezhnev. 'It won't be grand enough.'

Suslov proposed the Diamond Collection in the Kremlin, where treasures from the Tsarist era were displayed. Brezhnev scoffed.

'Podgorny and I saw a display in Iran which made ours look pitiful. No!'

Ideas were running thin. Podgorny tried again, suggesting a visit to the Diplomatic Academy. No one responded.

'I vote we stick with the airport,' Brezhnev concluded. 'We don't have to keep chasing after the Chinese. We Russians are a cultured people, after all . . .'.

The item was over. Chernyaev slipped away.[30]

Three days later, in Washington, Dobrynin called on Kissinger. It had been an intense few days in the White House, following developments in Vietnam. Kissinger and his colleagues in the Special Actions Group had been poring over the options. With few American soldiers left on the ground, and South Vietnamese forces in disarray, the only means to thwart the communist assault was an air offensive against North Vietnam. But this would be a major escalation in the war, with domestic and international repercussions, including for the forthcoming summit between Nixon and Brezhnev, and perhaps for ratification of Brandt's treaties in Bonn.

To smooth their relationship, Kissinger had invited Dobrynin and his wife Irina over to the White House. He wanted to show to the ambassador a film which the Chinese had made of the visit, and which Zhou Enlai had sent as a gift. Kissinger also brought along his parents. Louis Kissinger had been a schoolteacher in Germany, with a girls' school at Furth, in Bavaria. He specialized in literature, teaching Goethe and Heine. A few weeks after the Nazis took power, in 1933, he was sacked. The family fled to America, just before persecution of Jews intensified with the events of Kristallnacht, in November 1938. Some thirty members of Kissinger's wider family were killed during the years of Nazi dictatorship.[31]

The screening went well. Dobrynin and his wife warmed to the Kissingers. But Vietnam cast a shadow. At the end, the ambassador pulled his counterpart aside for a private word. Moscow was concerned about what America might be about to do against the north.

Kissinger was firm, reminding Dobrynin of their previous conversations. If there was an offensive, Washington would be obliged to take drastic measures. That situation had now arisen.[32]

The next morning, Dobrynin visited the State Department. President Nixon was hosting a signature ceremony for the Biological Weapons Convention. This treaty had been agreed between the United States, the Soviet Union and the United Kingdom. It built on the Geneva Convention, banning production and use of bacteriological weapons.

The signing ceremony took place in the main auditorium. Nixon spoke, in front of ambassadors based in Washington. He used his remarks to make a point about resisting aggression between countries. The reference to Vietnam was not lost on his audience.

As he spoke, Nixon spotted Dobrynin. Afterwards, he walked over to greet the Soviet ambassador and the two men exchanged a few words.

The president emphasized that he stood behind what Kissinger had told his counterpart. In handling the crisis in Vietnam, Washington and Moscow must keep themselves under control, and avoid damaging their own relations.

On the spur of the moment, Nixon added a personal suggestion. Dobrynin had told Kissinger that his wife Irina would like to meet Pat Nixon, and talk about the forthcoming visit to Moscow. The president said that she would be delighted to take up the offer.[33]

Two days later, Irina Dobrynin came to the White House for tea. She and her husband had met before the Second World War, as engineering students working in an aircraft factory. Pat welcomed her to the presidential quarters.

Nixon and Kissinger both briefed Pat in advance. They encouraged the First Lady to be enthusiastic about the visit, and say that she hoped it was not poisoned by events in Vietnam.

The two women reminisced about Pat's previous visit to Moscow, in 1959. It was on this occasion that her husband had held the so-called 'kitchen debate' with Khrushchev. Pat said she hoped that nothing would happen to prevent this next visit from taking place.

Irina leaned forward, and squeezed the hand of her hostess.

'Oh yes, yes!' she said, and nodded vigorously in agreement.[34]

'I want you to play them like they play us.' Nixon was briefing Kissinger, ahead of another meeting with Dobrynin. 'Say how gracious we are – how pleased Mrs Nixon is with the graciousness of Mrs Dobrynin, and all that. Because now that the die is cast, we are going to play this in the most vicious way that we can with those bastards.'[35]

The president and his national security adviser had gone through a rough patch. The offensive by North Vietnam was gaining ground. Communist forces had reached the ancient city of Hue, site of a vicious battle four years before. Other key population centres fell to the advance. Watching from Saigon, General Abrams warned that the South Vietnamese might be on the verge of collapse.

The Americans responded with bombing raids against the north. It produced little respite. As the war intensified, domestic turmoil erupted back in the United States. Protests broke out once more on university campuses. The Senate Foreign Relations Committee voted to terminate funding for American forces in Vietnam from the end of 1972. Nixon talked darkly with his advisers about standing aside from the presidential election, in favour of a candidate who might better unify the country.[36]

Against this backdrop, Kissinger visited Moscow in late April. Nixon wanted his emissary to concentrate on Vietnam alone, and pressure the Soviets into forcing the North Vietnamese back to the negotiating table. But the former academic found himself in meetings with Brezhnev and Foreign Minister Andrei Gromyko, discussing SALT and other topics which would dominate the agenda for the forthcoming summit. Back in Washington, Nixon grew suspicious. The time difference, and difficulties in passing secure communications between the two men, increased the strain. Haig, who remained back at the White House, found himself trying to calm both sides.

After Moscow, Kissinger returned to Washington briefly. He then flew back across the Atlantic, for a new round of secret talks with North Vietnamese envoy Lu Duc Tho. It was the first time that they had met in eight months. The encounter proved fruitless. Sensing victory on the battlefield, Hanoi was in no mood to negotiate.

Arriving back in Washington, Kissinger landed at Andrews Air Force Base, when he met with Haig. The two men flew by helicopter to the Washington Navy Yard. They boarded the presidential yacht *Sequoia*, and briefed Nixon. It was clear that the diplomatic path through Moscow to Hanoi had failed. More dramatic action was required.

North Vietnam was heavily dependent on supply of arms from the USSR. These arrived aboard Soviet ships, docking at the port of Haiphong. They were then moved by rail and road to inland Hanoi and other supply centres, before dispatch southwards to the front line. Decisive intervention to halt this flow would require American aircraft to drop naval mines on the waters outside Haiphong, to deny shipping access to the port, and to bomb the land communication routes.

Such action would be a major escalation in the war, akin to the American incursions into Cambodia during 1970. Bombing North Vietnam would bring civilian casualties. It would risk loss of American airmen, shot down by air defences provided by the Soviets. Already more than a thousand were held captive in the north, or missing in action. Both consequences would further stoke domestic opposition to the war. Johnson had attempted bombing against North Vietnam in 1968, only to pull back in the face of domestic and international criticism.

Moreover, it would jeopardize Nixon's visit to Moscow, and with it the prospect of détente. Faced with bombing against their own supply ships, the Soviets might well cancel the summit. In an election year, such cancellation would be a humiliation for Nixon.

As the moment for decision approached, Haig noticed that Nixon kept talking about 'crossing the Rubicon'. The president understood that it would be a decisive moment.

Two days after the meeting aboard the presidential yacht *Sequoia*, Nixon and Kissinger held a further conversation. It was the morning of Friday 5 May. This time they met in the Oval Office. The previous day, Haldeman and Kissinger had squared Treasury Secretary John Connally. As a Democrat, his support was particularly crucial.

The president was blunt. 'The United States of America at this point cannot have a viable foreign policy if we are humiliated in Vietnam. We must not lose in Vietnam. It's as cold as that. Right?'

'I agree,' replied Kissinger.

Nixon went on. 'And they have not given us any way to avoid being humiliated. And since they have not, we must draw the swords. So the blockade is on . . . If we draw the swords out, we're going to bomb those bastards all over the place.'

The decision was all but made. That afternoon, Nixon flew up to Camp David. He spent the weekend with Haldeman and Kissinger, making plans for the week ahead. Pat was also present along with his daughters Tricia and Julie. Nixon broke news of his decision to them.

The three men worked on drafts for a televised address. It included a passage with messages directed towards the Soviets. Kissinger thought the chances of avoiding a cancellation to the summit no better than 25 per cent. But a direct appeal over the airwaves might just help. Nixon returned after one late-night drafting session to find his wife waiting up. 'Don't worry about anything,' she said, and put her arms round him.[37]

Monday passed in a flurry of activity. In the morning, Nixon chaired a three-hour meeting of the National Security Council. Laird and Rogers expressed concerns, but were won round by Connally and Spiro Agnew, the vice president. The final decision on whether to go ahead was set for two o'clock that afternoon. When the deadline came, Kissinger joined Haldeman and Nixon at the president's hideaway, in the Old Executive Office. The chief of staff made a final plea to consider the negative impact on domestic opinion. Kissinger argued passionately against. Later, he wondered if the president had set him up to it, to ensure that his support was put on record.[38]

Throughout the day, Nixon kept tinkering with the text for his televised address. At 5.30 p.m., he had a haircut, followed by a light meal of wheat germ, a brief run on a treadmill and a cold shower. Finding himself in an unexpected lull, Kissinger filled the time by calling old friends on the phone. The broadcast was scheduled for nine o'clock in the evening. It was timed to coincide with peak viewing for the main networks.[39]

The cabinet assembled to watch the president. Two television sets were rigged up in the Cabinet Room. Both were tuned to NBC. There was light talk and joking as the members waited, but with apprehension in the air. The televisions were showing *Rowan and Martin's Laugh-In*, a popular comedy series that screened on Monday evenings.

Just before nine o'clock, Vice President Agnew invited the group to take their seats. They arranged themselves in two halves, each facing a different screen.

The president came on air. In the Cabinet Room, there was silence.

Nixon outlined the situation in Vietnam, and the action that he had ordered. He described the blockade of Haiphong, and the aerial bombardment of North Vietnam.

Then he turned to the Soviet Union.

America, he declared, respected the position of the USSR as a great power. But the cause of peace should not be jeopardized.

'Let us not slide back towards the dark shadows of a previous age,' the president declared. 'We, the United States and the Soviet Union, are on the threshold of a new relationship that can serve the interests not only of our two countries, but the cause of world peace.'

When the speech was over, those in the Cabinet Room continued to watch the television. NBC anchor John Chancellor was trying to make contact with correspondent Ed Stevens, based in Moscow. The link was unsuccessful.

Nixon walked in. He took his seat in the usual chair, and motioned for the sets to be switched off.

'We've crossed the Rubicon,' he declared, repeating the phrase which Haig had heard over recent weeks. 'This has to work.'[40]

On the other side of the Atlantic, in Helsinki, diplomat Gerard Smith was woken early with the news that bombing had begun. Still half-asleep, his mind leapt into activity. 'Here goes the ball game,' he thought. The Soviets would never be prepared to accept an arms deal now.[41]

In Moscow, the mood was tense. Diplomatic adviser Andrei Aleksandrov-Agentov watched on nervously as Brezhnev and Gromyko weighed up the risk of a backlash within the Politburo, if they went ahead with a summit. Kosygin and

Andropov were in favour, while Podgorny and Ukraine Party Secretary Pyotr Shelest argued that the USSR should give Washington a 'bloody nose' and pull out, even at the cost of undermining détente. To shore up his position, Brezhnev decided to hold a session with the Central Committee, appealing to a wider circle than the Politburo alone. In preparation, he retreated with a team of core advisers to a dacha outside Moscow which had belonged to the writer Maxim Gorky. The general secretary planned a speech invoking Lenin, who had argued for a policy of calculated engagement with the capitalist West during the early years of the Soviet Union. As the team prepared the text, Brezhnev was, recalled Aleksandrov-Agentov, a 'walking ball of nerves . . . smoking cigarette after cigarette'.[42]

The week rolled on. In Washington, Dobrynin and Kissinger met and spoke on the phone several times. The Soviet ambassador delivered a note protesting at damage to Soviet ships caught at Haiphong. But he also continued to talk about the summit agenda.

By the afternoon of Friday 12 May, Kissinger was more hopeful. He and Dobrynin met for nearly an hour, in the Map Room of the White House. Alongside negotiations on SALT, Dobrynin brought up a new topic. What gifts might be exchanged at the summit, between the president and the first secretary?

Brezhnev was ready to give Nixon a hydrofoil. The Soviet Union had developed new technology in the field. In return, Dobrynin hinted that the general secretary was keen on cars.

'Hell, yes,' declared Nixon, when Kissinger told him the news. 'We can give them an automobile.'

Haig was deputed to negotiate details with the Soviet embassy. Word was passed back that Brezhnev coveted a new El Dorado model, made by General Motors. The army officer called the company. The summit was on.[43]

'Why don't we go?' asked Brezhnev. 'So you can see it in the daylight?'[44]

It was the third day of the summit. Nixon had arrived in Moscow on Monday 22 May. He was staying at an apartment in the Kremlin, the first American president to do so. The first two days had been spent in a whirl of meetings and photo opportunities. Each afternoon saw the signature ceremony for a different bilateral agreement. On the Wednesday afternoon, Nixon and Brezhnev signed an agreement on cooperation in space exploration. It took place in St Catherine's Hall, in the Grand Kremlin Palace.

That evening, the general secretary was due to host dinner at his country dacha, outside Moscow. Since their encounter on the first day, alone in Brezhnev's office with only Soviet interpreter Viktor Sukhodrev, the chemistry had developed between them. Nixon thought the Soviet leader like a trade union boss in America, or Mayor Richard Daley of Chicago.[45]

As the two men left the ceremony, Brezhnev grabbed his American colleague's arm. He pulled him aside, into an elevator. It took them to the ground floor.

Outside, Brezhnev ushered Nixon into his Zil limousine. Only one of the secret service bodyguards made it in time to join them. Kissinger had intended to share a car to the dacha with Nixon, and brief him en route. Instead, he was obliged to scramble into a back-up vehicle. The motorcade sped off.

They flew out of Moscow. The cars hurtled along a special route reserved for senior officials, at the centre of the six-lane highway. Security vehicles followed, carving a zig-zag pattern to deter other drivers from getting in the way.

The guest house was located at Zarech'ye, close to the Moscow River. It nestled on a little rise, surrounded by birch groves stretching down to the river. As soon as they had arrived, the general secretary hurried his guest down to the waterfront. Twilight was just starting to set in. A hydrofoil was bobbing on the stream. The two men stepped into the craft, and it set off. Within moments, the speedometer was touching ninety kilometres an hour. Kissinger clambered into a following vessel, along with Soviet prime minister Aleksei Kosygin and interpreter Andrei Vavilov, deputy to Sukhodrev. The party clung on, laughing nervously as waves rolled out to the riverbanks.

An hour later, the party returned to the dacha. Nixon's secret service detail had caught up with the president. Kissinger found them in heated argument with their KGB opposite numbers. To forestall further abduction of their charge, the Americans had parked the presidential limousine across the dacha entrance, thus blocking the exit. The KGB were furious. Eventually, Kissinger brokered a deal. The secret service agreed to move their car, in return for agreement that Nixon would use it to return to the Kremlin at the end of the evening.[46]

Inside, Brezhnev was joined by his colleagues, Kosygin and President Nikolai Podgorny. Diplomatic adviser Andrei Aleksandrov-Agentov was there, along with Sukhodrev and Vavilov as interpreters. There was an awkward pause while Nixon and Kissinger waited for their aides, John Negroponte and Winston Lord, who had lost the main party during the dash out to the dacha. The two delegations sat around an oval conference table in silence. Eventually Negroponte and Lord entered, faces red with embarrassment.

So far during the summit, Nixon and Brezhnev had barely touched on Vietnam. Now, the Soviet leader invited his guest to address the topic. The moment had come.

Nixon took the cue. He explained that he had inherited a difficult situation. Since taking office, his administration had withdrawn 500,000 troops from Vietnam, and held private meetings with the North Vietnamese on thirteen occasions. But still peace was not in their grasp. 'They must decide,' he concluded, 'whether they want to stop the war or take the consequences of not stopping it.'

'Well, Mr President,' replied Brezhnev. 'We have indeed touched on a very, very acute and serious problem, because this is a problem of war.'

He went on. Vietnam was poisoning the international situation. 'Both our governments condemned Hitler when we fought together as allies,' Brezhnev declared. 'Now twenty-nine years since the end of that war there is another war.' De Gaulle had managed to end the conflict in Algeria. Why couldn't Nixon achieve the same in Vietnam?

Kosygin and Podgorny weighed in alongside. As they did so, Brezhnev marched up and down behind them, muttering.

'You're murderers,' snapped Podgorny. 'You have on your hands the blood of old men, women and children. When will you finally end this senseless war?'

Where Brezhnev and Podgorny had been angry, impassioned, Kosygin was icy and forensic. He recalled his own conversation with Johnson, back at Glassboro in 1967.

Kosygin had warned his host that more fighting would not bring a resolution. Johnson had been defiant, declaring that America could 'strangle' Vietnam. Five years later, a million Vietnamese had died, and no end was in sight. He concluded with an appeal to history. After so many presidents had failed, didn't Nixon want to be remembered as the 'man who succeeded in cutting through this knot'?

Nixon listened, his face flushed with anger. Kissinger was at his side. The national security adviser watched Aleksandrov-Agentov scribbling furiously in his notebook as the leaders talked. A thought dawned on him. The Soviet leaders were speaking for the record. Inside the communist bloc, fraternal governments would share accounts to each other of their dealings with the capitalist world. In practice, Brezhnev had little interest engaging with other socialist leaders, but on this occasion it was important to put on a good show. In lambasting Nixon, the Soviet leaders were demonstrating to Hanoi that they had not betrayed their fellow communists. It was the very approach that Chernyaev had watched the Politburo discuss in preparation for the summit, two months before.[47]

Podgorny was in mid-speech. Suddenly he stopped. Brezhnev said a few words, and then fell silent. For a moment, it was quiet in the room.

Nixon responded. Quoting the Civil War general, William Sherman, he noted that 'war is hell'. No one knew this better than the people of the Soviet Union, after what they had suffered in the Second World War.

'Our people want peace. I want it, too.' America was ready to negotiate in good faith.

It was 11 p.m. The discussion closed. Brezhnev ushered his guests upstairs, to the dining room, where they tucked into a four-course meal. Kosygin led the toasts, in Soviet cognac. Kissinger reckoned that he downed two glasses to each one that the Americans drank. Jokes and laughter flowed.

At one point Brezhnev turned to Sukhodrev. The interpreter had grown up as a child in London during the war, where his mother worked in the Soviet embassy, and spoke English fluently. He had interpreted with every Soviet leader since Khrushchev.

'Drink up,' Brezhnev declared, 'and your translation will get even better!'

As the Soviet leaders mellowed, they talked about their vast country. Lake Baikal in Siberia was the largest in the world, they explained, and the cleanest. And the most beautiful. Pride shone through their words.

Kosygin commented that it was a good sign if both sides could argue, and then enjoy a hearty dinner together. Nixon agreed. Honest discussion was essential. Kosygin nodded, and then offered another toast.[48]

It was past midnight. Nixon and Kissinger drove back into Moscow, travelling in the American presidential limousine operated by the secret service.

At the dacha meeting, the two leaders had agreed to make a final push on SALT. If agreement could be reached, it would be the culmination of the summit, and a tangible sign of the change in relationship which they sought. Earlier in the week, Nixon and Brezhnev had participated in a confused negotiating session, held in the general secretary's office on the third floor of the Kremlin. A large map of the world hung on one wall, with curtains drawn across sections that included secret information. Brezhnev seemed flustered by the detailed statistics on nuclear weapons, and offered concessions beyond those which his negotiators had previously been prepared to accept. The dynamic was made more complex by the ongoing, substantive negotiations between Gerard Smith and Vladimir Semenov, taking place in Helsinki. In Moscow, Gromyko and his officials broke off discussions for thirty-six hours, to take stock. At the dacha, Brezhnev agreed with Nixon that Gromyko would resume, with Kissinger, in the early hours of the morning.

Kissinger was tired. The summit was proving intense, unpredictable. Advance scheduling was impossible. The Soviets would suddenly call a negotiating session, at short notice. To add to the pressure, the Americans operated under the assumption that their living quarters were bugged. As a countermeasure, they had brought 'babbler' tapes, which could be plugged into a tape recorder, and played a cacophony of background noise to mask actual conversation from listening ears. But the sound was itself a distraction, and tested patience already worn thin by the pressures of the summit schedule. For the most sensitive conversations, Kissinger and Nixon resorted to sitting inside the presidential limousine, behind layers of armoured glass. Haldeman noticed that the national security adviser was tetchy, and sharp with his colleagues.[49]

Back in Moscow, Kissinger learnt of a new problem. Details of the Helsinki negotiations had leaked in *The New York Times*. These implied that the United States was about to concede numerical superiority in nuclear weapons to the USSR. Hardliners in Congress, including Senator 'Scoop' Jackson, had expressed concern. In a private cable, Haig warned that the Chiefs of Staff in the Pentagon took a similar view. The right-wing backlash that Nixon had feared seemed to be gathering pace.

The president was suffering from back pain. Upon return from the dacha, he had retreated for a massage from his physiotherapist, Dr Kenneth Riland. Kissinger knew that they had to speak. He found Nixon stripped to the waist, and lying on his front.

The former academic described the situation. The Soviets were holding out for a combination on limitations on submarine and land-born missiles which would retain a larger arsenal than the Americans had previously been prepared to accept. The issue had come down to which categories of Soviet submarines should be covered. At the same time, the Pentagon was urging the president to harden his negotiating position.

Nixon was clear. He would face down both sides. Kissinger was about to enter the negotiating session with Gromyko. Nixon instructed him to stall, unless the Soviets would accept his terms.

'Just do as best you can,' he told his adviser. 'And remember that as far as I'm concerned, we don't have to settle this week.'[50]

Thirty-six hours later, instructions arrived in Helsinki. In a final burst of marathon negotiations, Kissinger and Gromyko had closed the gap. A meeting of the Politburo on Friday morning confirmed agreement. The Soviets had accepted the American demand for a total ceiling of 740 on submarine-based missile launchers, but obtained a dispensation for those on older, diesel-propelled vessels, which carried shorter-range missiles. Both sides agreed identical instructions to send to Smith and Semenov, telling them to wrap up the draft agreement and travel to Moscow for final signature.[51]

The signing ceremony was due to take place in the Kremlin that evening. It was already lunchtime and the race was on. After two and a half years of negotiation, Smith, Semenov and their delegations had a final afternoon in which to finalize the agreements. Soviet and American diplomats confirmed the wording, article by article. These were in turn dictated over the phone to the US delegation office, where secretaries typed up the text on fine quality paper. As a formal treaty, the agreement was supposed to be formatted with double spacing between lines. But, with stocks of paper running low, the team was obliged to print the final sections in single-spacing. They finished at 4.30 p.m., just in time to rush to the airport.[52]

There, the two delegations scrambled aboard a US Air Force C-118 aircraft. After take-off, Smith ordered beer for his colleagues, Soviet and American. But the plane ran into turbulence. The treaty texts were spread out on a table in the cabin, next to bottles of beer. For a moment Smith feared that the drink would spill all over them.

The American diplomat reached for the aircraft logbook. He wanted to record the moment, as both delegations reflected on what they had achieved. Smith scribbled an entry, and passed the book to Semenov.

'This is a happy moment in my life,' wrote the Russian. He passed the book on.

Paul Nitze was the last American to sign. As a young man, he had visited the devastated Japanese city of Hiroshima, after the American attack that ended the Second World War. He had gone on to become an expert on nuclear weapons. 'I feel that only those of us,' he wrote, 'who were a part of it will ever fully know what was involved.'

The plane touched down in Moscow at 8.50 p.m. As the delegations left the aircraft, a Soviet official hurried up to Smith. He was required in the Kremlin at once. Meanwhile, an American diplomat told him that he must attend a press conference. Smith paused for a moment, but the Soviet was insistent. The American was hustled into a motorcade, along with Semenov. His bag disappeared. Nitze scooped it up, in a car bound for the US ambassador's residence at Spaso House.

As his motorcade approached the Kremlin, Smith caught sight of the Stars and Stripes flying over the battles and pointed towers. It was a heart-warming moment. But inside, his welcome was less cheerful. Nixon and Brezhnev were attending a banquet at Spaso House. Among those left in the American quarters at the Kremlin, no one seemed to know what was going on. Smith had not eaten all day, and started to feel faint.[53]

The signature ceremony was scheduled for 11 p.m. Haldeman could see that after a week of summitry Nixon was starting to tire. He hurried the dinner at Spaso

House through as fast as he could. The desert was a flaming baked Alaska. It had been prepared by Nixon's Filipino chef, and Brezhnev was thrilled. Afterwards, the pianist Harvey Van Cliburn provided entertainment, just as he had done at a dinner hosted by President Truman for Stalin and Churchill during the Potsdam Conference in 1945. Haldeman managed to wrap up the evening just after 10.30 p.m.[54]

While Brezhnev was enjoying dessert, Paul Nitze took a Soviet car over to the Kremlin. He arrived at the Vladimir Hall in the Grand Kremlin Palace, built during the reign of Tsar Nicholas I and the venue for the signature ceremony. Spectacular chandeliers were flanked by vast white arches and a domed ceiling. Nitze spied Semenov in a far corner, deep in conversation with his compatriots. After a few minutes Rogers entered, then Defence Minister Marshal Andrei Grechko, flanked by fellow Soviet generals. After that Brezhnev strode in, followed by Podgorny, Kosygin and other members of the Politburo. Nitze was struck at the grins, fixed onto their faces. They seemed like actors, he thought.

Kissinger and Smith entered. Nitze could see that they were ill at ease in each others' company. Nixon came in last, wearing a grey pinstripe suit. As the delegations approached the table where the documents awaited signature, Soviet officials jostled to be in prime position. The Soviet copy was in a red folder, that for the United States in a blue one. Nitze found himself elbowed to one side. Pat Nixon had slipped in at the back, and watched from behind a pillar.

As the two leaders signed the text, Kissinger hissed in Smith's ear. National security adviser and arms negotiator had held a joint press conference just beforehand. It had not gone well. The White House press corps, travelling with the president, had scented the last-minute concession to the Soviets over submarine-mounted missiles. Tired and irritated, Smith had done little to defuse the story.

'What were you trying to do?' whispered Kissinger. 'Cause a panic?'

The signatures were complete. The leaders and their officials clinked glasses, for a celebratory round of champagne. Brezhnev walked across to exchange a toast with Kissinger. A moment or two later, the Soviet leader turned, and made his exit. His officials followed. Nitze thought that they looked like a school of fish.

Within a few minutes, Smith and Nitze found themselves alone in the vast hall. The delegation head took a car back to Spaso House. Nitze walked through the Kremlin grounds and across Red Square, to the Hotel Rossiya where he was staying for the night.[55]

The next morning, Smith received a call at 6.30 a.m. It was Semenov. He had heard that the Americans would soon be leaving, and wondered if his counterpart would like to engage in some early morning sightseeing.

Though half-awake, Smith was delighted at the suggestion. He and Semenov wandered around Red Square, and across to Staraya Ploshad, where the Central Committee was located. Semenov lived close by. He suggested that the American might like to see his apartment. The two walked past a babushka, acting as warden at the entrance. Inside, Semenov showed his guest a collection of artwork and books. It included some modern Russian paintings. Without an interpreter present, Smith talked in halting Russian. Semenov produced a decanter of red wine. It was, he explained, produce from his dacha outside Moscow. He poured two glasses.

The American and his host exchanged a toast. It was still only half-past seven in the morning.

Over in the Kremlin, Kissinger was celebrating his forty-ninth birthday. The head of the KGB security detail presented him with a cake, prepared by Kremlin chefs. It was carried in by a waitress, who planted a kiss on Kissinger's cheek. Brezhnev had sent a bottle of 49-year-old Armenian brandy. For the national security adviser, the celebrations were a chance to relax. In the early hours that morning, he had been obliged to hold an impromptu press conference in a night club of the Rossiya Hotel. Haldeman was nervous that the story about SALT terms on submarines was running out of control. Half-dizzy with fatigue, Kissinger managed to give a strong performance. The genie seemed to be back in the bottle.[56]

The main part of the summit was over. Before leaving the USSR, Nixon and his wife were due to travel outside Moscow. On the morning after the signature ceremony, they flew up to Leningrad. The police had closed down much of the city centre. But the Americans could see crowds of people in the distance, peering from behind barricades.

During the Second World War, Leningrad had been besieged by Nazi forces. More than a million people died from fighting, starvation and cold. The composer Dmitri Shostakovich, whom Nixon had met at a formal banquet earlier in the week, composed his Seventh Symphony in tribute to the beleaguered city.

That afternoon, the president and First Lady travelled out of Leningrad, to the Piskaryovskoye Memorial Cemetery. It was in a suburb, close to what had been the front line. More than half a million people were buried at the site, most in mass graves. 'Here,' ran the inscription on the memorial plaque, 'lie fathers, sons, mothers, daughters ...'

The presidential party was visibly moved. A young woman acted as their guide. She showed Nixon a diary, kept by a 12-year-old girl called Tanya. It related how, one by one, her family had died. 'All are dead,' ran the last entry. 'Only Tanya is left.'

The guide explained that Tanya had herself perished a few days later. She, too, was buried in the cemetery.

Before leaving, Nixon inscribed a few words in the visitors' book. 'To Tanya and all the heroes of Leningrad,' he wrote. 'I hope it will never be repeated in all the world.'[57]

Back in Moscow, party aide Anatoly Chernyaev recorded his impressions of the visit. He had started to keep a diary a few months before, and already it had become an outlet to confide his innermost thoughts about the system in which he worked. Usually he was cynical about what he saw around him. But on this occasion he sensed a new mood.

'We've crossed a Rubicon,' he wrote, in an unconscious echo of the same image that Nixon had used about Vietnam. 'From these few days of 1972 men will date a new era of convergence, not in the worn-out phrase of our own ideology, but in a genuinely revolutionary and redemptive manner for humankind.'[58]

Notes

1 FRUS 1969–76 Vol. XVII, item 201, p. 796.
2 Eisenhower (1986), 509.
3 Kissinger (1979), 1050–1; Haig (1992), 262–3.
4 Nixon (1978), 560; Buchanan (2017), 236.
5 Holdridge (1997), 83–4; Kissinger (1979), 1055; Eisenhower (1986), 508.
6 Nixon (1978, 560; Haldeman (1994), 413.
7 FRUS 1969–76 Vol. XVII, item 196, p. 705–6.
8 FRUS 1969–76 Vol. XVII, item 194, p. 678.
9 Nixon (1978), 558.
10 FRUS 1969–76 Vol. XVII, item 194, p. 679; Kissinger (1979), 1061.
11 Haldeman (1994), 415–16.
12 FRUS 1969–76 Vol. XVII, item 194, p. 683–4; Nixon (1978), 563–4.
13 Haldeman (1994), 414.
14 Haig (1994), 259; Holdridge (1997), 86–7; Haig interview with Musgrave and Naftali, 30 November 2006, p. 18.
15 Haldeman (1994), 417; Buchanan (2017), 238.
16 Nixon (1978), 566.
17 Haldeman (1994), 418; Nixon (1978), 572.
18 Eisenhower (1986), 506–8.
19 FRUS 1969–76 Vol. XVII, item 197, p. 749.
20 FRUS 1969–76 Vol. XVII, item 197, p. 731.
21 Holdridge (1997), 94–5; Kissinger (1979), 1084–5.
22 Haldeman (1994), 422; Kissinger (1979), 1086.
23 FRUS 1969–76 Vol. XXXIII, item 242, p. 721.
24 FRUS 1969–76 Vol. XXXIII, item 242, p. 722–3.
25 Smith (1980), 321.
26 FRUS 1969–76 Vol. XXXIII, item 242, p. 732.
27 Aleksandrov-Agentov (1995), 210; Shevchenko (1985), 201–6.
28 Smith (1980), 360–1; FRUS 1969–76 Vol. XXXIII, item 246, p. 747–8.
29 Shevchenko (1985), 208.
30 Chernyaev diary 1972, p. 9–10, entry for 6 April 1972; Chernyaev (1995), 288–9.
31 FRUS 1969–76 Vol. XIV, item 88, p. 273–4; Ferguson (2015), 48, 80.
32 FRUS 1969–76 Vol. XIV, item 88, p. 273–4; Kissinger (1979), 1117; Dobrynin (1995), 243.
33 FRUS 1969–76 Vol. XIV, item 90, p. 279; Nixon (1978), 589; Dobrynin (1995), 243–4.
34 Eisenhower (1986), 512–13; Nixon (1978), 589.
35 FRUS 1969–76 Vol. XIV, item 196, p. 741.
36 Haig (1992), 285.
37 Nixon (1978), 602–3.
38 Kissinger (1979), 1184–6; FRUS Vol. XIV, item 204, p. 766–74; Nixon (1978), 603–4.
39 Nixon (1978), 604; Kissinger (1979), 1187.
40 FRUS 1969–76 Vol. XIV, item 208, 209, p. 783–8; Haldeman (1994), 456–7; Nixon (1978), 605–6; Kissinger (1979), 188.
41 Smith (1985), 382.
42 Aleksandrov-Agentov (1995), 224; Shevchenko (1985), 211–12; Dobrynin (1995), 248; Kornienko (2001), 185–6.
43 FRUS 1969–76 Vol. XIV, item 221, 223, p. 825–6, 829; Haig (1992), 288; Nixon (1978), 607; Kissinger (1979), 1193–5; Haldeman (1994), 459; Shevchenko (1985), 215.

44 Nixon (1978), 612.

45 Nixon (1978), 619. See Sukhodrev (1999), 267–70 for an account of the first meeting.

46 Nixon (1978), 612–13; Haldeman (1994), 463; Kissinger (1979), 1223–5.

47 Chernyaev (1995), 272, 290.

48 FRUS 1969–76 Vol. XIV, item 271, p. 1047–64; Nixon (1978), 613–14; Kissinger (1979), 1227–9; Sukhodrev (1999), 274–8; Aleksandrov-Agentov (1995), 228–30; Vavilov (2016), 36–9.

49 Haldeman (1994), 463.

50 Nixon (1978), 615; Kissinger (1979), 1229–33.

51 Smith (1985), 429–30; FRUS 1969–76 Vol. XIV, item 282, p. 1122–4; Kissinger (1979), 1241.

52 Nitze (1989), 323.

53 Smith (1985), 433–46; Nitze (1989), 324–6.

54 Haldeman (1994), 464; Nixon (1978), 616; Eisenhower (1986), 518–20.

55 Nitze (1989), 326–8; Smith (1985), 435–8; Nixon (1978), 616; Hillenbrand (1998), 310; Vavilov (2016), 55–6.

56 Smith (1985), 439; Dobrynin (1995), 255.

57 Nixon (1978), 616; Haldeman (1994), 465–6.

58 Chernyaev (1995), 465–6.

Chapter 7

HURTING EACH OTHER
(July–December 1972)

'Hey, look! Old Whaleboat.'

Press Secretary Ron Ziegler was walking down the beach. He hated the code name, which had been given to him by the secret service. But the rest of the White House staff loved the moniker, and it had stuck.

It was the afternoon of Saturday 17 June 1972. Ziegler, Chief of Staff Bob Haldeman and a small group of their colleagues were lazing in the sun at Key Biscayne, in Florida. President Richard Nixon was spending the weekend offshore, at the private retreat of his millionaire friend Robert Abplanalp, in the Bahamas.

The White House team had enjoyed a good few weeks. The president's visit to Moscow had been a success. Early in June, Senator George McGovern clinched the Democratic nomination with victory in the California primary. Nixon faced an opponent who favoured unconditional withdrawal from Vietnam, major reductions in defence and a massive increase in public spending. Early polls gave the incumbent president a twenty-point lead. The second term looked within sight.

Ziegler was dressed in swimming trunks. In his hand, he held a piece of paper. The press secretary passed it to Haldeman, while, behind him, a boy threw a Frisbee. The chief of staff watched it arc across the blue sky.

The paper was a wire service report. In the early hours of that morning, five men had been arrested inside the Democratic National Committee headquarters, at the Watergate Center in Washington. They were found with electronic equipment.

Haldeman smiled. It all seemed too ridiculous. In presidential races, bugging was commonplace. But why go after the Democrat National Committee? It was McGovern's campaign team, if anywhere, that useful intelligence might be had. And, with such a poll lead, it made little sense for the Nixon campaign to take the risk.

That evening, Haldeman took his wife Jo out to a restaurant. They dined on stone crabs, under the soft Florida night air. There had been no further word from Washington. Everything was calm.[1]

The next morning, Haldeman spoke over the phone with Nixon. The president was enjoying his vacation. He had been for a swim, and talked with Abplanalp's 12-year-old daughter about her pet turtles.

'What's this crazy item about the DNC?' he asked his chief of staff. Nixon had spotted the story in the *Miami Herald*.

Probably nothing, the two men agreed. It just didn't make sense. But the president suggested that Haldeman make a call, just to be sure.[2]

Jeb Magruder was also on vacation, in Beverley Hills, California. The 38-year-old was second in command at the Committee to Re-elect the President, Nixon's campaign organization, which was known by the acronym CRP. The call reached him at his hotel, from the White House switchboard. Haldeman wanted to talk.

When he came on the line, Magruder sounded nervous.

'Those guys were operating on their own, Bob. They just got carried away.'

'What guys?'

'McCord. He's our security man at CRP. He works for Gordon Liddy.'

Haldeman twitched. This sounded more serious. James McCord was a former CIA officer. Liddy had led the Plumbers team in the White House, and then moved across to CRP. If these two were involved, it could imply a chain back to the president.

Haldeman's tone became more urgent. Was Liddy involved, he asked?

'Well, I told you . . . uh . . . he was working with McCord.'

The chief of staff swung into action. His next call was to John Ehrlichman, the president's aide for domestic affairs. Ehrlichman had stayed behind in Washington to mind the shop.

The news was not good. That morning, *The Washington Post* carried the story as front page. There were more details about the break-in, and the men arrested. They had been caught wearing surgical gloves, and carrying equipment including forty rolls of camera film and over two thousand dollars in fresh $100 bills. A guard had spotted tape fixed over office doors to keep them open, and called the police.[3]

'We're in a bit of bind on this one, Bob,' explained Ehrlichman. 'One of those Cubans had a check on his person signed by Howard Hunt.'

Here was another angle. Howard Hunt had previously worked for Charles Colson, the presidential assistant who was supporting Nixon on his election campaign. Ehrlichman had already checked with Colson, who claimed no connection. He and Haldeman were not so sure. In recent months, Colson had established his own relationship with Nixon. The two men had started to meet privately, without Haldeman or Ehrlichman present. Haldeman thought he had cut a deal, that Colson would let him know about any instructions Nixon told him to execute.[4] But this sounded murky. Was something going on?[5]

Haldeman's next call was to Colson. He, too, sounded tense.

Colson explained. Hunt had moved across to CRP, to work for Liddy.

'You gotta believe me, Bob. It wasn't me. Tell the president that. I know he'll be worried.'

Nixon had planned to fly back to Washington that night. But a hurricane, named Agnes, was moving westwards across the Caribbean. Tropical storms struck Florida. Nixon decided to delay his departure until Monday evening. He used the extra day to take more exercise, swimming both morning and afternoon.

On the flight back, Haldeman briefed his boss. Nixon was relaxed, from the fresh air and exercise. He sipped at a beer, sitting in his private suite on *Spirit of '76*. Haldeman shared what he had learnt, about McCord, Liddy and Hunt. The president seemed detached, even bored.

'Silly damn thing,' he commented.

Haldeman slipped away, back to his wife in the rear section of the aircraft. The couple sat together, and looked out of the window. As the plane approached Andrews Air Force Base, they could see Washington, lit up in the darkness.[6]

The next morning, Haldeman was back at his desk in the White House. Outside, rain from Hurricane Agnes had drenched the city. The Potomac River burst its banks, flooding the fashionable suburb of Alexandria.

The buzzer rang. It was the president, wanting a word about the Watergate break-in.

A further conversation followed, in the afternoon. Nixon was mulling over the issues. The story had continued to feature in the morning newspapers. In the daytime bulletins, television networks focused on the Cuban angle. The Democrats had announced that they would bring a lawsuit against CRP.

'I feel like this is a nightmare,' commented Haldeman. 'Something like this just doesn't happen.'

The president was hopeful that the White House could distance itself from what had happened at CRP. At the same time, he wanted to hit back. His opponents had played dirty tricks in the past, but gone uncensored. In 1960, the Kennedy campaign had done so in key marginal states. Why was he getting rougher treatment?[7]

Nixon was due to hold a press conference later that week. In preparation, he had scribbled notes to himself. They were a reminder to stiffen his resolve.

'If I do good job bad press won't hurt me,' ran one line. 'If I do bad job good press won't save me ...'[8]

That evening, Haldeman and Nixon talked again on the phone. The Cuban angle had stuck in the president's mind. He was concerned about how the arrested men would pay for their legal fees, and wanted to get his friend Bebe Rebozo to channel money to them.

Then came another angle.

'Tell Ehrlichman this whole group of Cubans is tied to the Bay of Pigs,' Nixon told his chief of staff.

Haldeman was startled. Under the Kennedy administration, the CIA had armed a force of Cuban exiles who attempted to overthrow Fidel Castro's communist regime on the island. They landed at a spot on the southern coast, called Bay of Pigs, in April 1961. Within hours the invasion failed. It was a humiliation for Kennedy and his team. How this episode from a decade ago might be linked to Watergate was not clear.[9]

Two days later, Haldeman received another call. This time it was John Dean, special counsel at the White House. He was looking into the Watergate case, and thought that he had found a new angle.

Dean briefed Haldeman. The FBI was conducting an investigation, and had started tracing financial links. One led to money laundered through a bank in Mexico. The Bureau suspected, according to Dean, that there was a link between the break-in at the DNC and the CIA.

The special counsel had a suggestion. Could Haldeman speak to the CIA, and persuade them to lean on the FBI? It might close the investigation down.

As Dean spoke, Haldeman jotted down notes. 'Investigation out of control,' he wrote. 'Is at brink right now – either will open all up – or be closed.'

The conversation over, Haldeman put down the phone. He thought for a moment. Was this the connection with the Bay of Pigs that Nixon had mentioned? He needed to speak with the president.[10]

Haldeman walked through into the Oval Office. It was just past ten o'clock.

He explained to Nixon what Dean had told him.

'The FBI will stop if we could take this other step,' he said, referring to the option which Dean had outlined.

'Alright, fine,' replied the president. 'Right.'

'They say the only way to do that is a White House instruction,' Haldeman added, referring to Dean and Mitchell. 'And it's got to be to Helms and, ah, what's his name? Walters.'

Richard Helms had been CIA director since the mid-1960s. Vernon Walters was the former US Army general who had acted as Kissinger's intermediary with the North Vietnamese in Paris. He had recently moved across to the Agency as deputy to Helms.

'Walters,' repeated the president.

'And the proposal would be that Ehrlichman and I call them in,' added Haldeman.

'Alright, fine,' Nixon agreed.[11]

Three hours later, Helms and Walters arrived at the White House.

It was unusual for both the director and his deputy to be summoned together. Helms knew that there was little love lost between the president and himself. As vice president under Eisenhower, Nixon was implicated in the early stages of planning for the Cuban invasion. Once returned to the White House as president, Nixon had requested that the CIA turn over papers relating to the affair. Helms had stalled, scenting a political motive. The Bay of Pigs had been a fiasco for the Agency, and for the previous director, Allen Dulles. Helms had been installed as a clean pair of hands.

News of the Watergate break-in reached Helms on the Saturday evening. His response was equally cautious. At a meeting with his senior staff on Monday morning, he quizzed each in turn whether the CIA had been involved. All gave their word that the Agency was clear. 'Keep cool, do not get lured into any speculation,' he instructed them. 'Just stay the hell away from the whole damned mess.'

Before going to the White House, Helms shared a quick lunch with Walters at the Two Continents restaurant, in downtown Washington. His deputy was a seasoned operator. But he was new to the job, and Helms didn't want to expose him to the president's men before they had had a chance to talk through what might await them.[12]

Helms and Walters entered the White House through a basement door. An elevator took them to the second floor, where Ehrlichman had a meeting room. It was small. The two CIA officials and the two presidential aides crowded into the narrow space.

Haldeman was direct. Did the CIA have any role in the break-in?

No, replied Helms. It had none whatsoever.

The chief of staff went on. The White House was concerned that the FBI investigation might jeopardize CIA activity in Mexico. Walters should speak with FBI Acting Director Pat Gray, and warn him that further investigation by the Bureau could expose Agency assets.

Helms pushed back. He had already assured Gray that the CIA was not involved.

Haldeman pressed further. If the FBI didn't cease its investigation into the Mexican link, it could lead to an unravelling of Bay of Pigs activity. He was, Haldeman added, speaking on instruction from the president.

Helms reacted sharply. Ehrlichman was reminded of a scalded cat.

'The Bay of Pigs hasn't got a damned thing to do with this!' exclaimed the CIA director.

The meeting was over. Haldeman had given his instruction. Outside, in the car park, Helms spoke briefly with Walters. He didn't understand the reference to the Bay of Pigs. Perhaps Nixon knew something that he didn't.

Walters suspected as much. He knew from his experience in Paris that covert activities sometimes happened abroad without news reaching CIA headquarters. Undeterred, he drove over to the FBI, and passed the message to Gray.[13]

Back at the White House, Haldeman was content. He had delivered the message. He assumed that Helms would understand. It was less than a week since the Watergate story had first broken. Recording his diary that night, the chief of staff was optimistic. 'We seem to be in pretty good shape,' he reflected, 'at the moment, at least.'[14]

Ron Kovic was on a mission. A former sergeant in the US military, and crippled from the chest down, Kovic was determined to confront his former commander-in-chief.

The Republican Convention was scheduled to take place in Miami, in the last full week of August. The previous month, Democrats had met at the same venue. Their convention confirmed McGovern as presidential candidate. But it had been a chaotic, unruly business. Different interest groups hijacked the occasion. A gay couple in purple T-shirts was filmed kissing in the auditorium, and screened on national television. Poet Allen Ginsburg sat cross-legged under the podium, chanting mantras. On the final evening, delegates nominated thirty-nine personalities to join McGovern as vice-presidential candidate, including Mao Tse-Tung. Proceedings dragged on long into the night. The nominee only delivered his acceptance speech at half-past two in the morning, long after the prime slot for coverage in the evening news bulletins. A fortnight later, vice-presidential candidate Tom Eagleton was forced to drop out of the race after stories spun out of control that he had received electric shock treatment for depression. Traditional Democrat supporters began to splinter away from McGovern.

The White House was Nixon's to lose. McGovern was campaigning from the margins. For Nixon to win, and win by a landslide, he could reach to the political middle ground. In late July, the AFL-CIO trade union announced that it would not endorse McGovern. The president sensed a new majority, from both Republicans and blue-collar democrats. He was determined that his own convention in Miami should be a moment to seize this territory.

Kovic had a different vision. Born to a Catholic working-class home in Wisconsin, he joined the US Marines after graduation from high school. Kovic's father was Croatian, and his mother Irish. His inspiration was Kennedy's inaugural address in 1961, with the line, 'Ask not what your country can do for you, but what you can do for your country.' After basic training, the new recruit was sent to Vietnam.

In June 1968, on a second tour of duty, Kovic was wounded in a firefight near the Cua Viet River, in the demilitarized zone between North and South Vietnam. A heavy calibre round from a machine gun tore off his right heel, while a second shattered his lung and spine. Kovic was dragged off the battlefield on a stretcher. The soldier's birthday fell on the fourth of July. A few days short of 24, he had become paralysed from the waist down.

Back in America, Kovic fell into depression. Scars of Vietnam were etched into his mind, and his body. In the country to which he had returned, he found another struggle raging over Vietnam. Soon after the shootings at Kent State in May 1970, Kovic attended a peace rally for the first time. As demobilized soldiers returned from Vietnam, they joined a new organization, Vietnam Veterans Against the War. Kovic became an activist.

In the summer of 1972, Kovic and his fellow veterans made a plan. They would assemble in California, and drive to Florida. 'It is our last patrol together,' declared Kovic, 'and I know I will remember it as long as I live . . . we are going . . . to reclaim America and a bit of ourselves.' They travelled in camper vans and cars, with the Stars and Stripes streaming behind them. As a symbol of a country in turmoil, the flag was displayed upside down.

Nixon was due to address the convention on the last evening. He spent the weekend before at Camp David, putting final touches to his speech. On a walk around the grounds with Kissinger, he almost stepped into a manhole. Haldeman noticed a limp when he met the president the following morning.[15]

Pat had flown ahead to Miami, along with daughters Julie and Tricia. In a break with tradition, Pat appeared by herself before the convention delegates. She walked to the stage flanked by party co-chairs Bob Dole and Ronald Reagan, governor of California. Behind her hung vast photos of Pat and Richard Nixon together.

The audience broke into sustained applause. They waved home-made banners captioned 'Hi Pat!' In vain, the First Lady called for quiet. She tapped an outsized gavel on the podium. But the cheering went on, and on. Many were the kind of young people whom Nixon had wanted to draw into his campaign, neatly dressed offspring of the same, silent middle-class majority to whom he had appealed over Vietnam nearly three years before. 'Four more years! Four more years!' they shouted, waving their right hands in unison, with all four fingers outstretched.

Reagan came up to join her side. He grinned, and called for silence. Eventually the noise died down.

The schedule was already running late. Pat knew not to prolong her moment. 'Well,' she ventured. 'I stay in the wings and don't come out too often. So this is quite unusual for me . . . I shall remember it always.'

Outside the Convention Centre, protests were gathering pace. The veterans were joined by others from the anti-war movement. They included Yippies, the group who first protested in Chicago four years ago. The main venue was ringed with police, and buses parked end to end as a barrier. National Guard and Marines waited in reserve.

The veterans staged a march. Many wore fatigue jackets, with their medals of service. Their hair was long, and most had beards. Kovic was at the front of the column, with two other colleagues in wheelchairs on either side.

'Murder! Murder!' they shouted.

A chain-link fence barred their way to the Convention Centre, lined with police in riot helmets and holding batons. In protest, the demonstrators staged a mock theatre of death in war. Men and women had painted their faces white. They screamed and writhed on the ground, as though caught in a bombing raid.

As the day wore on, confrontation became violent. Demonstrators threw rocks and eggs, in clashes with the police. When Nixon arrived at the venue that night, tear gas hung in the air. It stung his eyes. The president had first joined a Republican convention as a candidate in 1952, as Eisenhower's running mate. Five campaigns on, he had reached a record matched only by Roosevelt. As a sitting president, aiming for a second term, it was the last that he would fight.

Inside the Convention Centre, there had been little drama. The major networks assigned reporters to cover the floor, whose job was to seek out differences between delegates. The Democrat Convention had been rich hunting ground, with genuine competition among the candidates to secure votes from delegates, and passionate debates over rights for women and gay people that ran into the early hours.

The Republican Convention offered few such opportunities. It was a tightly scripted and scheduled affair. Only one delegate voted against Nixon's nomination, out of almost 1,350 in Miami. CBS had assigned reporters Dan Rather and Roger Mudd to cover the event.

'So it's been kinda dull?' a fellow journalist asked Mudd, during a quiet moment on the convention hall floor.

'A little bit, yes,' acknowledged Mudd with a wry smile.

Nixon was due to speak at ten o'clock in the evening. As speakers warmed up the crowd, Mudd sensed that something was afoot. A group of veterans in wheelchairs were seated on one of the upper galleries to the chamber. It was Kovic and his companions. They had started to raise their voices.

'Do you hear me, people?' called Kovic. He was looking out, across the rows of delegates. People seemed to be avoiding his gaze.

'Do you hear me tonight? Can I break through your complacency?'

Applause for the speakers drowned out Kovic's voice. But Mudd had heard. He clambered over to the former sergeant, a camera crew with him.

'Can I have an inch of your compassion?' cried Kovic. The camera rolled.

A few minutes later, Nixon strode onstage. He was joined by Gerald Ford, minority leader in the House of Representatives. The backdrop behind both men was solid blue. Across America, an estimated 20 million viewers had tuned in.

The crowd erupted. It was, Kovic thought, the loudest roar that he had heard in his life.

'Four more years! Four more years!' shouted the delegates, fingers outstretched. They carried banners, spelling out the name of each state they represented in vertical letters.

Nixon grinned. This was his moment.

'Mr Chairman,' he began, 'delegates to this convention, my fellow Americans . . .'

The crowd roared again. Their applause echoed across the same floor from where, six weeks before, McGovern had given his own acceptance speech in the early hours of the morning.

'I address you tonight,' Nixon continued, 'not as a partisan of party, which would divide us, but as a partisan of principles, which can unite us.' This was the pitch that he hoped would forge a new political alliance.

Faint shouts rang out from the back of the chamber. It was Kovic and his fellow veterans.

'Stop the bombing!' they called. 'Stop the war!'

Security agents leapt towards them. Kovic felt himself pulled backwards. His wheelchair was being thrust away, out of the Convention Centre. He screamed as the agents propelled him. In the distance behind him, Nixon continued speaking.

The veterans were wheeled out of a side entrance. The door was barred, so that Mudd and his colleagues could not reach them.

Kovic started to shake. This was what he had come to Florida to do. The former sergeant had confronted the president, live on television.

Tears streamed down the veteran's face. It was time to go home.[16]

It was, Kissinger later reflected, a strange way to end a war.

The presidential adviser was back in France. It was his sixth encounter with Lu Duc Tho in the space of four months. Following the American bombing offensive against Hanoi and Haiphang harbour, the North Vietnamese had re-entered talks.

Progress had been slow. Kissinger and his assistant, Winston Lord, took to judging success by the quality of refreshments provided by their counterparts. Previously, these had been limited to soft drinks and *cha gio*, or Vietnamese spring rolls. By mid-August, wine and rice cakes had been added to the menu. Back in Washington, Nixon was sceptical. 'It is obvious that no progress was made and that none can be expected,' he noted on a record from Kissinger of his talks.[17]

Hanoi faced a difficult calculation. Victory over Saigon was impossible without full US military withdrawal from Vietnam. 'Fight to make the Americans get out,' Ho Chi Minh had declared, 'fight to make the puppets collapse.' McGovern was campaigning for the November election on a ticket of rapid disengagement. A Democrat victory would significantly strengthen North Vietnam's hand. But, with a strong showing at his party convention, Nixon had maintained a twenty-point lead in the polls. McGovern's chances were receding, and with it Hanoi's negotiating hand.

At the start of October, the North Vietnamese politburo debated the issue. The strategic objective remained withdrawal of US forces. If Nixon was going to remain in power, this would require a negotiated settlement. Outright victory on the battlefield did not look realistic. But was it preferable to reach a deal before the presidential election, or afterwards? They concluded that to wait was too risky. A re-elected Nixon administration might intensify the air war, forcing North Vietnam into a worse position. On 7 October, the politburo agreed that Lu Duc Tho should reach a deal with Kissinger. 'We must strive to end the war before the US presidential election,' ran his instructions. 'In order to accomplish this, we must take the initiative on the requirements of a solution.'[18]

The next day, Kissinger and Lu Duc Tho met. It was Sunday 8 October.

Previous encounters had taken place at Rue Darthe, in the Paris suburb of Choisy-le-Roi. But a CBS film crew had discovered the venue. The North Vietnamese provided a new location, in the country town of Gif-sur-Yvette, some twelve miles to the south of Paris. The house had been owned by the cubist painter Fernand Léger, who left it to the Communist Party of France in his will. The walls were still decorated with his vivid, abstract designs.

On the drive from the airport, Kissinger passed the racecourse at Longchamp, where a major race was due to take place that day. In opening pleasantries with Lu Duc, both men drew a parallel with their own endeavours. 'In France, they run the opposite way around the track than in America,' commented Kissinger.

'But we are making now a race to peace or to war?' countered Lu Duc.

'To peace,' replied Kissinger. 'We're behind the trees,' he added, in a reference to the steeplechase course at Auteuil, where riders compete on a section of the track shielded by foliage from spectators.

Al Haig sat at Kissinger's side, along with aides John Negroponte and Winston Lord. The soldier's stock was riding high. A month before, Nixon nominated him to the rank of a four-star general. Haig would be transferred after the election to a new post, as vice chief of the US Army. The Senate Armed Forces Committee had confirmed the promotion just before his departure for Paris. He had bypassed more than 240 officers with greater seniority. Nixon had asked Haig to accompany Kissinger. With a deputy who himself enjoyed the ear of the president, the national security adviser would need to watch his step even more carefully.[19]

Turning to business, Lu Duc invited Kissinger to speak first. But the former academic had noticed two large green folders sitting on the table before his counterpart. He stalled, waiting for Lu Duc to divulge what he had brought.

Talks broke for a pause in the early afternoon. Haig and Kissinger strolled around a nearby lake, with the rest of their delegation. Along the shore, groups of people were picnicking in the autumn sunshine. The Americans were too distracted to enjoy the scene. They were waiting for Lu Duc to make his move.

The session resumed at four o'clock. Lu Duc spoke first. 'We have listened carefully,' he explained. 'I think we can't negotiate in the way we are doing now.' It was time for a new proposal.

Referring to the papers in his folder, Lu Duc elaborated. Previous encounters had identified both military and political issues. On the military side, North and

South Vietnam would need to agree a ceasefire, while the United States committed to withdraw its forces, and North Vietnam returned American prisoners. The political side was deadlocked, over demands from Hanoi for a government of national unity in the South, which would include communist representatives. Lu Duc now dropped this demand, replacing it with a looser proposal for an Administration of National Concord, which would oversee the ceasefire process and future elections in the south. The ceasefire, he explained, could start from the end of the month.

This was it. Nixon had pledged to secure 'peace with honour' in Vietnam. The terms that Lu Duc had offered would, judged Kissinger, deliver that. The government led by Thieu in South Vietnam would remain intact, without communist involvement. The war would end, and the prisoners come home. Peace was within reach.

Calmly, Kissinger asked for a recess. He stepped aside into a separate room, along with Haig, Lord and Negroponte. Kissinger shook hands with his team. 'We have done it,' he commented. The deal, reflected Haig, was enough to save the honour of those who had fought and died in Vietnam.

The American team was staying on the Rue du Faubourg St Honoré in central Paris, at the residence of the US ambassador to France. That evening, Kissinger slipped out to take a stroll. He walked along the Left Bank, to the cathedral of Notre Dame, and then back through the Place de la Concorde. As he walked, he reflected on the events of the day. Peace had come, less dramatic but more thrilling than he might ever have expected. It was, he later concluded, the most satisfying moment of his time in public service.[20]

Kissinger faced a choice. He could continue the talks with Lu Duc, and turn the proposals contained in the green folders into a negotiated text acceptable to both sides. Or he could break off, and return to Washington for consultation with Nixon.

The presidential adviser was clear what he must do. A trip back to Washington would take time and lose momentum. Moreover, there was a domestic political risk. McGovern was due to give a major speech on Vietnam that Tuesday. The Democratic candidate was expected to confirm that he would pursue unilateral withdrawal, contingent only on release of American prisoners held in Hanoi. If Nixon's political advisers found out that Lu Duc had just made Kissinger a better offer, they would be tempted to leak the news, in a bid to boost their candidate's standing and undermine McGovern. That would set back the chances for a peace negotiation. Kissinger concluded that he must push on in Paris, alone. He cabled a terse update back to the White House. 'Tell the president that there has been some definite progress at today's first session,' the adviser reported. 'He can harbour some confidence the outcome will be positive.'[21]

For the next three days, the two delegations engaged in a marathon negotiation. For years, talks between them had been a stale rehearsal of each side's position. Now, they hastened to narrow their differences down to a single text. The final session, on Wednesday 11 October, lasted for sixteen hours, ending at two o'clock in the morning. Inspired by the drama of the moment, Kissinger's secretary, Irene Derus, insisted on acting as note-taker throughout.

At the end, Kissinger and Lu Duc offered short speeches of thanks.

'We have made great effort, and you too, you have made great effort,' concluded the North Vietnamese envoy. 'Through our effort, no doubt we will reach our objective of peace.' As the interpreter translated the words, Derus took them down in shorthand. 'We know you will be as dedicated in the pursuit of peace as you have in the fighting of a war,' responded his American counterpart.[22]

On Thursday, Kissinger and Haig returned to Washington. They went immediately to brief Nixon. It was evening. The president had spent the day on the campaign trail in Atlanta. He received the two men at his personal study, in the Executive Office Building. Chief of Staff Bob Haldeman joined them. Nixon sat in his easy chair, with his legs propped up, while the others occupied wooden chairs.

The president offered drinks. Kissinger asked for a scotch and soda, Haig for a martini. The security adviser held a red folder, marked 'secret', with the text that he had negotiated in Paris.

'Well, you got three out of three, Mr President,' he said, referring to the successes on China, the Soviet Union and now Vietnam. 'It's well on the way.'

Nixon was incredulous. 'You got an agreement? Are you kidding?'

'No, I'm not kidding,' replied Kissinger.

Haldeman looked on. Kissinger wanted to talk through the details, but Nixon wasn't listening. The president turned to Haig. He thought the general looked subdued.

'What about Thieu?' he asked.

'It isn't done,' Haig commented.[23]

The previous week, Haig had travelled to Saigon, as Nixon's envoy. He met with President Thieu. Tears had welled in the Vietnamese's eyes as Haig briefed him on the American plan for negotiations with the north. He sensed betrayal. 'Dr Kissinger does not deign to consider what we propose,' he told the visiting American. 'He just goes his own way.'[24]

Now, in briefing the president, Kissinger was upbeat. He and Lu Duc had agreed a schedule of shuttle diplomacy, to finalize the agreement with South Vietnam.

'The deal we got, Mr President, is so far better than anything we dreamt of. I mean I was absolutely, totally hard line with them.'

'Won't it totally wipe out Thieu, Henry?' asked Nixon.

'Yeah,' added Haldeman in support.

'Oh, no. It's so far better than anything we discussed.'

The four men broke for dinner, served in the outer room to the president's office. On Nixon's instructions, Manolo served wine. Haldeman took note. Usually the president reserved Château Lafite for himself, and gave others Californian wine. On this occasion, they all drank from the same bottle. It was a 1957 vintage.

A week later, it was Kissinger's turn to visit Saigon.

Ambassador Ellsworth Bunker met his plane at the airport. Bunker had served in Vietnam for five years. Aged 78, he had enjoyed a long career in business and government, as president of the company National Sugar, and then ambassador to

Argentina, Italy and India. Tall, thin, with horn-rimmed glasses and white hair swept back, Kissinger found him a reassuring presence.

Kissinger's encounter with President Thieu was less reassuring. At his first call on the presidential palace, Kissinger was kept waiting for fifteen minutes. Despite speaking fluent English, Thieu insisted on working through his interpreter, Hoang Duc Nha. Kissinger quickly noticed that his remarks were being translated in a shortened form.

'Either Vietnamese is a more concise language,' he noted, 'or Mr Nha is a master of abbreviation.'

'I am a master of contraction,' Nha snapped back.[25]

Over the next four days, Kissinger held a series of meetings with Thieu and his foreign minister, Tran Vam Lam. The South Vietnamese were not happy. Under the ceasefire terms agreed between Kissinger and Lu Duc, North Vietnamese forces would remain in the South, confined to their existing positions. The Americans hoped that, over time, support for communism would wither away. Hanoi would abandon its ambitions to secure control over the South. Thieu was less sanguine. He feared the North Vietnamese, and feared betrayal from the Americans.

Haig had remained back in Washington. Reading reports from Kissinger, he and Nixon became concerned. A deal which Thieu rejected would backfire, including with Nixon's conservative base in the United States. Nixon ordered Haig to instruct his boss in Saigon. 'Thieu's acceptance must be wholehearted,' the general advised. 'It cannot be a shotgun marriage.'[26]

Kissinger believed that he was walking a tightrope. To stop mid-course would risk disaster. Strained by the long-distance travel and diplomatic tensions, his patience started to wear thin. The time difference with Washington meant that instructions arrived too late for his daily sessions with the South Vietnamese. 'Washington must understand that this is not a Sunday school picnic,' he shot back to Haig. 'To wash out the final leg could cost us dearly.'[27]

But events were running away from Kissinger. Arnaud de Borchgrave, a senior editor with *Newsweek* magazine, had recently visited Hanoi. He secured an interview with Prime Minister Pham Van Dong, which was published as Kissinger was in Saigon. Van Dong leaked news of the deal reached in Paris, claiming that it amounted to victory for the communist side. Thieu, he declared, was 'overtaken by events.'[28]

Thieu reacted angrily. On Sunday 22 October, a fortnight after Kissinger and Lu Duc had first met at Gif-sur-Yvette, he held a stormy meeting with the former academic.

'I see that those whom I regard as friends have failed me,' he told his visitor from America. 'However great the personal humiliation for me I shall continue to fight.'

'Our principles have been the same as yours and we have defended them,' replied Kissinger. 'You have only one problem,' he added, in a veiled threat. 'President Nixon has many.'[29]

It was over. Under the schedule agreed between Lu Duc and Kissinger, the presidential adviser was due to travel onwards to Hanoi. That was now impossible. Without the South Vietnamese on board, agreement could not be reached. All that

1 President Richard Nixon and National Security Adviser Dr Henry Kissinger, 1972.

2. National Guardsmen advance towards student protestors at Kent State University, May 1970.

3. Nixon mingles with anti-war protestors at the Lincoln Memorial, May 1970.

4. West German Chancellor Willy Brandt kneeling at the Warsaw Ghetto memorial, December 1970.

5. Richard and Pat Nixon at the Great Wall of China, February 1972.

6. Nixon and Chinese Premier Zhou Enlai share a toast, February 1972.

7. Kissinger briefs the White House press corps that 'Peace is At Hand' in Vietnam, October 1972.

8. Kissinger and Soviet leader Leonid Brezhnev hunting outside Moscow, May 1973.

9. Nixon and Brezhnev en route to California aboard presidential aircraft *Spirit of '76*, along with Treasury Secretary John Connally and interpreter Viktor Sukhodrev, June 1973.

10. Brezhnev and interpreter Sukhodrev meet actor Chuck Connors at San Clemente, California, June 1975.

11. Nixon, Kissinger, Alexander Haig and new vice-president Gerald Ford in the White House, June 1973.

12. Premier Golda Meir and Defence Minister Moshe Dayan visit Israel troops on the Golan Heights after the Yom Kippur War, November 1973.

13. Writers Alexander Solzhenitsyn and Heinrich Böll meet after the former's exile from the Soviet Union, February 1974.

14. Nixon hugs his daughter Julie after announcing his resignation watched by sister Tricia and husband David, August 1974.

15. President Jerry Ford swaps his fur coat with Brezhnev, Vladivostok Summit,
December 1974.

16. Fleeing Americans board a US Marine Helicopter at Tan Son Nhut Airbase in Saigon,
Vietnam, April 1975.

remained was to park the negotiation as softly as possible, in the hope that a new initiative might be feasible after the election. The next morning, Kissinger returned to Washington.

On Thursday 26 October, a new blow struck. Kissinger called Haldeman at three o'clock in the morning to break the news. Following the *Newsweek* interview, the North Vietnamese had gone further. Radio Hanoi broadcast details of the draft agreement, claiming that it was only blocked by 'lack of good will and seriousness' from the Nixon Administration. Similar stories appeared in *The New York Times*. The election was less than a fortnight away. It looked like an attempt to influence the result.

For four years in the White House, Kissinger had stayed out of the public eye. Nixon's advisers feared that his German pronunciation would play badly on television.[30] But now his moment had come. In a hurried series of consultations with Nixon, Haldeman and Press Secretary Ron Ziegler, Kissinger agreed to do a press conference. The aim was to put the American side of the story on record, and in doing so forestall any advantage to McGovern from Hanoi's move.

The former academic walked to the lectern, in the White House Press Room. He was wearing a light grey suit and his distinctive heavy-rimmed glasses. Ziegler stood behind him. Haig leaned against a doorway, arms folded and with a white handkerchief neatly folded in his top pocket.

'We have heard now from both Vietnams,' Kissinger begun, in his heavy German accent. 'It is obvious that a war that has been raging for ten years is drawing to a conclusion.'

'We believe that peace is at hand,' he continued. 'By far the longest part of the road has been traversed.'

Afterwards, Ziegler reported back to Nixon. The national security adviser had given the press a headline. It demonstrated that the administration was negotiating in earnest, and that Hanoi's claims were misplaced. 'Your country owes you a great deal, Henry,' veteran journalist Scotty Reston told Kissinger on the phone after the press conference.[31] But it would also raise public expectations within America that the long ordeal over Vietnam might finally be coming to an end. And that might make it harder to press Hanoi for concessions when negotiations resumed after the election. 'This was really going considerably further than I would have gone,' Nixon grumbled in his diary.[32]

Haldeman took a different view. The previous day had seen significant escalation on Watergate. *The Washington Post* ran a story claiming that Haldeman had personally authorized use of CRP campaign funds for dirty tricks. It was the first time that the chief of staff had been directly implicated. But it was inaccurate. Working from a series of undercover tip-offs, journalists Carl Bernstein and Bob Woodward had failed to corroborate key details behind their story. The *Post* had, for the first time, overstepped the mark. Ziegler sprung a counteroffensive. At his daily press briefing, he accused the paper of 'shoddy and shabby' journalism.

Kissinger's press conference, thought Haldeman, helped move the story on further. Ten days out from the election, the White House looked back in charge.[33]

'Hubert, how are you?'

'Well fine, and I wanted to call up just to congratulate you on this historic victory.'

It was half-past one in the morning, on Wednesday 8 November 1972. Hubert Humphrey, Nixon's Democrat opponent in the 1968 elections, had phoned to offer congratulations for victory in the 1972 presidential contest.

The first results were declared the previous evening. It was decisive. Nixon had managed a clean sweep in the electoral college of all states except Massachusetts and Washington DC. The eventual tally in the popular vote would give him 60.7 per cent, against 37.5 per cent for McGovern. It was a wider margin of victory than any president had achieved except Johnson against his Republican opponent Barry Goldwater in 1964. The final campaign of Nixon's political career had ended in triumph.

In the midst of victory, the re-elected president felt oddly downcast. Over dinner, as the results came in, a crown on one of his top front teeth had snapped, and required emergency treatment. Later, Nixon retreated to the Lincoln Sitting Room. He put on a tape, with the soundtrack from *Victory at Sea*, a popular film from the 1950s about the naval campaign during the Second World War. Downstairs, in the West Wing, Haldeman and his staffers monitored results from around the country. As he spoke with Nixon over an internal phone, he could hear the music in the background. Brass played rousing notes against a base of strings and woodwind.

Just before midnight, McGovern sent a telegram conceding defeat. 'I hope that in the next four years you will lead us to a time of peace abroad and justice at home,' he wrote. 'You have my full support in such efforts.' As the Nixon family gathered round to read it, there were differing reactions. While Ed thought it gracious, Tricia and Julie were more sceptical. There was, they thought, something cold in the wording.[34]

Just after midnight, the president and First Lady drove to the Shoreham Hotel, to address a rally of Nixon's supporters. They did not stay long. Following a brief victory speech, Nixon returned to his motorcade.[35]

Back at the White House, various well-wishers made calls to offer congratulations. That from Humphrey touched the president. Nixon had respect for his former opponent. In 1968, as in 1972, the presidential election was fought out against the backdrop of Vietnam. Johnson's decision to halt bombing of the north just ahead of the poll had, Nixon believed, deprived him of a larger majority. But Humphrey himself had sought to strike a bipartisan tone over the conflict. Nixon thought it contrasted with McGovern's decision to position himself as a peace candidate.

'Well,' he told the senator, 'we'll get together and we'll work for the good of the country. That's the important thing.'

'Surely will,' replied Humphrey. 'And I didn't want to let this night go by without calling.'

After the call, Nixon summoned Haldeman and Colson. It was two in the morning. The group ordered bacon and eggs from the White House kitchen, with glasses of milk.[36]

The next morning, the White House staff gathered in the Roosevelt Room. It was eleven o'clock, but many still felt bleary from celebrations the night before. These were the men and women who had served Nixon for the previous four years, and shared in his victory.

Their boss walked in, followed by Haldeman. Kissinger thought that he looked grim. William Safire, the speech-writer, had a different impression. The president, he thought, seemed positive, almost youthful.

Nixon began to speak. He was, he said, proud of them. They had been accused of many things. The most common accusation was efficiency. 'We can plead guilty to that,' he quipped.

The president went on. He had been reading the biography of British prime minister Benjamin Disraeli, by the historian Robert Blake. Disraeli had compared his opponent William Gladstone and cabinet to a row of exhausted volcanoes. So, he explained, it was with a campaign team. 'It is the responsibility of a leader, despite our victories, to see that we do not climb to the top and look over the embers that once shot sparks into the sky.'

Safire liked the analogy, and the dramatic image. He took notes. Kissinger was less impressed. It all felt perfunctory, ungrateful.

Nixon rose, and left the room. Haldeman remained. He reached into his folder, and passed around photocopied forms.

The chief of staff explained. Each member of the White House should submit a letter of resignation. They should also state whether they wished to re-apply for a position.

Kissinger was appalled. 'I have already submitted my resignation in German,' he declared. 'The adjectives are at the end.'

Haldeman snapped back. 'It's the verbs that belong at the end, Henry. You don't even know how to construct a German sentence.'[37]

The first sign was a line of electronic blips, on the darkness of a radar operator's screen. It was the early evening of Monday 18 December 1972.

Dinh Huu Than was commander of the 45th Radar Company, in the North Vietnamese Army's Air Defence Corps. He and his soldiers were based at the village of Nghe An, on the coast some hundred miles south of Hanoi. The unit was equipped with P-12 early warning radars, supplied by the Soviet Union. The technology had originally been developed in the 1950s. It could detect air traffic at a range of up to 155 miles. Operators sat in a Zil transport truck, hunched over a circular, amber-coloured display screen. A second truck carried the search antennae. It was positioned 550 yards away from the command vehicle, as a precaution against air attack.

Dinh and his men watched the blips. The static pattern suggested that they were B-52 bombers. These were the largest strike aircraft in the US Air Force, capable of carrying a payload of thirty tons. Six bombers, flying in formation, could obliterate a 'box' on the ground two miles long, and half a mile wide.[38] When B-52s hit targets in South Vietnam, the shock reverberations could be heard in Saigon, thirty or forty miles from the target.

Typically, B-52 squadrons would approach North Vietnam by sea, over the Gulf of Tonkin. As they approached point 300, parallel with the lower half of the country, they would turn west, and move inland towards their targets. Dinh's men had become used to tracking such movements. But this time the blips kept moving northwards. After a few moments, Dinh realized what was happening. They were heading for Hanoi.[39]

It was the Nixon's last throw on Vietnam.

Following the election in November, Kissinger had resumed contacts with Lu Duc in Paris. Haig travelled to Saigon, in an effort to win more leeway from President Thieu. But neither side was prepared to give. Thieu refused to make concessions, while the North Vietnamese appeared to be rowing back from the draft agreement which they had offered in Paris the previous month.

Once again, the calculation was political. Nixon's landslide victory in the presidential race had not been matched by equivalent success in congressional elections. The Republicans had lost two seats in the Senate. They had made modest gains in the House, under leader Gerald Ford, but remained a minority in both. The new Congress would convene in early January. Most commentators expected that opponents of the war in Vietnam would demand to cut off funding. They might have sufficient votes to force the administration into a retreat. Hanoi anticipated a new position of strength.

By mid-December, Kissinger concluded that negotiations had run into the sand. At a meeting in the Oval Office, the presidential adviser chewed over the options with Nixon and Haig. It was deeply frustrating.

'They're shits,' fumed Kissinger, as he described his encounters with the North Vietnamese. 'I mean, they are a miserable, tawdry people. They make the Russians look good.'

'As of today,' he went on, 'we are caught between Hanoi and Saigon, both of them facing us down in a position of total impotence, in which Hanoi is just stringing us along, and Saigon is just ignoring us.'

The three men batted round the choices. It was time to change the dynamic. Nixon turned to Haig.

'Al thinks they want to settle,' he commented.

'I also think they want to settle, but – ' interjected Kissinger.

'Do you think they want to settle?' asked Nixon, looking at Haig.

Kissinger injected again. 'Mr President, they are –'.

Nixon repeated his question. 'Do you think they are going to?'

Haig spoke. As a battalion commander in Vietnam, he had watched B-52 air strikes hitting targets within a thousand yards of his soldiers' position. The bombs fell with a scream through the air, from aircraft flying at more than 30,000 feet above. As they exploded, the topsoil shook loose on the ground. It was a terrifying sight.

'If they get a good kick up the ass,' Haig commented.

The three men agreed. The United States would launch a major bombing offensive against Hanoi over the Christmas period, aimed at military and public infrastructure. Radio Hanoi would be among the targets. Operations would proceed around the clock, suspended only for a 36-hour period over Christmas Day.[40]

To set the scene, Kissinger gave a press conference. 'Peace can be near,' he warned, adjusting his words from the previous appearance in October, 'but peace requires a decision.' Bombing, the Americans hoped, would force Hanoi back to the negotiating table.[41]

The assault began on 18 December. It was a nerve-wracking period. North Vietnamese air defences were equipped with Soviet surface-to-air missiles, and coordinated by radar units such as that led by Dinh Huu Than. On the first night, three B-52s were shot down. By the third night, eight were lost. The North Vietnamese were getting the measure of their assailants. At the main B-52 base on Guam Island in the Pacific, US Air Force commanders plotted out bombing runs to avoid the most effective missile batteries. Meanwhile, in the United States, press and congressional politicians erupted in fury. 'The Rain of Death Continues' ran one headline in *The Boston Globe*. After a brief prospect of peace, America was back at war.

It was a lonely period for Nixon. Already, in the weeks after the election, he had withdrawn from public view. Only Haldeman and Ehrlichman, along with Kissinger and Haig, enjoyed regular access to the president. With the additional strain of the bombing offensive, the isolation became more intense.

Christmas Day was a depressed affair. Julie and Tricia were both travelling abroad with their husbands, leaving their parents to celebrate alone. When Pat suggested opening presents left by their daughters, her husband mumbled an excuse. The gifts remained untouched. Over their time in the White House, Nixon reflected in his diary, he and his wife had become 'more and more lonely individuals', unable to reach out to others when they needed a lift.[42]

Boxing Day brought sad news of a different kind. Harry Truman, thirty-third president of the United States, had died. He was 88 years old, and had suffered declining health.

The next day, both Nixon and former president Lyndon Johnson travelled to pay their respects at Truman's home town of Independence in the state of Missouri. Accompanied by their wives, Nixon and Johnson called on the Truman family at their home.

From there, the two men drove to the Truman Presidential Library, on the north side of the town. The former president's coffin was laid out in state, guarded by enlisted men from the US Army, Navy, Marines and Coast Guard. The Stars and Stripes were draped over the coffin. Nixon laid a wreath of red, white and blue carnations.[43]

The president had not been close to his predecessor. As a young congressman, Nixon had first made his name with attacks on alleged communist sympathizers inside the Truman Administration, notably the diplomat Alger Hiss. But, following Eisenhower, Truman was the second former president to die while Nixon was in the White House. Only Johnson was now left, among those who had shared the burdens of the highest office.

The previous day, word had reached the White House from Paris that the North Vietnamese were prepared to reopen talks. It looked as though the bombing campaign was having an effect. On the morning of his trip to Missouri, Nixon instructed Kissinger's staff to send back a positive reply.[44]

The next day was 28 December. Word came back from Paris. The North Vietnamese accepted the conditions that Washington had proposed for reopening talks, and a halt to the bombing. That afternoon, Nixon spoke on the phone with Kissinger. The presidential adviser was in Palm Springs, for a Christmas vacation. Both were elated.

'So this has been another spectacular for you, Mr President,' commented Kissinger.

'Yeah. Well, hell, we don't know whether it's that . . .' replied Nixon.

'Well, it took terrific courage to do it.'

'Yeah. Well, at least, it pricked the boil, didn't it?'[45]

Notes

1 Haldeman (1978), 3–8.
2 Nixon (1978), 625.
3 Dean (2014), 5–6.
4 Haldeman interview with Raymond Geselbricht, 13 August 1987, p. 87; Colson interview with Charles Graboske, 15 June 1988, p. 18.
5 Ehrlichman (1982), 8, 348; Haldeman (1978), 10–12; Haldeman (1994), 471–2; Colson (1976), 74–5.
6 Haldeman (1978), 12–14; Haldeman (1994), 473; Nixon (1978), 627–8.
7 Nixon (1978), 631–4; Haldeman (1978), 16–19; Haldeman (1994), 473; Dean (2014), 19–30.
8 Safire (1975), 358–9.
9 Nixon (1978), 634–65; Haldeman (1978), 23–5; Dean (2014), 30–1.
10 Haldeman (1978), 27–32; Dean (2014), 53–5; Haldeman (1994), 474; Haldeman interview with Raymond Geselbricht, 13 April 1988, p. 107–12.
11 Dean (2014), 55–8; Haldeman (1978), 32–4; Nixon (1978), 639–42.
12 Helms (2003), 1–8; Walters (1978), 587.
13 Haldeman (1978), 34–5, 37–8; Ehrlichman (1982), 350; Helms (2003), 9–10; Walters (1978), 587–9.
14 Haldeman (1994), 474.
15 Haldeman (1994), 496.
16 Kovic (1976), 152–59.
17 Kissinger (1979), 1315, 1319.
18 Doan, 141, quoted in FRUS 1969–76 Vol. VIII, p. 1076–7.
19 Haig (1992), 297–8.
20 FRUS 1969–76 Vol. IX, item 1, p. 1–25; Kissinger (1979), 1341–7; Haig (1992) 298–9.
21 Kissinger (1979), 1347–50; Nixon (1978), 691.

22 FRUS 1969–76 Vol. IX, item 6, p. 65–115 – quotes from, 113–14.
23 FRUS 1969–76 Vol. IX, item 9, p. 120–9; Haldeman (1994), 515–17; Haig (1992), 299–300; Kissinger (1979), 1360–1; Nixon (1978), 693.
24 Haig (1992), 294–5.
25 FRUS 1969–76 Vol. IX, item 27, p. 181–203.
26 FRUS 1969–76 Vol. IX, item 34, p. 219–20.
27 FRUS 1969–76 Vol. IX, item 35, p. 221—3.
28 Kissinger (1979), 1381.
29 Kissinger (1979), 1385–6; FRUS 1969–76, item 49, p. 260–4.
30 Klein interview with Naftali, 20 February 2007, p. 53.
31 Hastings (2018), 558.
32 Kissinger (1979), 1397–400; Haldeman (1994), 523–4; Haig (1994), 302; Nixon (1978), 705–6.
33 Woodward and Bernstein (1974), 184–6; Haldeman (1994), 523–34.
34 Nixon (1978), 715–17; Haldeman (1994), 530–1; Eisenhower (1986), 535–6.
35 Nixon daily diary, 7–8 November 1972.
36 Brinkley and Nichter (2014), 643–4; Haldeman interview with Raymond Geselbricht, 11 April 1988, p. 31.
37 Haldeman (1994), 532–3; Kissinger (1979), 1406–7; Safire (1975), 654–5; Ehrlichman (1982), 363; Woodward (2015), 137–8; Haldeman interview with Raymond Geselbricht, 13 April 1988, p. 63.
38 Hastings (2018), 563.
39 'The Christmas Bombing' by Marshall Michel, in *Air and Space* magazine, January 2001.
40 Brinkley and Nichter (2014), 665–704, quotes from, 677, 679 and 684; Nixon (1978), 733–4; Haig (1992), 308–9.
41 Kissinger (1979), 1446–51.
42 Eisenhower (1986), 539–40.
43 'Truman's Body Lies in State in His Library', in *The New York Times*, 28 December 1972.
44 FRUS 1969–76 Vol. IX, item 224, p. 827–9 and items 227 and 228, p. 836–45.
45 Brinkley and Nichter (2014), 722–30, quote on p. 725.

Chapter 8

SWEET RAIN
(January–June 1973)

Henry Kissinger arrived at the house in Gif-sur-Yvette on the morning of 8 January 1973. It was the same venue where talks with the North Vietnamese had come close to ending the war in Vietnam three months before, in October 1973. On that occasion, Lu Duc Tho and his compatriots had made a show of greeting the American delegation outside on the street, with warm handshakes and smiles for the journalists camped out across the road.

This time, the door opened silently, without any faces visible. It was only once he was inside that Kissinger met his hosts. With the door closed behind him, the North Vietnamese lined up to offer welcome greetings. In the wake of the Christmas bombing, they were sending a clear signal. To the outside world, Hanoi was holding firm. In private, the time had come to settle.[1]

Progress came quickly. The next day, Tuesday 9 January, was President Nixon's birthday. He was 60.

Around noon, Chief of Staff Bob Haldeman walked into his office, holding a classified cable from Paris.

'What happened?' asked Nixon.

'I think you should read this for yourself,' Haldeman replied.

Nixon put on his reading glasses. The cable was from Kissinger. His negotiations with Lu Duc that day had achieved a 'major breakthrough'. Peace was indeed now at hand.

The president was elated. He dictated a reply. 'What you have done today is the best birthday present I have had in sixty years,' Nixon declared.[2]

That evening, family and staff staged a surprise birthday party. Tricia, Nixon's daughter, suggested that they enjoy a cocktail together. She led her unsuspecting father to the Red Room, on the second floor of the White House. Once inside, the doors to the adjoining Blue Room opened, and some twenty of Nixon's friends and aides entered.

After drinks, the group sat down to a steak meal in the Blue Room. They ate from a dinner service commissioned by former president Woodrow Wilson, with a royal blue band on the dinner plates and gilt on the rim. Two candelabra were arranged on the table, between three bouquets of white flowers. Nixon was wearing a light blue casual jacket, while Pat, seated at the other end of the table, wore a dress in a similar shade.

Light-hearted toasts followed, from Nixon's friend Bob Alplanalp and others. When it came to Nixon's turn, his mood grew more serious. He raised a glass to the armed forces. 'God bless them and we'll prove that they were right,' he added. The reference to Vietnam was left unspoken.[3]

A couple of days later, Nixon jotted down his thoughts for the second term. He mapped out a series of headings, on his usual yellow legal notepad. 'Substance: Russia, China, MidEast, Europe,' ran the first. At the bottom, he added his own personal goals. 'Compassion,' he wrote, 'Understanding.'[4]

For the next week, with agreement reached in Paris, the Americans waited on Saigon. Would Thieu, who had vetoed the draft deal in October, do so again? Haig was sent to convey an ultimatum. Privately, Nixon and Kissinger were clear that if necessary they would go ahead without the South Vietnamese leader's backing.

Theiu finally signalled acceptance on Saturday 20 January. It was the morning of the inauguration ceremony in Washington, marking the re-elected Nixon's second term as president. He took the oath of office on the steps of the Capitol. Pat Nixon wore a light blue coat with a black fur collar, while the president had chosen a formal tie with grey and white stripes.

Watching him, Kissinger thought there was an oddly detached quality to his boss. 'Richard Nixon,' he recalled, 'moved as if he himself were a spectator, not the principal.'[5]

Afterwards, Nixon delivered his inaugural address. He hoped to strike an uplifting note. At the start of his first term, he reminded his audience Americans had been 'bleak in spirit'. Now the world was on the threshold of a new era of peace.

'We shall answer to God, to history, and to our conscience,' he concluded, 'for the way in which we use these years.'

Two days later, Kissinger returned to Paris. He and Lu Duc Tho were due to initial the final peace agreement the following day. Nixon would then deliver a televised address in Washington, announcing the end of the war.

As the president was working on a draft of his address with speech-writer Ray Price, he was interrupted with a message. Former president Lyndon Johnson had died. The Texan had suffered from heart pains in recent weeks. The end came with a heart attack at his ranch, in Texas. He and Nixon had spoken a couple of weeks before. Johnson explained that he had attended a University of Texas football game, and shouted too much in his excitement. Nixon offered his home at Key Biscayne in Florida for recuperation.

Johnson had spent his final years pondering over his legacy, and the war in Vietnam. He would play the song *Bridge Over Troubled Water* by musicians Simon and Garfunkel again and again, listening to the lyrics. When Nixon called, he asked about progress in the Paris talks.

'I just feel the torture that you're going through,' commented Johnson. 'I just wish I could help you.'

'Don't you worry,' replied Nixon. 'It's going to come out alright.'[6]

With the news of Johnson's death, various emotions struck Nixon and Price. Johnson had sent Price a copy of his memoirs for Christmas. The speech-writer felt a pang of guilt that he had not managed to thank the former president. Nixon thought of how Johnson had not lived to see the news of peace in Vietnam. The Texan had, he concluded, died of a broken heart, both physically and emotionally.[7]

The following evening, Nixon delivered a televised address from the Oval Office, announcing the peace agreement. It was ten o'clock. He wore a dark blue tie with white spots, and a lapel pin with the American flag.

The deal, he declared, had brought peace with honour. The prisoners of war would return within sixty days, and the independence of South Vietnam was upheld. But all parties must now ensure that it was a 'peace that lasts . . . and a peace that heals'.

Afterwards, Nixon went upstairs, to his private family quarters. Pat embraced him. Julie, Tricia and husband Ed were also there. They talked for a while. Then the president withdrew to the Lincoln Sitting Room, alone. He instructed that no phone calls be put through. Sitting in front of the fire, he ate a light supper, and listened to music.

Later, Nixon composed a short letter to Johnson's widow, Lady Bird.

'I only wish that Lyndon could have lived to hear my announcement,' he wrote. 'I know what abuse he took,' he added, 'in standing firm for peace with honour.'

With the deaths of Eisenhower, Truman and now Johnson, no previous president was still alive. Nixon was on his own. In the history of the Republic, only Presidents John Adams and Teddy Roosevelt had found themselves in a similar position, without living forebears who had experienced the burdens of highest office.

Twenty days later, on Monday 12 February 1973, the first prisoners arrived home.

It was called Operation Homecoming. By the end of the war, the Pentagon assessed that almost two thousand American servicemen had been captured or gone missing in Vietnam. The longest-serving were taken eight years before, during the initial phase of the US intervention. They were held in a number of camps inside North Vietnam, including the so-called 'Hanoi Hilton', in the capital city. Many had suffered degrading conditions and torture. Under the agreement reached in Paris, all were due to be returned within sixty days. The North Vietnamese identified 591 individuals to be repatriated; over 1,300 remained unaccounted for.

The first group of sixty left Hanoi on 11 February. They flew to Clark Air Base in the Philippines. On the flight, they enjoyed cigarettes and a white nutrient milkshake.

At the base, a red carpet had been rolled out in their honour, borrowed from the Manila InterContinental Hotel. America was observing a month-long period of mourning for the death of President Johnson. All flags on government buildings were flown at half mast. But Nixon agreed with Lady Bird that the returning prisoners of war deserved special treatment. At Clark, the Stars and Stripes flew from the top of the flagpole.[8]

US Navy pilot Commander Jeremiah Denton was the first to descend the aircraft steps. Captured in 1965, he had been paraded through the streets of Hanoi, and forced to take part in a televised press conference by his captors. During the interview, Denton blinked repeatedly, using his eyelid movements to spell out the letters T-O-R-T-U-R-E in Morse code. It was the first confirmation of conditions faced by the prisoners.

Denton walked to the end of the red carpet, where a microphone had been placed. He was dressed in a fresh dress uniform, in pale tropical khaki. He stood to attention, hands behind his back.

'We are honoured to have the opportunity to serve our country under difficult circumstances,' declared the officer. He spoke slowly, as his words echoed across the tarmac. 'God bless America.'

Others emerged from the plane. Some were on crutches. They saluted the flag, and many fell on their knees to kiss the ground.[9] Capt James Stockdale quoted a line from the ancient playwright Sophocles, about the sweetness of raindrops that greeted the traveller returning home.

From there, the men flew to Travis Air Force Base in California, and onwards, to homes across America. For those who had been away several years, it was a different country. The war, and the wider upheavals of the last decade, had melded society into a different shape from that which they remembered.

Outpourings of warmth washed over the former prisoners. Three years before, on Veterans Day in 1970, two college students in California had started a campaign to remember the POWs, by wearing metal bracelets inscribed with the name of an individual prisoner. More than 5 million were sold. Bob Dole, the junior senator for Kansas, wore one in memory of John McCain, a pilot and son of the naval theatre commander in the Pacific.[10] As the men returned home, strangers approached them, and presented the bracelets which they had worn.

But the warmth was not universal. Captain James Mulligan was a carrier pilot, and a veteran of both the Second World War and Korea. He had been shot down in March 1966, a week before his fiftieth birthday. Taken to North Vietnam, he was held in solitary confinement for over three years, and shackled with leg irons. Along with Denton and others, he belonged to a group in the Hanoi Hilton who called themselves the 'Alcatraz Gang'. The men supported each other, memorizing the list of names for all the prisoners in the camp to keep their minds active.[11]

Mulligan had left behind his wife Louise and six sons in Virginia. Along with other members of the Alcatraz Gang, he found himself troubled by what he found on his return to America. He had spent the months in solitary confinement reflecting on his country, and his Christian faith. But the values of duty and responsibility which sustained him in Vietnam seemed weakened back home.

When a reporter asked for his views about homecoming, Mulligan spoke out.

'I feel very strongly,' he declared, 'that it is about time we start raising the flag instead of burning it. I know people have strong feelings ... but we are all Americans.'[12]

'We have a cancer within – close – to the presidency, that's growing. It's growing daily. It's compounding. It grows geometrically now, because it compounds itself.'[13]

John Dean wanted to catch the president's attention. It was mid-morning, on Wednesday 21 March 1973. Dean was legal counsel to the president. When news of Watergate first broke, in the summer of 1972, Dean had overseen the White House operation to ensure that it did not undermine Nixon's campaign for re-election. He had done a good job. But now, nine months on, Watergate was back in the headlines.

Two weeks before, the Senate had voted unanimously to establish a select committee to investigate the Watergate affair. It would be led by Sam Ervin, a Democrat from North Carolina with almost two decades' experience as a senator. At the same time, the Justice Committee was probing in hearings around the confirmation of Pat Gray as a substantive replacement as director of the FBI for John Edgar Hoover, who had died a few months before. And, in a criminal case against Howard Hunt, Gordon Liddy and the operatives arrested over the break-in, presiding judge John Sirica was due to pass sentence.

Dean was in his early thirties, and had previously projected a crisp, neat confidence. As the investigation took its toll, Haldeman could see the strain in his colleague. He had, the chief of staff recalled, become a 'frightened young man, nervous and fidgety'.[14] From late February, Dean had been frequent visitor to the Oval Office. Even with this access, he remained concerned that Nixon still did not understand the full picture around Watergate. Ehrlichman thought the president was like a sea anemone, which recoils and closes when under threat.[15] It was, Dean believed, time to set out the facts clearly.

The cancer analogy had cut through to Nixon. He was listening now. Dean pressed on, explaining what his own investigations had unearthed. Haldeman had also joined them, sitting silently.

The core defence deployed by the White House over Watergate had been to distance itself, arguing that the matter had been handled by the Campaign to Re-Elect the President. Privately, money had been channelled to the defendants in the criminal case, on the expectation that they would remain silent. Some $430,000 had been dispersed, but this firewall was now unravelling. Gordon Strachan, an assistant to Haldeman, appeared to have been involved in the original decision to conduct a bugging operation against the Democrat National Headquarters. Meanwhile, Howard Hunt, one of those convicted, had demanded a further $125,000 to cover legal and other fees. It felt close to blackmail. Dean was concerned that the White House strategy was imploding.

'It'll cost money,' he told the president. 'It's dangerous.'

'Nobody, nothing,' he added, 'people around here are not pros at this sort of thing. This is the sort of thing Mafia people can do: washing money, getting clean money, and things like that we're – we just don't know about these things, because we're not used to, you know – we are not criminals and not used to dealing in that business.'

'That's right,' replied Nixon. He listened as Dean explained more about the difficulties.

'How much money do you need?' asked the president.

'I would say these people are going to cost a million dollars over the next two years,' answered Dean.

Nixon and Dean talked over the different names involved in the affair: Hunt, Liddy, Strachan, Bud Krogh, Chuck Colson, John Ehrlichman. Each knew things, and each would have a breaking point. Congress and the courts might spread their investigations further, probing into dirty tricks conducted by the team over the years.

Dean summarized the choices. 'There are two routes, you know,' he explained.

'One is to figure out how to cut the losses and minimize the human impact and get you up and out and way from it in any way . . . the other is go down the road – just hunker down, fight it at every corner, every turn, don't let people testify, cover it up is what we're really talking about.'

'And just take the heat,' concluded Nixon.

'And just take the heat,' echoed Dean.[16]

The meeting concluded just before noon. It had lasted nearly two hours. As Haldeman left the Oval Office, his assistant Larry Higby noticed a worried look on his face.

'What's the problem, Bob?' he asked.

Haldeman sat down at his desk, folded his hands behind his head, and looked up at the ceiling. He thought for a moment.

'Nothing new,' he said. 'Except the old man himself. I've never seen him this way.'

'What do you mean?' pressed Higby.

'He's acting strangely,' replied Haldeman. 'Something is really bugging him.'[17]

The next morning, Nixon walked over to the Executive Office Building. He joined a briefing on foreign and domestic policy, and then went to his private office. A few minutes later, Haldeman joined him. Both men had been reflecting overnight on the conversation with Dean.

Nixon mused over the cancer image. It suggested that the problem could be removed. Dean had implied that the time had come to sack people.

'The question is whether we really can,' reflected the president.

Haldeman wasn't sure. 'You go in,' he observed, 'and cut out all of what you think is cancerous and discover that it wasn't malignant.' 'There is nobody in the White House that's fireable,' he added.[18]

That afternoon, Nixon called another meeting. Dean and Haldeman were present. They were joined by Ehrlichman and John Mitchell, chair of the Committee to Re-Elect the President. Discussion lasted for almost two hours. Nixon chewed over the options once more.

Gradually, the group talked themselves round. The choices as Dean had framed them seemed too stark. Perhaps there was a middle way. The White House could offer to cooperate with the Ervin Committee, but then negotiate over how staff members might testify without breaking executive privilege.

'Let it hang out, so to speak?' asked Nixon.

'Well, it isn't really that – ' responded Dean.

'It's a limited hangout,' interjected Haldeman.

'It's a limited hangout,' agreed Dean.

'It's a modified limited hangout,' added Ehrlichman.

At the end, Nixon asked for a private word with Mitchell. His position was particularly exposed. His deputy, Jeb Magruder, appeared to be cooperating with the FBI investigation. The trail might soon lead to Mitchell himself.

Nixon was clear. He drew a contrast with Eisenhower, who had sacked his chief of staff, Sherman Adams, over accepting official gifts. Nixon wanted to protect his people. But they also had to protect themselves. 'I don't give a shit what happens,' he told Mitchell. 'I want you all to stonewall it, let them plead the Fifth Amendment, cover up, or anything else, if it'll save it – save the plan.'

The president went on. 'Up to this point the whole theory has been containment, as you know, John.'

'Yeah,' replied Mitchell.

'And now we're shifting,' explained Nixon. 'We're going to protect our people, if we can.'[19]

The code message was simple. The caller on the phone would tell journalist Robert Kaiser that he had forgotten his briefcase. It would be the signal that the meeting was on.

Kaiser had recently arrived in Moscow as correspondent for *The Washington Post*. He was joined by his colleague Hedrick Smith, who worked for *The New York Times*. Alexander Solzhenitsyn had agreed to give his first major interview with Western newspapers to the two men. It was a major scoop.

The arrangements were made through an intermediary, Zhores Medvedyev. The venue would be Alya's flat, on Kozitsky Lane in central Moscow. One evening a few days beforehand, Medvedyev showed the address to the two Americans from outside, and passed on final instructions. They should wear old clothes, to avoid drawing attention to themselves, and could bring their cameras and recording equipment, but wrapped up in copies of *Pravda* newspaper and a string bag, of the kind used by Muscovites for grocery shopping. Smith and Kaiser rehearsed what questions to ask their interviewee while skating at an outdoor ice rink, so as to avoid eavesdropping microphones.

The two men arrived at the flat just after noon, on 30 March. Solzhenitsyn himself answered the door, opening it a few inches while he surveyed the Americans. 'His eyes, dark and penetrating, peered out intently,' recalled Smith, 'searching, checking, questioning.'

Silently, the writer let them in. Alya was there, along with their 15-month-old son Ermolai. He led the guests through into his study, where the curtains were drawn. Smith had expected to be overawed by meeting such a literary giant, but Solzhenitsyn was warm and engaging. His face, thought the American, was like 'a well-worn table, its scratches, nicks and scars visible through a verneer'. Kaiser was transfixed by their host's eyes. He wondered if he had ever seen such a brilliant, dark shade of blue before.

Smith and Kaiser had come from the hard-hitting world of American journalism, with publications that had been at the heart of the Pentagon Papers affair the previous year. They were expecting the opportunity to question Solzhentisyn freely.

But the writer had very different ideas. He had already prepared a script for the interview, with both questions and answers, which he passed across to the two men, with a copy for each. For a moment, they were dumbfounded.

'This is outrageous,' the *New York Times* correspondent muttered. He even wondered if they should walk out.

'Let's read it first,' his colleague replied.

Solzhenitsyn had indeed been making plans. Over the previous year, the author had been in indirect contact with Karl Ragnar Gierow, secretary of the Nobel Prize Foundation, about holding a presentation of his prize in Moscow. Initially he had hoped that it might be possible to stage an award ceremony at the Swedish embassy, but the ambassador was wary about giving the dissident what would amount to a political platform. Instead, Solzhenitsyn hit on the alternative of an informal gathering at Alya's flat, with Gierow visiting Moscow to present the award in person. He had set a date, for mid-April, and sent out invitations to his friends, complete with instructions on how to enter the apartment block through different entrances, so as to avoid detection by the KGB. The interview with the *Post* and the *Times* would, he hoped, set the scene ahead of the event.

The Americans realized that they were dealing with a man of strong will. Solzhentisyn was, recalled Kaiser, 'one of those dominating human personalities that fill rooms'. And the chance to publish an exclusive interview was hard to pass over, despite the restrictions which Solzhenitsyn was seeking to impose. After a few minutes, the Americans agreed a compromise. They would read through the prepared text, and draw on the material, while asking some questions of their own. At Solzhenitsyn's insistence, they would also see whether other publications might consent to publish the text in full.

Smith and Kaiser thumbed through the text, checking at points with Alya, who had joined the group to help smooth over the initial tension. They had only been in the Soviet Union for a few months, and stumbled over the dense Russian script. But nonetheless they could see that it was a powerful cry to the outside world.

'You western people can't imagine my situation,' Solzhenitsyn had written. 'A kind of forbidden, contaminated zone had been created around me and my family.' He detailed the methods that the KGB used to disrupt his life, with surveillance teams and monitoring phone calls. It must, the writer surmised, add up to a sizeable operation, consuming time and staff which could be spent on better purposes.

'The Plan,' he concluded, 'consists of driving me out of this life or out of the country, tossing me into a ditch or sending me to Siberia, or having me dissolve in an alien fog.'[20]

For the Politburo, it wasn't quite that simple. On the same day that Solzhenitsyn met with the American journalists, Brezhnev was chairing a meeting of the group in the Kremlin. The KGB had been following Solzhenitsyn's plans for an award ceremony. Chairman Yuri Andropov had circulated a report in advance, concluding that the writer was 'a political opponent of the Soviet state', and recommending exile from the USSR.[21]

Brezhnev spoke first. He recalled the long struggle, through which the Soviet Union had risen to be a superpower over the last fifty years. 'We need to make it clear,' he declared, 'in a tangible way that we will not allow these people, the scum of human society, to poison our atmosphere.' The actions of Solzhentisyn and other dissidents risked stirring nationalist tensions, which could tear the USSR apart. Brezhnev counted Andropov among his closest colleagues. The KGB chief would call on him almost every day in the Kremlin, bringing with him a bulging file of secret information.[22] But on this occasion Brezhnev held back from commenting specifically on the proposal for exile in Andropov's report, instead inviting his colleagues to give their views.

Mikhail Suslov weighed in. He had served in the Kremlin since the 1940s, when he led the Communist Information Bureau (Cominform) and overseen expulsion of Yugoslavia from the Soviet bloc over ideological differences. 'An imperious man,' recalled one contemporary, 'whose gray-blue eyes peered through thick-lensed glasses . . . his meticulousness in doctrinal matters matched an ascetic personality.'[23]

Solzhenitsyn was, Suslov argued, a problem the Politburo had inherited from Krushchev. The previous general secretary had 'raised up [the writer] and praised him to the skies'. It was time to take action. But, mused Suslov, that need not involve exile. The key was to get him out of Moscow.

Nikolai Podgorny agreed. 'Solzhenitsyn is a hostile person, and should not be in Moscow. But I think he should not be sent out of the country.'

He was followed by Alexei Kosygin, who spoke in support. 'The main thing, of course,' commented the premier, 'is not a punitive policy, but rather a political-educational approach . . . Comrade Andropov himself should decide how to handle these people in accordance with our available laws.'

'If he resolves it wrongly,' Kosygin added, 'then we will correct him.'

Brezhnev closed the discussion. Andropov and Podgorny were tasked with removing Solzhentisyn from Moscow, in a way that accorded with Soviet law.[24]

Back in Alya's flat, the interview with Kaiser and Smith was coming to a close. It had taken four hours. Solzhenitsyn and his family posed for photos. With Alya and Ermolai, the writer beamed a smile. But when the Americans came to take his picture without the others, his expression changed.

'It's time to be serious,' said Solzhentisyn, his face hardening into a solemn look.[25]

The White House plan wasn't working.

Pressure was mounting on John Dean. On 22 March, the same day that Nixon and his advisers agreed to a strategy of guarded cooperation with the Ervin Committee, FBI nominee Gray had testified to the Senate Justice Committee against Dean. The presidential counsel had, he said, 'probably lied' in evidence that he gave to the FBI. Mitchell, Magruder and Dean all looked vulnerable. Under pressure, they might be tempted to tell what they knew in return for clemency. In early April, Nixon spent time away from Washington, in Key Biscayne, then San Clemente in Florida. But Watergate continued to pursue him. It had, he realized, assumed the position in the nation's political scene previously occupied by Vietnam.

Returning to the capital, the president hatched a new plan. He agreed with Ehrlichman and Haldeman that they would persuade Mitchell and Magruder to accept responsibility for the affair. The White House would present itself as stepping in to clean up the situation created by the Committee to Re-Elect the President. But Mitchell wasn't prepared to go along. Instead, he was tempted to shift blame towards the White House. 'He is an innocent man in his heart,' reported Ehrlichman to the president, 'and in his mind, and he does not intend to move off that position.'[26]

Talk turned to resignations. Dean now seemed a liability. Nixon wanted him to go. But the presidential counsel was not prepared to resign without Haldeman and Ehrlichman doing the same. And Dean knew enough for his testimony to cause real damage, if he chose to use it. There was, speech-writer Pat Buchanan warned Nixon, a 'Titanic mentality' around the White House. Staff would line up late each evening to buy the first overnight edition of *The Washington Post*, in which investigative reporters Bob Woodward and Carl Bernstein were publishing a steady stream of stories about the affair.[27] On Friday 27 April, the president flew down to Mississippi aboard *Spirit of '76* with John Stennis, a Democrat senator from the state. They were old friends, and talked in private on the flight.

'We say in our country that the rain falls on the just and the unjust,' warned Stennis. 'Time is running out.'[28]

Ehrlichman was aboard the same flight. He wandered forward to the cockpit, to see the view. As he watched the pilot, he felt a momentary impulse to end it all. It would, he mused, be easy enough to throw himself onto the controls. Within a minute or two, the plane would crash, and all their troubles would be over.

The presidential aide looked on for another moment, then turned round and walked back up the aisle to his seat.[29]

Nixon could feel the moment had come. That night, he flew back to Camp David. In the morning, fog had settled over the presidential retreat. He took breakfast, and worked for a while. Then he walked to the living room. Tricia was sitting there, in front of a blazing fire. She had travelled up that morning from Washington to see her father.

Tricia explained. The previous evening, she had been at the White House with Julie, Pat and brother-in-law David. They were all agreed that Haldeman must go. The family had become distrustful of the presidential aide, who they feared was manipulating his staff behind Nixon's back. But now they had set such feelings to one side. For Nixon's own sake, it was clear that his closest aides should resign.

Tears welled in Tricia's eyes as she explained. 'We also want you to know that we have complete confidence in you,' she added. 'If you decide not to take our advice, we will understand.'[30]

Deep in his subconscious, Nixon had been coming to the same conclusion. The attempt to put a firewall between his advisers had not worked. It was too difficult to distinguish who had known what, and when. And he could never be sure that those who might admit guilt would not turn on others. His only defence was to make a clean sweep.

Ziegler called Haldeman. The president wanted to see him, at Camp David. The chief of staff passed on the same instruction to John Ehrlichman.

The two men flew up together in a helicopter. Below them, the spring greenery was breaking through in the Maryland countryside. When they arrived, they were driven in a Navy vehicle, up to the encampment. The president's quarters were in Aspen Lodge. Haldeman entered first, while Ehrlichman waited outside.

Nixon reached out to shake Haldeman's hand. They had worked together for more than a decade, with the chief of staff only a buzzer's call away from his boss. But this was the first time Haldeman could recall shaking hands during his service. Haldeman thought his boss looked in bad shape. He was wearing a checked sports jacket, and his eyes were red.

A large window looked out on the pine woods that surrounded the retreat. Nixon motioned Haldeman over, to admire the view. The two men wandered out onto the flag-stoned terrace. They inspected the tulips, sprouting with new growth.

Back inside, Nixon started to talk. He was not, he explained, comfortable talking about religion. But each night since entering the White House he had kneeled to pray. He asked for guidance, and that the Almighty might help those in his administration going through hard times. A look of surprise crossed Haldeman's face as he listened.

Nixon broke the news. He added that he, too, might have to resign at some point. Haldeman was calm. He didn't agree with the decision, but he accepted it. Ehrlichman and he were expendable. The president must stay on to do his job.

Emotion washed over Nixon. He talked about Julie, and his conversation with her the previous day. Haldeman and Ehrlichman were, he said, the best men that he knew.

The chief of staff departed. A few minutes later, Ehrlichman entered. He thought the president seemed drawn, smaller. Nixon started to tell the same story that he had told Haldeman, about praying at night. Then he began to cry. Ehrlichman put an arm round his boss. 'Don't talk that way,' he said. 'Don't think that way.'

They walked out onto the terrace, into the fresh air.

'You'll have to resign,' Nixon said.

Ehrlichman nodded. He and Haldeman had served Nixon for more than a decade, since the campaign against Kennedy in 1960. They had seen him defeated, then rebuild and return to win the White House in 1968. They were architects of the crushing victory over McGovern the previous year. And now it was all over.

It felt, Nixon said, like cutting off his own arms. He offered money. His friend Bebe Rebozo could help with legal fees.

Ehrlichman shook his head. He was struggling to talk.

'Just explain this to my kids, will you?' he said, his voice tight with emotion. 'Tell them why you had to do this.'

'You have always been the conscience of my administration,' replied Nixon.

'If I was the conscience,' retorted Ehrlichman, 'then I haven't been very effective.'

He turned, and sharply walked away. As he did so, he dabbed at his eyes with a handkerchief.[31]

General Al Haig was enjoying a dinner at the officers' club in Fort Benning, Georgia. The club officer walked over with a message. The president was on the phone, and wanted to speak.

The general could guess what it was about. Two days before, Nixon had announced the resignations of Haldeman, Ehrlichman and Dean, in a televised broadcast, along with Attorney General Richard Kleindeinst. The president was looking for new people to replace them.

Haig had enjoyed the months since he left the White House. It was good to be back among the military, with friends and in a community that he knew well. His wife Pat was herself the daughter of a soldier, and enjoyed the military life. As Vice Chief of the Army, Haig was entitled to an elegant house. Pat had just finished decorating it.

The call had come through to the club office. Haig picked up the phone. It was Haldeman on the line, not Nixon.

'Al, I'm with the president now,' explained the former aide. 'He has asked me to tell you that he wants you to be his chief of staff in the White House.'

Haig paused for a moment. Then he spoke. If the president wanted him, he would do it. But he was not the right man for the job. It didn't require a soldier.

'Please ask the president to reconsider this,' he concluded.

'All right,' replied Haldeman. The call was over.

Haig returned to the dinner. A few minutes later, he was called again. Haldeman was once more on the line.

'Al, I've told the president what you told me,' Haldeman explained. 'He understands your reservations, but he wants you to do this.' It was an order.

'Then of course I must do it,' replied Haig.

The next morning, Haig took a plane from Fort Benning. It was a White House executive jet. The aircraft flew over Washington, giving a glimpse of the streets and public buildings of the capital city. It landed at Andrews Air Force Base.

Haig spent the morning at the Pentagon, breaking the news to his colleagues. In the afternoon, he was driven over to the White House. In the West Wing, FBI agents were stationed outside the rooms previously used by Haldeman, Ehrlichman and Dean. It was, Haig later learned, a first show of authority by the new attorney general, Elliot Richardson.

Haig walked into the Oval Office. Nixon seemed subdued. The general sensed anger and melancholy, but also determination. As Haig settled into the chair to the left of the president's desk, where Haldeman used to sit, a tinge of sadness crept through him. This was a different presidency to that which he had left just three months ago.[32]

General Secretary Leonid Brezhnev explained. A clean kill required a shot direct into the back of the neck. Striking the heart was not sufficient. The animal could charge for another 200 yards, even in its death throes.[33]

It was late afternoon, in early May. Dusk was just starting to draw in. The Soviet leader sat in a hunting tower, surrounded by pine woods. It was a box-shaped structure, two floors in height. A staircase with banisters stood on one side, leading to a small room with walls and roof built from planks of pine. There was a rough bench, while narrow horizontal windows looked out on the surrounding woodland. Foresters in green uniforms had laid bait, of grain and potatoes.

There were three men in the cramped hide. Brezhnev was joined by his interpreter, Viktor Sukhodrev, and by Henry Kissinger, national security adviser to President Nixon. The American wore a dark green hunting jacket, provided by his Soviet hosts, while Brezhnev was dressed in a simple smock, buttoned to the collar, with breast pockets on either side of his chest. When Dobrynin suggested that they looked like partisans in the Second World War, Brezhnev quipped back 'more like gangsters!' In contrast, Sukhodrev wore a quilted country coat, which along with his flawless English made him seem more Western than Soviet.[34] Outside, all was still. They waited.

Kissinger was in Moscow to prepare a summit. A year on from Nixon's visit, it was Brezhnev's turn to come to Washington. The trip was scheduled for late June. As a mark of personal warmth, the general secretary hosted preliminary talks at his country retreat, in Zavidovo, ninety miles north-east of Moscow. It was a great honour. The American party were told that the only foreign guests to visit before them were Marshal Tito of Yugoslavia and President Kekkonen of Finland. They found an encampment of chalets deep in the pine woods, heavy and oversized. Anatoly Chernyaev, who had come to know the place well from planning sessions with Brezhnev's inner team, called the architecture 'Soviet collective farm'.[35] On the first evening, the host cheerfully asked how much such a home would cost in the United States. When Kissinger suggested $400,000, the Soviet leader's face fell. Assistant Hal Sonnenfeldt hastily suggested that the price tag might be closer to $2 million. The Soviet leader looked more reassured.

The Americans arrived with a problem. At the Moscow Summit, the previous May, both countries had committed themselves to strengthen economic ties. A deal had been reached that autumn, settling outstanding debt from the Soviet Union over Lend-Lease aid provided by the United States during the Second World War. The next stage was a trade agreement between the two countries, in which America would extend the same terms, known at Most Favoured Nation (MFN), as with other, capitalist trading partners.

Domestic pressures against such a deal were mounting. Following the Israeli victory in the Six Day War, in 1967, increasing numbers of Soviet Jews applied for emigration to the country. Israel's position in the Middle East was more secure, and she occupied territory previously held by Jordan on the West Bank and Jerusalem. Others chose to move to the United States. Numbers increased rapidly. In 1968, just 231 Soviet Jews were granted exit visas. By the early 1970s, the numbers were well into the thousands.

For the Soviet leadership, this emigration was a new problem. Historically, Jews had suffered persecution under the Russian Empire, and in the Soviet era. This exodus helped to solve the problem. But it was also a challenge to the state. If Jews were able to leave the communist bloc and create a new life in the West, others would want the same opportunity. In August 1972, the Kremlin introduced an 'education tax' on émigrés. This imposed a charge on those who had attended universities, supposedly as reimbursement for the investment provided by the state. The rate was prohibitive, at up to twenty times an annual salary. It was designed to target Jews, who were more likely to have received tertiary education.

In the United States, domestic critics of Nixon's détente policy reacted in protest. On the left, liberals argued that it showed engagement with the Soviet Union had yielded no progress on human rights, while on the right conservatives argued that the Kremlin was still bent on confrontation with the West. Democrat Henry 'Scoop' Jackson, the hawkish senator from Washington State who had opposed Nixon's deal on SALT and the Anti-Ballistic Missile treaty, tabled an amendment opposing grant of MFN status to countries which restricted emigration. He assembled bipartisan support within the Senate, with almost three quarters of senators from both sides of the aisle.

Nixon and Kissinger had hoped to defuse the issue through private diplomacy. The Soviet Union had suffered a poor harvest, and needed the economic boost which trade with the United States could bring. In April, Soviet ambassador Anatoly Dobrynin passed on a pledge from the Kremlin leadership to remove the education tax. But Watergate had infected the mood in Washington. For Jackson and his supporters, this was not enough. They wanted the administration to go further, and secure a commitment that emigration would be unrestricted.

Kissinger arrived in Moscow with little to give. Early negotiations on a second SALT agreement had not made much headway. In the absence of progress on trade or arms reduction, the Americans settled for a watered-down version of an agreement proposed by the Soviets, on mutual commitments to reduce the threat of nuclear war. In the negotiating sessions at Zavidovo, Kissinger worked through the text with Brezhnev, trading jokes as they did so. The delegations sat around a rectangular table in Brezhnev's study, with pencils laid out in glasses and ashtrays for the host and Sukhodrev, who also smoked. The outcome, he recalled, was 'like a Russian matryoshka doll that has progressively smaller models nested inside each other'.[36] In the breaks between negotiations, the Americans remained wary about talking among themselves within range of Soviet listening devices. They resorted to using the balcony outside Brezhnev's own study.[37]

With the negotiations complete, Brezhnev had adjourned for a spell of boar hunting. He and Kissinger were now alone, with only Sukhodrev to interpret. Sonnenfeldt had gone to a separate hunting tower, with Foreign Minister Andrei Gromyko. The latter was himself not a huntsman, but had taken up the sport as a way of spending time with Brezhnev.[38]

As dusk fell, the boars approached. Kissinger was struck by the grace of their movements. Overcome by hunger, they edged towards the bait which had been laid out within easy range of the hide. A mother came first, then looked around as if giving a signal to her offspring to follow.

Brezhnev had explained to his guest beforehand that he did not hunt younger animals, but rather confined himself to the older males. As the party watched, one larger animal lingered back, watching from behind the trees. Brezhnev looked through the telescopic sight of his rifle, and pulled the trigger. The range was no more than fifteen yards. Seated behind, Sukhodrev felt that it amounted to murder. From his neighbouring hide, Sonnenfeldt also loosed off a shot, but misjudged the recoil from his hunting rifle, and landed a black eye.

As dark edged in, the general secretary took his guest to a second hide. It was deeper into the woods. Sukhodrev produced dinner from a bag, with gherkins, cheese, sausage and a bottle of Stolichnaya vodka. As they waited for another herd of boar to appear, Brezhnev talked.

It had been a good year for the Soviet leader. Watching from his post at the Central Committee, aide Anatoly Chernyaev noticed the change. The decision to press ahead with inviting Nixon to Moscow the previous summer had been driven by Brezhnev personally, and the subsequent success of the summit had given him confidence. At the Central Committee plenum the previous month, Brezhnev had consolidated his personal authority, as the pre-eminent leader in the Kremlin. In the run-up, Chernyaev and diplomatic adviser Aleksandrov-Agentov had weighed up whether the moment was indeed right to assert his position, and eclipse the triumvirate with Podgorny and Kosygin which had operated since the overthrow of Krushchev in 1964. They only realized the gamble had paid of when Mikhail Suslov, chief ideologue among the Politburo, used his own speech at the plenum to give full backing to Brezhnev.[39]

But deeper currents were at work. Soviet society remained constrained, frustrated by the lack of choice and consumer goods. The 'familiar, imposed way of life', as Chernyaev put it, no longer satisfied a new generation emerging from the years of recovery after the Second World War. 'There's nothing in the shops for ordinary people,' a secretary grumbled to him at work. 'No milk, no meat'.[40] But within the Soviet ruling class suspicion of the West and hostility to change ran deep. Arbatov called it a 'revolutionary inferiority complex'.[41] Shielded behind the privileges of private cars, superior food allowances and country dachas, the bureaucrats and generals were frozen in an outdated view of the outside world.

As they sat in the hunting tower, Brezhnev continued to talk with Kissinger. The presidential adviser fancied that he could discern different sides to the Soviet leader's personality, shifting between menace and sentimentality.

Brezhnev spoke darkly of China. His brother had worked there as a young man, before the split between Mao and Krushchev, at the start of 1960s. The Chinese were, he argued, treacherous, even cannibals. If they developed a nuclear capability on the same scale as the Soviet Union or the United States, the whole world would be at risk.

As they talked, wild boar once more started to edge towards the piles of bait. Brezhnev let off a couple of shots. But it was too dark and he missed. Kissinger was silently relieved. Hunting was not his thing.

Sentimentality took over. Brezhnev turned to talk of his war service, and his wife, Victoria Petrovna. After four years apart, they were reunited following defeat of Germany in the summer of 1945. Brezhnev described how he took part in the victory parade through Red Square, his major general's uniform soaked in a downpour of rain. His aides had often heard the story when their boss got tipsy, including how he had ended up in a restaurant with a fellow comrade later that night, and shot their pistols at the ceiling in celebration. When Stalin heard of the escapade, he supposedly commented 'for heroes – it's allowed!'[42]

Kissinger looked across at his conversation partner. His speech had become more halting, gentle. The menace had gone. Brezhnev was an old man, in search of peace.[43]

The returning prisoners of war had given Nixon a lift. Amid the darkening clouds of Watergate, the scenes of proud men returning unbowed from captivity had inspired him.

Colonel John Flynn was the senior ranking officer in Hanoi. He was an aviator, who first flew P-51 Mustang fighter planes during the Second World War. He had called on the president in early April, at the White House. With the veteran, Nixon felt able to open up, and talk about the pressures of his first term, as he sought to bring the Vietnam War to an honourable close. On one campaign stop, a 14-year-old girl had raised her middle figure as an insult to the president. It had left him shaken, wondering what the future had in store for America.[44]

Nixon and his wife Pat were determined to honour the returning prisoners in style. They decided to host a dinner at the White House. With wives and girlfriends invited as well, the gathering would include more than a thousand people. None of the public rooms were large enough to accommodate them. Pat oversaw preparations, with a huge marquee erected on the South Lawn. Food was prepared in the Pentagon kitchens, including strawberry mousse for dessert, made in huge blending machines. Individual place cards were written for each of 126 tables.

As the guests assembled, they wandered around the White House. Pat was determined that the presidential home should be open to the veterans. Many took souvenir photos of one another, and of their wives.

After dinner, Nixon offered a toast. He wanted, he said, to honour the wives. They were the true 'First Ladies of America'.

Colonel Flynn offered a reply, on behalf of the former prisoners. They were, he said, not a unique group of men. Rather, they were a 'random selection of fate', proud to be citizens of the United States. He presented Nixon with a plaque.

'Our leader,' it read. 'Our comrade – Richard the Lion-Hearted.'

Afterwards, a series of celebrities offered entertainment. Entertainer Bob Hope spoke first, then John Wayne, the actor and star of westerns. 'I'll ride into the sunset with you anytime,' he told his audience.

At the end of the programme, Nixon introduced Irving Berlin onto the stage. The composer and singer had just passed his eighty-fifth birthday. He had been too infirm to join dinner earlier in the evening, but now he was determined to play his part. Berlin burst into the song, 'God Bless America, My Home Sweet Home'. His voice was still firm and strong. The former prisoners wept and sang along with him.

Richard and Pat Nixon retired just after midnight. The president slipped away to the Lincoln Sitting Room, to be alone.

Half an hour later, the phone rang in Julie and David's room. It was Nixon, and he wanted to talk with his daughter.

She walked downstairs. Tricia was already there, while their father was smoking a pipe, and gazing at the fire. It was the only light in the room. He seemed drained. The evening had been a joyous occasion, and Nixon had felt a lift, with the satisfaction that in bringing peace his actions had also brought the men home. But now, alone, Watergate returned to his mind. He turned, and looked at his daughters.

'Do you think I should resign?' asked the president.[45]

<hr />

Notes

1 Kissinger (1979), 1462–3.
2 Nixon (1978), 746–7.
3 Eisenhower (1986), 541–2.
4 Nixon (1978), 765.
5 Kissinger (1979), 1471.
6 www.pbs.org/newshour/rundown/lbjs–last–interview/.
7 Price (1977), 68–9; Nixon (1978), 753–4.
8 Nixon (1978), 860–1.
9 Perlstein (2014), 2–3.
10 Dole interview with Naftali, 4 March 2008, p. 6.
11 'A POW Remembered and Found' by Patricia Brennan, *The Washington Post*, 24 December 2000; agatheringofeagles.com .
12 Perlstein (2014), 16.
13 Brinkley and Nichter (2015), 277.
14 Haldeman (1978), 234.
15 Ehrlichman (1982), 337.
16 Brinkley and Nichter (2015), 300–1. See also Nixon (1978), 791–9; Haldeman (1978), 237–40; Haldeman (1994), 591–2; Dean (2014), 308–36.
17 Haldeman (1978), 239–40; Dean interview with Naftali, 30 July 2007, p. 7.
18 Dean (2014), 339.
19 Brinkley and Nichter (2015), 338–71; Nixon (1978), 801–2; Haldeman (1994), 592–4; Dean (2014), 340–1; Ehrlichman (1982), 345.
20 Scammel (1986), 758–60; Solzhentisyn (1975), 329, 503–14; Smith (1977), 506–15; Kaiser (1976), 396–401.
21 Scammel (1995) doc. 67, p. 194–8.
22 Aleksandrov-Agentov (1995), 265.
23 Shevchenko (1985), 219–20. See also description in Aleksandrov-Agentov (1995), 261–3.
24 Scammel (1995) docs 68–9, p. 199–212.
25 Quoted in Scammel (1986), 760.
26 Brinkley and Nichter (2015), 427.

27 Buchanan (2017), 311.
28 Nixon (1978), 844.
29 Ehrlichman (1982), 389.
30 Nixon (1978), 845–6; Eisenhower (1986), 561–2.
31 Nixon (1978), 847–8; Ehrlichman (1982), 389–91; Haldeman (1994), 671–3; Haldeman (1978), 287–96; Price interview, 4 April 2007, p. 85.
32 Haig (1992), 332–6; Nixon (1978), 856–7; Haig interview with Brinkley and Naftali, 30 November 2006, p. 30.
33 FRUS 1969–76 Vol. XV, item 105, p. 368–9.
34 Price interview, 4 April 2007, p. 30; Vavilov (2016), 108–9.
35 Chernyaev (1995), 257–8.
36 Kissinger (1982), 281.
37 Kissinger (1982), 231; Vavilov (2016), 98–108.
38 Shevchenko (1985), 149.
39 Chernyaev (1995), 292–6.
40 Chernyaev diary 1973, p. 41; Chernyaev (1995), 327.
41 Arbatov (1992), 189.
42 Chernyaev (1995), 262.
43 Kissinger (1982), 232–4; Sukhodrev (1999), 291–6.
44 Brinkley and Nichter (2015), 400–3.
45 Eisenhower (1986), 564–9; Nixon (1978), 864–9; Ball interview with Naftali, 25 June 2007, p. 39.

Chapter 9

MONSTER RISING
(July–December 1973)

Leonid Brezhnev was excited. The Soviet leader had never visited the United States before, and now he was being feted by the superpower as an equal.

The official Ilyushin 76 which carried the general secretary arrived at Andrews Air Force Base on Saturday 16 June. Ambassador Anatoly Dobrynin was there to greet him, along with Secretary of State Bill Rogers.

Dobrynin had spent the previous weeks preparing the official programme with the White House. The Soviets had been impressed by the arrangements for secure communication which Nixon brought on his own visit to Moscow, the previous year, and were concerned to ensure that Brezhnev had equivalent provision. An advance party of Soviet technicians set up a network of radiotelephone links at different points, under the code name '*vizit*'. One was located in the White House itself. Another line ran to Dobrynin in the Soviet embassy. During the week before the visit, Brezhnev and his colleagues took to calling the ambassador on the slightest pretext, so as to check that the line was working. With an eight-hour time difference, calls arrived throughout the night. Deprived of sleep, Dobrynin was losing his patience with the new system.[1]

From Andrews, Brezhnev flew to Camp David. He spent two days at the retreat, recuperating from jet lag. It reminded him of his own hunting lodge at Zavidovo, where he had hosted Kissinger the previous month. The cabins were named after types of tree. Brezhnev lodged in Cornel, while Gromyko was in Birch, and his assistant Georgy Kornienko in Oak. The guests were presented with windcheater jackets, embroidered with their names and the presidential seal. When Nixon phoned to check that all was well, the Soviet leader was effusive. 'Thank you, thank you,' he repeated several times, in English.[2]

The formal welcome ceremony took place on Monday 18 June, at the White House. Brezhnev drew up outside the South Portico in his official limousine. The sun was shining. An honour guard was drawn up on the South Grounds, from the different services of the US military. They played the Star Spangled Banner, and the Soviet anthem. 'Unbreakable Union of Free Republics / Eternal Pride of Great Russia' rang the stirring lines, resounding across the American onlookers. The two leaders watched from a platform. They embraced, arms locked together as they looked out over the crowd. Many held Soviet and American flags, waving back at them.

After the national anthems, Nixon and Brezhnev walked over to inspect the guard. The Soviet could barely contain his delight. He bounded over to the crowd. As Nixon watched him shake hands with the spectators, he thought his counterpart would make a good American politician. He was a natural showman.

The ceremony had been planned with precision timing. Brezhnev's walkabout was not foreseen. As the Soviet leader worked the crowd, the White House chief of protocol nervously checked his watch.

'See,' said Brezhnev as he and Nixon walked back to the White House together, a full half-hour after the planned time. 'We're already making progress!'

Dobrynin felt a moment of thrill. The Soviet Union had arrived in Washington.[3]

Once inside, Nixon led Brezhnev to the Oval Office. They were accompanied by the Soviet interpreter, Viktor Sukhodrev. A pack of press photographers entered for a few minutes, in what White House schedulers called a 'photo opportunity'. Afterwards, the president and general secretary were alone, with just Sukhodrev as a bridge between them.

To break the ice, Brezhnev proudly showed Nixon his new cigarette box. The Soviet leader was trying to cut back on smoking. The box was locked, with a timer mechanism which only released every forty-five minutes. Inside was his favourite brand of Novost cigarettes made in the Soviet Union.

The two men began to talk. They swapped news of their families. Brezhnev had hoped to bring his wife or his son on the trip. But his wife had fallen ill, and their grandson was taking entrance exams for Moscow University. The family had decided to stay at home.

Conversation turned to relations between their two countries.

'If we decided to work together,' said Nixon, 'we can change the world.'

Brezhnev agreed. The personal relationship between them was crucial. He hoped that Nixon could visit the Soviet Union again, in 1974, and that they could maintain a rhythm of annual visits beyond that. The Politburo fully supported such an invitation.

Some people, Brezhnev added, thought that the two superpowers wanted to dominate the world. But that was not the case. The United States and Soviet Union could use their strength to play a constructive role.

'We should endeavour to look far ahead,' he concluded. 'Because if we can look far ahead, we can really create a basis of stable relationships and peace.'[4]

The private session was over. The accompanying delegations entered, with Foreign Minister Andrei Gromyko, Ambassador Anatoly Dobrynin, Secretary of State Bill Rogers and Henry Kissinger, the national security adviser. They had been waiting for a full hour outside, wondering what was going on. The schedule was falling even further behind. The Americans were getting twitchy, and so was Gromyko. As the delegations entered the Oval Office, he joked nervously that the two leaders had probably already settled everything between themselves.

Brezhnev seemed to pick up on the mood. He was wearing two watches, one set to Moscow time, the other to Washington. During the meeting, he kept checking his wrist. But the time difference threw him. Was Moscow ahead, or behind? Discreetly, Dobrynin and Gromyko corrected their boss.

'Are you looking at your watch?' asked Brezhnev at one point, glancing at Rogers. As the meeting stretched on into the afternoon, the Americans were starting to feel hungry.

'No,' replied Rogers. 'I was fascinated by your remarks.'

'Well then, Kissinger was looking at his watch,' shot back the Soviet leader.

'I was just sitting here minding my own business,' responded the presidential adviser.

'We have now put an end to old history,' declared Brezhnev to the group. 'And now we have made a start to new history. That is why this meeting is so important.'[5]

Eventually, the meeting concluded at half-past three. 'It is 10 p.m. in Moscow,' explained Nixon, 'and it is time to go to bed.' The American delegation escorted their Soviet guests out to the waiting convoy of limousines. Then they hurried back inside, for a late lunch in the White House mess.

From Washington, the party flew on to California. Nixon hosted the visitors at his home in San Clemente, Casa Pacifica. Both delegations travelled together on *Spirit of '76*. The Soviets pocketed complimentary items as souvenirs, including matchboxes decorated with the presidential seal. En route, the plane made a low pass over the Grand Canyon. It was just before nine o'clock, with the morning light playing on the rock formations below. Brezhnev was entranced. He had seen the view in westerns.[6]

Casa Pacifica was small compared to the White House. Nixon showed his guests around the house and gardens. He was visibly proud, especially of the view down to the Pacific. The modest, intimate surroundings created a different atmosphere to the formality of the White House, and even to Camp David.

Brezhnev was assigned to the bedroom used by Julie. It was decorated in blue and pink wallpaper, with a motif of lavender flowers and white wicker furniture. The Soviet advance team had even rigged up one of the secure phone lines to Moscow, much to Brezhnev's delight. Pat Nixon occupied a room across the hallway, while interpreter Viktor Sukhodrev was housed in the gardener's quarters. On a nearby Coast Guard base, a trailer housed air stewardesses from Brezhnev's own official plane. During his stay, the First Lady became aware of comings and goings, as this travelling entourage paid visits to the general secretary's room. Away from his wife and family, Brezhnev seemed to be enjoying the freedom provided by America.[7]

That evening, Nixon hosted a poolside reception for his guests. A mariachi band provided music. California governor Ronald Reagan was there, along with figures from Hollywood. Singer Frank Sinatra and actor Clint Eastwood both attended. So did various actresses, including Jill St John, who had played opposite Sean Connery in the James Bond film *Diamonds are Forever*, and was Henry Kissinger's date for the evening. As she shook hands in the greeting line with Brezhnev and Nixon, interpreter Andrei Vavilov whispered an explanation in the former's ear.

'Well, well, Henry,' murmured the general secretary in a heavy accent, and gave his host a nudge.

'You can't beat Henry,' replied Nixon.

Gromyko was more intrigued by Reagan. He offered a warm handshake in the greeting line. The governor, explained another guest quietly, had ambitions to make the move to Washington.[8]

The guests retired for dinner, and then for bed. But afterwards, at half-past ten, Nixon heard a knock on his door. It was a message from Kissinger. Brezhnev wanted to talk.

The president welcomed the Soviet leader in his upstairs study. It was a small tower room, overlooking the Pacific. Dobrynin, Gromyko and Kissinger joined them, along with Sukhodrev.

'I could not sleep,' explained Brezhnev, grinning. In California, the time difference with Moscow was now ten hours.

Wearily, Nixon invited his guest to talk.

The previous year, in Moscow, Brezhnev had used a late meeting at his dacha outside town to berate his guests over Vietnam. This time, the issue was the Middle East.

There was, Brezhnev explained, an opportunity to end a 'warlike situation'. The United States and the Soviet Union could conclude a new peace deal. Israel would retreat from the territorial gains that it had made during the war in 1967, in return for a truce with its neighbours. A subsequent agreement could be worked out over the status of the Palestinian people.

Kissinger fumed at this ambush. The Soviets had not warned their hosts that such a proposal was coming. And now they were asking the Americans to undercut their Israeli allies.

Brezhnev pressed. 'Perhaps I am tiring you out,' he said to Nixon, looking at his watch. 'But we must reach an understanding.' Might an informal gentleman's agreement be possible, on the principles required to reach peace?

The president pushed back. He was tired, head propped against a pillow. The Middle East was, he said, not as simple as that. Pragmatism was required. While he didn't want his visitor to return empty-handed, a gentleman's agreement was not possible.

As they watched, Dobrynin and Kissinger reflected. The delivery might be clumsy, thought the Soviet ambassador, but Brezhnev was giving a warning that trouble was coming in the region. Moscow could not keep her Arab allies in check indefinitely.

Kissinger was left with a bad taste from the exchange. Only a day before, both sides had signed an Agreement on Prevention of Nuclear War, which he and Brezhnev had negotiated during his visit to Moscow. But now, in effect, Brezhnev was threatening his hosts. Was this really how détente was supposed to work?[9]

The next morning, his hosts had a different kind of surprise for Brezhnev. Actor Chuck Connors was the lead in *The Rifleman*, a TV cowboy series which the general secretary loved. To Brezhnev's delight, he had visited San Clemente and presented him with a Stetson hat and two Colt 45 revolvers. The actor showed him how to twirl them in a quick draw, while Sukhodrev translated, cigarette in hand.

At the airport, Connors appeared again to say farewell. He was six foot five inches tall, and towered over Brezhnev. The Soviet hugged him, then suddenly Connors wrapped his arms around the other man, and lifted him off the ground. Around them, the KGB bodyguards gasped. Nobody had behaved like this with the general secretary before. But Brezhnev was thrilled. It was just the kind of spontaneous, theatrical gesture which he loved.[10]

While Brezhnev was in the United States, Senator Ervin had paused business. His committee had begun hearings into the Watergate affair in mid-May. They took place in the Caucus Room, within the Senate Office Building. Built in the first decade of the twentieth century, in an ornate French style, the walls were flanked by twelve columns with Corinthian plinths, and three large windows. The ceiling was inlaid with classical Greek patterns. The room had been the venue for major Senate committee investigations in the past, including those into the *Titanic* disaster, and the attack on Pearl Harbor.

Brezhnev left California on Sunday 24 June. The next day, action returned to Washington. The committee heard evidence from the most significant witness yet.

Legal Counsel John Dean had left the White House at the end of April, along with John Ehrlichman and Bob Haldeman. Now his moment had come to share what he knew.

Outside, the Washington summer pressed in. The temperature hovered around 80 °F. Inside, the former presidential counsel cut a trim figure. He was dressed in a light, summer suit, with a dark green tie and wore round, horn-rimmed glasses, which gave a thoughtful air to his youthful face.

Dean had prepared an opening statement, written out in longhand. It was 60,000 words in length. For the whole day, he read from his text, seated at a desk before Ervin and his fellow senators. Behind him sat his wife Maureen, her blond hair tied back in a bun, offset by round, white earrings and a cream poloneck sweater. They looked an attractive, serious couple.[11]

The cameras were rolling. From the start of the hearings, Ervin had arranged for ABC, CBS and NBC to film evidence sessions live. Later estimates suggested that 80 million people saw the coverage.

Dean had chosen his opening words carefully. Watergate was, he said, 'an inevitable outgrowth of a climate of excessive concern' for demonstrations and leaks, 'coupled with a do-it-yourself White House staff, regardless of the law'.

For the next three days, Dean was cross-examined by the committee. His testimony lasted for thirty hours. More details came out. The president had, Dean alleged, pursued a cover-up operation over Watergate since the story first broke a year before. Dean described his various encounters with Nixon, including his warning in mid-March that there was a 'cancer on the presidency'.

The capital was transfixed. After months of speculation about Watergate, fuelled by reporting from journalists Bob Woodward and Carl Bernstein in *The Washington Post*, here was the story told by a White House insider.

The hearings continued into July. In all, 155 witnesses were called to give evidence. Television coverage ran for more than 325 hours. Forced onto the back foot, Nixon waived executive privilege for current and former White House staff to appear in front of the committee. Ervin pushed for release of presidential papers as well. Dean's testimony, Nixon later reflected, had turned the tables. Some of what the former counsel said was slanted, or open to question. But that no longer mattered. Much of it was true, and it was the truth that the committee now sought. As Tennessee senator Howard Baker put it, 'What did the president know, and when did he know it?'

The biggest secret of all was about to come out.

Alexander Butterfield operated the White House taping system. The former air force officer was a classmate of Bob Haldeman from University College Los Angeles. In the wake of Nixon's 1968 election victory, Butterfield wrote to the chief of staff, seeking work. Haldeman liked Butterfield's discreet, organized approach. He took him on as a deputy. Butterfield ran the office, overseeing the elaborate system by which Haldeman kept a grip over paperflow within the White House.

In February 1971, Haldeman came into Butterfield's office. The president had given a new instruction. He wanted a system installed in the White House. It would enable secret recording of conversations in the Oval Office, the Cabinet Room, and by telephone. Nixon had an eye on history. He wanted every moment of his presidency on the record.

Butterfield was thorough. He turned to Al Wong, head of the secret service technical security team. Wong knew what was wanted. Johnson had installed a taping device at his desk, even showing it to Nixon during the transition between their presidencies. Kennedy had secretly taped meetings of his executive committee which handled the crisis over Cuba. The next weekend, Wong and his technicians set to work. Inside the Oval Office, five microphones were embedded in Nixon's desk, with more in the light fixtures over the mantelpiece. Wires ran down to a locked room in the basement, which contained Sony 500B tape recorders.

In March 1973, Butterfield left the White House. Over time, he had learned how to handle the president. He could sense when to interrupt Nixon, and when to stay away. But Butterfield didn't like the undercurrent, and suspected that something was going on. When the chance came up to become head of the Federal Aviation Administration, Butterfield took it. Four months later, it was his turn to take the stand in the Senate Caucus Room. The former officer was tall, with a neat side parting. He wore a dark suit and a striped tie. As he sat at the same table where Dean had spoken, his hands were clasped in front of him.

In the wake of Dean's testimony, the White House had released notes of the meetings between Dean and Nixon. The records were very detailed, even with verbatim quotes. Committee staffers suspected that they had been drawn from actual recordings of meetings. In preparatory questioning a few days before, held in private, they asked Butterfield a direct question. Under oath, he admitted that what they suspected was true. Now it was the turn of Fred Thompson, minority counsel, to expose the secret to the world. Thompson wore his hair long, swept back with sideburns.

'Mr Butterfield,' he asked. 'Are you aware of the installation of any listening devices in the Oval Office?'

Butterfield paused. The room was silent.

'I was aware of listening devices, yes, sir,' he responded.[12]

Thompson probed on the mechanics of the taping system. Then added a new question.

'As far as you know, these tapes are still available?'

'As far as I know . . .' replied Butterfield.

The secret was out. Until now, witnesses had not produced evidence which might directly incriminate the president. But the news that Nixon had recorded his own conversations offered a new angle. If the committee could get hold of the tapes, they might have the evidence they sought. The stakes had jumped to a new level.

'Tear it out! Now. Make sure it's done.'

Al Haig was assuming charge. It was the evening of Monday 16 July. The White House chief of staff had just watched Butterfield's testimony. Haig instructed his assistant, former soldier John Bennett, to remove the recording equipment. He also told him to seize the previous recordings, and hold them in a locked room. When Bennett had done so, he gave a key and safe combination to Haig. Only the chief of staff could now access the tapes.

Nixon was in hospital. The previous week, he had collapsed with a temperature and searing pain in his chest. White House doctor Walter Tkach diagnosed viral pneumonia. It was the first time that Nixon had taken sick absence since the start of his presidency.

With the tapes secure, Haig jumped in a car. Nixon was at the Naval Hospital in Bethesda, north of the city centre. The drive took forty-five minutes.

Time was short. The committee would move quickly to subpoena the tapes. But, until they did so, the recordings remained Nixon's own property, to do with as he wished.

Haig was direct. 'Mr President,' he said, 'it seems to me that you have two options. You can either keep the tapes or destroy them.'

Neither choice seemed attractive. The tapes told the story of a presidency. Neither man could remember every conversation that they contained, spread over the last two and half years. There might well be incriminating material. But, if Nixon destroyed the tapes, it would suggest that he had something to hide.

Later that night, Haig returned with legal advisers, Fred Buzhardt and Len Garment. The trio met with Nixon in his hospital room. It was cramped, with one small lamp to illuminate the scene. The president was out of bed, wearing a dressing gown.

Buzhardt favoured destroying the tapes. Garment wanted to preserve them as evidence. They began to argue. Nixon was tired, and still running a temperature.

'That's enough!' he snapped at the lawyers. 'Get out of here, both of you!'

Haig stayed behind. Nixon continued to chew over his options. He paced up and down. Like Buzhardt, Haig favoured destroying the tapes. Eventually, Nixon waved him away, too.

'I'll have to sleep on this,' he said.

'There's very little time, Mr President,' warned Haig. 'The tapes will be subpoenaed.'

The chief of staff returned the following morning. It was eight o'clock. Overnight, Buzhardt had received a letter from the special prosecutor appointed by the attorney general to investigate Watergate, requesting tapes that covered eight individual conversations with the president.

Nixon looked tired. Neither he nor Haig had slept much. But he had reached a decision.

The tapes were the truth. Nixon hoped that they would help him to prove his side of the story. 'The tapes are my best insurance,' he told his chief of staff. 'I can't destroy them.'

Nixon gazed into the middle distance. It was a telltale sign that he didn't want to hear the advice he was being given. There was, Haig thought, a glint of innocent hope in the president's eyes. Perhaps he really believed the tapes would save him.[13]

It was a blunt warning. 'Certain renegades and deluded people in our country,' declared the general secretary, 'have tried to sing in tune with our class and ideological enemies.'[14]

Brezhnev had warned Nixon that he would give a speech. During their private meeting in the Oval Office, two months before, the Soviet leader had mused that there was a 'deliberate attempt to spoil relations thrown in by certain people on the side'. He would, Brezhnev explained, make a 'big, serious speech' to tackle the idea that in pursuing détente the superpowers must reduce their own ambition to exert influence in the world. The Soviet Union could be a force to be reckoned with, and yet choose to work in partnership with the United States at the same time.[15]

The message came from an unlikely venue. Brezhnev was visiting Alma Ata, capital of the Soviet Republic of Kazakhstan. In the nineteenth century, the Russian Empire had colonized Central Asia, in a drive towards British India and the Persian Gulf. A century later, the region was divided into semi-autonomous republics inside the Soviet Union, governed by local communist parties. Far from the eyes of the Kremlin in Moscow, corruption was endemic.

The general secretary had consolidated his authority in part because the personal gamble he had taken to back détente with the United States seemed to be working. But engagement abroad could not mean weakness at home, either for the Soviet state, or for Brezhnev personally. In April, as part of his move to weaken Kosygin and Podgorny, the Soviet leader had promoted KGB chief Yuri Andropov to be a full member of the Politburo, along with Foreign Minister Andrei Gromyko and Defence Minister Andrei Grechko. For now, these men owed him a measure of loyalty. But if they sensed that the general secretary was a liability, they would be well positioned to sieze power in the same way that Brezhnev, Kosygin and Podgorny had unseated Khrushchev.

Andropov and the KGB had enjoyed a successful run. Efforts to rein in domestic opposition were bearing fruit. In the summer of 1973, the Fifth Directorate staged a show trial of two dissidents, Pyotr Yakir and Viktor Krasin. They were leading members of the group which had published a samizdat record of KGB actions, called *A Chronicle of Current Events*. Interrogators had extracted a concession from Krasin by inserting an undercover KGB agent as a stool pigeon into his cell. Worn down by pressure from his cellmate, Krasin opted to confess, and denounce the dissident movement. A further fifty-seven individuals were arrested, based on testimony from the two convicted prisoners.[16]

In mid-August, the day after Brezhnev's speech in Alma Ata, physicist Andrei Sakharov was summoned before the deputy general prosecutor in Moscow, with a warning to cease his contacts with foreigners.

Sakharov was furious. He responded by upping the ante, and held a press conference in his Moscow flat. Some thirty foreign journalists attended, sitting on chairs, stools and the bed in a front room lined with glass-fronted bookcases. The scientist read a statement, and then took questions. He was surprised at how fluently he was able to think on his feet.

'I like to think that the loyal character of my activities will ultimately be understood,' he explained to the group.

'Loyal to what?' asked one of the journalists.

'Loyal to the literal meaning of the word, namely lawful,' Sakharov shot back.

The scientist went on. The West was, he warned, running a risk with détente. It was pursuing nomalization in relations, while ignoring the plight of people inside the Soviet Union. The communist state was, Sakharov declared, 'a country wearing a mask that hides its true face'.[17]

A week later, the Kremlin retaliated. The newspaper *Pravda* carried a letter signed by forty members from the Academy of Sciences. Their former colleague had become 'an instrument of propaganda hostile to the Soviet Union'. Sakharov learned of the letter while on vacation in Batumi, on the coast of the Black Sea, with his son Alexei and new wife Elena. Already in his fifties, Sakharov had been learning to swim. Shaken at the news, he wandered along the beach, trying to persuade startled holidaymakers not to believe the propaganda, until Elena quietly hustled him away.[18]

Next it was the turn of Alexander Solzhenitsyn. Like Sakharov, the writer had felt the pressure from surveillance and intimidation by Andropov's men. In early August, the KGB arrested two women in Leningrad who had helped Solzhenitsyn type up copies of *The Gulag Archipelago*. The trail led to a copy of the text, hidden in an attic. Devastated, one of helpers, Elizaveta Voronyanskaya, hung herself.

Solzhenitsyn was determined to hit back. He had already smuggled out a second manuscript of the book to the West, ready for publication. Now the opportunity had come. 'I was in the saddle, at full gallop,' he recalled, 'the moment was of my choosing.'[19] He explained what had happened to Alya, his new wife.

'We'll have to detonate it, don't you think?' he asked.

'Let's do it,' she replied.

The next day, Solzhenitsyn met up with a trusted Swedish journalist. He passed on a statement, revealing the existence of the book, and the KGB's attempt to seize it. The book would, promised Solzhenitsyn, shortly be published in the West. The die was cast.

Solzhenitsyn followed with a private letter to the Soviet leadership. It was an appeal to return to the authentic roots of Russia, away from the industrialization and pollution of the Soviet Union. Art and literature should likewise be allowed to flourish. 'You will see,' he wrote, 'what a rich harvest it brings and how it bears fruit – for the good of Russia!'[20]

News of the impending publication shot across the world. *The New York Times* reported that *The Gulag Archipelago* would contain 'only true facts, places and the names of more than 200 people still alive'. Western media buzzed with talk of dissidents and what they had exposed about life in the Soviet Union. 'We are being asked to pay too high a price for détente,' commented the BBC, 'and to bolster up tyranny.'[21]

Ten days later, in mid-September, Sakharov struck out again. He published an open letter, to the US Congress. It was an appeal to pass the amendment tabled by Senator Henry 'Scoop' Jackson, linking the grant of MFN status on free trade to an open right of emigration for Soviet nationals. To deny such a right would, declared Sakharov, be 'tantamount to total capitulation of democratic principles in the face of blackmail, deceit and violence'. Congress faced a historic responsibility before mankind.[22]

It was a powerful blow. Ahead of the summit meeting with Brezhnev in June, Nixon and Kissinger had argued that the most effective way to secure emigration for Jews and other minorities from the Soviet Union was through quiet diplomacy. But here was an eminent, respected dissident, arguing that such tactics did not work. Jackson's campaign against détente had received a major boost.

Brezhnev, too, was trapped. To protect his own flank, he had authorized the clampdown on dissidents. But that had given them a moral authority, which they were now using against him in the West. 'The enemies of détente have stepped up their struggle,' warned Andropov in a report to the Central Committee. 'Left unresolved, the cases of Solzhenitsyn and Sakharov could linger for a very long time, with all the negative consequences we have mentioned.' With support for détente waning, Brezhnev would have little to show for the steps that he had taken. 'We have been tolerating their anti-Soviet activities for too long,' the general secretary told his colleagues, 'and that is wrong.'[23]

Watching from the CIA headquarters at Langley, outside Washington, analysts were more blunt. 'The outspokenness of these two men . . . places the Kremlin in a dilemma,' assessed a secret report. 'The initiative seems to have passed from the hunters to the hunted.'[24]

'Ignore the scandal,' ran Haig's dictum. 'Think of the country.'

The soldier had returned to a White House worn down by Watergate. The departure of Haldeman and Ehrlichman had removed an essential dynamo at the heart of the machine. Staffers were used to spending ten or twelve hours a day on the business of the presidency. But now, under the constant drumbeat of the Watergate investigation and press coverage, the working schedule stretched beyond that. Exhaustion was taking a toll.

In early August, a new front opened up. News broke of a bribery scandal involving Vice President Spiro Agnew when he had been governor of Maryland. The local state attorney launched an investigation. Witnesses started to come forward.

Henry Kissinger sensed his moment. His position was, as he saw it, both strong and precarious. As national security adviser, he acted with the authority of the president. But that authority was draining away in the mire of Watergate. Kissinger had long feuded with Bill Rogers, secretary of state. Nixon and Haldeman had planned to move Rogers, as part of a reshuffle at the start of the second term. Watergate had overtaken these plans. Now, in a White House unable to focus on foreign policy, they were back on the table.

Through July, press speculation mounted about Rogers' position. Dan Rather from CBS reported that the White House was considering a move. Haig made a recommendation to Nixon. Rogers should retire, and Kissinger move across to the State Department. Nixon flinched, unwilling to demand Rogers' resignation. Eventually, the secretary of state presented it himself, at a private Oval Office meeting in mid-August. A week later, as Nixon was floating in his swimming pool at San Clemente, he casually mentioned to Kissinger that he would nominate the national security adviser as successor.

The swearing-in ceremony took place on Saturday 22 September. The venue was the East Room in the White House. Chief Justice Warren Burger administered the oath. A small invited audience sat on chairs, drawn up in a semicircle around a platform and lectern. Kissinger's parents were there, and his children. So was Nancy Maginnes, his long-term girlfriend.

For the former Jewish refugee from Nazi Germany, it was an extraordinary moment. He and his family had arrived in America thirty-five years before, penniless and alien. Now the 50-year-old was taking the highest appointed executive office in his adoptive country.

Nixon appeared distracted and detached. He offered a few remarks.

Kissinger was, he noted, the first naturalized citizen to become a secretary of state. He was also, he added, the first since the war not to have a parting. Kissinger, who wore his curled hair combed back, ignored the reference in his own remarks. He had tried to write some notes in advance, but felt too tense. Instead, he spoke direct, on the spur of the moment.

There was, said Kissinger, no other country in the world where a man of his immigrant origins could rise to such office. In his youth, he had seen a society based on 'hatred and strength and distrust'. Now, in searching for peace, he hoped his own roots would help him to contribute. America, he concluded, 'has never been true to itself unless it meant something beyond itself'.

The new secretary of state glanced across at his parents, a former school teacher and his wife from Furth, in Bavaria. They looked as if they were in a dream.[25]

'You may have to calm some people down.'

It was Kissinger on the phone. The newly appointed secretary of state was in New York, for the General Assembly of the United Nations. He was staying at the Waldorf Towers. It was half-past ten, on the morning of Saturday 6 October 1973. The day was Yom Kippur, a holy festival in the Jewish calendar. Once again, the Middle East was on fire.

'Good,' replied Haig. 'I am sitting here with the president.'

Nixon was at Key Biscayne in Florida. Chief of Staff Al Haig was with him.

'OK. The Egyptians have crossed the Canal in five places, and the Syrians have penetrated in two places into the Golan Heights.' Kissinger was terse. 'We have to assume an Arab attack.'

'I think the president feels that way.'

'The open question,' added Kissinger, 'is it with Soviet collusion or against Soviet opposition?'[26]

It was the risk that Brezhnev had mentioned at San Clemente, in his late-night meeting with Nixon. But the attack had come out of the blue. Neither American nor Israeli intelligence had picked up signs of preparation by Egypt and Syria, until the very final hours before the assault was launched. When news first came through, Kissinger had called Dobrynin. But the ambassador said he, too, was in the dark.[27]

Nixon had flown to Florida for some respite from domestic politics. The noose around Spiro Agnew was tightening. The vice president had decided to take a gamble, offering to submit to impeachment proceedings from Congress. He calculated that he stood a better chance of reprieve from lawmakers in Washington than from the authorities in his home state of Maryland. Nixon had seen the evidence against him, of taking bribes, and concluded that it was damning. Privately, he authorized his staff to work with Agnew and Attorney General Eliott Richardson on a plea bargain.[28]

Pressure was mounting on Watergate, too. In May, following the departure of Haldeman, Ehrlichman and Dean, Nixon had authorized the attorney general to appoint a special prosecutor, the academic lawyer Archibald Cox. In constitutional terms, it was an awkward position. Cox was based within the Department of Justice, in the executive branch, and therefore came under the ultimate authority of the president. But, in securing his own nomination before the Senate, Richardson had pledged that Cox should be independent, able to pursue the Watergate case as he saw fit. Cox had interpreted his remit broadly, and branched out his investigation to examine unrelated issues, including Nixon's tax affairs, and spending by the secret service on security measures at San Clemente and Key Biscayne. As details of Cox's findings leaked into the press, the focal point of Watergate moved from Erwin's committee in the Senate to the special prosecutor.

Israel, Egypt and Syria had last gone to war in the summer of 1967. On that occasion, the smaller Israeli forces had secured a brilliant victory. Superior weaponry and tactics prevailed over the Arab states, who fielded equipment provided by the Soviet Union. The Israelis had achieved success through a devastating surprise attack. Now, Egypt and Syria were attempting the same trick.

Most onlookers assumed that, once again, the Israelis would triumph. But their forces had been caught out. In the final hours before the attack, Prime Minister Golda Meir and Defence Minister Moshe Dayan had ordered a partial mobilization. It was too little, too late.[29] Many soldiers were on leave, celebrating Yom Kippur with their families. In the early hours of Tuesday 9 October, the fourth day of the conflict, Kissinger was awoken by a call from Simcha Dinitz, Israeli ambassador in Washington. Could the United States, he asked, organize an urgent resupply of military equipment?

The next morning, at eight o'clock, Dinitz called on Kissinger at the White House. They met in the Map Room, on the ground floor. Dinitz explained the background. Israel was losing, fast. Almost fifty aircraft had been destroyed, and 500 tanks. It was clear that the Arabs had been supplied with Soviet weapons in the run-up to the war. The Israelis had captured anti-aircraft missiles with date markings only a few months old. Improved air defences allowed the Egyptians and Syrians to protect their ground forces, and concentrate on eliminating the exposed Israeli tanks. If news of Israel's vulnerability leaked, other Arab states might join in, for a final, decisive blow. The state founded twenty-five years before in the wake of the Second World War might be entering its final hours.[30]

Later that morning, Kissinger reached Dobrynin on the phone. If the Soviets were playing games, he warned, the whole relationship between Moscow and Washington was at risk. At just before five o'clock, Kissinger met with Nixon. The president had returned to the White House from Florida.

'The Israelis must not be allowed to lose,' stated Nixon bluntly. He instructed Kissinger to prepare plans for flying in supplies of new aircraft and tanks. They should include the new M-60 model, and laser-guided bombs.[31]

Minutes later, Agnew called on Nixon in the Oval Office. Both men knew that his vice presidency had reached the end of the road. They sat for a few minutes, in armchairs on either side of the fireplace. The investigation had not been a comfortable experience for the former governor of Maryland. The Inland Revenue Service had even started checking how much he had paid for his colourful neck ties. With Richardson, he had worked out a reduced sentence, on probation. There was no option but to take it, and resign from the office.[32]

As Kissinger scrambled with the Pentagon to fly military supplies to Israel, Nixon and Haig searched for a new vice president. Following Eisenhower's heart attack, in 1955, Congress had passed the Twenty-Fifth Amendment. This provided for appointment of a new incumbent if the post fell vacant during a presidential term, subject to a majority vote in both houses. With the Democrats in control of Congress, Nixon needed a candidate who could enjoy support from both sides of the aisle.

Gerald Ford had never expected to get the job. A congressman from Michigan, he had first been elected to serve in 1946, the same year as Nixon. With a steady manner and relaxed, warm manner, Ford made friends across the Hill. In 1965, he had become minority leader in the House. It looked as if it would be the culmination of his career. He had hoped to become speaker, but disappointing results for Republicans in the 1972 congressional elections denied him the prize, and his wife Betty was suffering from arthritis. Reluctantly, Ford had concluded that this term would be his last.

The call from Haig came on Wednesday afternoon. Ford hurried over to the Executive Office Building. He found Nixon in a relaxed mood, with a sports jacket and a pipe. His feet were propped up on a stool.

'Mr President,' exclaimed Ford. 'I've never seen you smoke a pipe!'

'Well,' answered Nixon, 'I do it when I'm alone, or when I'm with an old friend like you.'

It was an exploratory chat. Nixon explained his problem. The case against Agnew was compelling. As he listened, Ford was disgusted. Agnew had allegedly even accepted bribes inside the White House.[33]

That evening, news of the resignation broke. Washington was thrown into a frenzy of speculation. Who would succeed him? California governor Ronald Reagan was one possibility. Nelson Rockefeller, a former contender for the Republican nomination, was another. Few were ready to tip Ford.

Press Secretary Ron Ziegler alerted journalists. An announcement was due on Friday night. Nixon would call the nominee beforehand, at seven o'clock.

That morning, the president spoke with Kissinger. For an anxious three days, the secretary of state had struggled to galvanize the Pentagon into airlifting military equipment to Israel. Now, at last, the process was moving, with thirty C-130 transport aircraft due to fly the following day. But the race was on. The Soviets had already started sending their own supply flights to Egypt and Syria. As Kissinger briefed Nixon on the phone, he could tell that the president was distracted.[34]

Ford knew that Nixon would pick him. But the news was a closely held secret. He hadn't even told Betty. The congressman hurried home, to take the call at the appointed time from his house in Alexandria, on the other side of Potomac. It had two telephones. He found Betty on the main line, chatting to their son Mike, who was studying at a seminary in Massachusetts. There was a separate, private line in the Fords' bedroom upstairs. It was this phone that rang. Their daughter Susan answered.

'Dad, the White House is calling!'

Ford grabbed the receiver. Haig was on the line.

'The President wants to talk to you.' Nixon came on.

'Jerry,' he said. 'I want you to be vice president and I think Betty ought to hear what I am telling you.'

Ford explained. Only the line downstairs connected to a second handset. Could the president ring back, on the other number?

He dashed down to his wife.

'Betty, get off the phone!' he shouted. 'The president wants to call.'[35]

Two hours later, both men stood in the East Room of the White House. The television cameras were rolling. Nixon introduced his choice. He wanted it to be a surprise. But, as he built up to giving the name, he mentioned that his nominee had served for twenty-five years in the House of Representatives.

The audience was a crowd of Washington insiders, congressmen, senators and diplomats. They immediately realized who Nixon meant. Even before the president could state Ford's name, people started to applaud and shake his hand. The nominee thought it was like a party convention.[36]

Kissinger was also there. The secretary of state had excused himself from his work on the Middle East crisis to attend. As he watched, he sensed a wave of warm relief around the room. For a few minutes, the shadow of Watergate seemed to recede.[37]

Dobrynin, too, was there. Over the previous week, he had acted as a conduit between the Kremlin and White House. It was a delicate game. Both superpowers were calculating at what moment to impose a halt on their respective allies in the Middle East, and call on the UN Security Council to impose a ceasefire. All depended on the balance of advantage on the battlefield. Dobrynin suspected that Kissinger was playing the game with particular determination.

As Nixon left the East Room, he spotted the Soviet ambassador, and walked over. They exchanged a few words. The president said that he had a message for Brezhnev.

Both sides, he warned, were under pressure from those who opposed détente. 'We should not fall for that,' said Nixon, 'because the destinies of our peoples depend on it.' The president would, he emphasized, keep his side of the bargain.[38]

Prime Minister Golda Meir was not usually given to tears. Now in her mid-seventies, she had devoted her whole life to Israel, first as a young teacher on a kibbutz collective farm, then in the struggle for independence in 1948, and as leader of the young country since 1969. She had inherited the mantle from David Ben-Gurion, the legendary first prime minister of the Jewish state. In the opening days of the Yom Kippur War, she had held her composure, even as disaster beckoned. But as news arrived that the first American supply planes had at last touched down on Israeli soil, she cried. The tide was turning.[39]

Over the weekend, the airlift of American equipment accelerated. By early the following week, more than a thousand tons were arriving each day. Fighter aircraft crewed by Americans flew into Israeli bases, where they changed pilots and took off again moments later, straight into action against their Egyptian and Syrian opponents. The flow was greater than that achieved during the airlift to Berlin, in the early years of the Cold War.

With new tanks and aircraft, the Israelis were able to fight back. 'Golda,' reported the Israeli chief of staff, 'Dado' Elazar, to the prime minister, 'it will be all right. We are back to being ourselves, and they are back to being themselves.'[40] Army units counter-attacked on the Golan Heights, advancing towards the suburbs of Damascus, capital of Syria. In the Sinai Peninsula, between Israel and Egypt, tanks broke the Egyptian lines. With 2,000 tanks in combat, it was the largest armoured engagement since the battle of Kursk in 1943. On Tuesday 16 October, Israeli forces crossed the Suez Canal. Twenty-five thousand soldiers from the Egyptian Third Army were trapped on the far bank, cut off from their own bases. The pendulum had swung back dramatically towards Israel.

On Thursday 17 October, the Soviets petitioned the UN Security Council for a ceasefire. The same day, the Arab states decided to use a different weapon. The Organization of Petroleum-Exporting Countries (OPEC) announced that the key producer states in the Middle East would reduce output of oil. These countries had seen revenues fall since the devaluation of the dollar two years before, when the United States had left the gold standard. Now they had an opportunity to make amends. The price of oil jumped by 70 per cent, to over $5 a barrel.

Meanwhile, Nixon faced challenges of his own. On the day that he nominated Ford for the vice presidency, the Court of Appeals ruled on a demand from Cox to release tape recordings covering a series of key conversations in the White House about Watergate. The president had a week in which to comply, or challenge the verdict at the Supreme Court. Nixon was torn. To accept would risk jeopardizing executive privilege. Future presidents might find it impossible to conduct business in private.

The president hatched a plan. He would release edited transcripts of the recordings to Cox. These would be verified by John Stennis, the Democrat from Mississippi and chair of the Senate Committee on Standards and Conduct, who was an old friend of Nixon. This approach would allow the president to retain some control over what material became public.

The decision was not for the president alone. Cox would need himself to accept the compromise, as complying with the court ruling. So, too, would Eliott Richardson, the attorney general. The special prosecutor was under his authority. If Cox was to accept the compromise proposed by Nixon, it was for Richardson to persuade him.

Nixon and Haig held a series of conversations with Richardson. He was ambivalent. At moments, he seemed to accept the plan, and be ready to threaten Cox with dismissal. But, as the week progressed, his position hardened. As a young man during the war, Richardson had taken part in the D-Day landings in Northern France. He was prepared to stand his ground.

The clock was ticking. By the evening of Thursday 18 October, Nixon's patience was wearing thin. Haig reported that Richardson was still stalling. The court deadline expired at midnight the following day.

'No more tapes, no more documents, nothing more!' Nixon snapped. 'I want an order from me to Eliott to Cox to that effect, now!'[41]

The following evening, the White House put out a press release, announcing that the edited transcripts would be passed to Cox. The same night, Kissinger boarded a plane to Moscow. His mission was to negotiate a resolution for the UN Security Council on the Middle East. Later on, Haig reached Richardson on the phone. He was tired, and had been drinking. But his mind was made up. If Cox did not accept the plan, he would not sack him. Privately, Richardson had shared a quote from Homer's *Iliad* with the special prosecutor. 'Let us go forward together,' the Trojan warrior Sarpedon told his comrade Glaucus, 'and either we shall give honour to each other, or another to us.'[42]

Crisis loomed. Cox called a press conference early the following afternoon, at the National Press Club. It was a packed house. The special prosecutor was defiant. 'It's sort of embarrassing,' he told the assembled reporters. 'I don't want the President of the United States to tell me what to do.' The White House must provide the full tapes, unedited.

Haig called Richardson. The president wanted Cox fired. The attorney general refused, and resignation beckoned. Could he at least, asked Haig, wait until the crisis in the Middle East had subsided? Richardson refused. Two hours later, he called on the Oval Office, to submit his resignation.

Richardson's deputy was William Ruckelshaus. He, too, refused to sack Cox, and himself resigned. Robert Bork, the solicitor general, was next in line. He indicated that he was prepared to go through with dismissal of the special prosecutor.

As the crisis was running, Kissinger phoned from Moscow. The instructions he had received from Nixon directed him to negotiate a full settlement between Israel and her neighbours, rather than just a ceasefire. The secretary of state feared that he was walking back into the trap which Brezhnev had tried to set at San Clemente, for a quick deal which favoured the Arabs over Israel. He called Haig to protest.

'Will you get off my back?' Haig snapped back.

Kissinger had missed the latest news. 'What troubles can you possibly have in Washington on a Saturday night?' he asked, in a wounded tone.[43]

The story ran across the evening news bulletins. 'In my career as a correspondent,' declared NBC anchor John Chancellor, 'I never thought I would be announcing these things.' By the next day, as Kissinger and Brezhnev thrashed out a ceasefire agreement in Moscow, the press had dubbed it the 'Saturday Night Massacre'. Returning from a weekend on Long Island, speech-writer Raymond Price was shaken by the furore running in the capital. 'Washington,' reported *The New York Times*, 'had the smell of an attempted coup d'état,' while *The Times* of London talked of the 'whiff of the Gestapo in the clear October air'.[44]

The backlash broke over the White House. The switchboard was jammed with calls, from the public. Some 3 million contacted their representatives in Congress, to register anger at the president's actions.[45] By Tuesday 23 October, House Democrats had tabled twenty-one separate resolutions calling for impeachment. A series of newspapers called for Nixon's resignation. Ford's nomination to be vice president hung in the balance. The president was forced to back track. Charles Alan Wright, from his legal team, confirmed that the White House would hand over the tapes that Cox had requested, unedited.

'This president,' declared Wright, 'does not defy the law.'[46]

It was an order. Around the world, US military forces were instructed to move to Defence Condition level 3, or DEFCON 3 for short. In peacetime, the usual state of readiness was level 5. Level 1 signified imminent nuclear war. Level 3 was heightened readiness, with air force units prepared to move at fifteen minutes' notice. It had only been used once before, during the Cuban Missile Crisis in 1962.

Kissinger was in control. It was the late evening of Wednesday 24 October. Following his weekend visit to Moscow, the Security Council in New York had passed a ceasefire resolution for the Middle East, numbered 339, with the support of both the Soviet Union and the United States. But events on the ground were unravelling. Overnight, renewed fighting had broken out between the Egyptian Third Army, trapped in the Sinai Peninsula on the eastern side of the Suez Canal, and encircling Israeli forces. The Israelis claimed that the Egyptians were resuming their offensive. The Egyptians said the Israelis were seeking to obliterate their surrounded troops.

The previous day, Kissinger had briefed his staff at the State Department. Détente, he said, had enabled him to strike a deal in Moscow with Brezhnev. But, he added, 'we have never believed that we could substitute charm for reality.'[47] Now real events were forcing the pace once again. On Wednesday morning, as news flashed through from Sinai, a message arrived from Brezhnev, relayed by Dobrynin to Kissinger over the phone. The general secretary was blunt. Washington had been unable to rein in 'actions of provocation' by their Israeli allies. The Americans needed to respond, fast.[48]

By evening, events were spiralling out of control. In New York, the Egyptian foreign minister had called for both superpowers to intervene. Minutes later, another message arrived at the White House from Brezhnev. Israel was 'brazenly challenging' the Security Council. The superpowers should immediately dispatch military contingents to Egypt, and halt the fighting. If Washington could not join such action, Moscow would go alone. Kissinger noted that, once again, the general secretary had addressed the letter with a plain 'Mr President', dropping his usual salutation 'Esteemed'.[49]

This was a serious challenge. Dobrynin later learnt of the background. During a series of late-night Politburo meetings in Moscow, Brezhnev found himself cornered by Defence Minister Marshal Andrei Grechko, supported by Premier Nikolai Podgorny. It was time, declared the marshal, to stage a 'demonstration' of Soviet military strength in the region. Gromyko and Kosygin argued against, but Brezhnev felt obliged to give ground to these opponents of détente.[50]

In Washington, Kissinger and Haig realized the significance of Brezhnev's message. In the years after the 1967 war, Washington had sought to draw Egypt out of the Soviet orbit. In 1972, in a dramatic gesture, President Sadat had expelled Soviet military advisers from the country. Brezhnev's proposal was a ploy to reassert Soviet influence. Intelligence reports suggested that Soviet airborne troops had been placed on alert, and ships were moving across the Mediterranean. At worst, these forces could end up in direct confrontation with the Israelis. Action seemed imminent.[51]

Haig briefed Nixon.

'We've go a problem, Al,' the president responded. 'This is the most serious thing since the Cuban Missile Crisis. Words won't do the job. We've got to act.'

Kissinger proposed convening the National Security Council. Normally, it was chaired by the president. But Nixon was exhausted from the Watergate affair. That day, the House Judicial Committee had announced it would proceed with inquiries about impeachment of the president. Haig brokered a compromise. The secretary of state would lead the meeting, but it would take place in the White House Situation Room, under presidential authority.[52]

Deep in the basement, Kissinger met with his cabinet colleagues. Defence Secretary James Schlesinger was there, along with Chief of the Joint Staff Admiral Moorer, Haig and Brent Scowcroft, an air force officer who was covering the national security role in the White House, following Kissinger's appointment to the State Department. From time to time, Haig slipped out of the room, apparently to keep the president briefed on discussion.

The secretary of state was frank. Moscow seemed to be taking advantage of Nixon's domestic weakness to 'throw détente on the table'. Haig thought that Soviet military moves might start at dawn in the Middle East, only a couple of hours away. Rapid, firm action was critical.

Their colleagues agreed. Worldwide, US military forces would move to DEFCON 3. In the Mediterranean, the aircraft carriers *John F Kennedy* and *Franklin D Roosevelt* were directed to move towards Egypt. In the Pacific, B-52 bombers were recalled from Guam, and the 82nd Airborne Division, based at Fort Bragg in North Carolina, was placed on standby. At the Soviet embassy, Dobrynin first heard the news over the radio. Washington was sending a clear signal.

The group also agreed a reply to Brezhnev, drafted by assistant Hal Sonnenfeldt. It was in the president's name.[53]

In every crisis, reflected Kissinger, there comes a critical moment. The protagonists stand on the brink. Working with Nixon had taught him that, at such moments, there was no advantage in holding back. Full determination was required. But equally, once the moment was passed, moderation must take over, and the opponent offered a way out. 'Grandstanding is good for the ego,' Kissinger mused, 'but bad for foreign policy.'[54]

By the following afternoon, it was clear that such a moment had come. All sides were looking for a solution. Israeli military action had abated. President Sadat indicated that he would accept a peacekeeping mission composed of other members from the United Nations. In an effort at de-escalation, Brezhnev wrote a further letter to Nixon, announcing that he would send seventy Soviet ceasefire monitors.

In the White House, Nixon, Kissinger and Haig were elated. American firmness had faced down the Soviets. Israeli had survived the most threatening weeks in its history since the foundation of the state in 1948. Even under the cloud of Watergate, Washington could still influence the world.

Dobrynin was less sure. At lunch a couple of days later, Deputy Secretary of State Kenneth Rush gave him a private account of the National Security Council meeting. It sounded as though, mired in Watergate, the president had delegated foreign policy to his subordinates. Kissinger, said Rush, had seemed agitated, anxious to prove American authority. To Dobrynin, it looked as though détente was moving to the back burner.[55] Watching from Moscow, diplomatic adviser Alexei Aleksandrov-Agentov had a similar impression. It was, he later reflected, the most difficult moment in Brezhnev's dealings with Washington.[56]

The same evening, Friday 26 October, Nixon gave a press conference in the East Room of the White House. The president opened with a statement on events in the Middle East. He praised the handling of the crisis, including the move to DEFCON 3. But the press had already decided on their angle. The alert was, journalists contended, an attempt to deflect attention from Nixon's domestic woes.

Following Nixon's statement, Dan Rather from CBS rose to his feet. He goaded the president with a series of questions about Cox and impeachment.

Nixon tightened his fists, eyes flaring. Television reporting, he declared, was 'outrageous, vicious, distorted'. Ordinary viewers were being pounded night after night. A nation's confidence was being eroded. He glared at Rather.

Robert Pierpoint was a colleague at CBS. Later in the press conference, he picked up on Rather's line of questioning. What was it about television, he asked, that so angered the president?

'Don't get the impression that you arouse my anger!' snapped Nixon.

'I'm afraid, sir,' replied Pierpoint, 'that I have that impression.'

The president clenched his hands behind his back. He stared at Pierpoint. 'You see,' he responded, 'one can only be angry with those he respects.'[57]

Pat and Julie were watching upstairs in the presidential quarters, on television. As Nixon lashed out at the press corps, they winced. At home, they knew a different side to the president. But others, watching across America, did not. What would they be thinking?[58]

'May [God] answer you in time of trouble ...'

It was a line from Psalm 20. Minority Leader Gerald Ford was standing in the chamber of the House of Representatives, where he had served for twenty-five years. In front of him was Chief Justice Warren Burger, dressed in his legal robes. Betty was next to her husband, holding a Jerusalem Bible. It had been a gift from their son Mike, a candidate for the priesthood.

The date was Thursday 6 December. It was six o'clock in the evening. An hour before, the House had voted by 387 votes to 35 in favour of Ford's nomination. The Senate had given approval the previous week by a similar margin. The constitutional process created under the Twenty-Fifth Amendment was complete. It was the first time that a new vice president had been appointed while an administration was in office.

Ford took the oath, repeating the words after Burger. An audience of House members looked on. 'I will support and defend the constitution of the United States,' he declared, 'against all enemies, foreign and domestic ... so help me God.'

The audience burst into applause. Ford stepped forward to the microphone.

'I am a Ford, not a Lincoln,' he declared. 'My addresses will never be as eloquent at Mr Lincoln's.' His former colleagues burst into laughter. This was the Jerry Ford that they knew and respected.

Ford went on. 'As a man of Congress,' he declared, 'let me reaffirm my conviction that the collective wisdom of our two great legislative bodies, while not infallible, will in the end serve the people faithfully and very well . . . I say a fond goodbye.'

From the Capitol, Ford was driven to the White House. He found Nixon in the Oval Office.

'Congratulations,' said the president. 'It's good to have a teammate at last.'[59]

Ford entered a White House reeling under events. In mid-November, lawyers established that the subpoena for release of tapes covered a crucial meeting on 20 June 1972, between Nixon and Haldeman. It was the conversation just after news of the break-in first surfaced, in which the two men discussed the potential CIA angle. To compound the problem, a section of the tape had been erased. The deletion appeared to have happened while Rose Mary Woods, Nixon's secretary, was transcribing the recording. The sound quality of the tapes was poor, and Woods had spent hours in a painstaking process of playing and replaying to catch the dialogue they contained. Eighteen and a half minutes had been lost. When news of the erasure broke, Washington erupted into further speculation. Had the president made a deliberate attempt to destroy evidence?

Investigations spread into Nixon's financial and tax affairs. In a press conference held at Disney World in Orlando, Florida, Nixon lashed out once again at the press pack that hounded him. 'I am not a crook,' he declared, face set in a grimace. For many, his claim carried a whiff of guilt.

At the same time, America was experiencing a new phenomenon. The embargo imposed by OPEC countries on oil exports to the United States and Europe in the wake of the Yom Kippur War was starting to bite. Prices spiralled, pushing the country towards an energy crisis. Over two decades of steady growth and new consumer products, the post-war American economy had grown dependent on cheap oil. Now that had come to a sudden, juddering halt. In a television address, Nixon announced energy-saving measures, with speed restrictions on the highways and reduced opening hours for petrol stations. Defeated on the battlefield by American weapons, the Arabs had found a way to strike back.

For Nixon's family, the atmosphere inside the White House was becoming suffocating. Rumours surfaced in the press that the president was drinking, or reliant on medication. Pat Nixon's postbag doubled in size, so that she was receiving some five hundred letters from the public each day. A year before, Julie and her mother had persuaded the secret service that they might take evening strolls around downtown Washington. The area was a frequent scene of muggings and crime, but with their protection team the two women could walk safely. Pat wore a scarf to avoid being recognized. Amid the pressures at home, these walks became a moment of respite.[60]

The Ford family, too, was adjusting to life under guard. The secret service installed bulletproof windows and new wiring at their house in Alexandria. They dug up the driveway, reinforcing it so that it could carry an armoured limousine.

But there were some benefits, too. Susan Ford was 16 years old. She enjoyed going out in the evening, and her parents found it hard to enforce a curfew time. With agents monitoring her movements twenty-four hours a day, Gerald and Betty were better able to keep track of their daughter.[61]

A fortnight into the new job, Christmas beckoned. As vice president, Ford was entitled to his own aircraft, Air Force Two. In a nod to fuel shortages, he chose a Convair 580, slower and smaller than the jet which Agnew had used. Ford, Betty and their four children took it for a Christmas break at the ski resort of Vail in Colorado. The vice president paid a first class fare for each of his family. It was a memorable celebration. Ford loved skiing, and the snow was on fine form.[62]

For the Nixon family, Christmas was a more sombre occasion. They elected to spend it in the White House. Outside, the usual tree lights were dimmed, to save on electricity. David and Julie spent the morning with his parents in Pennsylvania, and then drove over to join the rest of the family. During the previous weeks, Julie had sought to do more press engagements and public events, in support of her father. She was worn out, and had a rising temperature. By late afternoon, she retired to bed.

Dinner was in the Red Room. Rose Mary Woods was there, along with Bob and Cynthia Milligan, young friends of David and Julie. The president talked wistfully about his own first Christmas away from home, at Duke University Law School. He could not afford the fare home. A professor had taken pity, and invited him in for dinner.

Afterward, Richard and Pat Nixon went upstairs, to see Julie. They sat on chairs by the bed, in a darkened room. On the spur of the moment, Nixon decided that they should fly to San Clemente for the New Year. To save fuel, they would travel on a commercial airliner.

The flight was not a comfortable experience. Ed and Tricia accompanied the parents, sitting together in the first-class cabin. Around them, fellow passengers were transfixed with curiosity.

California brought little comfort. The weather was cold, and the family was obliged to warm the house at San Clemente with electric heaters, moved from room to room to save on costs.

They were joined by Bebe Rebozo, Nixon's old friend. During the autumn, Rebozo had himself been drawn into the fray over Watergate, appearing in front of the Erwin Committee. On the last day of the year, the two of them talked in the living room, alone. Outside, the Pacific Ocean was grey.

The president turned to Rebozo. He asked the same question that he had put to his daughters seven months before, after the dinner with the prisoners released from Vietnam. Should he resign?

'No, you can't,' replied his friend. 'You have to fight.'

Later that night, after seeing in the New Year, Nixon reached for a notepad. It was a gift from Pat, bound in tortoiseshell. He scribbled down his choices – fight, or prepare for resignation. Then he wrote another line.

'The answer – fight.'[63]

Notes

1 Dobrynin (1995), 278–9, 281; Vavilov (2016), 133–4.
2 Nixon (1978), 877; Sukhodrev (1999), 298–305; Vavilov (2016), 132–3.
3 Dobrynin (1995), 276; Nixon (1978) 877–8: Kissinger (1982), 290–1.
4 Nixon daily diary; Brinkley and Nichter (2015), 762–9. For cigarette box, see also Scowcroft interview, 29 June 2007, p. 8; Sukhodrev (1999), 331.
5 FRUS 1969–76 Vol. XV, item 124, p. 496–506; Kissinger (1982), 291–3.
6 Nixon (1978), 881; Kissinger (1982), 294; Sukhodrev (1999), 305–6; Vavilov (2016), 150–1.
7 Eisenhower (1986), 570; Sukhodrev (1999), 307–8; Vavilov (2016), 139–41.
8 Gromyko (1989), 280; Dobrynin (1995), 282–3; Vavilov (2016), 163–4.
9 FRUS 1969–76 Vol. XV, item 132, p. 538–42; Kissinger (1982), 297–9; Nixon (1978), 884–6; Dobrynin (1995), 283; Sukhodrev (1999), 311–12.
10 Vavilov (2016), 168–9.
11 Dean interview with Naftali, 30 July 2007, p. 37.
12 Woodward (2015), 168–9; Butterfield interview with Naftali, 12 June 2008, p. 41–5, 50.
13 Haig (1992), 371–81; Nixon (1978), 901; Haig interview with Brinkley and Naftali, 30 November 2006, p. 33.
14 Quoted in Breslauer (1982), 215.
15 Brinkley and Nichter (2015), 768.
16 Andrews (1999), 408–13.
17 Sakharov (1990), 385–6; Rubenstein and Gribanov (2005), 148–50; Lourie (2002), 252–4; Kaiser (1976), 391–2.
18 Sakharov (1990), 386; Smith (1997), 547.
19 Solzhenitsyn (1975), 349–50.
20 Thomas (1998), 399–400; Pearce (1999), 222–5.
21 Solzhenitsyn (1975), 352.
22 Kaufman (2000), 272.
23 Rubenstein and Gribanov (2005), 153–8. See also Scammel (1995) doc. 92, p. 259–63 for record of Politburo on 17 Sept 1973, and doc. 92, p. 259–63 for Andropov's report.
24 CIA memo of 26 September 1973, *Sakharov and Solzhenitsyn: A Soviet Dilemma*, at www.cia.gov/library/readingroom.
25 Kissinger (1982), 431–2; Nixon (1978), 907; Haig (1992), 344–5.
26 FRUS 1969–76 Vol. XXV, item 106, p. 309–12.
27 Dobrynin (1995), 289; Kissinger (1982), 451; FRUS 1969–76 Vol. XXV, item 100, p. 289–91.
28 Nixon (1978), 915–18.
29 Meir (1975), 355–7; Dayan (1976), 375–7.
30 Kissinger (1982), 491–2; FRUS 1969–76 Vol. XXV, item 134, p. 392–6.
31 Kissinger (1982), 495; Nixon (1978), 922; FRUS 1969–76 Vol. XXV, item 140, p. 411–13; Haig (1992), 411; Schlesinger interview, 10 December 2007, p. 33–5.
32 Nixon (1978), 922–3.
33 Ford (1979), 102–3.
34 Kissinger (1982), 508; FRUS 1969–76 Vol. XXV, item159, p. 444–6.
35 Ford (1979), 105–6; Nixon (1978), 927.
36 Cannon (2013), 213.
37 Kissinger (1982), 511.
38 Dobrynin (1995), 291.

39 Meir (1975), 362.

40 Meir (1975), 363.

41 Haig (1992), 391–9; Nixon (1978), 929–31; Haig interview with Brinkley and Naftali, 30 November 2006, p. 49.

42 Haig (1992), 402; Farrell (2017), 521, with quote from *Iliad* book 12.

43 Kissinger (1982), 552; see also Scowcroft interview, 29 June 2007, p. 17.

44 Price (1977), 258–9.

45 Cannon (2013), 139.

46 Nixon (1978), 937.

47 FRUS 1969–76 Vol. XXV, item 250, p. 695.

48 FRUS 1969–76 Vol. XXV, item 258, p. 709–10.

49 Kissinger (1982), 583–4; FRUS 1969–76 Vol. XXV, item 267, p. 734–5.

50 Dobrynin (1995), 295; Aleksandrov-Agentov (1994), 203–6; Kornienko (2005), 202–8.

51 Kissinger (1982), 583–4.

52 Kissinger (1982), 585–6; Nixon (1978), 938; Haig (1992), 415–16. See also Haig interview with Musgrave and Naftali, 30 November 2006, p. 27.

53 FRUS 1969-76 Vol. XXV, item 269, p. 737–41; Kissinger (1982), 587–91; Haig (1992), 416–17; Dobrynin (1995), 297–9; James Schlesinger interview, 10 December 2007, p. 37; Scowcroft interview, 29 June 2007, p. 21; Haig interview, 30 November 2006, p. 43, 57–8.

54 Kissinger (1982), 526; 595.

55 Dobrynin (1995), 298–9.

56 Aleksandrov-Agentov (1994), 206.

57 Ambrose (1991), 258–9.

58 Eisenhower (1986), 589.

59 Ford (1979), 112–13.

60 Eisenhower (1986), 598–9; see also Gwendolyn King interview, 23 May 1988, p. 37.

61 Ford (1979), 113–14.

62 Cannon (2013), 161.

63 Nixon (1978), 970; Eisenhower (1986), 603–9.

Chapter 10

THE HUMILIATED MAN
(January–June 1974)

'Welcome aboard the Egyptian-Israeli shuttle!'

It was evening, on Sunday 13 January. SAM 86970, a United States Air Force Boeing 707, was preparing for departure from Ben Gurion airport in Tel Aviv. Joe Sisco, assistant secretary in the State Department for the Middle East, welcomed the travelling press party aboard Henry Kissinger's latest venture. Shuttle diplomacy had a name.

Three months before, the Yom Kippur War between Israel, Egypt and Syria had ended in an uneasy ceasefire. Israeli forces remained in occupation of a large area on the western bank of the Suez Canal, within seventy miles of Egypt's capital, Cairo. On the eastern bank, the Egyptian Third Army was encircled. To the north, Israel held the Golan Heights, a strategic upland on the Syrian border. Israeli tanks were within striking distance of Damascus, the capital of Syria. Both the Soviet Union and the United States had poured weapons back into the region, replacing the tanks and aircraft lost by each side during the brief, violent conflict.

While Israel held the Suez Canal, Egypt was in a stranglehold. Shipping through the waterway carried oil and other goods between east and west, so was critical for the national economy. But the Arab states had the Western world in a bind, too. The OPEC oil embargo, introduced in the wake of the war, was hurting. Energy prices had almost quadrupled. Restrictions introduced by governments on consumption were biting.

In Geneva, UN Secretary General Kurt Waldheim hosted talks to resolve the stand-off. Kissinger joined the opening session. He quoted an Arab proverb, 'That which is past is dead.'[1] But progress was slow. To accommodate the Arabs' refusal to recognize the state of Israel, separate tables were arranged in a hexagonal shape. Syria refused to take part. Within days, the talks were paused while Israel held an election, postponed from October due to the war. They produced an inconclusive result, with the governing Labour Party led by Prime Minister Golda Meir losing seats but clinging onto power.

In early January 1974, Israeli defence minister Moshe Dayan visited Washington. He had a proposal. Israeli was prepared to trade land for peace. Over two days of meetings with Kissinger, Dayan outlined his plan. Israeli forces would withdraw back across the Suez Canal, to a line some twelve miles to the east of the waterway.

The Egyptians could reoccupy this vacated territory. But between both sides, a United Nations peacekeeping force would provide a buffer zone. And each would be prohibited from deploying heavy weapons in the immediate vicinity of the line between them.[2]

Dayan had fought all his life for the state of Israel. Born on a kibbutz in 1915, he took part in the wars against Egypt in 1956 and, as commander of the Israeli Defence Forces, in 1967. Earlier, fighting with Britain against the Vichy French in Syria during the Second World War, he had suffered injury to his left eye. As Dayan scanned French positions through binoculars, a sniper's bullet struck the lens, smashing glass fragments into the eye socket. The soldier wore a black eye patch to conceal the wound.[3]

The plan that Dayan offered was an implicit deal. Israel sought security. At the start of the war in October 1973, Egypt had sprung a surprise attack, by amphibious assault across the Suez Canal. For a few days, the very survival of the Israeli nation hung in the balance. Dayan was himself under pressure for his failure to spot the move in advance and order a defensive mobilization. Tel Aviv was now trading withdrawal against conditions, with a UN buffer force, which would make it much harder to repeat such a move. While Egypt and Israel would still formally remain hostile states, the principle of land for peace would be established. The Sinai Peninsula, which lay between the Suez Canal and Israel, was Egyptian sovereign territory, occupied by Israel during the war in 1967. In future, further withdrawals might pave the way for a substantive peace deal between the two sides.

Kissinger sensed his moment. But landing Dayan's plan would require speed, and personal contact with the two sides. The White House was in little position to support. During his New Year break in California, President Nixon had largely retreated from national view. His sixty-first birthday, on Wednesday 9 January, was a subdued affair. Friends presented him with a cake. As he was serving out pieces, the president managed to slip, smearing his jacket sleeve with icing. His Irish setter, King Timahoe, was summoned to lick it clean.[4]

With Nixon lying low, the initiative would have to come from the secretary of state. Five days after meeting Dayan, on Friday 11 January, Kissinger arrived at Aswan, where Egyptian president Anwar Sadat was spending the winter months.

Like Dayan, Sadat was a soldier. He graduated as an officer of the Egyptian Signal Corps in 1938, when the country remained under British domination. Nearly twenty years later, he was one of a group around Colonel Gamal Nasser, who seized power in 1952. Nasser championed Egyptian nationalism and unity across the Arab world, standing as a champion against the West, and against Israel. Following his death in 1970, Sadat assumed the presidency.

Kissinger was struck by the man he found. Sadat was softly spoken, choosing his words carefully as he drew on a pipe. His English was formal, even stilted. Sadat had been imprisoned by the British, and taught himself the language while in jail. His eyes narrowed as he spoke. Listening, Kissinger found himself strangely calmed by the poise and dignity projected by the Egyptian leader. Sadat, too, was encouraged. He felt, he later recalled, as if he was 'looking at the real face of the United States, the one that I had always wanted to see'.[5]

Sadat might have lost the war, but he remained in a position of strength. The oil embargo had changed the equation, and left America hurting. Whereas Nasser had been humiliated by defeat in the 1967 conflict, the Yom Kippur War had given Sadat an opportunity. Israel's aura of invincibility had been punctured. She had come seeking peace. Kissinger should, he said, go ahead, and do so quickly.

For the next week, Kissinger and Joe Sisco travelled between Aswan, Tel Aviv and Jerusalem. The Boeing 707 was their flying office and bedroom. In the forward quarters, a secure communications facility linked the secretary of state to Washington, and American embassies in the region. Further back, the fuselage was divided into offices, a conference room and seating for travelling journalists. The flight between Egypt and Israel took two hours. On each journey, Sisco and his supporting team scrambled to prepare position papers and briefing notes for the next stage of the negotiation, using small portable typewriters and a photocopier.[6]

The American objective was simple. To work, Dayan's plan must be translated into technicalities: withdrawal lines, troop numbers and definitions for each category of military equipment. But the greater challenge was trust.

'You drive a tough bargain,' commented Kissinger during his first visit to Tel Aviv, following the encounter with Sadat.

'Either he wants to fight or he wants peace,' retorted Dayan.[7]

The Israeli warmed to the Jewish-American envoy. Kissinger had quickly mastered the detail of the battlefronts, and displayed an energy and drive which Dayan admired. But he could also see that Kissinger was struggling with the complexity of the task. At points in their meetings, the secretary of state would slump into silence, with his legs outstretched and chewing on a yellow pencil as he mulled over the next move.[8]

By Wednesday 16 January, Kissinger was back in Aswan. It was the third visit of the week. The previous night, the Americans had held a marathon negotiating session with the Israelis. Dayan still had to convince his cabinet colleagues. Prime Minister Golda Meir in particular was worried. The Yom Kippur War had changed her, and her administration. Every report of casualties from the fighting, she later recalled, had felt like 'a knife being twisted in my heart'.[9] Following the elections, her government was in a weakened position. An independent enquiry had been launched to investigate why Israel had failed to spot Arab preparations for attack. The electorate, recalled fellow cabinet minister Yitzhak Rabin, were 'exhausted, mourning their dead, and having difficulty in digesting recent events'.[10]

Kissinger met with Sadat in his study. It was eight o'clock in the evening. As the American described Meir's position, he found the Egyptians in equal distress. Foreign Minister Mohammed Gamasy was threatening to break off negotiations.

Sadat often reflected on what his years of imprisonment under the British had taught him. It was, he later wrote, a lesson in the need to recognize when life had changed. An individual could only hope to make progress once they had accepted that change required an underlying shift in mindset. The negotiations with Israel had reached just such a point.[11]

The Egyptian president looked at Kissinger. He and Meir had not communicated directly before. Now, he said, he had a message for her. He asked the secretary of state to write it down.

'You must take my word seriously,' he dictated. 'When I threatened war, I meant it. When I talk of peace now, I mean it.'[12]

Two days later, on Friday 18 January, Kissinger returned to Aswan for the final time. He had a deal. The Israeli cabinet had accepted the withdrawal agreement. In return, Sadat pledged that the Arab countries would lift the oil embargo.

Kissinger and Sadat posed for photos in the garden of the president's house. Afterwards, he took the American back into his study. When they were alone, Kissinger handed him a piece of paper. It was a reply from Golda Meir.

'Both our peoples need and deserve peace,' the Israeli prime minister had written. 'Let me reiterate what you said in your message. When I talk of a permanent peace between us, I mean it.'

Sadat put down the letter. He removed his reading glasses. Then he rose, walked across to Kissinger and kissed the American on both cheeks.

That afternoon, the Boeing 707 flew a short journey north. Sadat had arranged for the American visitors to spend the night in Luxor, capital of ancient Egypt. Since the war, Egypt had been under blackout restrictions. That night, they were lifted, and the ancient ruins at Karnak bathed in a son et lumière demonstration. Kissinger and his colleagues wandered among the pillars and sculptures covered in hieroglyphics. They were the legacy of an ancient civilization. Would their own efforts, the Americans wondered, leave an equivalent trace for future generations?[13]

Jerry Ford was on his guard. The vice president had enjoyed his first weeks in the new job, and the family vacation at Vail over Christmas. But returning to Washington in the New Year, he could sense that events were moving.

Republicans were starting to wonder if the president was a liability. Fifteen months before, he had been re-elected with a record landslide in the electoral college. Even then, his election had brought little advantage for Republican candidates running alongside him for Congress. But now, with mid-term elections looming in the autumn of 1974, House and Senate members were asking themselves if worse might be in store.

Former treasury secretary John Connally picked up rumours of a plot, circulating on the Hill. The protagonists apparently wanted to force the president out over the summer, and replace him with Ford. Connally tipped off Nixon. 'Some of them are men you think are your very good friends,' he warned darkly. Chief of Staff Al Haig checked with Barry Goldwater, veteran Republican senator from Arizona and former candidate against Lyndon Johnson in 1964. He denied knowledge.[14]

Ford faced a difficult role. He believed that he owed loyalty to the president. But remaining loyal did not mean that he was required to play an active role in defending Nixon's conduct. In mid-January, Ford addressed a farmers' convention in Atlantic City. He used a script for his speech provided by Nixon's staff, attacking 'extreme partisans' who sought to crush the president. Hours after delivering the speech, Ford learnt of the eighteen-and-a-half minute gap, in the tape recording of Nixon and Haldeman. He resolved to employ his own speech-writers in future.[15]

A few days later, Nixon called his vice president into the Oval Office. He started to talk. Ford had a busy schedule, and kept discreetly glancing at his watch. An hour and more passed, while Nixon rambled away. But Ford hardly felt that he could walk out on the president. He started to feel sorry for this haunted man, trapped inside the White House.

Nixon explained his hope that the tapes would exonerate him. He offered to show Ford the evidence. His vice president politely declined. After his experience at Atlantic City, he wanted to keep his distance from Watergate.[16]

Nixon was running out of people to talk to. To save fuel, he and Pat suspended trips up to Camp David. Julie and David had taken a house in Bethesda, loaned from his friend Bebe Rebozo. Their parents took to coming over in the evening, bringing a pre-cooked dinner from the White House kitchens with them. The garden was full of azaleas, and a haven for birds. A cardinal and a blue jay were frequent visitors. Each evening, they would turn up around the same time as the president. The family group sat in a glass-covered porch, watching them. Pat pointed out flowers in the garden, hoping to distract her husband from his cares. He took to reminiscing about the road trips they had made in the early years of their marriage. He hoped they might be able to go travelling again one day.[17]

In Congress, however, there was little such small talk. Watergate dominated conversation, and a new front was opening up. Under the constitution, Congress held the power to impeach a president, forcing him to stand down from office. A vote by straight majority was required in the House, and two thirds in the Senate. Only one attempt had been in the history of the Republic, against Andrew Jackson, successor to Abraham Lincoln. That had failed by one vote in the Senate. Now Republicans and Democrats alike were talking about whether the power could be used against Nixon.

The constitution defined grounds for impeachment as treason, bribery or 'other high crimes and misdemeanours'. The case against Jackson had been clear-cut, based on his violation of the Tenure of Office Act. That against Nixon was more ill-defined. Did the murky trail of concealment that followed the Watergate break-in really amount to a crime committed by the president himself?

On Wednesday 6 February, the House voted to take a first step. By 410 votes in favour, and just ten against, congressmen passed House Resolution 803. This gave authority to the Judiciary Committee to conduct an investigation into whether there were sufficient grounds for a case against the president. Days before, Nixon had given a defiant performance in his annual State of the Union address. But a majority of committee members were Democrats, and impeachment seemed to beckon.

The day before the vote, Democrats took a seat from Republicans in a by-election in Pennsylvania. Then, on 18 February, they seized Ford's old seat in Michigan, vacated by his move to the vice presidency. It was in Democrat hands for the first time in sixty-four years.

Soon afterwards, Ford met with Nixon. They talked about the election results. The president thought that spiralling inflation had caused the Republicans' defeat.

'No, Mr President,' replied Ford. 'It's Watergate that's responsible.'[18]

There was a ring at the door. Writer Alexander Solzhenitsyn was at home with his wife Alya and their 5-month-old son Stepan. Alya went to answer. She opened the door, keeping it on the chain.

It was two men. They said that they were from the public prosecutor.

The date was Tuesday 12 February. A month earlier, Brezhnev had presided over an emergency meeting of the Politburo. *The Gulag Archipelago* had been published in the West to widespread acclaim. Physician Andrei Sakharov welcomed the book as a stone that would shatter the wall dividing mankind.

The Politburo took a different view. 'It is filthy anti-Soviet slander,' Brezhnev told his colleagues. 'This hooligan Solzhenitsyn is out of control.' Nonetheless, the dilemma of what to do with the writer remained. Andropov favoured summary deportation into exile. The alternative was a trial inside the Soviet Union, along the lines used against other dissidents. Kosygin and Podgorny both argued for this course, which would allow the authorities to claim that due process had been followed. Gromyko reminded his colleagues of an additional angle, with the European Security Conference which had recently opened in Vienna. Negotiation of a final settlement on borders left at the end of the Second World War had been a long-standing Soviet objective, and would be a significant gain from détente. A backlash in the west over deportation of Solzhenitsyn might derail that goal.

Eventually, the group agreed on a two-phase approach. Andropov was authorized to initiate legal proceedings against Solzhenitsyn, while exploring whether any foreign countries might subsequently accept him into exile.

'We did not worry about acting against the counter-revolution in Czechoslovakia,' concluded Brezhnev. 'We survived it all. And I think we'll live through this.'[19]

Over the following weeks, the Soviet press launched a series of attacks on Solzhenitsyn and his new work. It was, declared the press agency Tass, a 'lampoon paid for in hard currency'. Behind the scenes, the KGB subjected the author to a barrage of menacing phone calls and hate mail. When *Washington Post* journalist Hendrick Smith called at his flat, he had to pick his way through police stationed outside, 'like swimming through jellyfish', as he later recalled.[20]

Discreetly, Solzhenitsyn and his wife made preparations for the arrest that they assumed was coming. Further copies of his writing were smuggled out on microfilm, and a bag of possession packed to take with him to prison. Now, with the knock at the door, that moment seemed to have arrived.[21]

Alya went upstairs to alert Alexander. He came to the door, and loosened the chain.

The two men burst in. Six others piled behind them. Some wore police uniform, some were in plain clothes. They pushed past a table in the hallway and a child's pram. Solzhentisyn and Alya shrank back.

'So that's your game, is it?' shouted the author. 'So that's your game?'

A large man in fur coat stepped forward with an official folder. 'I'm Senior Counselor Zvenov,' he declared. 'You must come with me.' He held out a pen for Solzhenitsyn to sign the arrest warrant.

Eventually, the writer relented. After a hurried scramble to locate the bag of possessions and put on a sheepskin coat, Solzhenitsyn turned to Alya. 'Look after the children,' he mumbled. Then the men bundled him outside, and into a waiting car. It sped off down Pushkin Street, towards Moscow's Lefortovo Prison.[22]

A day later, Solzhenitsyn was once more in a car. This time it was heading northwards on the Leningrad Highway. The prisoner sat on the back seat, flanked by KGB officers. They drove through the slush of winter snow, past bleak concrete apartment blocks draped with banners carrying communist slogans. At Khimki, the car passed a monument to the Soviet defence of Moscow in 1941, with metal girders arranged in the shape of vast anti-tank barriers. There the car turned off the highway. It was the road for Moscow's Sheremetyevo Airport.

The Aeroflot flight had already been waiting for three hours. Passengers were told that the delay was due to fog. The car drew up on the tarmac, and Solzhenitsyn was led into the forward compartment of the plane. Seven KGB men accompanied him, in plain clothes, along with a doctor. They ushered him into a seat and helped him to fasten the belt. An air stewardess dressed in a dark blue Aeroflot uniform offered sweets.

'Have a sweet or two,' urged the officer sitting next to him. 'They really help at take-off.'

As the plane flew westwards, Solzhenitsyn wondered what awaited him. It was clear that he was leaving the Soviet Union, for the first time since he had joined the advance on Germany as a soldier during the war. Once out of the country, would the KGB kill him off quietly? The men around him looked hardened, thuggish. Solzhenitsyn imagined a darkened car meeting them when they landed, then execution in the hidden basement of some Soviet embassy building. When the writer rose to use the aircraft toilet, they insisted that he leave the door open. It was, Solzhentisyn sensed, a precaution to ensure that he did not try to take his own life.

The flight descended, through clouds. As the aircraft came in to land, Solzhenitsyn could make out a river, and industrial buildings.

Once on the ground, he looked out of the window again. Above an airport terminal building there was a large sign: Frankfurt am Main. Solzhenitsyn was in West Germany.

A fortnight earlier, Chancellor Willy Brandt had suggested in a press conference that West Germany might offer asylum to the dissident writer. Andropov spotted an opening. In private correspondence with Brezhnev, the two men agreed to accelerate the two-phase plan identified by the Politburo, and move directly to exile Solzhenitsyn through a simple administrative decree revoking his Soviet citizenship. Within days, a KGB emissary flew to Bonn and agreed a deal with Brandt's adviser Egon Bahr.[23]

'Put his hat and coat on him!' barked one of the men. 'Get him out!'

As Solzhentisyn prepared to walk down the steps from the aircraft, a man stepped in front of him. He handed over five West German banknotes, in DM100 denominations.

'May I enquire to whom I owe this money?' asked the writer, in mock show of politeness.

'You don't, you don't,' replied the man.

Solzhenitsyn left the aircraft, and walked down the metal steps. A crowd was waiting at the bottom. None of the men followed him.

'Welcome, Herr Solzenitsyn . . .' A woman offered a bunch of daffodils. A man in a suit ushered him into a black Mercedes. His name was Peter Dingens, a former press attaché at the West German embassy in Moscow.

The car travelled northwards, along the autobahn. Then it climbed into the Eifel Hills, in the Rhineland towards the French border. The sky darkened as evening approached. At a small hamlet called Lagenbroich the car halted. Solzhenitsyn climbed out.

A hearty man with a moustache was standing outside a cottage. It was Heinrich Boll, the German author. The two men were old friends, and greeted each other with a hug before going inside.

Outside a crowd of journalists waited, with photographers and cameras. Even *Washington Post* correspondent Robert Kaiser was there, having broken his skiing holiday in the Alps to get to the story.[24] They wanted to hear from the acclaimed writer, now released from the Soviet Union. Boll and his guest stepped back outside, for an impromptu press conference.

'I said quite enough while I was in the Soviet Union,' explained Solzenitsyn. 'Now I shall be silent for a while.'[25]

Since February, the House Judiciary Committee had moved ahead with its investigation into the case for impeachment against the president. Under chair Peter Rodino and his deputy John Doar, the committee took a different approach to the Ervin Committee in the Senate the previous year. Both men thought that the senators had overstretched their hand, with televised, public hearings. They preferred a low-key style instead. Doar established his team in the old Congressional Hotel, with round-the-clock security and details of the investigation split up between teams as a precaution against leaks.

Leon Jaworski had succeeded Archibald Cox as special prosecutor. Like Rodino and Dour, he favoured a more discreet approach. As a representative for the Department of Justice, he faced a different decision. Rodino's committee was required to assess whether there was sufficient evidence to impeach the president, through a trial by the Senate. Jaworski must decide whether to indict Nixon in legal proceedings, leading in all probability to a case in front of the Supreme Court.

Through the spring, the White House tried to stay ahead of both investigations, and break their momentum. Both Jaworski and Rodino faced decisions with huge consequences. Rodino needed to win the support of a majority on his committee, while Jaworski required agreement from a grand jury, meeting in closed session, to proceed with an indictment. Nixon's legal team calculated that a show of cooperation, supplying documents and select tape recordings, might be sufficient to win over a majority. On 6 March, the White House announced that it would share with Rodino all the material that it had already supplied to Jaworski. Seven hundred pages of documents and nineteen recordings were handed over.

But partial disclosure only stoked the appetite for more. In early April, the House Committee voted to issue a subpoena, demanding another forty-two tape recordings. A week later, Jaworski issued his own subpoena, requesting sixty-four recordings. Rodino followed with a further demand, for 142 more tapes.

Nixon was in a bind. His ratings continued to fall. For the first time, a poll by Harris suggested a thin margin of the general public favoured impeachment. Continuing to withhold tapes would look as if the president had something to hide. But to give them up would breach the principle of executive privilege, and expose Nixon to further demands.

The solution, once more, was to meet the investigations halfway. In autumn 1973, Nixon had toyed with the idea of releasing transcripts, redacted to avoid the most compromising passages, and presented as a voluntary disclosure which would not breach executive privilege. Now, cornered by Rodino and Jaworski, he returned to the same option.

The House Committee had set a deadline to comply with the subpoena, of 25 April. As the date approached, the White House team was thrown into a frenzy of transcribing and editing selected passages from the tapes. Nixon himself reviewed each section. He had instructed his staff to publish only those sections relating to 'presidential actions'. The guideline was intended to ensure that rambling, preparatory conversations caught on the tapes would not be taken out of context. But as the lawyers worked through the tapes, they realized that it was hard to draw a clear-cut distinction. Nixon's style was to engage in long, open-ended debate. Pinpointing genuine moments of decision was difficult.

Press Secretary Ron Ziegler worried about bad language. With his family, Nixon was well spoken. But with trusted aides his language became coarser. As a soldier, Haig thought it still pretty mild. But Ziegler was concerned about offending the sensitivities of those very voters across Middle America on whose support the president relied. He removed the swear words from transcripts, replacing them with a prim moniker 'expletive deleted'.[26]

Time was pressing. The White House pushed back against the original deadline, which was extended for a further five days. Secretaries worked through the night, typing up the final version of the transcripts. The full text stretched to 1,300 pages. Nixon kept re-editing, ordering the removal of additional material. Cross references and indexes became confused in the scramble to prepare the final document for publication. Staffer Frank Gannon thought the result like the novel *Ulysses*, with streams of Nixon's monologues that would be impenetrable or misunderstood.[27]

Nixon wanted to present the transcripts on television. Ziegler's strategy was to put the president out on the front foot, shaping the public narrative with a bold stroke. Haig briefed the cabinet in advance, playing an excerpt from one tape to demonstrate how difficult the process of transcription had been. Publication would follow a few hours later, once Nixon's address had seized the headlines and news bulletins.

Nixon spoke from the Oval Office at just past nine o'clock, on the evening of Monday 29 April. He sat at his desk, dressed in a dark grey suit and tie. The transcripts were stacked on a table beside him, in thirty-eight blue folders decorated with the presidential seal.

'Good evening,' began the president. He spoke calmly, reading from his notes, eyes glancing up at the camera from time to time.

The address lasted for more than half an hour. In measured terms, Nixon set out the reasons which had led him to accept publication of the tapes, and what they contained.

'In giving you these records, blemishes and all,' he declared, 'I am placing my trust in the basic fairness of the American people.'

'I know,' Nixon added, 'that through the long, painful and difficult process revealed in these transcripts, I was trying in that period to discover what was right and to do what was right.'

Nixon concluded with a line from Lincoln. 'I do the very best I know how – and I mean to keep doing so until the end.'

Seasoned observer Theodore White thought it one of the most impressive television speeches of Nixon's career. The president was composed, his appearance conveyed gravity.[28]

Public demand for the transcripts was insatiable. The next morning, queues stretched round the US Government Printing Office, as people waited to buy copies of the transcripts, on sale for $12.25. Within a week, 3 million had sold. *Newsweek,* the *Chicago Tribune* and *The New York Times* all published serialized versions. National Public Radio delivered a full reading, right through all thirty-eight volumes. The public were transfixed. Here was an unvarnished glimpse into the White House, bad language and all.

By early May, it was clear that the venture had backfired. Public figures and newspapers across America slammed the president. William Safire, presidential speech-writer now turned columnist, called his former boss 'guilty of conduct unbecoming a president'. The Christian evangelist Billy Graham claimed that he felt nauseous when he read the transcripts.[29] Two weeks after publication, a Harris poll found a clear majority now favoured impeachment.[30]

In the offices of the House Judiciary Committee, telegrams flooded in. 'Impeach the [Expletive Deleted]!' they declared. Peter Rodino could sense his moment.

Henry Kissinger was tired. So was his new bride, Nancy Maginnes. The couple had first met in the summer of 1964, when they both worked on Nelson Rockefeller's presidential campaign. Kissinger was recently separated from his first wife, Annaliese. Ten years later, in March 1974, he and Nancy married. It was a simple, private ceremony, presided over by a family court judge.

A month later, Henry was back in the Middle East. Preliminary contacts with Israeli and Syrian diplomats suggested that there might be an opening to reach a peace deal over the Golan Heights. In the Yom Kippur War, Syrian forces had stormed Israeli positions on the hills, which separated the Damascus plain from the Sea of Galilee. The Israelis launched a counteroffensive in the closing days of the war. Armoured forces created a salient, stretching almost to the suburbs of Damascus.

Kissinger arrived in the region at the end of April, with Nancy accompanying him. For the next month, the secretary of state followed the same path of shuttle diplomacy between Damascus and Tel Aviv which he had pursued with Cairo at the start of the year. Nancy cut a dashing figure on the trail. Ten years younger than her husband, and tall with auburn hair, journalists followed her around at each stop. At the King David Hotel in Jerusalem, she swum up and down the pool, followed by a secret service agent.[31]

Golan proved a harder negotiation than that over Sinai, four months before. The basic principle was the same. Israel would pull back to an agreed line, in return for limitations over deployment of forces in the vicinity by either side, supervised by UN monitors. But the military calculus was more complex. While Sinai was open desert, the Golan Heights were more rugged terrain, with settlements dotted across rocky hills. Both sides feared the other might gain advantage by occupation of a key hilltop, as a springboard for future conflict.

At a political level, the balance was equally difficult. Israeli leader Golda Meir's premiership was stumbling to a close, wounded by a public inquiry into the war and a crumbling parliamentary majority. Defence Minister Moshe Dayan had become a reviled figure, harangued and even spat on in public.[32] In Damascus, Syrian president and former air force chief Hafez al-Assad proceeded with extreme caution. He had assumed power as part of a military junta in the wake of the upheaval in Jordan four years before, when Syrian military support to the Palestinian fedayeen (guerillas) was defeated by the Jordanians. A misstep in concessions to the Israelis could expose Assad to the same fate.

In late May, the negotiations moved to a crescendo. Kissinger had brought the parties close to agreement over two lines – red for Syria and blue for Israel – which marked the furthest deployment of their forces. Between them, a UN observer force would monitor compliance. Behind, limitations would be placed on how many men, tanks and artillery each side could position within reach of the other. Each concession, often just a few hundred yards in one direction or the other, had to be 'wrested from their very souls', recalled Kissinger. It was a gruelling experience. Meetings ground on late into the night. Nancy was suffering from stomach ulcers with the strain. The press pack travelling aboard Kissinger's plane joked that they were like hostages, and took to wearing lapel badges demanding their freedom.[33]

Monday 27 May was Kissinger's fifty-first birthday. He was in Damascus. The previous night, the secretary of state had been mired in last-ditch talks with Assad until three o'clock in the morning. It seemed futile, and Assad appeared to be slipping away. Removing forces from Sinai and now Golan was, he told his guest, like 'deflating various balloons', which would reduce the pressure on Israel. A country constructed on Zionism was doomed to failure. Israel was using Nixon's weakness as a result of Watergate to pressure Washington into forcing a bad deal on the Arabs.[34]

Fortified by a birthday cake from his staff, Kissinger returned in the morning to bid Assad farewell. They met in his private quarters. There was just one adviser on each side in attendance, along with Isa Sabbagh, the Arab-American interpreter who had worked with Kissinger throughout the shuttle.[35]

The conversation started in a detached, wistful tone. The two men agreed a brief statement, confirming that the talks would be put on pause. Kissinger suggested a reference to the 'warm hospitality' that he had received, joking that it had caused him to put on ten pounds. Assad laughed.

The statement agreed, Kissinger rose to say farewell. Assad did likewise. As they reached the door, he turned to his guest. Sabbagh translated.

He had, Assad said, enjoyed their human contact. Could he perhaps make a gesture, 'out of loyalty, out of fondness'? Might they revisit the positioning of the red line one last time?

Kissinger was in the final stages of exhaustion. This was his twelfth visit to Damascus on the trip. Over the last week, he had spent almost forty hours in sessions with the Syrians, and almost as much with the Israelis. But here, through his tiredness, he sensed an opening. Assad had, he later noted, 'played out the string to absolutely the last millimetre'.[36]

The Syrian explained. To sell a settlement to his own side, he must be seen to have maintained a presence in those parts of Golan which Syria had controlled before the Yom Kippur War. There were two villages on hilltops within the buffer zone between the two sides. Could they agree to add small loops to the line, which would allow Syria to position a limited number of men in these locations? It would give 'moral, psychological' reassurance, not a military advantage.

That night, Kissinger flew back to Tel Aviv. He met the Israeli cabinet after midnight. Golda Meir was there, along with Defence Minister Moshe Dayan and Yitzhak Rabin, the former ambassador to Washington who had recently been elected in a party leadership contest to take over from Meir, defeating rival Simon Peres. The handover was scheduled to take place at the end of the month.

The Israelis had a different problem. Two weeks before, Palestinian terrorists had seized a school in the northern Israeli town of Ma'alot. Ninety schoolchildren were taken hostage, along with their teachers. When Israeli commandos stormed the building, sixteen were killed. The nation was stunned, in shock and mourning. To carry a deal with Israeli public opinion, Assad would need to give assurances that Palestinians would not be able to operate from bases on the Golan Heights.

Over the next two days, Kissinger returned to Damascus for a final time, and then back to Tel Aviv again. The two sides had closed the deal. He called on Golda Meir and her cabinet at 2.30 a.m. 'It's alright,' the secretary of state said as he walked into her office. 'That's it. We've done it.'[37] A few hours later, Nixon made a formal announcement from the White House briefing room. The shuttle was finally over.

That evening, Golda Meir held a reception in her office. She was 76. Meir had emigrated from her native Ukraine to America in her youth, and then to Palestine. Her political career had spanned the entire lifespan of the state of Israel, since creation in 1948. Now, after five years as prime minister, it was coming to a close.

Meir offered a few words. The agreement with Syria would, she hoped, allow mothers and young wives in both countries to 'sleep at night without terror'. Perhaps it would even be the start of a lasting peace between Israel and her neighbours.

Kissinger, too, had emigrated to America as a Jew in his youth. With Meir, he sensed the affection of a Jewish mother towards her wayward son. He spoke briefly in reply. Then he turned to bid his hostess farewell. As he did so, he offered her a kiss on the cheek.

Meir could not resist a final quip. She had watched Kissinger being embraced by Arab leaders, as he travelled to their capitals in his search for peace. Now it was her turn.

'I have been afraid,' she told Kissinger, 'that you kissed only men.'[38]

Major General Walter Tkach was not used to be summoned by the president.

The officer was a surgeon with the US Air Force. He had served as assistant White House physician during the Eisenhower years, and become friendly with the Nixon family. When Richard Nixon assumed the presidency, he returned as senior doctor. The job had few demands. Apart from his bout of pneumonia the previous summer, Nixon had enjoyed good health during his time in the White House. The president was strict about his physical regime and diet.

Nixon had called Tkach to his room. It was late evening on Monday 10 June 1974. The presidential party was in Salzburg, for a stopover en route to the Middle East. Nixon had been planning the trip for months. As Kissinger pursued his shuttle between Damascus and Tel Aviv, Nixon urged him to suggest a visit to his hosts. Assad warned that, until a deal was reached, it would be premature. But now, with agreement over both Sinai and the Golan Heights, Nixon seized his moment. He would be the first president to visit the region since Franklin Roosevelt passed through Egypt on his way to the wartime conferences with Stalin and Churchill.

When Tkach entered, Nixon rolled up his trouser leg. The flesh underneath was red and swollen. The surgeon quickly recognized the symptoms. It was phlebitis, or inflammation caused by a blood clot. The condition was serious. If the clot became dislodged, it could travel to the vital organs, and prove fatal.

The surgeon's advice was clear. Travel was an unnecessary hazard. The president should check into hospital, and return to Washington once the condition had stabilized.

Nixon was dismissive. 'The purpose of this trip is more important than my life,' he told the surgeon. 'I know that I'm taking a calculated risk.'

That night, Nixon shared news of his condition with Pat and his secretary Rose Mary Woods over dinner. His leg was raised on an ottoman stool. There was, he assured them, nothing to worry about.[39]

Two days later, Nixon was in Egypt. The party arrived in Cairo to huge crowds, lining the streets from the airport into the centre of the city. President Sadat rode in an open-top car alongside his guest, as the crowds shouted 'Nixon! Nixon!' It was, the Egyptian told him, 'a real welcome from the heart.'

The next day, the two men travelled to Alexandria, by train. More crowds thronged the track during the three-hour journey. Press Secretary Ron Ziegler estimated that they numbered 2 million. People shouted, women chanting in a high-pitched warble. The two presidents rode in an antique carriage with an open balcony at the end of the train, waving to the onlookers. The temperature was over 100 °F. As the carriage jolted along the track, Nixon and Sadat clung to a handrail overhead.

The pain in the president's leg throbbed. Out of the corner of his eye, he spotted a hearse, driving along a road parallel with the railway line. For a moment he wondered if Haig, whom he had warned about his condition, had made arrangements in case it proved fatal.

'Thank you Nixon!' read one banner held by the crowd. 'We trust Nixon!'

As the train approached Alexandria, the two men briefed a group of journalists travelling with them. One asked what contribution the United States could make towards peace in the Middle East.

In reply, Sadat referred to the banners they had seen.

'President Nixon never gave a word and didn't fulfill it,' he said. 'He has fulfilled every word that he gave.'[40]

From Egypt, the party travelled to Saudi Arabia. In the royal palaces where they lodged, the travelling party found that the air conditioning had been turned down to glacial temperatures. Pat Nixon was reduced to spending the night in a marble bathtub, which was marginally warmer than her bed, wrapped in all the blankets she could find.[41]

The party flew on to Damascus. It was the first time a US president had visited Syria. As *Spirit of '76* crossed the border, four MiG jets from the Syrian Air Force appeared in the sky. Looking out of the window, staffer Steve Bull turned to National Security Adviser Brent Scowcroft.

'Brent, what is that?' he asked.

'Oh, shit!' replied the airforce officer.

Up in the cockpit, Pilot Ralph Albertazzie had received no prior notice of this escort. For a few anxious minutes, he threw the presidential aircraft into a series of evasive manoeuvres. Inside the cabin, staffer Larry Eagleburger had been writing a note for Kissinger on arrival protocol. 'You will get off the plane right behind Mrs Nixon,' he jotted down. Then, as the plane swerved into another steep bank, he added the words 'I hope . . .'.[42]

Safely on the ground, President Assad embraced his guests with a welcome to match that which they had received in Egypt. Canons fired a twenty-one gun salute, and soldiers with fixed bayonets lined the road from the airport. In the distance, through a shimmering haze, the visitors could make out the Golan Heights. At dinner that evening, they were treated to a whole roast lamb with an apple in its mouth. 'Let us open a new page,' declared Assad in his welcome toast.

Outside, in the kitchens, presidential valet Manolo Sanchez talked with his hosts. The welcome seemed genuine. Americans were always smiling, said one, whereas Russians looked grim.

The next morning, Assad escorted his visitor back to the airport. During the trip, Nixon's phlebitis had eased somewhat. But, as he watched Nixon on his travels,

Kissinger sensed a growing detachment, conveyed in a waxy, glazed expression on his face. The journey had brought relief from the pressures of Watergate, but no escape.[43]

Now, at the airport, the time had come to part. During his visit, Nixon warmed to his Syrian host. Assad struck him as a man of substance, even with a touch of mystique. His large, domed forehead reminded Nixon of his speech-writer Pat Buchanan.

Asad reached forward. He kissed Nixon on each cheek.[44]

Spirit of '76 returned to Washington on Wednesday 19 June. Vice President Gerald Ford welcomed Nixon back at the White House. He quoted an Arabic proverb, 'May Allah make the end better than the beginning.'

The American capital continued to boil with speculation over Watergate. The House Judicial Committee had almost completed a review of evidence received over the case for impeachment, including the tape transcripts. Decision would follow, but there were mixed signals on which way the committee members might break.

The following Tuesday, Nixon was off on his travels again, bound for Moscow. He had spent the long weekend at Camp David, away from the media. News of his phlebitis had leaked out, and questions about the president's health added to those about Watergate. Some wits joked that Nixon was flying to the Soviet Union to claim asylum.

Brezhnev welcomed the president in person, at Vnukovo aiport. He strode across the tarmac to greet Nixon. It was their third summit meeting. The two men reviewed an honour guard, drawn from the different armed forces of the Soviet Union. In the distance, a crowd waved flags from both countries.[45]

Back in Washington, the backdrop to détente was darkening. Critics in Congress, led by Senator Henry 'Scoop' Jackson, were seeking to constrain the administration on several fronts. Jackson continued to press for assurances that the Soviet Union would allow Jews to emigrate in greater numbers, in return for granting free trade with the United States. Publication of *The Gulag Archipelago* and the exile of Solzenitsyn increased the moral case for a tougher line against Moscow. In an interview with veteran broadcaster Walter Cronkite, the writer had warned Americans against pursuing a 'pseudo-détente' with the USSR.

Meanwhile, both Jackson and the Pentagon manoeuvred to limit negotiating options over arms control. Talks in Geneva over a new agreement on SALT had become bogged down. Veteran negotiator Paul Nitze resigned in frustration. Then, on the day after he returned from the Middle East, Nixon faced a bruising meeting of the National Security Council, at which Defence Secretary James Schlesinger and the joint chiefs took an unexpectedly tough line. It was, Nixon confided in his diary, a 'real shocker'.[46]

With Nixon and Kissinger boxed in back home, there was little scope to make progress on substance at the summit. The White House was still determined to reinforce the positive image of Nixon projected during the Middle East tour. But the travelling American press party was keeping a close eye. At a grand dinner in the Kremlin on the first evening, Nixon gave a warm toast, speaking of the personal relationship between the two leaders. Soviet news agency Tass translated the phrase as 'relations that have grown up between us'. American journalists seized on the reference, which could be taken to imply that Nixon's personal contribution was less central to détente than hitherto. Press Secretary Ron Ziegler tried to correct the reference, but the impression stuck.[47]

Brezhnev was still determined to give his guest a warm reception. 'It is too early to put a full stop to this process,' he told Nixon at the opening session of the talks. Progress would require them to 'overcome obstacles and negative accretions of the past'.

Nixon agreed. 'The more we find areas to work together, the more we make the relationship binding,' he noted. 'It takes small as well as large threads.'[48]

On Saturday 29 June, Brezhnev travelled down with Nixon and Kissinger to his holiday retreat, on the Crimean coast. They flew aboard the general secretary's TU-104. Brezhnev was thrilled with his new telephone, which made calls from the plane. He phoned his wife, and passed the handset to Nixon to pass on his greetings. Ambassador Dobrynin had missed the flight, as he had slipped back to his apartment in Moscow to collect some belongings. He managed to catch a lift aboard *Spirit of '76*, which also flew down to the Crimea. Speech-writer Pat Buchanan took a photo of the Soviet diplomat, posing in Nixon's chair on board the presidential aircraft.[49]

The villa was situated in a suburb of Yalta, called Oreanda. Sensitive to parallels with the wartime gathering between Roosevelt, Stalin and Churchill, at which the Western leaders had acquiesced in Soviet domination of eastern Europe, the White House advance party persuaded their hosts to rename the location. In a small act of détente, the presidential motorcade discreetly bypassed Yalta town. The Americans arrived at their destination to find freshly painted signs, naming Oreanda as a town in its own right.[50]

The next day, Brezhnev took Nixon out for a cruise on his motorboat. The two men sat in the stern of the vessel, chatting in the sun with their jackets off, while KGB staff in sailor suits served refreshments. Kissinger, Gromyko, Haig and Dobrynin joined them. The sea was choppy, and at one point some plates slid off the table. A few hundred feet away, other members of the presidential party were given a more liquid reception on a separate boat. Major George Joulwan, a presidential aide from the Marine Corps, was due to receive promotion to Lieutenant Colonel that day. Vodka flowed among the group in celebration, and the toasts become more raucous. Buchanan and his fellow speech-writer Ray Price were having a great time.

'Fuck the KGB!' declared one of the American party, slamming down his empty glass on the table.

There was an awkward silence.

Then one of the Russians laughed, followed by another. 'Fuck the KGB!' one shouted.

'Fuck the CIA!' shot back another.

Several hours later, the American party arrived back at shore. They ran into Nixon and his host, returning from their own cruise. Brezhnev was in a fulsome mood. He threw his arms around Buchanan in a hug. Haig shot the ragged group a dark look.[51]

Back in Moscow, Nixon was due to deliver a television address to the Soviet people. Price had been labouring over the script. The president had told his speech-writer that he wanted to appeal to a 'community of spirit' between the two nations.

The two men grappled for an image that would make this theme more tangible. Two years before, Nixon had signed an agreement on cooperation in space during his last visit to Moscow. American astronauts were now training alongside their Soviet counterparts, in preparation for a joint mission. It was, Nixon told his television audience, a journey made possible by 'careful planning, by precise engineering' towards a common goal. Peace would come the same way, step by step.[52]

The next afternoon, Nixon was due to leave Moscow. Brezhnev joined him in the presidential limousine for the drive out to the airport. He was wearing a dark suit with four buttons down the front, and his two medals for Hero of the Soviet Union and Hero of Socialist Labour. Gromyko, Podgorny and Kosygin all crammed into the car as well. The drive took almost half an hour. Brezhnev's colleagues did most of the talking, while the general secretary sat in silence.

The car arrived at Vnukovo. Nixon and Brezhnev walked together towards *Spirit of '76.*

The president said that he was sorry that Brezhnev was not travelling back with him, to Washington. The host said that he had had the same thought, during the car ride. There was an air of sadness to him, even disappointment. Brezhnev had held high expectations for the summit, and now it was over.

Nixon turned shook hands with the Soviet leaders in turn. Then he climbed the steps to the plane. At the top he gave a final wave, and tossed a fountain pen with the presidential signature to Viktor Sukhodrev as a gift. The interpreter caught it neatly. Then Nixon stepped into the cabin, and looked around.

'Well,' said the president. 'We're home again.'[53]

Notes

1   Shlaim (2000), 321.
2   FRUS 1969–76 Vol. XXVI, item 1, p. 3; Kissinger (1982), 800–3; Dayan (1976), 464–5.
3   Dayan (1976), 50.
4   Ambrose (1991), 290–1.
5   Kissinger (1982), 637–9; Sadat (1978), 291.
6   Kissinger (1982), 818–21.
7   FRUS 1969–76 Vol. XXVI, item 4, p. 13.
8   Dayan (1976), 476.

9   Meir (1975), 360.
10 Martin (1998), 463.
11 Sadat (1978), 303.
12 Kissinger (1982), 836.
13 Kissinger (1982), 844–6.
14 Haig (1992), 442; Nixon (1978), 978.
15 Ford (1979), 115–16.
16 Ford (1979), 116–17.
17 Eisenhower (1986), 610–11.
18 Ford (1979), 117.
19 Quoted in David Remnick article 'The Exile Returns' in *The New Yorker*, 14 February 1994. See also Scammel (1995) doc. 99, p. 283–92.
20 Smith (1977), 515.
21 Solzhenitsyn (1975), 383–402.
22 Solzhentisyn (1995), 406–11.
23 Scammel (1995) doc. 120, p. 342–6.
24 Kaiser (1976), 402.
25 Solzhenitsyn (1975), 442–51.
26 Woodward and Bernstein (1976), 124–5; Haig (1992), 451–2.
27 Woodward and Bernstein (1976), 136.
28 White (1975), 296.
29 Perlstein (2014), 234.
30 White (1975), 298.
31 Issacson (1992), 591.
32 Peres (1995), 180–1.
33 Kissinger (1982), 1109, 1086.
34 FRUS 1969–76 Vol. XXVI, item 74, p. 300–16; Kissinger (1982), 1096; Scowcroft interview, 29 June 2007, p. 23.
35 FRUS 1969–76 Vol. XXVI, item 75, p. 316–34; Kissinger (1982), 1097–9.
36 Kissinger (1982), 1098.
37 Meir (1975), 374.
38 Kissinger (1982), 1108.
39 Woodward and Bernstein (1975), 213–14; Haig (1994), 458–9; Eisenhower (1986), 628.
40 Nixon (1978), 1011; Thomas (2017), 487; Haig (1994), 459; Woodward and Bernstein (1975), 216–17; Kissinger (1982), 1128; Scowcroft interview, 29 June 2007, p. 22.
41 Eisenhower (1986), 631.
42 Buchanan (2017), 370; Kissinger (1982), 1132; Haig (1994), 459–60; Bull interview with Naftali, 25 June 2007, p. 28.
43 Kissinger (1982), 1125.
44 Nixon (1978), 1013–14; Eisenhower (1986), 632; 'Nixon Warmly Welcomed on Arrival in Damascus', *The New York Times*, 16 June 1974; Kissinger (1982), 1132.
45 Nixon (1978), 1027; Woodward and Bernstein (1975), 222.
46 Nixon (1978), 1024–5; Kaufman (2000), 278–9; Kissinger (1982), 1151–61; Nitze (1986), 337–41.
47 Woodward and Bernstein (1975), 224–5. See Smith (1974) for account of the dinner.
48 FRUS 1969–76 Vol. XV, item 186, p. 899–910.
49 Nixon (1978), 1029–30; Dobrynin (1995), 312–13; Buchanan (2017), 374.
50 Eisenhower (1986), 609; Price (1977), 296–7.

51 Nixon (1978), 1032–3; Buchanan (2017), 375–6; Price (1977), 297–8; Sukhodrev (1999), 317–18; Vavilov (2016), 202–3.
52 Price (1977), 294; 'President Nixon's Address to the Soviet People', at nixonfoundation. org.
53 Nixon (1978), 1039; Vavilov (2016), 217–18.

Chapter 11

AWFUL WISDOM
(July–December 1974)

It was the moment when Al Haig knew the game was up.

The chief of staff arrived at his office at the White House on the morning of Monday 29 July. The previous week had brought two further blows over Watergate. The Supreme Court reached a unanimous verdict that Nixon be required to hand over all the tapes subpoenaed by Special Prosecutor Leon Jaworski. The ploy of publishing edited transcripts had failed. Two days later, the House Judiciary Committee voted by a heavy margin to recommend impeachment proceedings. Six of the seventeen Republican members lined up alongside Democrats in favour.

At the same time, Nixon's legal team – Fred Buzhardt and James St Clair – had become concerned over one of the tape recordings. It related to the conversation between Nixon and Haldeman on 23 June 1972, a few days after news of Watergate first broke. Haig asked the lawyers to prepare a transcript.

As he sat at his desk in the West Wing, Haig read the text. On paper, the words were stark, unequivocal. Nixon had given Haldeman instructions for the CIA to intervene with the FBI and halt the investigation.

President: 'Say, look the problem is that this will open the whole Bay of Pigs thing, and the President just feels that, ah, without going into the details – don't lie to them to the extent to say there's no involvement, but just say this is a comedy of errors . . . . They should just call the FBI in and . . . don't go further into this case period. Well, can you get it done?'

Haldeman: 'I think so.'

Haig knew that the tape changed everything. The lawyers agreed. The recording was clear, compelling evidence. They could not withhold or delay it. And, once it became known, the case against Nixon would be devastating.

The next day, the lawyers briefed the president. Once Nixon had absorbed the news, Haig offered his own advice. 'I just don't see how we can survive this one,' he told the president. 'We have to face facts.' Nixon nodded, but said nothing.

Outside the Oval Office, Haig realized that he would have to act. The president's days were numbered. As chief of staff, he must help Nixon come round to accepting his fate. And he had to make quiet preparations for an orderly transition of power.

Haig's first call was to Kissinger. Relations between the two men had been strained at times. In Moscow, they bickered over who should occupy a bedroom in the Kremlin next to Nixon. But now they realized that they would have to work together. Kissinger was the senior member of the cabinet, and would be crucial to a transition. The situation was, Haig explained, terminal.[1]

Next, Haig spoke to the closest White House advisers: Press Secretary Ron Ziegler, and speech-writers Pat Buchanan and Ray Price. He showed them the transcript. They all agreed that Nixon's fate was sealed. Piecing together events over recent months, Buchanan suspected that Nixon had learned of the tape earlier that year. It was the reason that he had dug in over release of the recording. That evening, Haig discreetly summoned Price into his office. He asked the aide to start work on a resignation speech.[2]

By Thursday morning, 1 August, Nixon had made his decision. He called Haig into the Oval Office.

'Al, it's over,' he told his chief of staff.

Without the votes in Congress, impeachment was inevitable. The president had decided that he must resign. But he wanted to spend a last weekend at Camp David, bringing his family round to the choice that he had made. He instructed Haig to work with Price on the resignation speech, and to warn the vice president what was coming.

Haig met with Gerald Ford that morning, in his office in the Old Executive Office. Ford's own chief of staff, Robert Hartmann, was also present. Haig did not trust Hartmann, and spoke only in code. The vice president should, he said, be prepared for 'changes in your life'. They might come soon.

Later that afternoon, Haig managed to track down Ford alone, at his office on the Capitol. The vice president thought his visitor looked even more tired than he had done that morning. This time, Haig was frank.

'Are you ready, Mr Vice President, to assume the presidency in a short period of time?'

'If it happens, Al, I am prepared,' replied Ford.

Haig explained. A tape had come to light with new evidence and Nixon had decided to resign. Then Haig turned to a more delicate subject. Buzhardt had prepared a list of options for how the transfer of power might take place. They included the sensitive issue of whether Nixon might pardon himself, or be pardoned by his successor. Haig handed over a short note, summarizing the options. Ford asked a couple of questions, to clarify his understanding.

The conversation had made things seem more real. Haig felt a wave of sadness pass over him. As he rose to take his leave, the two men embraced.

That night, Ford shared the news with his wife Betty. They talked until after midnight. Both believed strongly that Ford should not offer a view on the options set out by Buzhardt. At last, the couple retired to bed. Still awake, they lay in the darkness, holding hands. Then they started to pray.

'God, give us strength and wisdom, give us guidance as the possibility of a new life confronts us.

'We promise to do our very best, whatever may take place.
'In Jesus' name we pray.'[3]

The sixty-four tapes requested by Jaworski were released on Monday 5 August. They included that of 23 June 1972, with the conversation between Nixon and Haldeman.

Inside the White House, Haig has assembled staffers to brace them for what was coming. If they could no longer give their loyalty to the president, he explained, they must give it to the country. His voice cracked as he spoke, and many of those listening were in tears. When the chief of staff had finished speaking, they broke into applause.

Outside, the news broke over Washington like a bombshell. On Capitol Hill, support for Nixon was draining away by the hour. Senator Barry Goldwater had been a firm defender of the president. Now, as he read the tape transcripts, he was consumed with rage. Here was proof that the president had lied.[4]

That evening, Nixon took his family out for a cruise on the *Sequoia*. It was a beautiful summer evening, but Pat and the girls seldom found such outings a relaxation. The ship was on full view from the banks and bridges along the Potomac River, where journalists were camped out, leaning over the parapets to snap pictures. Julie felt it was like a deathwatch. But they recognized that the president needed some respite. Over dinner, the group tried to keep the conversation going, and Nixon reminisced about life in the White House. Afterwards, he retired to his cabin. His phlebitis had flared up again.

As the craft meandered downstream, Haig called over the radiophone. Secretary Rose Mary Woods answered, while the others hovered in the background. It was an update on the position in Congress. Afterwards, she went down to Nixon's cabin to pass on the news.

At half-past seven, the yacht docked at the Navy Yard. As he disembarked, Nixon shook hands with Lieutenant Commander Combs, the supervising officer.

'It has been wonderful,' said the president.[5]

The position in Congress was crucial. While Nixon could still rely on a majority of Republicans to support him, he was protected against a vote to go ahead with impeachment, or indeed an eventual verdict of presidential guilt. But the tapes had swept away his final defences. The following morning, in a meeting of the cabinet, Republican Party Chair George Bush dropped the first suggestion that Nixon might need to resign.

By Wednesday, it was clear the die was cast. Haig arranged for a delegation of senior Republicans to call on the president. The group comprised of Hugh Scott, leader in the Senate, Barry Goldwater, and Congressman John Rhodes, leader from the House. This trio arrived at five o'clock, through the basement entrance. Haig caught a word with them before they entered the Oval Office. He advised them to present facts, not advice.

Goldwater acted at spokesman. He was blunt.

Nixon asked how many votes he might have in the Senate. Goldwater suggested between sixteen and eighteen. Scott put the figure at no higher than fifteen.

'I don't have many alternatives, do I?' responded Nixon.

The three visitors were silent.

'There'll be no tears from me,' the president reassured them. 'I haven't cried since Eisenhower died.'[6]

Afterwards, Nixon went up to the family quarters for dinner. The group gathered in the Solarium, their favourite room. Julie and Tricia were both there, along with their husbands, David and Ed. Pat looked composed, but the girls could tell from the raised angle of her head that she was feeling the strain. Earlier in the week, the girls had made a last-ditch effort to talk their father out of resignation. But, since the outing on the *Sequoia* two days before, they and Pat had quietly begun to accept the inevitable. The three of them had spent the time packing up belongings. Now, joined by Nixon, the group ate dinner off trays, and tried to keep the conversation light. Presidential valet Manolo Sanchez let the dogs in, and the others fed them with tidbits.

After dinner, there was a knock at the door. It was Olli Atkins, the White House photographer. The president had asked him to join them, for the record. Pat tried to explain that she couldn't face having a picture taken, but Nixon was insistent. Awkwardly, the group posed in a line, holding hands. Pat and the girls were fighting back tears.[7]

Afterwards, Nixon retired to the Lincoln Sitting Room. At his request, Kissinger joined him. As he entered, the secretary of state found memories of previous encounters in the same place flooding through his mind. Before, the small, book-lined study had conveyed a sense of concentrated power. Now it was filled with silence and solitude.

For two hours, the two men talked. Their conversation meandered across their efforts together in foreign policy over the previous six years. Kissinger thought the president shattered, but still in control of himself. He sought to consol his companion. History would offer a less severe judgement on Nixon's achievements.

It was close to midnight, and Kissinger rose to leave. As the two men walked down the corridor to the elevator together, Nixon stopped outside the Lincoln Bedroom. He explained that each evening he would kneel briefly in this spot, recalling the Quaker tradition that he had inherited from his mother. Might they pray together now, he asked?

Kissinger was not a religious man. But he agreed, and they entered the room together. It contained relics from Lincoln's presidency, including a copy of the Gettysburg Address in the former president's own handwriting.

Kissinger felt a deep sense of awe. As they prayed together, he found himself remembering the words of Agamemnon, in the eponymous tragedy by Aeschylus. The ancient playwright had talked about pain bringing wisdom, drop by drop, even against the will of men. Those lines were a favourite of Robert Kennedy. The presidential candidate had quoted them in April 1968, in response to news of

Martin Luther King's assassination. Two months later, he himself was dead. Now Kissinger found the same lines reverberating in his head, as he prayed in Lincoln's former abode.[8]

Since the previous week, Ray Price had been working on a resignation speech. While news of Nixon's plans remained private, he was obliged to keep his assignment hidden, deflecting requests for more routine work with excuses. Plans and timelines kept shifting.

Eventually, on Tuesday afternoon, Haig had confirmed the schedule. The president expected to make a televised address from the Oval Office, on Thursday evening. Price and Haig talked quickly, as the chief of staff gobbled down a late lunch at his desk, of sandwich, fries and a Pepsi-Cola. They both thought that Nixon should deliver a healing speech, which would pave the way for his successor to bring the country back together.

For the next forty-eight hours, drafts flowed between Price's office in the Old Executive Building, and Nixon's private hideaway in the same block. Following his meeting with Kissinger, Nixon chewed over the text once more. A few hours later, he placed a call through to Price's home. It was 4.15 a.m. The speech-writer had only turned into bed a couple of hours before, and was exhausted.

The president sounded animated. He apologized for calling at night. But he had been thinking. He wanted to make a speech that looked to the future, reminding his audience what still remained to be done. Price made some notes, and Nixon hung up.

Fifteen minutes later, the phone rang again. Nixon had been thinking some more. His speech, he explained, should talk about the need to reduce the threat of war, not just limit it. Mankind should turn away from making weapons, to building the benefits of a stable peace.

A few minutes later, the phone rang again. By now, Price was up, and working on his text. He finished a revised draft at half-past eight.

More summons to the Oval Office followed during the day. Seeing Nixon behind his desk, Price was shocked. The president was drawn and haggard. He wondered if Nixon had managed to sleep at all.[9]

The broadcast was scheduled for that evening, at nine o'clock. Price submitted his final draft at six. That evening, before his speech, Nixon was due to meet with the cabinet. Forty-six colleagues had assembled in the Cabinet Room. Nixon walked in, and took his usual chair. It was just after eight o'clock.

Nixon started to speak. A sob broke from one of his audience, then another. Soon, men were crying openly. The president continued, then looked at his watch. He had been speaking for almost half an hour. Eventually, the emotion became too much. Nixon burst into tears.

'I just hope that I haven't let you down,' he said, in a broken voice.

An aide escorted the president from the meeting. Haig found him in a small room, next to the Oval Office. He was looking over Price's text, for a final time. Haig was worried that, after the emotion of the cabinet meeting, Nixon would not be able to make it through the broadcast. The president took a deep breath, then turned to his chief of staff.

'Al, don't worry,' he said. 'I just can't stand it when other people cry.'

The Oval Office was set up for filming. A crew from CBS had assembled lights and cameras. Nixon would speak from his desk. The president entered a few minutes before the broadcast was due to start. Apart from the crew, there was only a secret service agent in the room. Nixon had asked that others, including his family, remain outside.

Over in the Old Executive Building, Price was due to watch the speech on television, in legal adviser Fred Buzhardt's office. His former colleague and speech-writer William Safire had joined them for the occasion. But Buzhardt was struggling to get his set working. The minutes were ticking down to nine o'clock. Eventually someone fetched another television from a nearby office. As the screen lit up, the group could make out a familiar scene. Nixon was sitting behind his desk. He wore the same blue suit that he had worn for his first televised broadcast in Moscow, during the summit two years before. He had chosen it specially, because the thinner fabric was cool under the hot television lights.

'Good evening,' began the president.

Nixon went on. He explained the developments of recent days. Without a base of support in Congress, it would be wrong to continue the process.

'Therefore,' he continued, 'I shall resign the presidency effective at noon tomorrow.'

Price's text was on the desk in front of him. But Nixon hardly looked down as he spoke, explaining the decision that he had just announced. His resignation would, he hoped, hasten a 'process of healing' which was desperately needed across the country. Looking back, he recalled the pledge made in his first inaugural speech to advance peace among nations. The world was, he believed, a safer place as a result of his actions.

'All our children have a better chance than before of living in peace rather than dying in war,' he concluded. 'This, more than anything, is what I hope will be my legacy.'

The lights dimmed and the broadcast was over. Price looked at his watch. It was 9.16 p.m.[10]

Nixon rose and the camera crew stood back. As the speech drew to a close, Kissinger had slipped into the back of the room. Now he walked with the president back to his quarters. He reminded Nixon of what he had said during their conversation on the Wednesday night. History would judge Nixon a great president.

They reached the door, where Julie was waiting for him. Before going inside, Nixon turned to face Kissinger.

'That depends, Henry,' he said, 'on who writes the history.'[11]

The next morning Nixon woke with a jolt. It was six o'clock. He ordered a breakfast of corned beef hash and poached eggs from the White House kitchen. Then he returned to the Lincoln Sitting Room. He had one more speech to write.

He settled down with a yellow notepad. On the table before him lay a pile of books, presidential memoirs. They contained slips of paper, where Nixon had marked out passages that caught his attention.

There was a knock at the door. It was Haig. Apologetically, he produced a typed sheet of paper, and placed it on the desk. It contained one line.

'I hereby resign the Office of President of the United States.'

Nixon took his pen, and signed. Afterwards, when Haig had left, he remembered a new reference that he wanted to use, from Teddy Roosevelt. He asked one of his staff to fetch some biographies of the former president which were in his study over in the Old Executive Building.

The president was due to address his cabinet and White House staff for a final time, at half-past nine, in the East Room. He had decided that the occasion should be televised. Officials had worked through the night to prepare, laying cables and setting up chairs.

The moment had arrived. David, Julie, Tricia and Ed were waiting in the hallway, outside the Lincoln Sitting Room. Pat joined them. She was wearing a pink and white dress, and dark glasses. The First Lady had been up all night, sorting through packing. She looked exhausted. Nixon, too, was ashen. He was holding one of the biographies of Teddy Roosevelt. After saying farewell to the Residence staff, he passed the book to Ed.

The family walked to the elevator, and descended to the ground floor. An aide briefed them. Everything had been choreographed. There were names, taped to the floor, so they would know where to stand. When he mentioned television cameras, Pat and Tricia flinched. They had not expected to be filmed. But Nixon was insistent.

The group paused for a moment. Pat and the girls were struggling to control their emotions. Tricia suggested that they take three deep breaths, to calm themselves. The doors leading into the East Room swung open. Marine Lieutenant Colonel Jack Brennan made the announcement.

'Ladies and Gentlemen, the President of the United States and Mrs Nixon!'

The Nixon family walked forwards. In front, an audience of over four hundred had gathered. Cabinet members and senior staffers sat on chairs. Speech-writer Pat Buchanan and his wife Shelley had arrived late, and stood at the back of the room. As the group entered, everyone rose to their feet, clapping waves of applause. In a daze, the group found their places on the stage. Nixon stepped forwards to a microphone, while Tricia reached out for her mother's hand. The applause went on.

Eventually, the clapping died down. Nixon looked out at the faces in front of him. But it was too much. Colleagues from over the years were red-eyed, tears streaming down their faces. He focused on the cameras instead.

The president started to speak. He talked about his roots, his childhood and parents in California. Then he talked about his mother. There would be no books written about her, he said, but she was a saint.

Turning to Ed, Nixon took the volume about Teddy Roosevelt. He pulled out a pair of thick, black reading glasses. It was the first time that he had worn them in public. Looking on, Kissinger wondered if it was a deliberate gesture of vulnerability. The secretary of state was in tears. But he found himself angered, too, that his emotions were being stirred at such a heart-breaking sight, perhaps deliberately.

Nixon had chosen the words that Roosevelt had written when his first wife died. 'When my heart's dearest died,' he read, 'the light went from my life forever.'

Looking up from the book, Nixon elaborated his point. Roosevelt had written these words as a young man. But he had gone on to rebuild his life, and to serve the country as president. Greatness came only when people were tested, and found a way to climb back from the deepest valley to the highest mountain.

'Remember,' he concluded. 'Others may hate you, but those who hate you don't win unless you hate them, and then you destroy yourself.'

It was over. Nixon walked away from the podium, and out of the East Room. Gerald Ford and his wife Betty were waiting discreetly in a side room. He stepped forward, and held out his hand.

'Good luck, Mr President,' said Nixon. 'I know the country is going to be in good hands.'

'Thank you, Mr President,' replied Ford.

The two couples walked outside. There was a red carpet, leading across the South Lawn to the Marine One helicopter. Pat whispered to Betty. 'You'll see so many of these red carpets,' she warned, 'and you'll get so you hate them.'

They reached the helicopter. The two men shook hands, and the women kissed. Ford felt the departing president touch his elbow, holding the grip for a moment. It was, he thought, a gentle way to wish him good luck.

Nixon climbed the steps to the aircraft. He turned for a moment, and stood facing the crowd. He held both arms outstretched, fingers extended in his favoured V-for-Victory sign. Then he turned back, and climbed inside.

The rotors spun, and the helicopter lifted into the air. Watching from the ground, Ford reached out to squeeze his wife's hand. 'We can do it,' he said. 'We're ready.'

As the couple walked back to the White House alone, Kissinger realized the prayer that he should have offered two nights before, in the Lincoln Bedroom. Ford was a good man, with a stout heart. Under his stewardship, Kissinger hoped that America would rediscover its faith, and that fate would be kind to this new president.[12]

Just before midday, it was the turn of Gerald and Betty Ford to enter the East Room. He was wearing a dark tie, with light diagonal stripes. Betty wore a light blue dress, with white trimming, and her dark hair in a neat perm.

The room was packed. Chief Justice Warren Burger was there, along with Kissinger as senior member of the cabinet. Half an hour before, Kissinger had formally taken receipt of Nixon's letter of resignation. Now Berger administered the oath of office of the new president. Applause echoed through the room. In the front row, Ford's children clapped vigorously.

The new president walked to the podium, and began to speak. It was not, he explained, an inaugural address. He came to the presidency in extraordinary and troubling circumstances. Rather, he wanted to give 'a little straight talk among friends'. As with Nixon, two hours before, his speech was broadcast live on television.

Ford noted that he had neither campaigned for the position, nor been elected to it. It was a time to come together, between political parties, and serve the needs of the people. 'My fellow Americans,' he announced, drawling the vowels in his Midwest accent. 'Our long national nightmare is over ... Our great Republic is a government of laws and not of men.'

As he drew to a close, Ford introduced a different note. He asked his audience to remember Nixon and his family in their prayers. 'May our former president who brought peace to millions,' he declared, 'find it for himself.'

Then came the final line. 'God helping me,' declared the new president, 'I will not let you down.'

The room erupted into applause. Ford stepped away from the podium, to join his wife. He put an arm around her shoulder. Then, as the applause continued, they stepped forward and away from the stage.[12]

Jerry Ford was comfortable making decisions. His 'lifetime batting average', as he put it, was high. He liked to consult a few people whose views he trusted, reflect and reach a view.[14] Where Nixon had chewed over the issues for hours, testing arguments and playing devil's advocate with his staff, Ford preferred clarity. Three weeks into his presidency, he could sense that was needed more than ever.

The first weeks had gone well. Ford's arrival was a breath of fresh air after the long ordeal of Watergate. The straight-talking new president from Michigan cut a fresh image. *The Washington Post* published a photo of him bouncing on a trampoline at Camp David, in shirtsleeves with arms outstretched. He and Betty danced the night away at a state dinner for King Hussein of Jordan, to the song 'Bad, Bad Leroy Brown' by Jim Croce. Newspapers crowed about his down-to-earth style. Betty opened up in her first interview about her struggle with chronic pain, and sessions with a psychiatrist. It had, she said, allowed her to voice 'a lot of entrenched feelings that were locked inside'.[15]

The politics were working for Ford, too. His first address with Congress, on the Monday after he took office, was interrupted by waves of applause. 'I do not want a honeymoon with you,' he told his former colleagues. 'I want a good marriage.' Approval ratings for the new president soared to over 70 per cent.

But a shadow remained. What should Ford do about Nixon? The former president had retreated to San Clemente, a broken man. Back at the White House, many of his staff remained. Ford had opted to keep on Haig for a transition period, working alongside his own chief of staff Robert Hartmann and other newcomers. Tensions simmered between the two teams. And, locked away, the tapes and files from the Nixon Administration still remained inside the building. One member of Ford's team rumbled a late-night attempt to ship them to California, using army trucks under order from Haig. Precedent from previous incumbents suggested that they were Nixon's personal property. But the thirty-seventh president was an unprecedented case. With Special Prosecutor Leon Jaworski weighing up whether to indict the former president, Ford judged that the materials could not be released to Nixon until his legal position was clarified.

The questions started to mount. On Wednesday 28 August, Ford held his first press conference. Like his inauguration, it took place in the East Room of the White House. The new president hoped it would be an occasion to talk about the economic challenges facing America, with inflation soaring from the impact of the oil crisis. But the first question, from Helen Thomas of UPI, cut straight to Watergate. Should Nixon have immunity from prosecution, and was Ford prepared to grant a presidential pardon?

Ford stumbled for an answer. He had, he said, been reflecting in his prayers over recent days. Then he tried to close the question down. No charges had yet been made. It would be 'unwise and untimely' to make a commitment.

The press conference lasted for almost half an hour. Questions kept coming. Was pardon an option? Would Ford consider it? Was he in touch with Jaworski? No, said the president. Jaworski should make his own decision. There was no contact.

Afterwards, Ford walked back to the Oval Office. He was furious. When he took office, the former congressman hoped to establish a more open relationship with journalists. He envisaged holding a press conference every two or three weeks. Judging by this first experience, these encounters risked being dominated by Nixon. And his answers could be presented as contradictory. If Ford was not in touch with Jaworski, why did he disclose that he had been reflecting on the matter in recent days? The press would surely scent a story. Was Ford contemplating a pardon, even before an indictment was made?[16]

Two days later, Ford met with his closest team in the Oval Office. Haig and Hartmann were both there, along with aide John Marsh and lawyer Philip Buchen. The Ford team was concerned to find Haig with the group. They suspected that he remained loyal to Nixon.

Haig, for his part, had jostled with Hartmann during the early weeks of the new administration. Ford refused to designate a single figure to run the White House, preferring to operate with individuals directly, as 'spokes on a wheel'. Haig disliked Hartmann's abrasive style, and felt he was seeking to control access to the president. At a personal level, it had been a difficult time for the former chief of staff. Exhausted from Nixon's resignation, Haig wrestled with a sense of guilt that he could have done more to deliver a different outcome.[17]

Ford swore the group to secrecy. He talked a little about the press conference, and his frustration. Then he paused for a moment, while he filled his pipe.

'I am very much inclined,' the president continued, 'to grant Nixon immunity from prosecution.'

There was a stunned silence. A clock ticked in the background.

Haig rose to his feet. His association with Nixon would, he suggested, make it improper for him to continue as part of the conversation. Ford told him to stay. He went on, explaining his reasons. Trial of the former president would be a 'degrading spectacle'. A full legal process could take years, whereas the country needed to move on.

Ford was, he added, 'ninety-nine percent' sure. But he would welcome other views.

Marsh spoke first, then Buchen. They were both cautious. Even if the logic was right, the timing was wrong. Buchen urged Ford to extract a deal from Nixon, with a statement of contrition, and agreement to hand over his papers to the United States. Hartmann counselled that Ford should wait. Polling suggested a majority wanted Nixon on trial. 'I don't need the polls to tell me whether I am right or wrong,' snapped back Ford.

Over the next week, private messages flowed back and forth between Washington and San Clemente. Buchen had found a legal precedent. In 1915, President Woodrow Wilson had pardoned a New York newspaper editor over an indictment for contempt of court. The Supreme Court upheld the pardon, ruling that the president could pardon an individual even when there was no conviction or admission of guilt. This would be the model for Nixon. In return, the tapes and files would be moved to a federal facility in California. Nixon would hold one key to the vault, the other would be kept by the General Services Administration.

Buchen held exploratory conversations with Nixon's legal team, and with Jaworski. The special prosecutor offered no comment, but privately was relieved. A pardon would spare him the decision over whether to move forward with indictment.

By Friday 6 September, the plan was agreed. Benton Becker, a young lawyer working with Buchen, flew out to San Clemente to confirm the details. He found Nixon aged, shrunken in his suit and rambling in speech, at times incoherent.

'You've been a fine young man,' the former president said as Becker took his leave. 'You've been a gentleman. We've had enough bullies.'

Nixon offered his visitor a presidential tiepin and cufflinks. They were, he said, the last ones he had. Tears welled up in his eyes. Back in the Oval Office, Becker gave Ford a shocked account. The president had spent a light-hearted Saturday, hosting Dobrynin in the White House, along with a visiting party of Soviet cosmonauts and the ambassador's 5-year-old granddaughter, Katya. Ford and the little girl posed for photos together on either side of a globe, stretching their hands round towards one another. Now, talking to Becker that evening, the atmosphere was more sombre. The young lawyer feared that the former president might not have long to live.[18]

The next day, Ford was due to deliver a televised address. He wore a dark blue tie with light stripes, and sat at the same desk from which Nixon had announced his resignation, less than a month before.

The new president was direct. He had come to a decision. He was certain, in his mind and in his conscience, that it was the right thing to do. Already in the job he had learned that difficult decisions came to his desk.

The plight of Nixon and his family was, Ford explained, 'an American tragedy in which we have all played a part. It could go on and on, or someone must write the end to it.'

A text of the pardon lay on the desk. Ford read it out, and then, taking his pen in his left hand, added his signature.

As the red recording lights on the cameras went off, Ford felt a wave of relief. It was done. America could move on.

Within minutes, the reaction had begun. Phone calls flooded into the White House. Protestors gathered in Lafayette Square, near the church where Ford had prayed only hours before. Jerry TerHorst, press secretary to Ford, had resigned that morning when he heard the impending news. His departure gave journalists a new angle. Who else in the White House knew about the decision? Who disagreed with it? At an engagement in Pittsburgh the next day, students shouted 'Jail Ford!' at the new president. By the end of the week, his approval ratings had slumped more than twenty points.

Ford was a veteran. He had been in politics long enough to know that his initial popularity could not last. But this turnaround was quicker and more brutal than even he had expected. The honeymoon was over.

Vladivostok was an unlikely venue for superpower diplomacy. The city nestles in an enclosed bay, on the Pacific coast of the Soviet Union. It was established in 1860 by a Tsarist military expedition. The settlement grew in size during the late nineteenth century, mirroring the development of San Francisco, Sydney and other new cities around the rim of the Pacific. During the Russian Civil War, in 1919–20, an intervention force of American troops briefly occupied Vladivostok, along with Japanese and the Czechoslovak Legion, an exile unit formed for the liberation of their homeland in Europe.

General Secretary Leonid Brezhnev and Foreign Minister Andrei Gromyko had been quick to make contact with Ford after Nixon's resignation. They hoped that the new president would maintain the same policy of détente established by his predecessor. In his first letter, days after Ford's appointment, Brezhnev had suggested that the two men hold an early meeting 'on neutral ground' before the end of year.[19] Ford was due to visit Japan and South Korea, in his first presidential visit overseas. A stopover at Vladivostok, in the same region, would round off the tour.

Air Force One touched down on 23 November 1974, at a Soviet air force base some fifty miles from Vladivostok. (Ford disliked *Spirit of '76*, and has restored the old name for the presidential aircraft.) It was a bleak setting. Heavy snow forced their hosts to abandon the usual guard of honour. The Americans found Brezhnev and Gromyko huddled in a wooden stand, on the edge of the bleak, white airfield. They had arrived only hours before, after the blizzard forced their plane to stay over the previous night in Khabarovsk, on the Chinese border. The aircraft hangers were all concealed underground, as a precaution against attack. At least the president was dressed for the cold. Dobrynin had offered Ford his own hat, made from beaver fur, when he set off from Washington. Ford added a wolfskin coat, purchased during a stopover in Alaska.[20]

The two delegations boarded a train. This was to take them to a resort called Okeanskaya, just outside the city. It was a heavy, ornate construction which seemed to date from Tsarist times. Brezhnev and Ford squeezed into a dining car, along with their entourage. The Soviets served tea and cognac, with pastries. As the carriages trundled across the Siberian landscape, both men tried to make small talk.

Ford looked out of the window, at low hills in the distance. Were they, he asked, suitable for agriculture?

Brezhnev looked uncertain. He came from Ukraine, at the other end of the Soviet Union. Some land was suitable, he said, but the heavy winters were a problem.

Kissinger helped himself to the pastries. At first he was coy about doing so. But they were good, and the secretary of state couldn't resist. By the end of the journey, he had eaten three platefuls.[21]

The delegations arrived at Okeanskaya. It was a sanatorium, used by off-duty military from the Soviet Pacific command. There was a single stone building, surrounded by wooden huts. Ford thought it like a YMCA camp in the Catskill Mountains. Kissinger, who occupied one of the huts, worried about the metal stove provided for heating. It was old, and threw off sparks. He feared that the building might catch fire.[22]

Both sides had come to Siberia keen to make progress, after the disappointment of Nixon's visit to Moscow and the Crimea that summer. Ford and Kissinger still believed that a deal on arms control would be valuable. The SALT agreement, signed in 1972, would expire in 1977. Both superpowers were developing new weapon systems, due for deployment after that date. The Soviets were catching up with technology for MIRVs, which allowed several nuclear warheads to be launched from a single missile. Soviet missiles were heavier than US ones, and thus could potentially carry a greater number of warheads. Defence Secretary James Schlesinger, who had insisted that Nixon hang tough in Moscow, now thought there was scope for a deal, fixing numbers on both launchers and MIRVs beyond 1977. With his back thus covered in Washington, Ford could afford to negotiate.

At the same time, relations between the two countries had entered heavy going on trade and human rights. Kissinger had spent much of the year in parallel negotiation with Dobrynin and Senator Henry 'Scoop' Jackson, over conditions for greater emigration by Soviet Jews, in return for granting the Soviet Union trade under MFN terms. Kissinger reached a private understanding with Dobrynin and Gromyko, that Moscow would not impede such emigration. In October, Jackson revealed the agreement in a press conference at the White House. Brezhnev was furious, and the deal fell through.

The talks at Okeanskaya lasted for two days. Ford was a different operator to Nixon. Whereas his predecessor preferred to pitch his remarks at a general level, and leave the negotiation on detail to Kissinger, the new president was more hands-on. On the first day, he led his team in negotiations until after midnight. During breaks, the American delegation would walk around outside, braving the cold to confer on tactics out of range of Soviet listening devices. Watching from a distance, diplomat Georgy Kornienko could see that Ford and Kissinger were engaged in intense debate. By the end, Brezhnev signalled a position that Ford, Kissinger and Schlesinger had all agreed America could accept:

an equal numerical limit on launchers and MIRVs for both countries, set to last for the next decade.

As a sign of goodwill, Brezhnev showered his guest with presents. He produced a rack and several pipes, carved from wood. Then, during another break, he handed over a picture of Ford, made by a local artist from different kinds of wood. It was based on a magazine photo, and bore little similarity to the president.

'This portrait makes me much more handsome,' commented Ford diplomatically. 'Mrs Ford will think she is married to a new man.'

Perhaps the original photo wasn't very good, Dobrynin added politely.[23]

With the main talks over, Brezhnev took his guest for a drive into Vladivostok. As a naval base, the city was normally closed to foreigners, and for that reason the travelling American press pack were not allowed to accompany the president. They complained strongly, and eventually the Soviets consented to organize a separate bus tour.[24]

It was late afternoon, and already growing dark. Crowds lined the streets, waving at the leaders' motorcade, and Ford waved back out of the window. The limousine bounced up and down the steep streets leading down into the bay, which reminded Ford of San Francisco. As the vehicle headed back towards Okeanskaya, the general secretary leaned across and took the president's hand in his own. He began to talk about the trauma of the Second World War.

'I do not want to inflict that on my people again,' he explained.

As a young man, Ford had served with the US Navy during the war in the Pacific. He agreed with Brezhnev. The talks had made significant progress, he added.

'I agree,' replied Brezhnev. 'This is an opportunity to protect not only the people of our two countries but, really, all mankind.' He continued to hold Ford's hand.

The two delegations returned to the airfield by train. As Ford bade farewell to his host at the foot of the aircraft steps, he noticed Brezhnev eyeing his Alaskan wolfskin coat. The general secretary had spotted it earlier during the visit, and asked Ford about the fur. Now the president sensed his moment. He took the coat off, and handed it to his host. Brezhnev put it on, smacking his lips with delight. Sukhodrev, himself wearing a sheepskin coat, looked on and smiled.

'Let it be a momento of our meeting,' said Ford. Brezhnev grinned.

Then the president turned, and mounted the steps to board Air Force One.[25]

It was the seventy-third Nobel Prize ceremony. Each year, since 1901, the awards were presented in a lavish ceremony held in the hall of the Royal Swedish Academy of Music, and attended by the Swedish monarch.

10 December 1974 was no exception. Members of the judging panel and prize recipients entered to a fanfare, dressed in white tie and tailcoats. The stage was covered in a rich blue carpet, emblazoned with a single letter 'N' at the centre to commemorate Alfred Nobel, the scientist and benefactor of the prizes. Red chairs were laid out in a semicircle. King Carl XVI Gustaf sat on the right-hand side. Aged 28, the young monarch had acceded to the throne a year before, on the death of his father.

This year the panel had an unusual award to make. Alexander Solzhenitsyn had received the Nobel Prize for Literature four years before, in 1970, but had been unable to make the journey from the Soviet Union to collect the honour in person. Now, exiled in the West, he was free to travel to Stockholm. The bearded Russian entered with the rest of the official party. Like them, he wore formal dress. His wife Alya sat in the audience, in a light blue jacket and pearl necklace. She had flown to join her husband a few weeks after his departure from the Soviet Union in February.

The permanent secretary of the academy gave a laudatory speech. He referred to the aspiration that Alfred Nobel recorded in his will, to see frontiers between countries dismantled.

'Your presence here today,' he declared, 'does not mean that frontiers are at last abolished.' But it was a sign of hope, however distant and forlorn, than the day would at last come when a frontier would 'be as it should be – merely a line on a map'.

That evening, the prizewinners were honoured with the traditional Nobel dinner, held in Stockholm's City Hall. 1,300 guests sat at long tables in the main courtyard, called the Blue Hall. The menu was a blend of French and Scandinavian cuisine. Guests dined on a starter of smoked salmon, followed by roe deer steaks and orange sorbet for dessert.

Solzhenitsyn gave a speech of thanks. He addressed the audience in Russian.

Many laureates had been recognized before him, the writer noted in a wry introduction, but perhaps none had caused the Academy so much bother. Nevertheless, the delay brought one advantage. Solzhenitsyn had already lived with the award for four years, and seen how it had transformed his life.

'It has prevented me from being crushed,' the writer told his audience. 'It has helped my voice to be heard in places where my predecessors have not heard it for decades.' For that, he gave heartfelt thanks to the Academy. There was a silent community back in Russia, Solzhenitsyn added, who joined him in that thanks. An artist's work could not be contained by politicians. The Academy had set him free.[26]

Notes

1 Kissinger (1982), 1198.
2 Buchanan (2017), 380; Price (1977), 324.
3 Haig (1994), 475–84; Ford (1979), 2–10.
4 White (1975), 21–2.
5 Nixon (1978), 1063–4; Eisenhower (1986), 644; White (1975), 22; Woodward and Bernstein (1975), 491–2.
6 Nixon (1978), 1073; Haig (1994), 498–9.
7 Nixon (1978), 1074–5; Eisenhower (1986), 649–50.
8 Kissinger (1982), 1207–10; Nixon (1978), 1076–7.

9   Price (1977), 339–47; White (1975), 29; Woodward and Bernstein (1975), 425; Price interview, 4 April 2007, p. 104–6.

10 Nixon (1978), 1082–4; Price (1977), 347; Haig (1994), 503.

11 Nixon (1978), 1084; Kissinger (1982), 1212.

12 Nixon (1978), 1086–90; Haig (1994), 504–5; Eisenhower (1986), 653–6; Kissinger (1982), 1213–14; Ford (1979), 39–40; Buchanan (2017), 383; White (1975), 33.

13 Ford (1979), 40–1.

14 Ford (1979), 175.

15 Quoted in Perlstein (2014), 281.

16 Ford (1979), 157–8.

17 Haig (1994), 510–11.

18 Ford (1979), 169–72; Werth (2006), 305–7; Dobrynin (1995), 325–6.

19 FRUS 1969–76 Vol. XVI, item 7, p. 15–16.

20 Dobrynin (1995), 328; Kissinger (1999), 286–7; Aleksandrov-Agentov (1994), 234–7; Sukhodrev (1999), 320–3.

21 FRUS 1969–76 Vol. XVI, item 90, p. 320–9; Kissinger (1999), 288–9; Ford (1979), 213–14.

22 Ford (1979), 214; Kissinger (1999), 290–1.

23 FRUS 1969–76 Vol. XVI, item 92, p. 351–69; Ford (1979), 217; Kornienko (2001), 199–201.

24 Sukhodrev (1999), 323.

25 Ford (1979), 218–19; Sukhodrev (1999), 323–5.

26 'Alexander Solzhenitsyn – Banquet Speech' at www.nobelprize.org.

Chapter 12

HORIZON OF DREAMS
(January–December 1975)

'Let us not talk of détente and past achievements. I am concerned for the country and for you.'

Defence Secretary James Schlesinger was blunt. It was the morning of Wednesday 9 April 1975. President Gerald Ford was chairing a meeting of his National Security Council and there was just one item on the agenda – the situation in Vietnam.

At first, the Paris Agreement brokered between Secretary of State Henry Kissinger and North Vietnamese leader Le Duc Tho in January 1973 had looked as though it would hold. But within months the position had begun to deteriorate. Hanoi had used the cover afforded by a cessation in hostilities to strengthen its network of trails and arms dumps in South Vietnam. Clashes continued between the two sides. Meanwhile, in Washington, Congress had passed an act in June 1973 prohibiting US military action in or over Indochina. Financial assistance to the South Vietnamese, which also required congressional approval, was slashed. Weakened by Watergate, Nixon had been unable to mount an effective counter-case. The Paris Agreement would only hold if the United States remained fully behind Saigon, with the ultimate threat to intervene again if required. That guarantee had come unstuck.

At New Year 1975, Hanoi struck. North Vietnamese forces overran the capital of Phuoc Long province, some fifty miles from Saigon. It was the first time that a regional centre had fallen to the communists. By the end of March, they had cut South Vietnam in two, seizing the port of Da Nang and cutting off the Central Highlands from the rest of the country. President Thieu ordered his forces to fall back into defensive positions around Saigon. At the same time, Khmer Rouge forces in Cambodia launched a new offensive, aimed at the capital Phnom Penh.

The National Security Council was gathered in the Cabinet Room of the White House. Ford invited CIA director William Colby to open the meeting with an update on events. His assessment was sombre. Previously, analysts had assessed that Hanoi would pause to consolidate its position before a final assault on Saigon, perhaps waiting until the following year. Now, agents with access to the North Vietnamese command were reporting that Hanoi was emboldened to press home its advantage. The strategic balance, Colby concluded, 'decisively favours the communists'. If Saigon fell, America's global standing and the trust of her allies would hang in the balance.

Kissinger was even more stark in his assessment. As architect of the Paris Agreement, he felt its demise particularly keenly. Defeat in Vietnam would bring fallout around the world. 'We will see the consequences,' he warned, 'though they may not come quickly or in any predictable manner.'

The group reviewed what options were left. Further resistance by Saigon would require an emergency injection of US funds. A request for $300 million was already before Congress. General Fred Weyand, Chief of Staff to the US Army, recommended raising this to $722 million, which he judged might be sufficient to sustain a defensive perimeter in the south. Schlesinger pushed back. South Vietnam was lost, he argued. Instead, Ford should look to the future, and make a 'Churchillian speech' that would rally Congress and the American people to the longer struggle ahead.

Ford was not persuaded. It had been the right policy, he concluded, to resist communism in South East Asia. Washington would not abandon that stand now.

The president's appeal to Congress brought no change. A few days later, the Senate Foreign Relations Committee met with Ford, Schlesinger and Kissinger, also in the Cabinet Room. National Security Adviser Brent Scowcroft joined them. New York senator Jacob Javits led the group, which included Frank Church of Idaho and Joe Biden from Delaware. They were adamant. Congress would, said Javits, support an evacuation from Saigon, but 'not one nickel for military aid'.[1]

Two days later, on 17 April 1975, Phnom Penh fell. In neighbouring South Vietnam, communist forces closed in on Saigon. Under direction from Kissinger and Schlesinger, a series of US Air Force flights evacuated non-essential American personnel from the embassy and military liaison office, along with those South Vietnamese who had worked for US forces, and were at most risk of retribution from the North Vietnamese. This latter category numbered into tens of thousands, and, amid increasing panic, it was difficult to establish who was legitimately owed safe passage. Emotions ran high. Two junior State Department officers who had served in Saigon, Lionel Rosenblatt and Craig Johnstone, returned to the country without official leave, to help those with whom they had worked to escape.

On Friday 28 April, advancing communist forces reached the outskirts of Tan Son Nhut airport. Rocket attacks made further flights impossible. In Washington, fourteen hours behind, it was late evening on the previous day. Contingency plans had been prepared to pull out the last cohort of Americans, numbering some thousand, by helicopter from the embassy and other locations, in the heart of the city. Naval carriers were based offshore, with marines ready to fly in and safeguard this final stage. On the ground, Ambassador Graham Martin was deeply torn. He had lost his own son in Vietnam, and was committed to the cause which he represented, while fearing that evacuation would trigger a final panicked collapse.

Ford and Kissinger spoke over the phone.

'About six and a half or seven hours left,' explained the secretary of state. 'I think it can be done. I just think we have no choice.'

'Well, tragic as it is, I think this is what has to be done,' replied Ford. 'Tell him to do it.'

'Under these conditions we can't take any more Vietnamese,' added Kissinger.

'All right. Get the order under way and it sickens me.'

'Mr President, we carried it as far as it could be carried and maybe a few hours beyond it and you know we need to have no regrets. It's the best that could be done.'[2]

The evacuation was code-named Operation Frequent Wind. As a prearranged message, Saigon Radio played the tune 'White Christmas' by Bing Crosby in the early hours of Saturday 30 April. It was a signal for remaining Americans to assemble at the embassy and military liaison office. CH-53 Sea Stallion and CH-46 Chinook helicopters clattered across the city, carrying heavily armed troops from the 9th Marine Amphibious Brigade. Once on the ground, they secured landing sites at both locations, clearing parking lots by crashing vehicles into the surrounding walls to create enough space. Outside, crowds of Vietnamese were gathering, demanding passage out. Those with high priority status were allowed through. The marines laid out petrol barrels around the perimeter, ready to ignite if the mob burst in.[3]

The first evacuation flight departed just after 3 p.m. Helicopters left at ten-minute intervals. Passengers were ordered to abandon all but essential hand baggage. Despite his orders from Washington, Ambassador Martin was determined to keep including Vietnamese on the flights, and by 6.30 p.m, over six thousand Americans and locals had been lifted out. On the carriers offshore, chaotic scenes developed as aircraft piloted by South Vietnamese attempted to land on the deck, or crashed into the sea. Inside the compounds, there were harrowing scenes. One evacuee reported seeing mothers throw their babies over the 14-foot perimeter wall, in the hope that they might be taken on a flight out. Others offered their jewellery or bodies in return for escape. For the young marines standing guard, it was a traumatic experience.

Back in the White House, Ford and Kissinger waited on news. The secretary of state sat alone, turning over the sequence of events in his mind. He thought of the elation around reaching agreement in Paris, just over two years before. At the time, it had seemed like peace with honour. Might a different outcome have been possible?[4]

As night fell in Saigon, the scenes outside the embassy compound became more frantic. Ford authorized a final wave of nineteen evacuation flights, before the operation was terminated. Ambassador Martin had previously argued to stay behind with two volunteers from his staff. The president and secretary of staff, fearing that he would be taken hostage, ordered him to depart. At 5 a.m., the ambassador boarded a flight. 'Tiger Out' radioed the pilot in confirmation, using the military code word assigned to Martin.

As the final helicopters pulled out, the detachment of eighty marines who had been guarding the perimeter fell back to the main embassy building, closely followed by the mob. They climbed onto the roof, blocking the stairwell behind them with metal lockers torn from the wall, and fire extinguishers.

Amid the chaos, the navy pilots conducting the evacuation had mistaken the call sign for Ambassador Martin's flight as confirmation that the full airlift was complete, and neglected to collect this last group of troops. For a further two hours, the marine detachment waited on the roof. Dawn broke over Saigon, while small arms fire sounded from the streets around. It was clear that the North Vietnamese were drawing close. The men passed round a bottle of whisky for comfort.

Eventually, just before 8 a.m., the helicopters returned. The soldiers removed their flak jackets and equipment to save weight, and scrambled aboard. The very last to leave the rooftop was Gunnery Sergeant John Valdez, who commanded the troop. As the men lifted up into the sky, they could see Saigon below, ablaze with fires.

'I felt very low,' recalled one member of the detachment. 'I felt like it was the end of the world.'[5]

'It's the only way of saving the earth,' declared Solzhenitsyn. 'Instead of a world war to have a détente, but a true détente.'

The Soviet author had come to Washington. Over the months since his award of a Nobel Prize, life had not been easy. Solzhenitsyn told the American journalist Hedrick Smith that exile was a kind of 'spiritual castration'.[6] He and Alya had moved to Zurich with their four young children, living in an anonymous house in the suburbs. But the KGB were quick to track him down. Solzhenitsyn was befriended by a Czech couple, Frantisek and Valentina Holub, who were undercover intelligence officers posing as émigré dissidents. At their first meeting, Valentina offered a bouquet of roses and lilacs, claiming to have come from Ryazan, where the author had once worked as a school teacher.

Solzhenitsyn enlisted the Holubs to help with editing his work. Quietly, they passed back reports to KGB chief Yuri Andropov in Moscow. On his orders, the intelligence service sought to undermine the exile's morale and trust in those around him and his family. Fake parcel bombs were sent to their home, and rumours planted that people within his circle had betrayed him to the KGB.[7]

The author had come to Washington for a break. His visit was at the invitation of the American Federation of Labour (AFL), to address a gathering of union leaders at the end of June 1975. AFL President George Meany and Secretary Lane Kirkland introduced the occasion, before a dinner audience at the Hilton Hotel of two and a half thousand. Defence Secretary James Schleschinger and his predecessor, Melvin Laird, were on the platform with the guest, along with former Secretary of State Bill Rogers. Solzhenitsyn, Meany explained, was not a crusader, nor a politician, nor a general, but an artist, who had demonstrated 'the power of the pen, coupled with courage, to free men's minds'.

The guest was dressed in a dark green suit, high-collared and buttoned up. He spoke in Russian for almost an hour, gesticulating with his right arm, while his left held notes. A translator provided simultaneous interpretation through the microphone.

The world, said Solzhenitsyn, needed America. After the trauma of Vietnam, some voices were arguing for 'peace and quiet at any cost'. Americans wanted to be left alone, to drive their big cars, enjoy tennis or golf, and mix cocktails. But concession and compromise would not bring security. A true détente with the Soviet Union could only be built on genuine disarmament, a free society on both sides, committed to peace, and an end to ideological propaganda.

America was a young country, the speaker concluded, with great qualities of strength, generosity and magnanimity. But these same qualities left Americans trusting and vulnerable.

'Do not let yourselves become weak!' declared Solzhenitsyn, as waves of applause broke over the hall. 'Do not let yourselves be taken in the wrong direction!'[8]

In the White House, Solzhenitsyn's visit presented Gerald Ford with a dilemma. A media storm broke over whether the president would meet with the dissident author. Secretary of State Henry Kissinger counselled against. Deputy Chief of Staff Dick Cheney and his boss, Donald Rumsfeld, put the opposite case, arguing a meeting would help offset 'the illusion that all of a sudden we're bosom-buddies with the Russians'.[9] Eventually, a late invitation was extended to the writer. Already rebuffed, Solzhenitsyn refused.[10]

The exile's speech had stoked an issue of substance, too. Over the previous two years, negotiators from the United States, Soviet Union and European countries had been engaged in a so-called Conference on Security and Cooperation in Europe (CSCE). These talks had originally been convened in response to Soviet leader Leonid Brezhnev's call for a final settlement of territorial matters left from the Second World War. The Western allies had successfully widened the agenda, to cover internal matters on press freedom and human rights as well, in what was dubbed a 'third basket' (alongside territorial integrity and military security). Brezhnev was keen to sign a final agreement during the summer of 1975, to mark the thirtieth anniversary since the Second World War, and negotiators were well advanced in clearing the last sticking points, with a summit scheduled in Helsinki for the end of July, at which Ford, Brezhnev and others were due to sign the final text.

In his speech, Solzhenitsyn had denounced the draft agreement as a 'funeral of eastern Europe'. Critics of détente rallied behind his opposition. Senator Henry 'Scoop' Jackson hosted the exile to address a congressional group, including conservative Republican senator Jesse Helms. Solzhenitsyn warned that, while Western statesmen talked of détente, the Soviet Union was 'put[ting] the finishing touches on an even more novel and important improvement in the system of punishment'.[11]

Further afield, another politician was watching closely. California governor Ronald Reagan had supported Richard Nixon over détente. But following the arrival of Ford, he sensed an opportunity. Since January, Reagan had taken to delivering weekly radio addresses to the nation. It was a platform to set out his conservative agenda for free market economics at home, and a tougher stance abroad. Many suspected that the governor was testing the water for a presidential run. Ford had himself declared that he would be a candidate in early July, but when the sitting president found himself embroiled in controversy over his refusal to meet with Solzhenitsyn and the draft Helsinki agreement, Reagan seized the opportunity to criticize him openly for the first time.

'I am against it,' declared the governor, referring to the CSCE agreement, 'and I think all Americans should be against it.'[12]

'You've lost weight.'

'You look like you have, too.'

It was the morning of Wednesday 30 July 1975. Gerald Ford was welcoming Leonid Brezhnev to the American ambassador's residence in Helsinki. It was the same neo-Georgian mansion overlooking the Baltic Sea where Gerard Smith and Vladimir Semenov had thrashed out the SALT deal three years before. The drawing room had a fireplace and large windows. Glasses and jugs of water were laid out along a large rectangular table.

Brezhnev was pleased at his weight loss. Earlier that summer, the CIA had picked up snippets to suggest that the Soviet leader was suffering from health problems. He had suffered a stroke on the way back from his meeting with Ford in Vladivostok. His teeth were causing him trouble, and at the Victory Day parade in May on Red Square to mark the anniversary of the Second World War his behaviour had been erratic.[13]

'I've been stabilized,' he explained to the Americans as press photographers took pictures of the group.

'You look excellent,' replied Ford.

'I'm about 78 kilograms,' added Brezhnev proudly.

'I'm stable within the ten kilogram range,' commented Kissinger with a laugh.

In front of the cameras, the good cheer continued. Two weeks before, American Apollo and Soviet Soyuz spacecraft had managed a link-up in space. The two countries had constructed a joint module, with the seal between the craft finely engineered to ensure a smooth fit. Once docking was complete, astronauts Thomas Stafford and Alexei Leonov greeted each other with a handshake. It was, Ford told Brezhnev, a symbol of progress between the two countries.

With the photographers gone, discussion became more serious. Originally, the two sides had hoped to conclude a further agreement on arms control at Helsinki, and to make progress on talks over conventional forces, with limits on deployment within Europe and longer notice times for each side to warn the other about military exercises. But preparatory meetings between Kissinger and Soviet foreign minister Andrei Gromyko had exposed significant differences. And Solzhenitsyn's visit to America had brought a new factor into the equation. When the meeting turned to problems over emigration for Soviet Jews, which continued to be a contentious issue, Ford felt obliged to refer to the émigré writer. As he did so, Kissinger got up to use the bathroom.

'I am not leaving because you mentioned that name,' offered the secretary of state.

There was an awkward round of laughter.

'Mr General Secretary,' explained Ford, 'Solzhenitsyn has aligned himself with those who are very severe critics of the policy you and I believe in, détente.' He named Henry 'Scoop' Jackson and union leader George Meany. As president, he wanted to see that policy continue. Détente could and would work, and be made irreversible. But lack of progress on substance fuelled its critics.

Brezhnev was dismissive. Solzhenitsyn was, he said, 'nothing more than a zero for the Soviet Union'.

Ford returned to the charge, more forceful this time. He had come to Helsinki despite domestic criticism of this decision to do so, because he believed in détente. The majority of people in America hoped for more progress. If that happened, the critics could be brushed aside. But 'I repeat with quiet emphasis,' he added, 'détente must be made irreversible.'

The meeting had felt heavy going. At one point Soviet diplomatic adviser Andrei Aleksandrov-Agentov slipped a note to interpreter Alexei Vavilov. 'They are squeezing words out of each other as from toothpaste tubes,' he observed laconically.[14]

Afterwards, both leaders left for the main gathering, of the CSCE. Finnish president Urho Kekkonen acted as host, in the vast, modern Finlandia hall. Thirty-five countries were represented, mostly at head of government level. Prime Minister Harold Wilson of the United Kingdom was there, along with Pierre Trudeau of Canada, Chancellor Helmut Schmidt of West Germany and President Giscard d'Estaing of France.

The conference lasted for three days, with speeches from each leader in turn. During their preparatory meetings, Kissinger and Gromyko had agreed to limit the time slot allocated to each speaker. Otherwise, calculated Kissinger, the occasion might drag out for a whole week.[15]

The leaders took the stage in order determined by lot. Wilson and Trudeau both spoke early on. The Americans thought their speeches good, though they were struck at Wilson's rumpled suit, with specks of dandruff.[16] Brezhnev was due to take thirteenth place, while Ford was twenty-sixth. It meant that the president had to sit through the first two days of the gathering, listening to others, before he could speak himself.

Brezhnez was joined in the Soviet delegation by Gromyko, diplomatic adviser Andrei Aleksandrov-Agentov and interpreter Viktor Sukhodrev, who wore a loud pin-striped suit and tie decorated with flowers. Behind the scenes, the Soviets had equal concerns about the Helsinki Accords to their American counterparts. Aleksandrov-Agentov had presided over agonized debates at Brezhnev's dacha between his advisers, including party aide Anatoly Chernyaev. The greatest concern was over the so-called 'third basket', on human rights and media freedom. If the Soviet Union signed up to commitments on these, might it not amount to caving in on Western pressure in a way that made any pledges on the territorial integrity of post-war borders worthless? Rival versions of Brezhnev's speech had been prepared by the Foreign Ministry and Aleksandrov-Agentov's group.[17]

When Brezhnev's turn came he strode slowly to the lecture, decorated with a large bouquet of white flowers. He reached into a pocket and pulled out a pair of metal-framed glasses, then looked down at his notes. The audience watched from rows of desks, each delegation named by country, and listening to a translation through headphones.

Brezhnev spoke in a deep voice, slurring slightly over his words. He started by recalling the history of Europe, 'drenched plentifully' with the blood of two world wars. Agreement had required compromise. He highlighted the commitments on press freedom. In an information age, he warned, the media could serve the cause of peace, or spread the 'poison of discord' between countries and peoples.

In conclusion, Brezhnev said, there were no winners or losers in the conference, no victors and vanquished. 'It has been a victory of reason,' he added. 'Everyone has won.'

Once back in his seat, he slipped a note to Aleksandrov-Agentov. 'Andrei Mikhailovich – how did it go?' read the note. 'Be honest!'[18]

The next day was Ford's turn. He, too, began by talking about the past. There had, he noted, been too many 'narrow escapes' from conflict over the last thirty years. The American people remained committed to the cause of peace.

Détente must, he explained, be everyone's business, in Europe and elsewhere. 'But détente can only succeed,' he added, 'if everyone understands what détente actually is.'

It was a response to the challenge that Solzhenitsyn had thrown down in Washington a month before. Borrowing the threefold structure which the Soviet author had used, Ford framed an answer to his own question. Détente was, he explained, an evolutionary process, in which challenges remained. It was about progress in steady steps, not declarations. And it had to be a two-way street, in which each side accepted mutual obligations.

'History will judge this conference,' he concluded, 'not by what we say here tomorrow, but by what we do tomorrow – not by the promises we make, but the promises we keep.'[19]

Three days later, after brief visits to Belgrade and Bucharest, Ford returned to Washington. Once again, he found himself in controversy. Many commentators hailed the speech in Helsinki as his best yet. But opponents of détente slammed the CSCE as a 'new Yalta', in the words of *The Wall Street Journal*. Meanwhile, his wife Betty gave an interview to the CBS programme *60 Minutes*, which broke new ground for a First Lady. She appeared to endorse marijuana use, welcomed the recent Supreme Court decision to allow abortion, and supported the right of her daughter to have a sexual relationship before marriage.

Conservatives rose in fury. The president's approval ratings fell by more than twenty points in the space of a fortnight.[20] A year on from Nixon's resignation, Ford was looking vulnerable.

The news caught up with Andrei Sakharov as he visited the home in Moscow of his friend Yuri Tuvim, in early October. He had dropped by for a few hours rest over a quiet cup of tea. But foreign correspondents tracked him down, along with fellow dissidents Lev Kopolev and Vladimir Voinovich. Sakharov had been awarded the Nobel Peace Prize.

It had been a tense autumn for the physicist. Over the previous year, his wife Elena's eyesight had deteriorated badly, with a cataract in one eye, and glaucoma in the other. It was clear that she needed specialist medical treatment. A group of six Nobel laureates petitioned the Soviet leadership on her behalf from abroad, including the veteran French human rights activist René Cassin and Heinrich Boll, the author who had greeted Solzhenitsyn on his arrival in Germany. Eventually, as a goodwill gesture on the eve of the Helsinki conference, Elena was allowed to travel to Italy for treatment. But the KGB continued to harass the couple. Just before she left Moscow, an anonymous package arrived with horrific photos of mutilated eye sockets, stabbed through with sharp objects. *Washington Post* correspondent Robert Kaiser thought that the ordeal had visibly aged the physicist, and caused him to put on weight.[21]

'Andrei Sakharov is a firm believer in the brotherhood of man,' ran the citation from the Nobel Committee in Oslo.'[He] has warned against the dangers connected with a bogus détente, based on wishful thinking and illusions.'

Caught unawares by the news, Sakharov offered a few words in response. It was, he said, an honour shared by all those prisoners of conscience, who had sacrificed their freedom to defend others. His remarks were filmed by video camera, and the tape quickly carried out on a flight to the West, to reach news bulletins around the world.

Back in his own apartment, phone calls and messages of congratulation poured in. A diplomat from the Norwegian embassy arrived with a bunch of roses and a message from his ambassador. Norway would, it said, provide any assistance required for Sakharov to visit Oslo and receive the prize in person.

The next day, Sakharov gave a more organized press conference. He read a prepared statement, and confessed that he was 'happy and proud' at the award. With this and the commitments made in Helsinki, Sakharov hoped that the outside world could hold the Soviet Union to account over its record over human rights.

Across Moscow in his headquarters at the Lubyanka, KGB chief Yuri Andropov watched events with alarm. Earlier that summer, he had made a rare public speech warning over the risks posed by provisions on human rights in the Helsinki agreement. Sakharov's international standing had taken another lift. It was essential that the Soviet authorities move quickly to discredit him.

Advised by Andropov, the Politburo made its choice. Like Solzhenitsyn before him, Sakharov would not be permitted to travel to the West and receive his award. When Sakharov submitted his application for a visa, he was informed of the decision.

Angrily, Sakharov phoned a journalist from Agence-France Presse. KGB operatives were listening in. 'This decision is an insult not only for me, but also for the Nobel Committee,' declared the physicist. 'This is a challenge to world opinion.'[22]

A familiar voice came over the telephone line. It was Ronald Reagan. Ford was sitting at his desk in the Oval Office, on an afternoon in mid-November 1975.

'Hello, Mr President,' began the governor. He went straight to the point.

'I am going to run for president. I trust we can have a good contest, and I hope that it won't be divisive.'

'Well, Governor,' replied Ford. 'I'm sorry that you are getting into this.' A race for the Republican nomination would, he explained, 'take a lot of money, a lot of effort and it will leave a lot of scars'.

'I don't think it will be divisive,' countered Reagan. 'I don't think it will harm the party.'

'Well,' said Ford curtly, 'I think it will.'

There was no more to be said. In the three months since his return from Europe, Ford had continued to go through a bad patch. During September he had survived two assassination attempts in quick succession, in Sacramento and then San Francisco. Relations with Moscow came under further pressure, over Soviet intervention to the civil war in Angola, and failure to renew sale of American grain, which had been part of the package of agreements struck between Nixon and Brezhnev. In October Ford tried to regain the political initiative with a reshuffle of his cabinet, moving liberal Nelson Rockefeller aside from the vice presidency, and replacing James Schleschinger as Defence Secretary with White House chief of staff Donald Rumsfeld. But the manoeuvre deepened the impression of a president struggling to assert his authority. Reagan sensed that his moment had come.

The morning after his phone call to Ford, Reagan announced his decision at the National Press Club in Washington. His candidacy would, he said, be healthy for the nation and his party. America was sinking into economic decay. Ten years before, she had enjoyed military superiority. Now, the United States was in danger 'of being surpassed by a nation that has never made an effort to hide its hostility to everything that we stand for'.

Announcement made, Reagan set off on a whirlwind tour, to set out his case to the country. That afternoon he flew to Florida, then back northwards to New Hampshire, and on to North Carolina, Illinois and California. A week later, he appeared on the ABC show *Issues and Answers*, with journalists Bob Clark and Frank Reynolds. Relaxed and folksy in style, the former actor turned politician made a sharp contrast to Ford.

Clark asked about his conversation with the president. It was true, Reagan admitted, that Ford expressed concern about divisions in the party. But both men were determined to avoid that happening.

His interviewer then turned to détente. As president, what would Reagan do?

It was a worthy idea, replied the candidate. But it needed to be a two-way street. The United States was giving away too much, while the Soviet Union was engaged in a rapid build-up in its military capability. This was not in the spirit of détente.

'None of us wants confrontation,' Reagan concluded. 'We want a world that can find areas where we can discuss our problems and talk about them.'[23]

The Sakharovs had a solution. Elena was already in the West, following treatment for her eye condition in Italy. She had stayed on to recuperate at the home of a friend in Florence. When the local Soviet consulate tried to confiscate her passport, Elena resisted. With the Nobel Prize ceremony due to take place in December, Elena could prolong her stay, and travel to Oslo to receive the award on her husband's behalf.

The event called for two sets of remarks from the recipient – an acceptance speech, and then a longer lecture on the following day. As the date approached, Andrei Sakharov busied himself with drafting. He found the lecture simple to compose, under the title *Peace, Progress and Human Rights*. But the acceptance speech was more difficult. Other concerns pressed in on him. In late November, his daughter Lyuba gave birth to a first child, stillborn. Sakharov was distraught. In his apartment, dissidents and foreign correspondents in Moscow kept interrupting for interviews or advice. One young man asked for help, claiming that he had been incarcerated in a mental hospital, and followed Sakharov on a train journey out to his country dacha. When the physicist shook him off, the man threw himself under a passing train and was killed. Sakharov was left unsure whether the event was genuine, or another manipulation by the KGB.

Elena flew to Oslo on Tuesday 9 December, the day before the ceremony. The previous evening, Sakharov had boarded a train in Moscow for Vilnius, capital of the Soviet republic of Lithuania. That summer, his friend Sergei Kovalev had relaunched the samizdat publication, *A Chronicle of Current Events*. The authorities had reacted sharply, and subjected Kovalev to a series of threats and heavy-handed interrogations. He was now standing trial, with the venue moved to Vilnius in an effort to reduce publicity.

Sakharov had agreed with local dissidents in Lithuania that he would attend as a show of support. Under the law, he was entitled as a Soviet citizen to sit in the courtroom. But when the trial opened the following day, officials stalled, keeping Sakharov and his supporters waiting in the lobby outside. Traveling on a bus that morning, the physicist had noticed how Lithuanians shied away when they realized that he was a Russian. But now, in the court building, locals came up to thank him for coming. KGB henchmen looked on, and from time to time scuffles broke out.

That afternoon, the judge declared a recess in the trial. Sakharov went to the house of Viktoras Petkus, a fellow dissident and authority on Lithuanian history. Since arriving in the city, he had tried to reach Elena over the telephone, only to find the lines were cut off. Now, gathered in Petkus' home with the supporters whom Sakharov met at the courthouse, the group switched on the radio. It was the award ceremony, broadcast from Oslo.

There was a trumpet fanfare. Aase Lionaes, a Norwegian Labour politician, gave some introductory remarks, speaking in Russian. Then Elena came to the stage. Sakharov could hear her footsteps over the radio, as she mounted the platform, and then her voice. It sounded so familiar and yet distant, as though coming from another world.

Elena explained the circumstances. Her husband could not attend the ceremony, but was instead at the trial of his friend Kovalev in Vilnius. So she was speaking on his behalf.

Like Brezhnev and Ford in Helsinki, four months before, Sakharov's acceptance speech opened with reference to the Second World War. That catastrophe had left a deep personal feeling on people across Europe. As a result, there was a 'general human longing for peace, for true détente, for genuine disarmament'.

As Elena spoke, reading through thick glasses issued after her surgery, the words were steady and clear. Watching, Norwegian artist Victor Sparre was reminded of the character Antigone from ancient tragedy, 'proud and beautiful . . . the incarnation of resistance to the tyrant'.

Elena continued to read. Acknowledging the citation from the Nobel Committee, she noted the link between defence of peace and that of human rights. The award was a 'great personal joy and gift'. It was also an act of intellectual courage, in recognizing the views of a man whose views did not coincide with that of his state.

Above all, she said, reading her husband's words, 'I also see in it a manifestation of tolerance and of the true spirit of détente.' The award was, she declared, an honour and source of hope to all those imprisoned for acts of conscience in the Soviet Union and eastern Europe.

The audience burst into applause. As the broadcast ended, Sakharov was ushered into a room next door by his Lithuanian friends, for a traditional celebration of cake and toasts.

Ten days later, Elena returned to Moscow. Sakharov and his family went out to Sheremetyevo Airport to meet her, along with a crowd of friends and foreign correspondents. After her long absence from the Soviet Union, customs officials insisted on a thorough search through her baggage. The group were obliged to hang around for several hours, while books and tapes were removed from her possession. Andrei and Elena filled the time with an impromptu press conference. Caught on the hop, KGB officers assigned to watch the couple tried to break it up with a group of cleaning ladies, vigorously mopping the floor in different directions.

Night was drawing in. Finally released by the authorities, the Sakharovs climbed into a car. They had managed to hang on to an Italian edition of *My Country and the World*, Andrei's latest work to be published in the West. The crowd of friends and supporters filled other cars, and the motorcade set off.

They drove down the Leningrad Highway, on the way into central Moscow. Snow lay on the ground. Tall Soviet apartment blocks lined the sides of the road, and in the distance illuminated red stars glinted above the towers of the Kremlin. It was the route that Alexander Solzhenitsyn had taken nearly two years before, on his journey into exile. But, for Andrei and Elena, the road led in the opposite direction. They were coming home.[24]

Notes

1   Kissinger (1999), 531; Ford (1979), 255.
2   Kissinger (1999), 1107.
3   'In the First Person – Saigon 1975' by Tom Glenn, from *Studies in Intelligence* Vol. 59 no. 4 (December 2015).

4   Kissinger (1999), 541–2.
5   'Last US Marines to leave Saigon describe chaos of Vietnam War's end', *Chicago Tribune*, 30 April 2015; Fall of Saigon Marines Association, at fallofsaigon.org.
6   Smith (1977), 516.
7   Andrew (1999), 415–17.
8   Text of speech as published by AFL-CIO, *Free Trade Union News*, July–August 1975.
9   FRUS 1969–76 Vol. XVI, item 156, p. 612–13.
10 Ford (1979), 297–8; Kissinger (1999), 648–52.
11 Kaufman (2000), 292.
12 Perlstein (2014), 488.
13 FRUS 1969–76 Vol. XVI, item 154, p. 608–9. For an account of Brezhnev's stroke in Vladivostok, see Sukhodrev (1999), 325.
14 FRUS 1969–76 Vol. XXXIX, item 329, p. 958–65; Vavilov (2016), 240–3.
15 FRUS 1969–76 Vol. XXXIX, item 284, p. 836.
16 FRUS 1969–76 Vol. XXXIX, item 330, p. 966–7.
17 Chernyaev (1995), 307–8, 316.
18 Aleksandrov-Agentov (1994), 249.
19 Helsinki conference speeches at www.cvce.eu.
20 Perlstein (2014), 494.
21 Sakharov (1990), 426–8; Kaiser (1977), 395.
22 Sakharov (1990), 429–32; Rubenstein and Gribanov (2005), 190–6.
23 Papers on Reagan candidacy announcement, at fordlibrarymuseum.gov.
24 Sakharov (1990), 418–20, 433–41; Lourie (2002), 272–5, 279.

SELECT BIBLIOGRAPHY

Document Collections
Foreign Relations of the United States (FRUS):

Johnson Administration, 1964–8

Vol XVII: Eastern Europe, 1964–8

Nixon and Ford Administrations 1969–76

Vol I: Foundations of Foreign Policy, 1969–72
Vol VI: Vietnam, January 1969–July 1970
Vol VII: Vietnam, July 1970–January 1972
Vol IX: Vietnam, October 1982–January 1973
Vol X: Vietnam, January 1973–July 1975
Vol XII: Soviet Union, January 1969–October 1970
Vol XI: South Asia Crisis, 1971
Vol XIII: Soviet Union, October 1970–October 1971
Vol XIV: Soviet Union, October 1971–May 1972
Vol XV: Soviet Union, June 1972–January 1973
Vol XVI: Soviet Union, June 1972–August 1974
Vol XVII: China, 1969–72
Vol XXIV: Arab–Israel Dispute, 1969–72
Vol XXV: Middle East and Arabian Peninsula, 1969–72; Jordan, September 1970
Vol XXVI: Arab–Israel Crisis and War, 1973
Vol XXXIII: SALT I, 1969–72
Vol XXXIX: Foundations of Foreign Policy, 1973–6

David C. Geyer and Douglas E. Selvage (eds), *Soviet–American Relations: the Détente Years, 1969–1972* (State Dept, Office of the Historian, 2007)
F. S. Aijazuddin, *The White House and Pakistan: Secret Declassified Documents 1969–1974* (Karachi: Oxford University Press, 2002)
Christopher Andrew and Vassily Mitrokhin, *The Mitrokhin Archive: The KGB in Europe and the West* (London: Penguin Press, 2000)
Jaromir Navratil (ed.), *The Prague Spring 1968* (Budapest: Central European University Press, 2006)
Joshua Rubenstein and Alexander Gribanov (eds) *The KGB File of Andrei Sakharov* (New Haven: Yale University Press 2005)
Michael Scammel (ed.), *The Solzhenitsyn Files* (Carol Stream IL: edition q, 1995)
Wilson Centre Archive: Cold War International History Project (www.wilsoncenter.org/program/cold-war-international-history-project)

Presidential Libraries
Lyndon Baines Johnson Library – Daily Diary
Richard M. Nixon Library – Daily Diary
Gerald R. Ford – papers on 1976 election campaign

Transcripts
Douglas Brinkley and Luke Nichter, *The Nixon Tapes, 1971–1972* (Boston: Houghton
    Mifflin Harcourt, 2014)
    The Nixon Tapes, 1973 (Boston: Houghton Mifflin Harcourt, 2015)
Daniel S. Stackhouse, *Telephone Diplomacy: The Secret Talks Behind US-Soviet Detente
    During the Cold War, 1969–1977* (CreateSpace Independent Publishing Platform,
    2014)

Oral Histories
Nixon Presidential Library
Timothy Price interviews with:

   Pat Buchanan (4 April 2007)
   William Safire (27 March 2008)

Timothy Naftali and Douglas Brinkley interviews with:

   Steve Bull (25 June 2007)
   Alexander Butterfield (12 June 2008)
   Charles Colson (17 August 2007)
   John Dean (30 July 2007)
   Robert Dole (4 March 2008)
   Daniel Ellsberg (20 May 2008)
   Alexander Haig (30 November 2006)
   Herbert Klein (20 February 2007)
   Egil 'Bud' Krogh (5 September 2007)
   Ray Price (4 April 2007)
   James Schlesinger (10 December 2007)
   Brent Scowcroft (29 June 2007)

Charles Graboske interview with Charles Colson (15 June 1988)

Raymond Geselbricht interview with:

   Bob Haldeman (11 April 1988, 12 April 1988, 13 August 1988)
   Gwendolyn King (23 May 1988)

Diaries and Letters
Anatoly Chernyaev, *Diary 1972, 1973* (nsarchive.gwu.edu/anatoly-chernyaev-diary)
Caroline Moorehead (ed.), *The Letters of Martha Gellhorn* (New York: Henry Holt and
    Company, 2006)
H. M. Haldeman, *Haldeman Diaries: Inside the Nixon White House* (New York: Berkley
    Books, 1994)
Robert Ferrell (ed.), *Inside the Nixon Administration: The Secret Diary of Arthur Burns,
    1969–1974* (Lawrence: University Press of Kansas, 2010)

Newspapers
Chicago Tribune
Free Trade Union News
Harpers
The New York Times
Rude Pravo
Time
The Washington Post

Memoirs
Andrei Alexandrov-Agentov, *Ot Kollontai do Gorbacheva* (Moscow: Mezhdunarodnoye
    Otnosheniye, 1994)
Georgy Arbatov, *The System: An Insider's Life in Soviet Politics* (New York: Times Books,
    1992)
Charles Bohlen, *Witness to History, 1929–1969* (New York: W. W. Norton and Co., 1973)
Elena Bonner, *Alone Together: The Harrowing Story of Elena Bonner and Andrei Sakharov's
    Internal Exile in the Soviet Union* (London: Vintage Books, 1988)
Leonid Brezhnev, *Memoirs* (Moscow: Novy Mir, 1978)
Luba Brezhneva, *The World I Left Behind* (New York: Random House, 1995)
Pat Buchanan, *The Greatest Comeback: How Richard Nixon Rose from Defeat to Create the
    New Majority* (Random House, 2014)
    Nixon's White House Wars (New York: Random House, 2017)
Anatoly Chernyaev, *My Life, My Times* (Moscow: Mezhdunarodnoye Otnosheniye,
    1995)
Clark Clifford, *Counsel to the President: A Memoir* (New York: Random House, 1991)
Charles Colson, *Born Again* (Grand Rapids: Chosen Books, 1976)
Moshe Dayan, *Story of My Life* (London: Weidenfeld & Nicolson, 1975)
John Dean, *Blind Ambition: The White House Years* (London: HarperCollins, 1975)
    The Nixon Defence: What He Knew and When He Knew It (London: Penguin 2004)
Anatoly Dobrynin, *In Confidence* (New York: Times Books 1995)
Alexander Dubcek, *Hope Dies Last* (New York: Kodansha, 1993)
John Ehrlichman, *Witness to Power: The Nixon Years* (New York: Simon & Schuster,
    1982)
Julie Eisenhower, *Pat Nixon: The Untold Story* (New York: Simon & Schuster, 1986)
Gerald Ford, *A Time to Heal: The Autobiography of Gerald R. Ford* (New York: Harper &
    Row, 1979)
Raymond Garthoff, *A Journey Through the Cold War: A Memoir of Containment and
    Co-existence* (Washington DC: Brookings Institute Press, 2001)
Andrei Gromyko, *Memoirs* (New York: Doubleday and Co., 1990)
Alexander Haig, *Inner Circles: How America Changed the World* (New York: Warner Books,
    1992)
H. R. Haldeman and Joseph DiMona, *The Ends of Power* (London: W. H. Allen and Co.,
    1978)
Richard Helms, *A Look Over My Shoulder: A Life in the Central Intelligence Agency* (New
    York: Presidio Press, 2003)
Martin Hillenbrand, *Fragments of Our Time* (Athens GA: University of Georgia Press,
    1998)
John Holdridge, *Crossing the Divide: An Insider's Accounts of the Normalization of US–
    China Relations* (Lanham: Rowman & Littlefield, 1997)

Henry Kissinger, *White House Years* (New York: Little, Brown and Company, 1979)
    Years of Upheaval (New York: Simon & Schuster, 1982)
    Years of Renewal (New York: Touchstone, 1999)
    On China (London: Penguin 2012)
G. M. Kornienko, *Kholodnaya Voina: Svidelstvo Yeyo Uchastnika* (Moscow: Olga Press, 2001)
Ron Kovic, *Born on the Fourth of July* (New York: Akashic Books, 1976)
Egil Krogh, *Integrity: Good People, Bad Choices and Life Lessons from the White House*
    (New York: Public Affairs Books, 2007)
Golda Meir, *My Life* (London: Weidenfeld & Nicolson, 1976)
Paul Nitze, *From Hiroshima to Glasnost: At the Centre of Decision: A Memoir* (London:
    Grove/Atlantic, 1989)
Richard Nixon, *RN: The Memoirs of Richard Nixon* (London: Sidgwick & Jackson, 1978)
Shimon Peres, *Battling for Peace: My Memoirs* (London: Weidenfeld & Nicolson, 1995)
Raymond Price, *With Nixon* (London: Viking Press, 1977)
Yitzhak Rabin, *The Rabin Memoirs* (Berkeley and Los Angeles: University of California
    Press, 1979)
James Reston, *Deadline: A Memoir* (New York: Random House, 1991)
Anwar el-Sadat, *In Search of Identity: An Autobiography* (London: Collins, 1978)
William Safire, *Before the Fall: An Inside View of the Pre-Watergate White House* (New
    York: Doubleday and Co., 1975)
Andrei Sakharov, *Memoirs* (London: Vintage, 1992)
Arkady Shevchenko, *Breaking with Moscow* (New York: Alfred Knopf, 1995)
Gerard Smith, *Disarming Diplomat* (Lanham: Madison Books, 1996)
    Doubletalk: The Story of SALT I (Lanham: University Press of America, 1985)
Alexander Solzhenitsyn, *The Oak and the Calf* (New York: Harper & Row, 1975)
Viktor Sukhodrev, *Moi Yazhik, Moi Drug: Ot Khrushcheva do Gorbacheva* (Moscow: OST
    Olympia, 1999)
Kenneth Thompson (ed.), *The Nixon Presidency: Twenty-Two Intimate Perspectives of
    Richard M Nixon* (Lanham: Rowman & Littlefield, 1987)
Andrei Vavilov, *Nixon's Comrades: A Kremlin Notetaker Remembers* (CreateSpace
    Independent Publishing Platform, 2016)
Vernon Walters, *Secret Missions* (New York: Doubleday and Co., 1978)
Casper Weinberger, *In the Arena: A Memoir of the 20th Century* (Washington DC:
    Regnery Publishing 2001)

Journalist Accounts
Alistair Cooke, *Letter from America 1946–2004* (London: Allen Lane, 2004)
David Frost, *Frost/Nixon* (London: Macmillan, 2007)
Robert Kaiser, *Russia: The People and The Power* (New York: Athenaeum, 1976)
Hedrick Smith, *The Russians* (New York: Ballantine Books, 1977)
Theodore White, *The Making of A President 1968* (New York: Harper, 1969)
    The Making of A President 1972 (New York: Harper, 1973)
    Breach of Faith: The Fall of Richard Nixon (New York: Scribner, 1975)
Bob Woodward and Carl Bernstein, *All The President's Men* (New York: Simon & Schuster, 1974)
    The Final Days (New York: Simon & Schuster, 1976)
Bob Woodward, *Secret Man: The Story of Watergate's Deep Throat* (New York: Simon &
    Schuster, 2012)
    The Last of the President's Men (New York: Simon & Schuster, 2015)
Zbynek Zeman, *Prague Spring: A Report on Czechoslovakia 1968* (London: Penguin, 1969)

Biographies

Jonathan Aitken, *Nixon: A Life* (London: Weidenfeld & Nicolson, 1993)

Stephen Ambrose, *Nixon Vol. I: The Education of a Politician, 1913–1962* (New York: Simon & Schuster, 1988)

    Nixon Vol. II: The Triumph of a Politician, 1962–1972 (New York: Simon & Schuster, 1989)

    Nixon Vol. III: Ruin and Recovery, 1973–1990 (Touchstone Books, 1992)

Douglas Brinkley, *Dean Acheson: The Cold War Years, 1953–1971* (New Haven: Yale University Press, 1992)

James Cannon, *Gerald R. Ford: An Honourable Life* (Ann Arbor: University of Michigan Press, 2013)

Robert Daley, *Nixon and Kissinger: Partners in Power* (New York: HarperCollins, 2007)

John Farrell, *Richard Nixon: The Life* (New York: Random House, 2017)

Jonathan Fenby: *The General: Charles de Gaulle and the France He Saved* (New York: Simon & Schuster, 2010)

Niall Ferguson, *Kissinger 1923–1968: The Idealist* (London: Allen Lane, 2015)

Seymour Hersh, *The Price of Power: Kissinger in the Nixon White House* (New York: Summit Books, 1983)

Walter Isaacson, *Kissinger: A Biography* (New York: Simon & Schuster, 1988)

Robert Kaufman, *Henry Jackson: A Life in Politics* (Seattle: University of Washington Press, 2000)

George Lieberman, *The Last Diplomat: John D. Negroponte and the Changing Face of US Diplomacy* (London: I.B. Tauris, 2012)

Richard Lourie, *Sakharov: A Biography* (Lebanon NH: Brandeis University Press, 2002)

Chris Matthews, *Kennedy and Nixon: The Rivalry that Shaped Postwar America* (New York: Touchstone, 1996)

Zhores Medvedev, *Andropov* (London: Penguin, 1983)

Joseph Pearce, *Solzhenitsyn: A Soul in Exile* (New York: HarperCollins, 1999)

Michael Scammel, *Solzhenitsyn: A Biography* (London: Paladin Grafton Books, 1986)

Bartholomew Sparrow, *The Strategist: Brent Scowcroft and the Call of National Security* (New York: Public Affairs Books, 2015)

Anthony Summers, *The Arrogance of Power: The Secret World of Richard Nixon* (London: Viking Penguin, 2000)

D M. Thomas, *Alexander Solzhenitsyn: A Century in His Life* (New York: St Martin's Press, 1998)

Evan Thomas, *Being Nixon: A Man Divided* (New York: Random House, 2016)

Timothy Weiner, *One Man Against the World: The Tragedy of Richard Nixon* (New York: Henry Holt and Company, 2015)

Historical Accounts

Gunter Bischof, Stefan Karner and Peter Ruggenthaler (eds), *The Prague Spring and The Warsaw Pact Invasion of Czechoslovakia in 1968* (Lanham: Lexington Books, 2009)

George Breslauer, *Krushchev and Brezhnev as Leaders: Building Authority in Soviet Politics* (London: Unwin Hyman, 1982)

Dusko Dober, *Shadows and Whispers: Power Politics Inside the Kremlin from Brezhnev to Gorbachev* (New York: Random House, 1986)

David Farmer, *Chicago 1968* (Chicago: The University of Chicago Press, 1988)

Martin Gilbert, *Israel: A History* (New York: Doubleday, 1998)

Max Hastings, *Vietnam: An Epic Tragedy 1945–1975* (London: William Collins, 2018)

Walter Isaacson and Evan Thomas, *The Wise Men: Six Friends and the World They Made* (New York: Simon & Schuster, 1986)

Mark Kurlansky, *1968: The Year that Rocked the World* (London: Jonathan Cape, 2004)

Margaret Macmillan, *Nixon and Mao: The Week that Changed the World* (New York: Random House, 2008)

Norman Mailer, *Miami and the Siege of Chicago* (New York: Random House, 1968)

John Newhouse, *Cold Dawn: The Story of SALT* (New York: Henry Holt and Company, 1973)

Luke Nichter, *Richard Nixon and Europe: The Reshaping of Postwar Atlantic World* (New York: Cambridge University Press, 2015)

Dan Parry, *Moonshot: The Inside Story of Mankind's Greatest Adventure* (London: Ebury Press, 2009)

Rick Perlstein, *Nixonland: The Rise of a President and the Fracturing of America* (New York: Simon & Schuster, 2008)
The Invisible Bridge: The Fall of Nixon and the Rise of Reagan (New York, Simon & Schuster, 2014)

Charles River, *The 1968 Democratic National Convention: The History of America's Most Controversial Convention* (Ann Arbor: Charles River Editors, 2016)

Avi Shlaim, *The Iron Wall: Israel and the Arab World* (New York: W. W. Norton and Co., 2000)

Barry Werth, *31 Days: The Crisis that Gave Us the Government We Have Today* (New York: Nan A. Talese, 2006)

Ernest Yanarella, *The Missile Defence Controversy: Technology in Search of a Mission* (Lexington: University Press of Kentucky, 2002)

Miscellaneous Articles, Websites etc.
www.cia.gov/library.readingroom – Sakharov and Solzhenitsyn
www.cvce.eu – on Helsinki Accords
www.fallofsaigon.org – on final US evacuation from Vietnam
www.gatheringofeagles.com – on Vietnam POWs
www.kentstate1970.org – on Vietnam protest shootings
www.midway-island.com – on Nixon/Thieu meeting
www.nixonfoundation.org – on Nixon speeches
www.nobelprize.org – on Nobel award for Solzhenitsyn
www.ohioheroes/org/inductees/2008/newlin.htm – on Medal of Honour awards
www.presidentialpetmuseum.com – on Nixon dogs
www.pbs.org/newshour/rundown – on Lyndon Johnson final interview
www.radio.cz/en/section/archives – on Prague Spring
Marshall Michel, *The Christmas Bombing* (Air and Space, January 2001)
Richard Mobley, *US Joint Military Contributions to Countering Syria's 1970 Invasion of Jordan* (National Defence University Press, Joint Forces Quarterly No. 55, 2009)
David Remnick, *The Exile Returns* (The New Yorker, 14 February 1994)

INDEX

Acheson, Dean 26–7, 33, 39–40, 77–9
Agnew, Spiro 49, 53, 115, 173–6, 184
82 Airborne Division (US) 54, 181
101 Airborne Division (US) 31
Aleksandrov-Agentov, Andrei 115–18, 159, 182, 229–30
Andropov, Yuri 13–14, 57, 60, 63, 68–9, 93, 99, 110–11, 116, 152–3, 170–2, 192–3, 226, 231
  see also KGB
Anti-Ballistic Missile Defence (ABM) 43, 51–3, 64, 68, 75, 79, 108, 158
  see also SALT
Apollo (space missions) 24, 35–6, 46, 68, 103, 228
Arab–Israel Wars see Six Day War (1967); Yom Kippur War (1973)
Assad, Hafez 197–201

B-52 (US warplane) 27, 46–7, 139–41, 181
Bay of Pigs (Cuba) 54, 89, 126–9, 207
Ben Gurion, David 58
Berlin (East-West tensions) 25, 43, 64, 68, 71, 73, 75, 77–8, 91, 97, 98, 110, 177
Berlin, Irving 161
Bernstein, Carl 137, 154, 167
Biden, Joe 224
Biological Weapons Convention 112
Boll, Heinrich 194, 231
Bonner, Elena 59, 69–70, 98–9, 171, 231–4
Brandt, Willy 58, 63, 68, 77, 91, 98, 110, 112, 193
Bretton Woods System 94
  see also Gold Standard
Brezhnev, Leonid 2, 4–6, 8–10, 11, 14–15, 24, 42, 57, 68–9, 70–1, 77–8, 91, 97–8, 99, 108–22, 152–3, 156–60, 163–7, 170–2, 174, 177, 179–82, 192–3, 201–3, 218–20, 227–30, 232, 234
  attitude towards dissidents 57, 99, 152–3, 170–2, 192–3

background and early career 71, 160
  with Ford 218–20, 228–9
  relations with Politburo 68–9, 109, 110–12, 115–16, 152–3, 180, 192, 229
  relationship with Nixon 91, 116–18, 119–22, 163–7, 177, 201–3
Buchanan, Pat 19, 40, 154, 201–3, 208, 213
Bunker, Ellsworth 27–8, 31, 65, 67, 135
Burns, Arthur 94–5
Bush, George 209
Butterfield, Alexander 168–9

Cambodia (including US military incursion) 46–8, 51, 54, 65–6, 73, 76, 80, 111, 114, 223
Campaign to Re-elect the President (CRP) 126–7, 137
Cassin, Rene 99, 231
Ceaucescu, Nikolai 36, 75
Central Committee (Soviet) 60, 69–70, 73, 110, 116, 121, 159, 172
Central Intelligence Agency (CIA) 6, 65, 89, 96, 126, 127–9, 172, 183, 202, 207, 228
Cernik, Oldrich 1–3, 9–10, 14–15, 29
Charles, Prince 58, 80
Cheney, Richard 227
Chernyaev, Anatoly 69, 110, 118, 122, 157, 159, 228–9
Chicago (1968 Democrat Convention) 7–8, 15–16, 19, 131
China (relations with US) 21, 26, 71–2, 74–6, 85–91, 99, 103, 106–8, 111, 135, 146, 159
Chronicle of Current Events (Soviet) 171, 233
Churchill, Winston 25, 105, 121, 199, 202, 224
Clay, Lucius 77
Clifford, Clark 6–7
Colson, Charles 89, 126, 139, 150

Conference on Security and Co-operation
in Europe (CSCE) 192, 227–31, 234
Congress (US) 20, 42, 52, 56, 81, 119, 140,
150, 172, 174–5, 179, 183, 190–1,
201, 208–9, 212, 215, 223
involvement in Watergate 150, 179,
191, 201, 208–9, 212
views on arms control 42, 52, 119, 172,
201
views on Vietnam 56, 65, 140, 223–4
Congress, 24th Party (Soviet) 69–70, 73, 77
Connally, John 66, 94–5, 114–15, 190
Connors, Chuck 166–7
Cooke, Alistair 8, 16
Cowan, Glen 71–2
Cuba Missile Crisis 4, 9, 12, 42, 79, 168, 180

Daley, Richard 7–8, 15–16, 116
Dayan, Moshe 175, 187–9, 197
De Gaulle, Charles 57–8, 63, 105, 117
Dean, John 127–8, 149–50, 153–4, 156,
167–8, 174
Democratic Party (US) 7, 15–16, 52, 58,
108, 125, 127, 130, 134, 175, 179,
191, 207
Department of Defense (US) *see* Pentagon
Dobrynin, Anatoly 3–6, 23–7, 32, 39, 42,
56, 64–5, 68, 73–5, 79–80, 91, 97–8,
112–13, 116, 157–8, 163–4, 166,
174–5, 177, 180–1, 202, 217–20
background and early career 3–4
contacts with Dobrynin 24–6, 32, 56,
64–5, 68, 74–5, 90–1
Dole, Robert 130, 148
Dubcek, Alexander 1–3, 8–10, 14–15, 23,
29–30

Ehrlichman, John 20, 48, 81, 88–9, 96, 99,
100, 126–9, 141, 149–150, 154–6,
167, 173–4
involvement with "Plumbers" 81, 89,
96, 99, 100
role in Watergate 126–9, 149–50,
154–5, 156, 167, 173–4
Eisenhower, Dwight 20, 28, 37, 39, 58, 80,
95, 128, 131, 141, 147, 151, 175, 199,
210
Ellsberg, Daniel 81, 89, 96
see also Pentagon Papers

Ervin, Sam 149–50, 153, 167–8, 174, 184,
194

First Infantry Division (US) 36
First World War 10, 36, 51, 67, 71, 92
Ford, Betty 176–7, 182, 184, 208, 214–15,
230
Ford, Gerald 47, 89, 131, 140, 176–9,
182–4, 190–1, 201, 208, 214–20,
223–5, 227–31, 238
appointment as Vice-President 176–9,
182–4
becomes President 208, 214–15
contacts with Brezhnev 218–20,
228–31
domestic politics challenges 215–18,
219, 227–8, 230, 231–2, 234
oversees withdrawal from Vietnam
223–5

Gandhi, Indira 58
Gandhi, Mahatma 105
Gold Standard 94–5, 98, 178
Goldwater, Barry 20–1, 138, 190, 209–10
Graham, Billy 49, 73, 196
Grechko, Andrei 29–30, 68, 109–10, 121,
170, 180
Gromyko, Andrei 4, 43, 52, 63, 68–9, 90–1,
96–8, 110, 113, 115, 11–20, 158,
163–4, 166, 170, 180, 192, 202–3,
218–19, 228–9
background 96–7
contacts with US 96–8, 113, 119–20,
158, 163–4, 166, 202–3, 218–19,
228–9
role in Politburo 63, 68–9, 110, 115,
170, 180, 192
Gulag Archipelago, The 11–12, 171–2, 192,
201
see also Solzhenitsyn

Haig, Alexander 22–3, 27–8, 49–50, 55, 65,
67, 74, 80, 90, 100, 103, 106, 108–
109, 113–16, 119, 133–7, 140–1, 146,
156, 169–70, 172–3, 174–6, 178–81,
190, 195, 200, 202–3, 207–8, 209,
211, 213, 215–16
background and military service 22–3,
140–1

Involvement in Watergate and Nixon's
  resignation 169–70, 172–3, 174–6,
  178–9, 190, 195, 207–8, 209, 211–13,
  215–16
role on China 103, 106
role on Middle East 55, 174–6, 180–1,
  200
role on Soviet Union 108–9, 113–16,
  119, 202–3
role on Vietnam 27–8, 49–50, 65, 67,
  80, 113–15, 133–7, 140–1, 146
Haldeman, Robert
  20–1, 23–4, 28, 31, 35, 37–40, 46, 49,
  58, 63, 66, 68, 71, 73, 78, 81, 88–91,
  93–5, 103–8, 114–15, 119–22, 125–9,
  130, 135, 137, 138–9, 145, 149–50,
  154–6, 167–8, 173–4, 183, 190, 207,
  209
  background and relationship with
    Nixon 20–1, 39, 46, 71, 78, 91,
    107–8, 120–2, 139, 154–5
  involvement in Watergate 81, 89–90,
    125–7, 127–9, 149–50, 154–6, 167–8,
    183, 190, 207, 209
  role as White House Chief of Staff 21,
    31, 38–40, 49, 68, 73, 77, 103–4, 114,
    122, 139, 173
Harriman, Averell 6, 25, 27
Heath, Edward 58
Helms, Jesse 227
Helms, Richard 6, 47, 65, 128–9
Helsinki 41–3, 51, 109, 115, 119–20,
  227–31, 234
  as venue for SALT negotiations 41–3,
    51, 109, 115, 119–20
  Helsinki Accords 227–31, 234; *see also*
    CSCE
Hirohito, Emperor of Japan 58
Hoover, John Edgar 89, 149
Hopkins, Harry 25
Hunt, Howard 89, 95–6, 126, 149–50
Humphrey, Hubert 6, 8, 16–17, 19, 138
Hussein, King of Jordan 53–4, 56, 215

Intercontinental Ballistic Missile (ICBM)
  42–3, 51, 79
  see also SALT negotiations
International Monetary Fund (IMF) 98
  see also Bretton Woods System

Israel 53–6, 58, 99, 174–6, 177–81, 187–90,
  196–9
  see also Six Day War (1967) and Yom
    Kippur War (1973)

Jackson, Henry 'Scoop' 52, 109, 119, 158,
  172, 201, 219, 227, 229
Jackson-Vanik amendment 172, 201,
  219
Jaworski, Leon 194–5, 207, 209, 216–17
Johnson, Lyndon Baines 4–8, 16, 19–23,
  27, 38, 42, 52, 55, 81, 114, 118, 138,
  141–2, 146–7, 168, 190
  involvement with Vietnam 6, 7, 16, 19,
    27, 38–9, 81, 114, 138, 147
  relations with Nixon 146–7
  views on Soviet Union 4–6, 118

K2 (mountain) 85
Kaiser, Robert 70, 98, 151–3, 194, 231
Kekkonen, Urho 157, 229
Kennedy, Edward 52
Kennedy, Jackie 66–7
Kennedy, John Fitzgerald 4–6, 20–1, 23, 25,
  47, 54, 66, 76, 81, 94, 97, 127, 130,
  155, 168
  presidential term and assassination 5,
    66, 94
  relations with Nixon 19–20, 66–7
Kennedy, Robert 4, 7–8, 17, 210
Kent State University (1970 shootings)
  48, 130
KGB (*Komitet Gosudarstvennoi
  Bezopastnosti* – Soviet Union) 1,
  3, 9, 11–14, 24, 41, 43, 57, 60, 63,
  69–70, 92–3, 98–9, 110–11, 117, 122,
  152–3, 167, 170–2, 192, 202, 226,
  231, 233–4
  role against dissidents 11–14, 41, 57,
    60, 69–70, 92–3, 152–3, 167, 170–2,
    192–3, 226, 231, 233–4
  see also Andropov
Kissinger, Henry 19–28, 31–2, 36–9, 42–3,
  45–7, 49, 51, 53–6, 58, 64–9, 73–7,
  79–81, 85–92, 94, 97, 99–100, 103–8,
  112–22, 128, 130, 132–7, 139–46,
  157–60, 163–6, 172–81, 187–90,
  198–202, 208, 210–12, 214, 219–25,
  227–9

background and family 20–1, 112, 173–4
contacts with Dobrynin 24–6, 32, 56, 64–5, 68, 74–5, 90–1
relations with Haig 22–3, 55, 178, 208
relations with Nixon 19–22, 88, 139, 173, 200–1, 210–12, 214
role on China 74, 75–6, 85–9, 103–8
role on Middle East 53–6, 166, 174–9, 180–1, 187–90, 196–9, 200–1
role on Soviet Union 24–6, 32, 42–3, 51, 53, 64, 68–9, 73–5, 79–80, 90–1, 112–22, 157–60, 163–6, 172, 175–9, 180–1, 201–2, 219, 227, 229
role on Vietnam 26, 27–8, 31–2, 36–7, 38–9, 45–7, 49, 65–7, 114–15, 128, 132–5, 136–7, 140–2, 145–6, 223–5
Kosygin, Alexei 5–6, 8–10, 24, 42, 51, 68–9, 91, 97, 115, 117–18, 121, 153, 159, 170–1, 180, 192, 203
relations with Brezhnev 5, 9, 68, 159, 170–1
Kovic, Ron 129–32
Krogh, Egil 'Bud' 89, 95–6, 150
Khrushchev, Nikita 4, 9, 11, 20, 42, 57, 69, 97, 113, 118, 153, 159, 171

Laos (1971 US military incursion) 46, 65–7, 72–3, 95, 111
Laird, Melvyn 27–8, 31, 38, 47, 49, 55–6, 65, 115, 226
Liddy, Gordon 95–6, 126, 149, 150

McCain, John (father) 31, 46
McCain, John (son) 31, 148
McGovern, George 8, 16, 108, 125, 129–30, 132, 134, 137, 138, 155
Macmillan, Harold 58
McNamara, Robert 6–7, 38, 80
Malraux, Andre 105
Mansfield, Mike 76–8, 89–90
Mansfield Amendment 76–8
Mao Tsetung 72, 74, 88, 104–6, 107, 129, 159
Marine Corps (US) 65, 73, 130–1, 202, 213–14, 224, 226
Meir, Golda 55, 175, 177, 187, 189–90, 197–9
MIRV (Multiple Independent Re-Entry Vehicle) 42–3, 51, 109, 219–20
see also SALT negotiations

Mitchell, John 22, 47, 66, 81, 89, 128, 150–1, 153–4
involvement in Watergate 128, 150–1, 153–4
Moorer, Thomas 55–6, 65, 100, 181
'Moratorium' protests on Vietnam 37–8
Most Favoured Nation (MFN) status (US-Soviet trade) 157–8, 172, 219
Mudd, Roger 131–2

Nasser, Gamal 188–9
National Security Council (NSC) 5, 22, 27, 51, 55, 78, 115, 181, 201, 223,
New York Times 8, 12, 40, 49, 53, 59, 70, 80, 85, 88–9, 100, 119, 137, 151–2, 172, 179, 196
Nitze, Paul 120–1, 201
Nixon, Julie 19, 39, 48, 80, 100, 114, 130, 138, 141, 147, 154–5, 161, 165, 182–4, 191, 209–10, 212–13
Nixon, Pat 19, 67, 80, 100, 103–4, 106–7, 112–14, 121, 130, 141, 145–7, 154, 160–1, 165, 182–4, 191, 199–200, 209–10, 213–14
Nixon, Richard 19–28, 31–2, 35–40, 45–7, 51–9, 63–8, 71–81, 85, 87–99, 94–101, 103–9, 111–13, 115–22, 125–42, 145–7, 149–51, 153–9, 163–6, 168–70, 172–84, 188, 190–1, 194–203, 207–19, 223, 227, 230, 232
background and early career 19–20, 50–1
candidate in presidential elections (1960) 20
candidate in presidential elections (1968) 19–20
candidate in presidential elections (1972) 129–32, 138–9
contact with Soviets 23–6, 51–2, 63–4, 67, 76–9, 90–2, 96–8, 108–9, 112–22, 157–61, 163–6, 180–2, 201–3, 219, 232
contact with China 74–6, 85, 87–8, 103–8
involvement with Middle East 53–6, 166, 174–7, 180–2, 197–201
marriage and family 80, 99–101, 141, 145–6, 161, 184

Watergate and Resignation 125–9,
    149–51, 153–5, 168–70, 178–9,
    181–4, 190–1, 194–6, 201, 207–14,
    215–17
relations with Eisenhower 20, 39, 58
relations with Ford 176–7, 183, 191,
    204
relations with Johnson 141–2, 145–6
relations with Kennedy 20, 67–8
relations with Kissinger 19–22, 88,
    210–11, 212
role on Vietnam 26–7, 31–2, 36–40,
    45–52, 65–7, 72–3, 80–1, 113–16,
    132–7, 145–7, 223
Nixon, Tricia 19, 49, 80, 100–1, 114, 130,
    138, 141, 145, 147, 154, 161, 184,
    210, 213
    Wedding 80
Nobel Prize (for Literature) 56–57, 59, 152,
    220–1, 226
Nobel Prize (for Peace) 230–31, 233–4
Non-Proliferation Treaty (NPT) 42
North Atlantic Treaty Organisation
    (NATO) 76

Ostpolitik 63, 77
    see also Brandt

Partial Test-Ban Treaty (1963) 42
Pasternak, Boris 56–7
Pentagon (US) 80–1, 89, 96, 100, 108, 119,
    147, 151, 156, 160, 175–6, 201
Perle, Richard 52
'Ping-Pong' diplomacy (US/China) 71–2,
    74
'Plumbers' 96, 100, 126
    see also Ehrlichman, Liddy and Hunt
Podgorny, Nikolai 3, 5, 8–10, 24, 42, 69, 97,
    111, 116–18, 121, 153, 159, 170–1,
    180, 192, 203
Polaris (nuclear missile system) 108
    see also SALT
Politburo (Soviet) 2, 4, 6, 9–10, 14, 51, 57,
    63, 68–70, 91, 99, 110–11, 115–16,
    118, 120–1, 152–3, 159, 164, 170,
    180, 192–3, 231
    dynamics and internal tensions 68–9,
    115, 170, 180
Pompidou, Georges 58–9

Poseidon (nuclear missile system) 108–9
    see also SALT
'Prague Spring' 2, 10, 14, 23
    see also Cernik, Dubcek, Svoboda
Price, Ray 146, 179, 202–3, 208, 211–12

Rabin, Yitzhak 55–6, 189, 198
Rather, Dan 65, 131, 173, 182
Reagan, Ronald 130, 165–6, 176, 227–8,
    231–2
Republican Party 20–1, 24, 47, 52, 58, 77,
    129–31, 138, 140, 176, 190–1, 207,
    209, 227, 232
Reston, Scotty 8, 40, 88, 137
Rodino, Peter 194–6,
Rogers, William 23–4, 27–8, 31, 38, 47, 49,
    55–6, 65, 68, 77–8, 89, 97, 103–4,
    115, 121, 163–5, 173, 226
    tensions with Nixon and Kissinger
    24–5, 38, 64, 68, 77, 173
Roosevelt, Franklin 24–5, 36, 39, 77, 88, 93,
    97, 131, 199, 202
Roosevelt, Teddy 139, 147, 213–14
Rostropovich, Mstislav 57
Rumsfeld, Donald 227
Rusk, Dean 5–6

Sadat, Anwar 180–1, 188–90, 199–200
'*Samizdat*' (Soviet) 11–12, 59, 171, 233
Safeguard (missile defence system) 52–3,
    108
    see also ABM and SALT
Safire, William 40, 48–9, 93–5, 139, 196,
    212
Sakharov, Andrei 12–14, 40, 59–60, 69–70,
    98–9, 171–2, 192, 230–4
SALT (Strategic Arms Limitation Talks)
    42–3, 46, 51–3, 64, 68–9, 71, 73, 75,
    78, 90–1, 97, 100, 108–9, 113, 116,
    119, 122, 158, 201, 219, 228
    completion and signature of SALT I
    Agreement 119–22
Sanchez, Manolo 49–50, 71, 92, 101, 135,
    200, 210
Schlesinger, James 181, 201, 219, 223–4
Second World War 3, 10–11, 14, 20, 25, 28,
    41, 47, 51, 76, 85, 94, 97–9, 109–10,
    112, 118, 120, 122, 138, 148, 157, 159,
    160, 175, 188, 192, 220, 227–8, 234

Selassie, Haile 58
Semenov, Vladimir 43–4, 46, 51–2, 79, 108,
    110, 119–21, 228
Senate (US) 6, 20, 23, 50, 52–3, 58, 76, 78,
    89, 101, 113, 133, 140, 149, 153, 158,
    167–8, 174, 178, 182, 190, 192, 194,
    209–10, 224
  involvement in Watergtae 149, 167–8,
    174, 178, 190, 194, 209–10
Shelest, Pyotr 9, 116
Shevadnadze, Edvard 77
'Silent Majority' speech 40, 45–6
Sisco, Joe 53–56, 187, 189
Six Day War (Arab-Israel) 53, 157, 166–7,
    175, 180, 189
Smith, Gerard 43–4, 51–3, 68, 78–80,
    108–10, 115, 119–21, 228
Smith, Hedrick 13, 151–3, 192, 226
Solzhenitsyn, Alexander 11–13, 40–1,
    56–7, 59–60, 92–3, 99, 151–3,
    171–2, 192–4, 221, 226–31, 234
Sonnenfeldt, Helmut 78, 91, 157–8, 181
Stalin, Josef 3, 12–13, 25, 41, 59, 68, 70, 99,
    111, 121, 160, 199, 202
State Department (US) 20–2, 24–6, 78–9,
    85, 109, 112, 173, 180–1, 187, 224
Stennis, John 154, 178
SLBM (Submarine Launched Ballistic
    Missile) 42–3, 51, 108
  see also SALT
Sukhodrev, Viktor 116–18, 157–9, 164–6,
    203, 220, 229
Supreme Court (US) 89, 178, 194, 207,
    217, 230
Suslov, Mikhail 110–11, 153, 159
Svoboda, Lubvík 10–11, 14, 29–30

Thieu, Nguyen Van 31–2, 35–7, 134–6, 140,
    146, 223
Tho, Le Duc 45–6, 113, 132–6, 140, 145–6,
    223

Thompson, Llewellyn 'Tommy' 79, 109
Thompson, Robert 38–9
Tito, Josip 157
Trident (nuclear missile system) 108
Truman, Harry 6, 26–7, 77, 97, 121, 141,
    147

United Nations 4, 14, 174, 181, 188
Universal Declaration of Human Rights
    99

Vladivostok (US/Soviet Summit) 219–20,
    228

Walters, Vernon 37, 45, 128–9
Warsaw Pact 1–2, 23, 36, 76
Washington Post, The 74, 126, 137, 151–2,
    154, 167, 192, 215, 231
Watergate 125, 127–9, 137, 149, 153,
    158, 160–1, 170, 173–4, 177, 181,
    184, 191, 197, 201, 207, 215–16,
    223
  see also Nixon, Haldeman and
    Ehrlichman
Wheeler, Earle 'Bus' 6, 23, 27, 31, 47, 55
White, Theodore 7, 20, 196
Wilson, Harold 58, 229
Wilson, Woodrow 145, 217
Wolfowitz, Paul 52
Woodward, Bob 137, 154, 167, 185

Xuan Thuy 37, 45

'Yippies' 7–8, 15, 131
Yom Kippur War (Arab–Israel) 174–5,
    177–8, 183, 189, 196, 198

Zhou Enlai 74, 85–7, 103–6, 107–8, 132
Zhuang Zedong 72
Ziegler, Ron 63, 88, 103–5, 125, 137, 154,
    176, 195, 200, 202, 208